# PUBLIC FINANCE IN A
# DEVELOPING COUNTRY

# PUBLIC FINANCE IN A

# DEVELOPING COUNTRY

## *El Salvador — A Case Study*

*By*

*Henry C. Wallich* and *John H. Adler*

With the collaboration of
*E. R. Schlesinger, Florence Nixon,*
and *P. J. W. Glaessner*

GREENWOOD PRESS, PUBLISHERS
NEW YORK                    1968

# PREFACE

THE ECONOMIC IMPORTANCE of public finance is growing rapidly in underdeveloped countries as a result of the increasing emphasis upon social services and economic development. While much progress is being made, the costs of modern policies have often placed heavy pressure upon the far less modern revenue systems that still exist in many of these countries. The result, in some cases, has been an instability of fiscal and monetary affairs that may have slowed the process of development. An intensive study of the public finance problems of underdeveloped countries therefore seems desirable, directed toward finding ways of balancing rising social and economic aspirations with available resources. We are greatly indebted to the government of El Salvador for giving us an opportunity to make a small contribution to this problem, which is being faced only gradually by economists.

It is fortunate that our study of Salvadorean public finances could take place in an environment where great disproportion between needs for expenditure and fiscal resources is not in evidence. El Salvador has enjoyed fiscal and monetary stability for many years, even though it has had to suffer some of the consequences of the recent world-wide inflation. The stability has made possible an examination of the impact of the Salvadorean fiscal system upon the economy undistorted by maladjustments of internal origin.

This study represents an attempt to appraise El Salvador's public finances in the light of present-day economic knowledge and techniques. The task was facilitated by the relatively simple structure of the Salvadorean economy and fiscal system. We have been able to reach conclusions and insights that would be very difficult to attain in a country with more complex features. In some respects, it is true, the progress of the study was hampered by the lack or uncertainty of statistical information. Many basic data, among them the national income estimates and various price indexes, had to be developed by Salvadorean technicians, in collaboration with the authors, expressly for this study. Thus many of the conclusions reached are highly tentative in character. There is good reason, however, to believe that although many of the quantitative results are subject to a wide margin of error they are justifiable in qualitative terms.

Even where the results must be considered rather uncertain, it is hoped that the analysis retains some value because it draws attention to certain economic effects and relationships and because it emphasizes the need for further study. Growing interest in the study of economic questions in El Salvador, as manifested in the recent establishment of the Faculty of Economics, should stimulate the pursuit of many of the questions here left unanswered.

The study is presented in three parts: (1) a summary; (2) the body of the study, consisting of description and analysis; and (3) technical appendices. The summary, which evaluates the results of the entire study, is contained in Chapter I. This is followed by a brief description of the Salvadorean economy in Chapter II, where an attempt is made to show the structure of this economy in terms of the composition of the gross national product and of the balance of payments. Chapters III to V describe the processes of budget formulation and execution and present a brief summary of the revenue system and of government expenditures; these chapters are backed by extensive descriptive material in their respective appendices. Chapter VI endeavors to view Salvadorean fiscal affairs in an international perspective through comparisons with other countries, among them Guatemala, Mexico, Chile, Denmark, and New Zealand.

Chapters VII to XIII constitute the main analysis. Here an investigation is made of the effects of taxation and government expenditure upon the structure and growth of production and upon the welfare of the consumer. The experience of the government is reviewed, with regard to the cost of revenue collections, the seasonal variations in revenues, and particularly the cyclical flexibility of revenues and expenditures. There follows an analysis of the effect of the fiscal system upon the composition, distribution, and magnitude of the national income. The possibilities of anticyclical policy are reviewed, as well as the impact of public finances upon the currency. The final chapter deals with some aspects of the public debt.

The appendices support and amplify some of the chapters.

The entire study could never have been carried out without a great deal of outside help and advice for which we gratefully acknowledge our indebtedness. The number of persons who have aided us is too large to permit full enumeration, and we must limit ourselves to acknowledging only the most outstanding contributions. Ing. Manuel Valdés contributed greatly to the organization of the study, as well as to the solution of many technical problems. Dr. Manuel Tosco gave us invaluable help in statistical matters, and we greatly regret that the revised cost-of-living index prepared by him arrived too late to be utilized. Messrs. Dalponte, Mena Ariz, and Serrano assisted in the preparation of many of the basic economic and monetary statistics. We also owe a debt of gratitude to many Salvadorean public officials and businessmen, and particularly to the officers and staff of the Banco Central de Reserva, for the time and patience which they devoted to our questions.

In the United States, we have to thank our friends and colleagues in the fields of fiscal policy and Latin American economics, most of them located in the international agencies, the United States government, and the Federal Reserve System. We have also been aided greatly by the friendly comments of our colleagues in the Federal Reserve Bank of New York, particularly Arthur Bloomfield, George Garvy, and Robert Rosa. For the editing of the Spanish version of the study, we are deeply indebted to Dr. Jorge Sol, who undertook this difficult job with painstaking care and whose many valuable suggestions went far beyond the normal functions of an editor in correcting factual errors and shaping the structure of the whole work. We are also grateful to our secretaries, who put in many hours of overtime work in typing it, to Winthrop W. Case, who edited the English version, and to Dr. Alfonso Rochac, who gave the Spanish text a final scrutiny and prepared the subject index.

The present study was completed and submitted to the Government of El Salvador in the spring of 1949. It is gratifying to note that considerable economic progress has been made by El Salvador since that time and that a number of desirable developments referred to in this study as lying in the future have meanwhile materialized.

The Spanish version of the study was issued by the Fondo de Cultura Económica of Mexico City, in 1949, under the title of *Proyecciones Económicas de las Finanzas Públicas — Un estudio experimental en El Salvador.*

July 1951                                                    H. C. W.
                                                             J. H. A.

# CONTENTS

## PART ONE

## PART TWO

# PART THREE: APPENDICES

# TABLES

# PART ONE

# CHAPTER I

## SUMMARY AND EVALUATION

THE FISCAL STRUCTURE of a country naturally reflects the basic features of its economy. El Salvador is an export economy, with coffee, the chief crop, constituting about 82 per cent of total exports. Although the production of coffee is the economically and politically dominant activity of the country, it accounts for only about 12 per cent of the total gross national product, which amounted to 435 million colones ($174 million) in 1946. A sizable part of the gross national product is derived from agricultural activities only loosely connected with the market economy, with the result that large sectors of the population are relatively self-sufficient in most of the basic needs.

These facts go far to determine the structure of the fiscal system and particularly the tax system. The government has to rely heavily upon taxes on foreign trade and other indirect taxes; income taxes and other direct taxes yield only small amounts. The total tax capacity of the economy is limited by the same circumstances. At the same time, the country's relative self-sufficiency helps to explain how, despite the vulnerability of its export economy, it has been able to withstand economic fluctuations successfully enough to maintain a balanced budget, a stable exchange rate, and freedom from exchange control for over fourteen years.

Various interesting aspects of the Salvadorean fiscal structure are revealed by comparisons with other countries. Of the total revenues of the Salvadorean national government in 1946, 10.7 per cent was derived from direct taxes and 53.2 per cent from taxes on foreign trade, as compared with 14.1 per cent and 43.2 per cent, respectively, for Guatemala, and 23.7 per cent and 30.8 per cent for Mexico. Total expenditures of the national government in 1946 amounted to 10.4 per cent of the national income, compared, for instance, with 13.7 per cent for Mexico and 16.2 per cent for Chile.[1] Of these expenditures, 35.5 per cent in El Salvador may be classified as being directed toward social and cultural ends and economic development, compared with 52.6 per cent in Guatemala, and 28.4 per cent in Peru.

These facts, taken from Chapters II and VI of this study, provide the background for the following summary of the analytical Chapters VII to XIII. This summary will encompass the impact of the fiscal system upon business, the consumer, and the government; its effect upon the national income and the currency, and its relation to anticyclical policy and the debt. From this summary it will be clear that fiscal matters do not present problems of especial urgency in El Salvador; some recommendations for reforms that seem to follow from this study's analysis are presented in the separate Recommendations and Suggestions.

## 1. THE IMPACT OF THE FISCAL SYSTEM UPON BUSINESS (CHAPTER VII)

Salvadorean business enterprises feel the immediate impact of the tax system through various indirect taxes entering into business costs, through the taxation of business profits, and in a favorable sense, through tariff protection. The immediate impact of government expenditures is felt in the demand of the government for the products of business and in the competition that the government occasionally offers in the purchase of imported materials and in the labor market. It may be stated at the outset that these effects are, on the whole, slight. The indirect effects of the fiscal system upon business, through its influence upon consumption and saving as well as upon risk and incentives, are likewise not very great; these are taken up in Chapter X, which deals with national income.

### EFFECTS OF TAXES UPON BUSINESS

A variety of minor taxes are levied upon Salvadorean business activities, in the form of production, license, and other imposts.

[1] For notes pertaining to these figures, see Chapter VI. All "national income" data relating to El Salvador must be understood to refer to gross national product.

Other taxes entering into business costs are the duties upon imported goods used by business, which may be estimated at about one half of total import duties paid. Both types of taxes probably are wholly shifted to the consumer. Direct taxes are levied upon business enterprises in the form of a very light property tax and, in the case of corporations, of an income tax that is identical with the personal income tax (except as noted below). No distinction in taxation is made between business and private income or property, and the amount of property and income taxes paid by business enterprises therefore cannot be estimated, but it is bound in any case to be small; the shiftability of these taxes is uncertain.

Finally, three taxes are levied upon business enterprises in place of income taxes, the enterprises or their owners being therefore exempted from income taxes: (1) the coffee export tax (the largest single tax levied in 1946 on a single product); (2) the cotton tax; and (3) the sugar tax. Since the coffee tax cannot be shifted forward to the world market and the foreign consumer, it is absorbed by the coffee producer, or possibly shifted backward in part to the coffee worker. Since the tax lacks the progressive character of the income tax and falls with the same proportional weight upon large and small producers, its substitution for the income tax works a certain hardship upon the latter. On the other hand, the rates of the coffee export tax have usually been adjusted rapidly in response to changes in coffee prices in order to avoid undue burdens, and the administrative advantages of this tax therefore tend to compensate for its deficiencies.

The cotton and sugar taxes levied on the processors in place of income taxes, on the other hand, can be shifted to the consumer (and the first probably has been entirely shifted to the consumer since the removal of the price ceilings on yarn), owing to the high protection that cotton and sugar products enjoy in the domestic market. The processors thus are probably freed almost entirely from tax liabilities in connection with their business activities. In view of their small number, it is doubtful whether the administrative advantages of the cotton and sugar taxes are sufficient to compensate for these deficiencies.

The special positions that the tax system creates for coffee, cotton yarn, and sugar producers appear to represent the most striking effects of taxation upon Salvadorean business (Chapter VII, Table 31). In view of the universally modest level of the tax rates and the usually satisfactory level of business profits, it seems unlikely that taxation should have significantly affected the volume and direction of productive investment, except as a consequence of tariff protection.

### EFFECTS OF GOVERNMENT EXPENDITURES UPON BUSINESS

The Salvadorean government devotes a moderate portion of its revenues to the purchase of the products of Salvadorean business. The purchases, however, have been distributed over a wide range of products and it is not clear to what extent any particular industry has been stimulated thereby.

Through its expenditures, the government also offers competition to business in the labor market and in the purchase of materials. During the late war and postwar years this competition seems to have been quite intensive, particularly with regard to construction labor and materials. This is the visible expression of the inflationary effects that a large government budget may have at times of full employment, even though the budget be fully balanced by taxation.

In the sale of goods and services, the government competes with private business only on a limited scale. The most important cases appear to be a "yard stick" textile plant and the Lempa power project. Neither project so far has operated on a scale that would permit an appraisal of the results.

### THE TARIFF AND THE STRUCTURE OF PRODUCTION

Tariff protection has been of great importance for the sugar, textile, cotton, and henequen industries. Duty exemptions for machinery employed by new industries likewise have been important for several industries. Since, however, a detailed analysis of these policies would lead far into the field of commercial policy, only limited attention could be devoted in this study to this effect of the tax system upon business. Comments on certain features of the tariff will be found on page 303, in Appendix D.

INFLUENCE OF THE FISCAL SYSTEM ON BUSINESS ORGANIZATION

The tax system appears to discriminate to some extent against the corporate form of organization. Taxes upon corporate income are levied at the same rates that apply to personal incomes. Since the various shareholders in many instances are probably in lower tax brackets than the corporation, the aggregate tax liability upon their respective shares in the income of the business, if it were conducted in the form of a partnership, would probably be less than the tax liability of the corporation. In view of the advantages that the corporate form of organization appears to offer an underdeveloped country for the formation of capital and the adoption of efficient business practices, this discrimination against corporations seems undesirable.

## 2. THE BUDGET AND THE CONSUMER (CHAPTER VIII)

All taxes must ultimately be borne by individuals who are consumers, whether in the form of direct taxes or in the form of higher prices or lower wages. Salvadorean taxes are therefore analyzed here with respect to the following characteristics important to the consumer: their shiftability; their progressiveness; and their avoidability. Then the total tax burden resting upon consumers with different income levels and occupations is estimated. Finally, estimates are presented of the weight of taxes upon important consumption items and of the variation in the "real" tax burden during cyclical fluctuations.

### "SHIFTABILITY" OF TAXES

Three groups of taxes may be distinguished according to their degree of shiftability: (1) those that in the main are *not* shifted; (2) those that in the main *are* shifted; and (3) an intermediate group of uncertain shiftability. The unshiftable group consists chiefly of income, inheritance, and personal-property taxes, and accounted in 1946 for only 12.8 per cent of total taxes. The shiftable group, consisting chiefly of consumption and import duties, accounted for 69.7 per cent. The "intermediate" group, in which the coffee export tax is the dominant factor, accounted for 17.5 per cent.

## PROGRESSIVENESS OF TAXES

A second important distinction from the consumer's point of view is the degree to which taxes are (1) progressive, i.e., increasing more than in proportion to a rise in the consumer's income; (2) merely proportional; or (3) regressive, i.e., increasing less than in proportion to a rise in the consumer's income. The group of "progressive" taxes, consisting mainly of income and inheritance taxes, accounted in 1946 for only 11.6 per cent of total tax revenues. The degree of progressiveness, however, was quite marked. The "proportional" taxes, among which the coffee tax was of primary importance, accounted for 18.9 per cent, while the "regressive" taxes, consisting mainly of consumption taxes and import duties on goods used by business, accounted for 43.4 per cent. There was also found to exist a "mixed" group, consisting chiefly of import duties on consumer goods and certain shifted taxes, that appear to be regressive in the lowest brackets and progressive in the upper brackets. This group accounted for 26.1 per cent of total tax revenues.

## "AVOIDABILITY" OF TAXES

Since a considerable volume of taxes is levied upon goods that are not strictly "necessities," the consumer can legitimately avoid paying such taxes by avoiding the consumption of these luxuries and semi-luxuries. While a clear-cut distinction between luxuries and necessities cannot of course be made, a reasonable appraisal seems feasible. From this it appears that a family with an income of 8,000 colones annually that is a "heavy" consumer of cigarettes, liquor, imported textiles, and other imported luxuries could reduce its total tax burden by approximately one half through eliminating these forms of consumption.

## THE CONSUMER'S TAX BURDEN

Undoubtedly the most important aspect of the entire tax system from the consumer's viewpoint is the total tax burden that it imposes upon him through direct taxation and through taxes shifted to him in the form of higher prices or lower earnings. An estimate was made of the tax burden borne by typical families in different income brackets and in different walks of life, the estimate endeavoring to take into account all direct and indirect taxes with the appropriate assumptions as to tax shifting. It shows that the total tax burden for the year 1946 appears to have ranged from a low of 6.1 per cent of family income for a rural laborer's family with an annual income of 600 colones, to over 21.2 per cent for a businessman's family with over 100,000 colones income. For families with 3,000 colones income, the burden averages 7.8 per cent; for those with 4,800, it averages 9.8 per cent (Table 36).

It appears that the aggregate tax structure, despite the heavy impact of regressive consumption taxes, is progressive — a conclusion that is of primary importance for an appraisal of the tax system. However, taking into account various qualifications that must be made, one may conclude that the impact of the taxes that actually are being collected is probably somewhat less progressive than the computed tax liabilities indicated above.

### WEIGHT OF TAXES UPON SELECTED COMMODITIES

In order to assess the tax burden upon various commodities important to the consumer, the taxes (usually specific) levied upon them have been calculated in *ad valorem* equivalents. For domestically produced goods, the weight of taxes in 1946 was found to range from 67.7 per cent for cigarettes to 1.7 per cent for cotton goods. In the case of imported products, those taxes of which significant amounts were collected ranged from 42 per cent upon gasoline to 12.9 per cent upon drugs and medicines.

### CYCLICAL VARIATIONS IN TAX BURDEN

The tax burden that falls upon the consumer has been considerably affected by the inflation prevailing in recent years. Specific taxes, i.e., those levied not upon the inventory value of the taxed objects but on their quantity or similar characteristics (import duties, for instance, are mainly specific), have decreased in weight. Income taxes, on the other hand, which are levied on the *money* income at progressive rates, have become more burdensome. A study of the weight of import duties shows that the *ad valorem* equivalent of the duties upon import goods purchased by a family with an annual income of 3,000 colones fell by about one third between 1940 and 1946. On the other hand, it was found that in 1946 the "real" value of the basic income tax exemption of 3,000 colones had been reduced by inflation to the equivalent of 2,143 colones in terms of 1942 prices. In practice, however, delays in assessment and collection, as well as other factors, undoubtedly have greatly mitigated the increase in the income tax burden shown by these calculations.

### 3. The Government's Experience under the Fiscal System (Chapter IX)

There are several aspects of the fiscal system that are of special interest to the government for the purpose of fiscal administration and policy. The questions studied from this particular viewpoint comprise (1) the cost of tax collection; (2) the seasonal variation in tax revenues; (3) the "cyclical flexibility" of revenues, i.e., the fluctuations in revenues resulting from fluctuations in national income; (4) the relation of stable and flexible expenditure; (5) the "real" income of the government in times of inflation (i.e., revenues recomputed in terms of constant purchasing power) compared with the "real burden" for the taxpayer; and (6) the potentialities of the revenue system for higher yields.

#### COST OF COLLECTING TAXES

The total cost involved in the collection of approximately 50,000,000 colones of tax revenues in 1947 was 2,350,000 colones, or 4.7 per cent. The cost of collecting major individual revenues ranged from 3.6 per cent for export and import taxes to 18 per cent for inheritance and gift taxes. It rose as high as 64.4 per cent for *matrículas de comercio*, which, however, also serve certain nontax purposes. The percentages in all cases are high. This does not mean, however, except with respect to some petty taxes, that the effort to collect revenues has been encountering diminishing returns. It appears, on the contrary, that an expansion of the staff of the Bureau of Internal Revenue, together with an overhaul in its procedures, would be well worth while in terms of additional revenue collected.

### SEASONAL VARIATION IN TAX REVENUES

A seasonal index of tax revenues is useful for the control of expenditures during the course of the fiscal year, since it helps to decide whether a deviation of actual revenue collections from budget estimates reflects seasonal influences or a more basic trend. The pattern of monthly receipts in El Salvador has been somewhat unstable, owing both to frequent changes in the coffee export tax and to changes in the coffee export season. Nevertheless, it is interesting to note that during the last eight years there seems to have existed a distinct pattern with a peak in the first few months of the year and a low toward the end of the year. The range of seasonal fluctuations during this period was of the order of 20 per cent above and 15 per cent below the monthly average.

### CYCLICAL FLEXIBILITY OF TAXES

A study of the interrelation of tax revenues and national income during the period 1939–1946 (in monetary terms) shows that revenues tend to rise more or less in proportion to national income. However, the low level of imports and hence of import tax collections during the war years, and their extraordinary upswing thereafter, have considerably intensified fluctuations during the recent boom. The net result has been a postwar increase in revenues probably considerably more than in proportion to the rise in national income. The effects of this "built-in flexibility" of the tax structure have been enhanced by the "administrative flexibility" of certain revenues such as the coffee export tax, the rates of which can easily be adjusted upward or downward in response to economic changes. The result of the high cyclical flexibility that the tax system has exhibited in recent years is that the budget may have become unusually vulnerable to a cyclical contraction. In other words, a sharp decline in national income might conceivably produce a dangerously large budget deficit — a deficit that might be greatly in excess of such "anticyclical" deficit spending as might perhaps be justifiably undertaken under such conditions.

### STABLE AND FLEXIBLE EXPENDITURES

The expenditures of the Salvadorean government may be divided into two groups: those that are devoted chiefly to administrative purposes of a relatively stable character and those that serve purposes such as public works and the like, which inherently are capable of considerable variation. It was found, nevertheless, that during the recent inflations the two types of expenditures increased in roughly the same proportion. When the two groups were "deflated," however, by dividing the administrative expenditures by an index of the level of average government salaries and the variable ones by an index reflecting the cost of construction labor and materials, it was found that the fluctuations in the "real" value of these respective expenditures were very different. While the fixed expenditures increased slightly in "real" terms from 1939 to 1946, the variable ones in "real" terms actually declined, owing to the much sharper rise in their unit cost. The experience seems to demonstrate that rising expenditures for public works during a cyclical upswing, quite apart from their inflationary effect, are likely to be uneconomic. On the other hand, the sharp increase in payments on the public debt during the inflation year 1946 appears to have been an advantageous move not only for anticyclical purposes but also for the purpose of obtaining maximum value for money spent.

### "REAL" INCOME OF GOVERNMENT AND "REAL" COST OF TAXES TO TAXPAYER

The increase in the unit cost of all government services, deflated by the respective indexes, shows that the great apparent rise in government revenues from 1939 to 1946 was largely an illusion. In monetary terms, revenues rose 119 per cent, but in "real" terms the rise was only 55 per cent. If the increase in debt repayment in 1946 is eliminated, there remains a net "real" increase of only 10 per cent. In 1947 and 1948, however, a rather large increase seems to have occurred, but the lack of data does not allow an exact determination of the "real" value of the government receipts in these years.

The cost-of-living index, however, rose even more than the unit cost of government services. In other words, the purchasing power of money in the hands of the consumer, as measured by the cost-of-living index, declined more than that of money in the hands of the government. The consumer thus realized a "saving" upon the government services that he "bought" with his taxes. The extent of the "saving" in 1945 can be estimated at about 21 per cent of the total tax burden. Account must be taken, however, of the fact that these "savings" were to a large extent the result of the decline in purchasing power of the salaries of the government employees.

### CAPACITY OF TAX SYSTEM FOR HIGHER YIELDS

The question of whether or not the tax system would be capable of producing higher yields may be treated without implying that such higher taxation would at present be desirable. In fact, despite the low ratio of government services to national income and the obvious need for additional social, cultural, and developmental expenditures, a rise in the tax burden could be justified only if assurance existed that the proceeds would be devoted to these purposes. Past experience provides no such assurance, for it appears that increases in revenues have been shared proportionately by most or all government services. Nevertheless, situations may arise, such as a sharp drop in revenues, that would make recourse to additional taxation imperative.

A very large increase in taxation probably would be difficult to accomplish, since the state of development of the economy makes it impossible for the government to absorb a very high proportion of national income. It is obvious, however, that a reasonable increase in the present very modest ratio of taxes to national income is possible. It could be accomplished by (1) more effective administration of existing taxes; (2) increases in the rates of existing taxes, which in most instances (the chief exception being certain import taxes) are moderate; and (3) expansion of the present tax system, which still is far from tapping effectively all the sources of revenue available to modern government. The statement of these objective facts, it may be repeated, implies no judgment whatever as to the advisability of increasing the total tax burden.

### 4. THE BUDGET AND THE NATIONAL INCOME
### (CHAPTER X)

The preceding discussion of the impact of the budget upon business, the consumer, and the government leads up to a study of its general effect upon national income. The effects which are of particular interest are those upon (1) the balance of payments, through government expenditures abroad; (2) capital formation; (3) the distribution of national income; and (4) the size of the national income.

#### THE BALANCE OF PAYMENTS

In recent years the government's expenditures abroad for public debt service, consular and diplomatic service, and imports for its own use have fluctuated around an average of 15 per cent of total expenditures. Debt service and consular and diplomatic expenditures appear to have undergone only relatively minor variations in response to increases in government revenues (except for the large increase in debt payments connected with the resumption of service in 1946). Imports for government use, on the other hand, have increased considerably with rising government income. The ratio of aggregate government expenditures abroad to total government expenditures has shown a tendency to remain constant during periods of changing revenues, or perhaps to decline, although such expenditures naturally are subject to the government's policy decisions.

A comparison with the private sector indicates that for both sectors the ratios of expenditures abroad to total expenditures are of the same order of magnitude. The comparison further suggests, however, that an increase in taxation and government expenditure, accompanied by a corresponding reduction in the income and expenditure of the private sector, would result in a net decline in total imports, if past expenditure patterns of both sectors continued to rule.

In a broader sense, the budget influences the balance of payments also through its influence upon total national income, and through the restrictive effects upon exports and imports, respectively, of export and import taxes. No quantitative appraisal of these effects has been possible, however, beyond the general impression that the coffee export tax does not seem to have reduced materially the volume of exports.

### CAPITAL FORMATION

Only very limited information is available on the proportion of government expenditures devoted to capital formation, i.e., to investment in roads, buildings, plant and equipment, and the like. It appears that during the period 1940–1947, this proportion fluctuated around 12 per cent. There is no clear evidence that the proportion has tended to rise with rising government revenues.

A comparison of the rate of governmental capital formation with the corresponding rate of the private sector, for which only very vague estimates are available, indicates that the government's rate may be relatively higher by a small margin. On the basis of past expenditure patterns, however, there is no strong reason to assume that an increase in taxation and government expenditures, accompanied by a corresponding reduction in the income and expenditure of the private sector, would result in an increase in total capital formation, unless the additional taxes fell predominantly upon the lower income groups who save and invest little. But the introduction of new taxes, even if they are borne by the entire economy and not only by the low income groups, would result in an acceleration of the rate of capital formation, provided that the yield of such additional taxes is utilized fully, or at least primarily, for such (investment) purposes.

### DISTRIBUTION OF NATIONAL INCOME

Since taxpayers do not necessarily share in the benefits of government services in proportion to the amount of taxes they pay, the combined effect of taxation and free availability of government services is to redistribute to some degree the national income. It is extremely difficult to calculate the quantitative

extent of this redistribution since there is no certain way of estimating the degree to which different individuals benefit by government services. Nevertheless, it seems desirable to make some
rough appraisal since all budgetary operations in fact imply
some decision on the part of the government involving redistribution of the national income.

The order of magnitude of this redistribution has been estimated on the basis of three alternative assumptions. If the results of the most plausible of these assumptions are accepted, it
appears that for the lowest income group the benefits from government services are approximately 20 per cent greater than
the tax burden, while for the highest income group the benefits
are about 20 per cent less than the taxes. The other alternatives
yield different results, but in each case it appears that the tax
system does tend to redistribute income slightly in favor of the
lower income groups.

### THE SIZE OF THE NATIONAL INCOME

The fiscal system may increase national income both by increasing aggregate demand, if unemployed resources are available, and by creating incentives and facilities for long-term economic development. It is generally recognized that aggregate
demand can be increased, not only through the familiar method
of deficit spending but also through a balanced budget, because
normally part of the government's revenues are derived from
taxpayers who otherwise would have spent this money abroad
or allowed it to go into idle savings. It also is recognized, however, that an increase in aggregate demand can increase national
income only if unemployed or "underemployed" resources are
available. Under conditions of approximately full employment,
the budget can change the composition and distribution of the
national income but cannot immediately increase its magnitude
in "real" terms. An increase in government expenditures under
conditions of full employment, even though fully balanced by
additional tax revenues, in fact tends to have inflationary effects.
It seems probable that the increase in the Salvadorean budget
in recent years has resulted in competition between the govern-

ment and the private sector of the economy for factors of production which, since there was full employment, has tended to intensify the prevailing inflation.

The second way in which the budget can increase the national income is through developmental expenditures aiding long-term development. The Salvadorean government's developmental expenditures have ranged from 10 per cent of total expenditures during the late thirties to 20 per cent during the middle forties. It appears to have been the government's policy to stimulate development, not by the direct creation of new industries and enterprises, but by creating conditions in which private enterprises could expand and develop. The government has built roads and established credit facilities and is now planning a major power project; it has provided tariff and quota protection to some industries and has created a tax system which, by and large, avoids interference with incentives to enterprises. With minor exceptions, the government has not followed the policy of many other Latin American countries which, through "fomento" institutes and otherwise, have directly promoted industrialization. The success of the Salvadorean "indirect developmental approach" so far has been fairly moderate. This does not indicate that the approach holds out no promise, but it appears that more comprehensive and better balanced policies, involving emphasis on credit, the creation of a capital market, technical instruction and training, storage and marketing facilities, and tariff reform, may be necessary to make the policy fully effective. None of these measures, moreover, would prevent the government from adopting, in addition, the "direct developmental approach," if it should so decide.

## 5. FISCAL POLICY DURING ECONOMIC FLUCTUATIONS (CHAPTER XI)

Increasing attention has been paid in recent years to the effects of economic fluctuations and to the possibility of compensating action on the part of the government. Although the opportunities for anticyclical policy in El Salvador are limited, they deserve some attention.

### CHARACTERISTICS OF ECONOMIC FLUCTUATIONS
### IN EL SALVADOR

In El Salvador, as in other export economies, economic fluctuations have been the result mainly of the ups and downs of world markets. Despite its heavy dependence upon coffee exports, however, the country has shown remarkable resistance to international fluctuations. The impact of the cycle has been mitigated by the predilection of the United States consumer for El Salvador's mild coffee, by the resilience of the large subsistence sector which forms the basis of the country's economy, and by the conservative character of its banking system. If there is a weak spot, it may well prove to be the high cyclical flexibility of tax revenues, which in monetary terms have risen sharply during the latest upswing and may suffer a corresponding contraction in case of a depression.

### OBJECTIVES FOR SALVADOREAN ANTICYCLICAL POLICY

There is little that a small export economy can do to counteract international fluctuations, but some scope for action exists, and attention must be given particularly to avoidance of action that would aggravate fluctuations. Interest in anticyclical policy usually centers upon measures to mitigate depressions, but for an export economy the most decisive actions are those that are taken during the upswing. It is during the period of rising exports, incomes, and money supply that the monetary authorities must endeavor to limit credit expansion and to accumulate a sizable exchange reserve while the fiscal authorities must seek to avoid large increases in the budget and to pay off government debt or accumulate a Treasury surplus. If they succeed in these endeavors, they will have accomplished the immediate aim of relieving the pressure of inflation upon the lower income groups and also the longer-run aim of strengthening the economy against a future depression.

### LEGISLATION FOR ANTICYCLICAL POLICY

While these anti-inflation aims are difficult to realize in practice, they do not present any inherent difficulties of principle.

About measures to counteract a depression, on the other hand, it is difficult to generalize. The authorities will have to endeavor to reconcile two objectives that are inherently in conflict. On the one hand, they will find themselves impelled to give immediate assistance to the economy, through public works, purchases of crop surpluses, credits to distressed producers and property owners, and related measures. On the other hand, they must prevent these inherently expansionary measures from endangering the soundness of the monetary and fiscal system. It may be pointed out that in a country where tax revenues have shown a high degree of cyclical flexibility, the budget deficit that is produced automatically by the shrinkage of revenues in a severe depression may well be so great as to exceed what is tolerable, even from the viewpoint of an aggressive compensatory policy. In that case, it may well be that the government will have to place emphasis upon salvaging the fiscal and monetary structure at the expense of plans for anticyclical fiscal policy.

## 6. The Budget and the Currency (Chapter XII)

Government finances, more than almost any other factor, are decisive for the soundness of the currency. El Salvador's conservative fiscal and monetary policies are largely responsible for the country's maintenance of a currency that has been completely stable in terms of gold since 1934, and at all times free from exchange controls — a distinction almost unique in Latin America. Very little therefore needs to be said herein about the effects of the budget on the currency.

### FISCAL OPERATIONS AND THE MONEY SUPPLY

The operations of the Salvadorean treasury have influenced the money supply through the direct issuance of subsidiary currency, loan operations with the banking system, and the movement of the treasury cash balance. The net impact has to all practical purposes been zero. This monetary neutrality of the government has permitted the Central Reserve Bank to conduct an orthodox policy of stable exchange rates and free exchange markets.

### ECONOMIC EFFECTS OF THE GOVERNMENT'S MONETARY NEUTRALITY

The economy has benefited from this conservative policy in terms of greater convenience for international operations, a preferred status as an export market for the United States, and certain anti-inflationary effects resulting from the free flow of funds and merchandise. On the other hand, it does not appear that exchange stability and freedom have been as successful as might perhaps have been hoped in stimulating the growth of savings and investment and the inflow of foreign capital. But this does not imply that the sacrifices, in terms of limitations on credit and public spending, that have been imposed upon the economy in order to secure stable and free exchanges have been in vain. There is no evidence that the economy has suffered as a result of these restraints. If progress in the direction of industrialization and diversification has not been rapid, this seems due primarily to the slowness of the spirit of enterprise in responding to the incentives offered by the government. Having pursued for a number of years a policy of stimulation of private enterprise, of which policy the maintenance of free and stable exchanges is a part, the country has acquired a certain stake in these conditions, and could change them only at a not inconsiderable loss. There is reason to believe that if these exchange policies can be continued, their effects may eventually become cumulative. Given the wholehearted cooperation of Salvadorean entrepreneurs, the approach pursued so far may be expected to call forth an increasing measure of development.

### 7. THE PUBLIC DEBT IN THE NATIONAL ECONOMY (CHAPTER XIII)

The public debt of El Salvador is very small and, in contrast to the public debts of many other countries, has exerted very little influence upon the economy. Its main aspects may therefore be summarized very briefly.

#### HISTORY AND PRESENT STATUS OF THE PUBLIC DEBT

Prior to 1922, the country's public debt was largely internal, but several substantial issues in 1922 made it predominantly an external one. The debt service incurred by these issues was onerous, and was suspended repeatedly during the hard years of the thirties. In 1946, a new basis for payment was established and the debt is now serviced regularly at interest rates of 3 to 4 per cent. In 1948, annual payments on the outstanding debt of 32.4 million colones amounted to 2.4 million colones.

#### GENERAL ASPECTS OF SALVADOREAN DEBT OPERATIONS

The burden of the present debt is very light, since annual service in 1946 amounted to little more than 3.7 per cent of exports and only 0.6 per cent of national income. The circumstances and policies that have resulted in so small a debt burden are of some importance. Particular interest attaches to the difficulty of tapping domestic savings, the avoidance of central bank financing, and the question of foreign borrowing.

*Difficulty of Tapping Domestic Savings.* The government has financed its public works program entirely out of taxes, without resort to loans. Since public works, if productive, increase the tax capacity of the country, there would probably be some justification for financing a limited part of such projects through loans from domestic investors. In the past, however, no such borrowing would have been possible because of the absence of a domestic capital market. The development of a capital market that would facilitate the utilization of savings by government and private enterprise would greatly strengthen the economy.

*Avoidance of Central Bank Borrowing.* El Salvador has consistently avoided central bank financing of the inflationary type so often practiced by other countries. This policy has greatly contributed to the maintenance of stable monetary conditions. It may be added, however, that small-scale purchases of government securities by the central bank, undertaken in the open market and on the bank's own initiative, are often valuable for the development of the capital market, and are generally regarded as quite safe from the monetary point of view as long as they remain small.

*Possibilities of Borrowing Abroad.* The annual service of 2.4 million colones on the existing foreign debt amounts to only 5.3 per cent of total budgetary expenditures (1946 figures) and, as already noted, 3.7 per cent of exports. The very modest character of this burden, together with the strength of the currency and the satisfactory condition of the budget, should put the country in a position to assume moderate additional foreign indebtedness, in the event that the government were to undertake to borrow abroad for productive purposes.

PART TWO

# CHAPTER II

# THE SETTING AND STRUCTURE OF THE ECONOMY

## 1. Composition and Distribution of the Gross National Product

THE PEOPLE OF EL SALVADOR, who occupy some of the most densely populated territory in Central America, carry on an economy based primarily on agriculture, and particularly on coffee. In 1946, some 2,047,000 Salvadoreans produced a gross

### TABLE 1

#### Gross National Product by Source of Income, 1946[a]

| Source of income | Gross product in millions of colones | Per cent of total gross national product |
|---|---|---|
| Agriculture | 199.9 | 46.0 |
|   Coffee | (53.0) | (12.2) |
|   Other agricultural | (146.9) | (33.8) |
| Forestry and mining | 17.4 | 4.0 |
| Construction | 15.0 | 3.4 |
| Industry | 46.0 | 10.6 |
| Interest payments and rents | 25.5 | 5.9 |
| Commercial services | 80.5 | 18.5 |
| Professional services | 11.5 | 2.6 |
| Government services | 23.0 | 5.3 |
| Other services | 16.1 | 3.7 |
| Total gross national product | 434.9 | 100.0 |

• The "gross national product" is the market value of all goods and services produced by the national economy, before deduction of depreciation charges.

The "national income" represents the aggregate earnings of labor and property arising from the current production of goods and services by the national economy

In El Salvador the national income probably is 5 to 10 per cent smaller than the gross national product, but no specific national income computations are available. Wherever, for brevity's sake, the term "national income" is used in connection with El Salvador, it is to be understood as referring to the gross national product. In some of the older writings, the term "national income" is sometimes applied to the revenues of the government, but needless to say this use of the word is quite out of keeping with present-day practice and is never employed in this study.

national product[1] that approximated 435 million colones ($174 million), equal to 218 colones ($87) per capita. Roughly 200 million colones or 46.0 per cent of this gross national product in 1946 came from agricultural and pastoral production, as is shown in Table 1.

Of this 200 million colones, the coffee crop, which is the dominating force in the economy, accounted for 53 million colones or 26 per cent. Other major agricultural products are such basic foodstuffs as corn, beans, maicillo, sugar, and rice, as well as henequen and cotton. Production in the extractive industries — mining and forestry — approximated 4 per cent of the gross national product, while residential construction constituted 3.4 per cent. Industrial production, consisting chiefly of textiles, alcoholic beverages, seed oils, hides and leather, rope, flour, cement blocks, and various minor products, contributed about 10.6 per cent. Interest payments, rents, and services, including those of the government, constituted a little more than one third of the total.

The estimated distribution of this 1946 gross national product of 435 million colones among Salvadorean family units (families of five) is shown in Table 2. The data indicate that of a total of

TABLE 2

GROSS NATIONAL PRODUCT BY FAMILY INCOME GROUPS, 1946[a]

| Family income in colones | Number of families | Per cent of total population | Average family income in colones | Per cent of gross national product |
|---|---|---|---|---|
| Under 600............ | 240,000 | 60.0 | 584.6 | 32.2 |
| 600–1,200............ | 120,000 | 30.0 | 877.5 | 24.2 |
| 1,200–2,400........... | 20,000 | 5.0 | 1,749.5 | 8.1 |
| 2,400–3,600........... | 10,000 | 2.5 | 2,911.4 | 6.7 |
| 3,600 and over........ | 10,000 | 2.5 | 12,528.0 | 28.8 |
| Total............ | 400,000 | 100.0 | 1,087.5[b] | 100.0 |

[a] The population of 2,000,000 is assumed to be composed of 400,000 families of five members each. For further details, see Appendix G.
[b] Average for all families.

[1] For derivation of these estimates, see Appendix A.

about 400,000 families some 360,000 families, or 90 per cent, had annual incomes of less than 1,200 colones ($480); and 240,000 families, or 60 per cent, had 600 colones ($240) or less. This latter group of 240,000 families, with incomes of less than 600 colones in 1946, are largely rural, and a large part of their income is nonmonetary.

It is apparent from Table 1 that the Salvadorean economy is in good part self-sufficient. A large part of the population is engaged in the production of domestic foodstuffs, either as a primary occupation or as a supplement to employment in the coffee industry. In addition, a large number of families are self-subsisting units, and therefore a considerable portion of the economy must be regarded as nonmonetary. Nevertheless, the low degree of industrialization and economic diversification implies that most commodities other than those needed for basic subsistence must be obtained from abroad and be paid for with exports. Thus, although exports account for only a small portion of the gross national product, averaging only about 15 per cent, as may be seen in Table 3, their qualitative significance for the economy is very great.

TABLE 3

EXPORTS COMPARED WITH GROSS NATIONAL PRODUCT
(*In millions of colones*)

| Year | Gross national product | Exports | Per cent of exports to gross national product |
|------|------------------------|---------|-----------------------------------------------|
| 1939 | 244 | 31.8 | 13 |
| 1942 | 279 | 46.2 | 17 |
| 1945 | 398 | 53.3 | 13 |
| 1946 | 435 | 65.4 | 15 |

This significance is enhanced by the fact that one of the country's dominant political interests, the coffee growers, is identified with the foreign trade sector. Despite the relatively low ratio of exports to gross national product, the Salvadorean economy must therefore be regarded as basically an export economy. An investigation of the structure and fluctuations of the balance of payments is thus an essential supplement to the preceding description of the country's economy in terms of its gross national product. This investigation will now be undertaken.

## 2. THE BALANCE OF PAYMENTS AND ITS INFLUENCE ON THE DOMESTIC ECONOMY

The main sources of El Salvador's international income and expenditure are summarized in Table 4. The data for the five years analyzed indicate that fully four fifths of total foreign exchange receipts were derived from exports of coffee. The state of El Salvador's balance of payments, and ultimately of the entire economy, therefore inevitably becomes a function of the volume and price of the coffee crop.

The risks to which mono-export economies usually find themselves exposed have been compensated, for El Salvador, by the following two special characteristics of the United States market where most Salvadorean coffee has been sold in recent years: first, the absence of United States interests pressing for protection; and secondly, the fact that El Salvador, along with Colombia and Guatemala, is one of the three chief producers of mild "blue" coffee, which is required by the United States for blending with hard Brazilian coffees. A drop in the price of this coffee relative to that of hard coffees greatly increases the volume that can be sold. In consequence of this high price elasticity of demand for its coffee, El Salvador has rarely experienced difficulty in disposing of its entire coffee output.

Despite the relative stability of the volume of exports, the "real" returns from exports fluctuate considerably, in accordance with changes in the price of coffee and in the general price level of import goods, i.e., in accordance with the terms of trade. For the years 1920–1947, a calculation of the terms of trade is presented in Table 5, which takes the average price of coffee as an index of the price of exports and the United States wholesale price index of commodities other than farm products and foods (in colón equivalent) as an index of the cost of imports. The index of the terms of trade shows, as one would expect, that in general these terms deteriorated for El Salvador during periods

## TABLE 4

### BALANCE OF PAYMENTS OF EL SALVADOR FOR SELECTED YEARS

*(In thousands of colones)*

| | 1937 Credits | 1937 Debits | 1938 Credits | 1938 Debits | 1945 Credits | 1945 Debits | 1946 Credits | 1946 Debits | 1947 Credits | 1947 Debits |
|---|---|---|---|---|---|---|---|---|---|---|
| **Current-account transactions** | | | | | | | | | | |
| Merchandise | 37,083 | 25,939 | 25,857 | 22,765 | 52,421 | 33,751 | 63,424 | 52,125 | 99,135 | 91,860 |
| Coffee exports | (35,313) | ... | (23,779) | ... | (46,733) | ... | (51,571) | ... | (84,253) | ... |
| All other merchandise exports | (1,770) | ... | (2,078) | ... | (5,688) | ... | (11,853) | ... | (14,882) | ... |
| Net exports of nonmonetary gold | 1,869 | ... | 1,476 | ... | 616 | ... | 1,564 | ... | 367 | ... |
| Travelers' expenditures[a] | 691 | 1,749 | 713 | 1,947 | 687 | 4,282 | 1,264 | 4,907 | 2,022 | 5,217 |
| Dividends and interest[b] | 202 | 2,659 | 109 | 900 | 250 | 1,313 | 465 | 2,053 | 536 | 2,986 |
| Government expenditures[c] | 150 | 516 | 200 | 569 | 250 | 645 | 400 | 1,108 | 824 | 1,915 |
| Contributions[d] | 50 | 100 | 150 | 50 | 1,032 | 60 | 726 | 70 | 683 | 91 |
| Other current-account items, including insurance[e] | 535 | 1,570 | 1,019 | 1,508 | 2,471 | 2,145 | 2,957 | 2,060 | 8,452 | 2,894 |
| Total current account | 40,579 | 32,534 | 29,523 | 27,740 | 57,725 | 42,015 | 70,800 | 62,323 | 112,018 | 104,963 |
| Total capital movements (net) | ... | 7,622 | ... | 1,239 | ... | 16,348 | ... | 9,921 | 1,040 | ... |
| Changes in gold holdings (net) | ... | 148 | ... | 44 | 233 | ... | 1,871 | ... | ... | 5,697 |
| Errors or omissions[f] | ... | 275 | ... | 500 | 405 | ... | ... | 427 | ... | 2,398 |

[a] Estimated tourist expenditures prior to 1947; for 1947 covers total travelers' checks, letters of credit, and foreign currencies, bought and sold by local banks for travel purposes. Also covers passages sold by the international air transport companies.

[b] Debits comprise interest paid on foreign debt, and dividend and profit remittances to foreign companies and residents. Credits consist of profits from local banks' investments in foreign stocks, and interest on bonds of the external debt.

[c] Debits comprise expenditures for maintenance of foreign services, missions, scholarships, etc. Credits cover foreign diplomatic missions and consulates.

[d] Estimated personal receipts and expenditures, for the most part, but also includes government receipts from abroad in the form of United States aid, and the like.

[e] Insurance consists only of premium payments to, and claim payments by, foreign life and fire insurance companies operating in El Salvador. Item also covers workers' savings remittances, pensions, foreign companies' administrative expenditures, commissions, communication costs, subscriptions, foreign lottery tickets, etc.

[f] Residue of other items.

Source: *Balanza de Pagos de El Salvador*, Banco Central de Reserva de El Salvador, 1948.

## TABLE 5

### INDEX OF TERMS OF TRADE, 1920–1947

| | Index of import prices[a] | Index of coffee export prices[b] | Index of terms of trade[c] |
|---|---|---|---|
| 1920................. | 160 | 142 | 89 |
| 1921................. | 104 | 107 | 103 |
| 1922................. | 102 | 140 | 137 |
| 1923................. | 103 | 150 | 146 |
| 1924................. | 99 | 197 | 199 |
| 1925................. | 102 | 200 | 196 |
| 1926................. | 99 | 195 | 197 |
| 1927................. | 94 | 147 | 156 |
| 1928................. | 92 | 181 | 197 |
| 1929................. | 91 | 154 | 169 |
| 1930................. | 85 | 86 | 101 |
| 1931................. | 74 | 84 | 114 |
| 1932................. | 87 | 68 | 78 |
| 1933................. | 88 | 73 | 83 |
| 1934................. | 97 | 97 | 100 |
| 1935................. | 97 | 102 | 105 |
| 1936................. | 99 | 97 | 98 |
| 1937................. | 106 | 110 | 104 |
| 1938................. | 101 | 93 | 92 |
| 1939................. | 101 | 101 | 100 |
| 1940................. | 103 | 87 | 84 |
| 1941................. | 110 | 107 | 97 |
| 1942................. | 118 | 146 | 124 |
| 1943................. | 120 | 161 | 134 |
| 1944................. | 122 | 162 | 133 |
| 1945................. | 124 | 171 | 138 |
| 1946................. | 136 | 227 | 167 |
| 1947................. | 168 | 283 | 169 |

[a] United States Bureau of Labor Statistics index of wholesale prices for all commodities other than farm products and foods, in colón equivalent (converted from original 1926 base in terms of dollars). Its base was shifted to 1934–1938 = 100. This index was selected because it is most representative of prices in those world markets where El Salvador made its purchases during 1920–1947. Prior to 1935, it is less representative than in subsequent years because of the large volume of Salvadorean trade with European countries. In the years since 1939 this index does not differ significantly from the index of the unit cost of imports which was used in Appendix B to deflate the export sector of the gross national product.

[b] Annual value of coffee exports divided by annual physical volume of coffee exports and adjusted to make the 1934–1938 average equal 100.

[c] Index of coffee export prices divided by index of import prices. A rise in the index means an improvement in the terms of trade for El Salvador.

## TABLE 6

### DISTRIBUTION OF SALVADOREAN EXPORTS BY DESTINATION

*(Per cent of total)*

| Period | Value of exports in millions of colones | United States | Canada | Honduras | Guatemala | Other Latin American Republics | Germany | Denmark Norway and Sweden | Other Europe | Africa Asia and Oceania |
|---|---|---|---|---|---|---|---|---|---|---|
| 1920–1924[a] | 34.0 | 38 | ..[b] | ..[b] | ..[b] | 4[c] | 6 | 22 | 26 | 4[c] |
| 1925–1929[a] | 39.4 | 17 | ..[b] | ..[b] | ..[b] | 2[c] | 31 | 21 | 23 | 6[c] |
| 1930 | 27.3 | 23 | .. | 1 | 1 | 2 | 29 | 17 | 27 | .. |
| 1931 | 22.7 | 15 | .. | .. | 1 | 2 | 29 | 18 | 35 | .. |
| 1932 | 14.0 | 17 | .. | 1 | 1 | 1 | 33 | 17 | 29 | 1 |
| 1933 | 20.3 | 21 | .. | 2 | .. | .. | 26 | 17 | 31 | 3 |
| 1934 | 24.0 | 27 | .. | 1 | 1 | 3 | 31 | 13 | 24 | .. |
| 1935 | 27.1 | 48 | .. | 1 | 1 | 1 | 13 | 16 | 20 | .. |
| 1936 | 25.2 | 57 | .. | 1 | 1 | 5 | 14 | 14 | 8 | .. |
| 1937 | 38.8 | 61 | 4 | 1 | 1 | 1 | 11 | 11 | 10 | .. |
| 1938 | 27.4 | 62 | .. | 4 | 1 | 2 | 10 | 15 | 6 | .. |
| 1939 | 31.8 | 60 | .. | 4 | 3 | 2 | 9 | 10 | 8 | 4 |
| 1940 | 30.6 | 75 | 1 | 4 | 1 | 2 | .. | 11 | 3 | 3 |
| 1941 | 28.0 | 79 | 7 | 5 | 4 | 3 | .. | 2 | .. | .. |
| 1942 | 46.2 | 82 | 5 | 4 | 4 | 4 | .. | .. | 1 | .. |
| 1943 | 56.3 | 80 | 2 | 5 | 4 | 8 | .. | .. | 1 | .. |
| 1944 | 57.5 | 73 | 12 | 5 | 2 | 4 | 2 | .. | 1 | 1 |
| 1945 | 53.3 | 85 | 6 | 3 | 2 | 3 | .. | .. | 1 | .. |
| 1946 | 65.4 | 71 | 9 | 8 | 4 | 4 | .. | 1 | 3 | .. |
| 1947 | 100.1 | 78 | 4 | 4 | 3 | 5 | .. | 2 | 4 | .. |

[a] Average.
[b] Not available.
[c] Partly estimated.

## TABLE 7

### DISTRIBUTION OF SALVADOREAN IMPORTS BY ORIGIN
#### (Per cent of total)

| Period | Value of imports in millions of colones | United States | Canada | Honduras | Guatemala | Other Latin American Republics | Germany | Great Britain | Other Europe[a] | Africa Asia and Oceania |
|---|---|---|---|---|---|---|---|---|---|---|
| 1920–1924[b] | 20.8 | 65 | ..[c] | ..[c] | ..[c] | 3[d] | 5 | 15 | 7 | 5[d] |
| 1925–1929[b] | 38.8 | 58 | ..[c] | ..[c] | ..[c] | 3[d] | 8 | 13 | 14 | 4[d] |
| 1930 | 23.9 | 49 | 1 | .. | 2 | 4 | 9 | 13 | 18 | 4 |
| 1931 | 14.9 | 50 | .. | .. | 2 | 7 | 9 | 12 | 17 | 3 |
| 1932 | 13.0 | 49 | .. | .. | 1 | 7 | 10 | 11 | 18 | 4 |
| 1933 | 16.2 | 46 | .. | .. | 1 | 5 | 12 | 14 | 17 | 5 |
| 1934 | 21.5 | 45 | 1 | 2 | 1 | 7 | 9 | 12 | 15 | 8 |
| 1935 | 22.7 | 38 | 1 | 2 | 2 | 5 | 25 | 14 | 13 | ... |
| 1936 | 21.1 | 39 | 1 | 1 | 2 | 3 | 33 | 11 | 10 | ... |
| 1937 | 26.0 | 40 | 1 | 2 | 1 | 3 | 31 | 11 | 11 | ... |
| 1938 | 22.9 | 47 | 1 | 3 | 1 | ... | 21 | 9 | 16 | 2 |
| 1939 | 22.1 | 53 | 1 | 3 | 1 | 3 | 17 | 7 | 15 | ... |
| 1940 | 20.3 | 67 | 2 | 3 | 1 | 5 | 1 | 8 | 12 | 1 |
| 1941 | 20.8 | 78 | 3 | 3 | 2 | 7 | 0.2 | 5 | 2 | ... |
| 1942 | 21.4 | 67 | 3 | 4 | 10 | 10 | ... | 5 | 1 | ... |
| 1943 | 29.9 | 68 | 2 | 3 | 5 | 16 | ... | 5 | 1 | ... |
| 1944 | 30.7 | 68 | 3 | 6 | 1 | 16 | ... | 3 | 3 | ... |
| 1945 | 33.8 | 68 | 3 | 6 | 1 | 17 | ... | 2 | 3 | ... |
| 1946 | 52.8 | 71 | 3 | 5 | 1 | 12 | ... | 3 | 5 | ... |
| 1947 | 92.3 | 78 | 2 | 3 | 1 | 6 | ... | 3 | 7 | ... |

[a] In the postwar period, consisted mainly of imports from the Low Countries and Scandinavia
[b] Average.
[c] Not available.
[d] Partly estimated.

of depression and improved during booms. It is interesting to note that in recent years, beginning in 1943, the terms of trade have been at a level that in terms of historical precedent is highly favorable to El Salvador.

Another important aspect of El Salvador's international position is the regional distribution of its export markets and its sources of supply, shown in Tables 6 and 7. As late as 1934, European countries, particularly Germany and the Scandinavian countries, were El Salvador's chief customers and suppliers. Europe accounted in that year for 68 per cent of all Salvadorean exports and 36 per cent of all Salvadorean imports. During the next few years, however — even before European trade was cut off by the war — both exports and imports shifted strongly toward the United States; in 1938 the United States took 62 per cent of the exports and supplied 47 per cent of the imports. In the postwar era the preponderance of the United States in Salvadorean trade has been even more pronounced, as is revealed by the fact that in 1947 the United States purchased 78 per cent of the exports and supplied 78 per cent of the imports.

This shift in the direction of Salvadorean trade has had the effect, so far, of insulating the country against European exchange and payments difficulties. During the early thirties, the trade pattern of El Salvador was "triangular," that is to say, the country purchased more from the United States than it sold there, and paid for the difference with dollars earned from an export surplus with Europe. The gradual spread of trade and payments restrictions in Europe during the thirties and the even tighter restrictions after the war would have put El Salvador in a difficult position had it not been possible to shift its trade toward the United States.

The present almost exclusive orientation toward the United States involves certain risks, because El Salvador, in effect, now depends upon the sale in a single foreign market of a single product which has only a limited domestic market and is characterized by a highly unstable price abroad. Owing, however, to the special advantages outlined above that are offered by the United States market to Salvadorean coffee, this risk is less than might at first appear. Moreover, the structure of the Salvadorean econ-

omy gives it a certain degree of protection against the consequences of severe changes in coffee prices. The country produces
most of its own basic foodstuffs; a large part of its imports are
therefore of a type that during bad times can be postponed. The
organization of the coffee plantations, furthermore, frequently
makes it possible for the worker to cultivate a small plot of land
upon which he can fall back in bad times. The Salvadorean economy is therefore on the whole less vulnerable to world-wide depressions than mono-export economies ordinarily tend to be. A
depression in world markets may reduce the standard of living
close to subsistence levels, but it does not mean mass unemployment and starvation because at that level the economy becomes
almost self-sustaining.

The aspects of Salvador's international economic position
dealt with so far all relate to the current part of the balance of
payments, which constitutes by far the most important segment.
Transactions on capital account are relatively unimportant, because foreign investment in El Salvador has remained small,
despite the relatively favorable conditions created by a free exchange market and stable exchange rates since 1934. While
these advantages have succeeded in attracting short-term foreign bank credit, long-term capital has entered the country only
on a small scale. The reasons for this must probably be sought
in the absence of large mineral resources and of opportunities
for large-scale plantation operations, which have been the typical outlets for foreign capital in the Caribbean area. The small
size of the market tends to discourage foreign investment for
production for domestic use. The default on the foreign debt
and the political uncertainties of recent years have reduced further the potential interest of foreign investors in El Salvador.

The low volume of foreign investments, on the other hand, has
relieved the Salvadorean balance of payments from the pressure
of heavy transfers of earnings on such investments. The favorable
implications of this circumstance, however, have frequently
been outweighed by the steady outflow of domestic funds to the
United States, which often has represented a far heavier drain.

## 3. ECONOMIC DEVELOPMENT

Until recently, the prosperity and advantageous competitive position of the Salvadorean coffee industry have tended to minimize the urgency of El Salvador's initiating a concerted effort toward diversification and industrialization. Lately, however, the pressure of population on limited land resources has become increasingly severe and now constitutes El Salvador's primary long-run economic problem. Its solution will probably have to be sought in a more balanced and intensive development of the country's resources through better agricultural methods and the establishment of small industries.

In recent years some gradual development in this direction has been evident. The output of cotton, sugar, henequen, and various foodstuffs has increased. A considerable number of industrial units, including textile plants, iron foundries, pharmaceutical plants, a vegetable-oil mill, and a sulphuric acid factory, have been established. The government has aided economic development through energetic road construction. A large hydroelectric project on the Lempa River is being planned. With the exception, however, of a textile mill owned by the *Mejoramiento Social* ("Social Betterment"), a quasi-governmental corporation, the government has not engaged directly in industrial development plans.

## 4. MONEY AND CREDIT

El Salvador has the almost unique distinction among Latin American countries of having maintained a stable exchange rate and a free exchange market since 1934. Since that time, the Salvadorean colón has been maintained at a rate of 2.5 to the United States dollar by the Central Reserve Bank (*Banco Central de Reserva*), which was created in 1934.

The banking system consists, in addition to the Central Reserve Bank, of three commercial banks, of which one is foreign-owned; the Mortgage Bank (*Banco Hipotecario de El Salvador*); a capitalization bank (*Capitalizadora de Ahorros S.A.*);[2] the Rural Credit Cooperatives with their central organization (*Fede-*

---

[2] A form of savings bank with insurance-policy features.

*ración de Cajas de Crédito*); and the Salvadorean Coffee Company (*Compañia Salvadoreña del Café, S.A.*), an organization which, without having been created as a credit institution, has on occasion engaged in sizable loan operations. In addition, there are numerous private lenders, including a few insurance companies, national as well as foreign, who operate in the country.

In general, both the short-term and the long-term credit needs of well-established businesses in leading branches of agriculture and industry are met in satisfactory volume and at reasonable rates. Enterprises in lines subject to a high degree of risk, however, as well as small economic units and individuals, particularly in agriculture, can secure credit only on onerous terms, or not at all.

The securities market is very little developed. The Mortgage Bank has succeeded in issuing a certain volume of *cédulas*, and some of the government's dollar bonds no doubt are owned locally. A satisfactory market for domestic government bonds or for the stocks or bonds of corporate enterprises still remains to be developed, however.

### 5. RECENT TRENDS

During the last eighteen years, the Salvadorean economy has undergone fluctuations similar to those experienced by other Latin American countries, although of lesser intensity. Table 8 shows the development of the gross national product, exports, government revenues, prices, and money supply, since 1930, reflecting very clearly the great depression of the early thirties, the recovery up to 1937, the less intense depression of the late thirties, and the wartime and postwar inflation. To illustrate the extent of these fluctuations, it may be noted that exports ranged from a low of 14.0 million colones in 1932 to a high of 38.8 million in 1937 and another high of 100.1 million in 1947. Government revenues for the same years ranged from a low of 14.8 million to highs of 20.0 and 50.3 millions in 1937 and 1947.

Except for the extreme gyrations of exports, it will be noted that the fluctuations were relatively moderate compared with those experienced by many other Latin American countries. This is due primarily to the relative stability that is inherent in

TABLE 8

SELECTED SALVADOREAN ECONOMIC DATA

| | Gross national product[a] (in millions of colones at current prices) | Total exports (in millions of colones) | Government tax revenues[b] (in millions of colones) | Wholesale price index (all goods 1937 = 100) | Total means of payment, including government deposits (in millions of colones, end of period) |
|---|---|---|---|---|---|
| 1930 | . . .[d] | 27.3 | 21.4 | . . .[d] | . . .[d] |
| 1931 | . . .[d] | 22.7 | 16.3 | . . .[d] | . . .[d] |
| 1932 | . . .[d] | 14.0 | 14.8 | . . .[d] | . . .[d] |
| 1933 | . . .[d] | 20.3 | 16.0 | . . .[d] | . . .[d] |
| 1934 | . . .[d] | 24.0 | 17.6 | . . .[d] | 24.1 |
| 1935 | . . .[d] | 27.1 | 18.6 | . . .[d] | 23.7 |
| 1936 | . . .[d] | 25.2 | 19.0 | 84 | 25.1 |
| 1937 | . . .[d] | 38.8 | 20.0 | 100 | 26.5 |
| 1938 | . . .[d] | 27.4 | 19.7 | 87 | 25.1 |
| 1939 | 244 | 31.8 | 18.8 | 73 | 26.0 |
| 1940 | 229 | 30.6 | 17.4 | 64 | 22.1 |
| 1941 | 232 | 28.0 | 17.6 | 80 | 29.3 |
| 1942 | 279 | 46.2 | 18.5 | 95 | 43.4 |
| 1943 | 351 | 56.3 | 21.5 | 114 | 63.2 |
| 1944 | 367 | 57.5 | 26.1 | 128 | 72.7 |
| 1945 | 398 | 53.3 | 26.7 | 148 | 86.6 |
| 1946 | 435 | 65.4 | 36.7 | 169 | 89.6 |
| 1947 | . . .[d] | 100.1 | 50.3 | 204 | 95.5 |
| 1948 | . . .[d] | . . .[d] | 47.4[c] | 239 | 95.3 |

[a] As estimated in Appendix B.
[b] For years prior to 1940, fiscal year tax revenues have been prorated on a calendar year basis.
[c] Budget figure for fiscal year 1948.
[d] Not available.

the economy despite its highly specialized character, and to the conservative monetary and fiscal policies pursued. There has been no large-scale deficit spending on the part of the government, and credit expansion by the banks has been very moderate despite the increase in reserves. At the end of 1948 the economy accordingly found itself free from the dollar shortage so prominent elsewhere and was in a strong position to meet the uncertainties of the future.

# CHAPTER III

## GENERAL ASPECTS OF GOVERNMENT FINANCE

THE FOCAL POINT of all government finance is the budget. It is in the budget that the plans and purposes of the government find expression and that their execution is controlled. All fiscal operations ultimately tie up with the budget.

In the present chapter, the budget will serve as guidepost to the various legislative and administrative aspects of Salvadorean government finance. Only a brief survey of the latter, however, can be given here, since full description, while interesting, would lead far beyond the scope of this primarily analytical study. The reader interested in a comprehensive though condensed discussion of these matters will find them assembled in Appendix C.

The budget and the fiscal functions centering upon it will be surveyed under five headings: (1) Preparation of the budget; (2) legislative enactment; (3) modifications after enactment; (4) execution of the budget; (5) controls. Particular attention will be given to the treatment that these key aspects are accorded in the Salvadorean legislation. Experience has shown that such legislation must be specially designed to overcome the numerous economic, political, and administrative complications and pitfalls that are apt to beset the progress of the budget from the planning stage to its final liquidation, since otherwise fiscal efficiency and control are bound to suffer. It may be said in advance that the Salvadorean legislation contains provisions adequate to cope with most of the problems that may arise.

### 1. PREPARATION OF THE BUDGET

The preparation of the budget is probably the most important single action of the government affecting the financial and general economic conditions of the country. Proof that this significance is recognized is the inclusion in the national constitution of some of the major legislative provisions regarding the budget.

Details are regulated by the Organic Budget Law (*Ley Orgánica de Presupuestos*).

Under the Budget Law, the Bureau of the Budget (*Dirección General del Presupuesto*) has primary responsibility for the preparation of the budget and for supervising its execution. The annual budgets prepared and liquidated by the bureau must account for all receipts and expenditures of public funds, no extra-budgetary operations being permitted. In accordance with a special provision of the constitution, the government since 1939 has included all receipts in a general fund, the special-fund practices previously prevailing having been abandoned in that year. The Budget Law contains detailed regulations to control the process of estimating government receipts. Estimates of revenues from existing taxes must not exceed the average of collections for the last five years. However, the law permits account to be taken of special developments that are likely to affect these mechanically computed estimates. The proceeds of new taxes may be freely estimated. All estimates must be prepared in cooperation with the Court of Accounts (*Corte de Cuentas*) and are subject to modification by the Ministry of Finance (*Ministerio de Economía*).

Estimates of expenditure requirements are submitted to the Bureau of the Budget by the various government departments and are adjusted by the bureau, again with the cooperation of the Court of Accounts and subject to modification by the Ministry of Finance.

The expenditure budget is divided into titles, and these into chapters; the latter subdivision is of particular importance because transfers of appropriations between chapters cannot be made without legislative approval. No global assignments of funds are permitted; each item must clearly indicate the purpose of the proposed expenditure. To facilitate control of disbursements during the course of the fiscal year, expenditures are divided into two categories, fixed and variable. For fixed expenditures, which consist mainly of salaries of government employees and other recurrent obligations, funds are automatically allotted to the disbursing agency by the Treasury and approved by the Court of Accounts on a monthly basis. For "variable expenditures," which comprise mainly the purchase of merchandise, payments for public works, and other irregularly occurring expenditures, funds are made available and approved only upon justification of the expenditure in each case. The distinction, while primarily administrative, will be frequently employed for analytical purposes in this study.

## 2. LEGISLATIVE ENACTMENT

The legislature, both before and after voting on the budget, may introduce modifications, but its freedom of action is circumscribed in various respects that give the executive some voice in the proceedings.

The budget as presented by the Bureau of the Budget and voted by the legislature must be balanced in the sense that aggregate revenues from all sources, including borrowing, must equal projected expenditures. Seasonal borrowing up to 10 per cent of budgeted revenues without special legislative approval is permitted by the constitution, but repayment before the end of the fiscal year is required. All other operations increasing the indebtedness of the government require legislative approval.

## 3. MODIFICATIONS AFTER ENACTMENT

Once the budget has been enacted, the executive can modify it, without legislative approval, in only two ways: (1) through simple transfer of credits within the same chapter, which is subject to the approval of the Bureau of the Budget and to various limiting conditions as to purpose and availability of funds; and (2) through exceptional credits, which may be appropriated directly by the executive in case of war and other catastrophes if the legislature is not in session. Supplementary appropriations may be requested by the executive from the legislature only during the second half of the fiscal year, subject to the approval of the Court of Accounts and the Bureau of the Budget.

Credit transfers and supplementary credits have been resorted to in every year since the enactment of the Budget Law. In all years the final budget of expenditures, after all modifications during the year, has been larger than the original budget. This practice, however, has not conflicted with the proper management of public finances, since expenditures have always remained within the limits of appropriated funds. On the other hand, the use made of transfers and supplementary credits has been quite liberal.

### 4. EXECUTION OF THE BUDGET

The revenues of the Salvadorean government are collected through three distinct administrative organizations: the Treasury (*Tesorería*), which controls the fourteen local tax administrations, the Bureau of Internal Revenue (*Dirección General de Contribuciones*), and the customs service (*Dirección General de la Renta de Aduanas*). All of the offices are divisions of the Ministry of Finance. Minor revenues accrue also through other government agencies and enterprises. Most of the indirect taxes are collected at the source, that is to say at the place of production (e.g. the liquor and cigarette taxes), or through the sales of tax stamps (e.g. the beer and soft-drinks taxes). Direct taxes are assessed on the basis of tax returns, and payment is requested through the issuance of a payment order (as in the case of the income and property-transfer taxes) or against a printed receipt (*boletos de Vialidad*).

The administration and the disbursement of public funds, in contrast to their collection, are the sole responsibility of the Treasury and its paymaster, under the control of the Court of Accounts. In order to obtain funds for disbursement, each government department must submit to the Finance Minister every second month a statement of fixed and variable expenditures which the budget provides for the particular department, and must request funds for the period in question. If the Finance Minister finds that the total of these requests is likely to exceed the funds available to the Treasury and to endanger budgetary equilibrium, he may request the department heads to lower their estimates. The final decision rests with the Cabinet. The disbursements, which are made by the paymasters in the various departments, are subject to the prior approval of the Court of Accounts, which checks them against the budget. Purchases of merchandise are handled through the General Purchasing Office (*Proveeduría General*), which maintains a merchandise warehouse. The payment of salaries of government employees is regulated by a permanent salary law which, however, during the recent inflationary period has been subject to repeated upward revisions.

## 5. CONTROLS

The control of government receipts and expenditures is the responsibility of the Court of Accounts, the functions of which are defined in the constitution. The court participates, with the Bureau of the Budget, in estimating budgetary receipts. It also prepares an annual report on the execution of the budget. The court furthermore must determine the legality of all purchases made by government departments and must countersign all purchase orders.

A survey of the pertinent legislation shows that the system of formal controls has been highly developed in El Salvador, if this term is understood to comprise those controls that ensure that all legal requirements are met. It may be added that the administration of the formal controls is practiced with great exactness and efficiency, as proved by the speedy completion of the budget liquidation and the accuracy with which all published accounts can be reconciled.

The pertinent laws also provide for the maintenance of "material" controls, this term being used to denote controls that go behind the legal justification of a given receipt or expenditure to scrutinize its economic appropriateness. The results of this type of controls do not appear, however, to have been as satisfactory as those of the system of formal controls, partly because of the inadequacy of the system itself and partly because of the failure to develop an effective technique to put this type of controls into practice. A similar weakness seems to hamper the controls designed to ensure the maintenance of an equilibrium of receipts and expenditures over the course of the fiscal year. As a result, a drop of revenues below budget estimates may fail to be translated with sufficient speed into an appropriate reduction of expenditures. On the other hand, the record shows that an excess of revenues over estimates has almost invariably been accompanied by a rapid increase in expenditures through supplementary appropriations. If any criticism can be made of the budget law in this respect, it is that it does not sufficiently restrain the tendency of expenditures to catch up with rising revenues, and thus on occasion permits the uneconomic use of funds.

The foregoing seem to be the only noticeable shortcomings of the budgetary legislation that experience has demonstrated since the legislation went into effect. In every other respect, the legislation seems to have produced the desired results. In appraising this satisfactory record, it must of course be remembered that the period of operation of the legislation has, despite many ups and downs, been free from extreme economic or political pressures.

# CHAPTER IV

## GOVERNMENT RECEIPTS

THE PRECEDING CHAPTER has presented a brief summary of the general administrative features of Salvadorean government finance. In this and the following chapters an attempt is made to analyze and appraise the financial operations of the Salvadorean government during the last decade. To view these operations in the broadest perspective, the subject is introduced with some general considerations about government finances.

### 1. OBJECTIVES OF GOVERNMENT FINANCE

The objectives of government finance can be summarized under the following headings:

(1) The maintenance of the basic machinery of government and the procurement of such services as governments generally provide for the citizens of their countries.

(2) The promotion of economic development, either by direct government action, such as the construction of highways, or indirectly through the combined effect of taxation and expenditures on the economic system.

(3) The improvement of social and cultural conditions, including not only specific purposes like education and public health, but also broad social objectives, such as a distribution of income that will ensure a balanced growth of the economy. These goals may be pursued both through tax policy and through expenditure policy.

(4) Stabilization of the economy in so far as possible, and compensation for fluctuations in general business activities, aiming at the maintenance of full employment. This may be accomplished both through an adaptation of taxation to changing economic conditions and through public works.

All government expenditures must be met by receipts from taxes or borrowing. All fiscal operations of the government therefore have two distinct aspects and pose two distinct sets of problems. The first pertains to the effects on the economy produced by the raising of the funds, whether by taxation, by borrowing, or through the sale of government property. The second concerns the effects on the economy of the expenditure of these funds, since every expenditure determines the allocation of manpower and materials between the private and the public sectors of the economy and exercises an influence upon the price level and the level of total economic activity. The question of the desirability of a particular financial action of the government — for instance, whether a specific tax should be raised or lowered, or whether expenditures on one of the objectives of government action should be increased or decreased — will have to take account of a range of complex alternatives. The principle that could be adopted for guidance in such decisions is that a marginal colón spent by the government, for any specific purpose, should produce the same satisfaction to the average taxpayer that it would have yielded had the taxpayer been able to spend it for his private benefit. This principle also may serve as the yardstick for judging the adequacy and efficiency of the fiscal system.

## 2. DEVELOPMENT OF THE PRESENT REVENUE SYSTEM

The present chapter discusses the first or revenue aspect of government finance. It presents a breakdown of all public reve-

TABLE 9

NATIONAL AND MUNICIPAL GOVERNMENT RECEIPTS OF EL SALVADOR, 1945–1947

|  | 1945 | 1946 | 1947 |
|---|---|---|---|
| *In thousands of colones* | | | |
| National............... | 29,057 | 39,503 | 53,620 |
| Lottery............... | 1,845 | 2,202 | 2,610 |
| Municipal............. | 3,512 | 3,940 | 4,276 |
| Total............. | 34,414 | 45,645 | 60,506 |
| *In per cent of total* | | | |
| National............... | 84.4 | 86.5 | 88.6 |
| Lottery............... | 5.4 | 4.8 | 4.3 |
| Municipal............. | 10.2 | 8.6 | 7.1 |
| Total............. | 100.0 | 100.0 | 100.0 |

# TABLE 10

## FIVE-YEAR AVERAGES OF GOVERNMENT RECEIPTS, BY SOURCE OF INCOME, 1900–1948

*In thousands of colones*

| | Import duties | Export taxes | Liquor taxes | Stamp taxes | Direct taxes | Property-transfer taxes | Various taxes, fees, fines | Consular fees | Govt. enterprises | Other receipts | Total |
|---|---|---|---|---|---|---|---|---|---|---|---|
| 1900–1904 | 3761.3 | 611.0 | 1918.6 | 107.9[a] | ... | ... | 267.9 | | | 258.3 | 6881.7 |
| 1905–1909 | 5204.9 | 774.6 | 2211.0 | 251.7 | ... | ... | 388.9 | | | 584.9 | 9416.5 |
| 1910–1914 | 6781.5 | 1320.9 | 2757.0 | 357.4 | ... | ... | 794.8 | | | 703.6 | 12715.1 |
| 1915–1919 | 4828.3 | 1959.5 | 2662.4 | 457.9 | 477.0[b] | ... | 642.8 | | | 753.8 | 11686.1 |
| 1919/20–1923/24 | 5972.3 | 1947.6 | 2402.7 | 536.2 | 712.8 | | 696.9 | | | 894.9 | 13163.1 |
| 1924/25–1928/29 | 11631.2 | 2460.8 | 4093.6 | 631.1 | 802.0 | | 1495.8 | | | 1090.0 | 22324.6 |
| 1929/30–1932/33[b] | 8854.8 | 3314.7 | 2798.4 | 572.1 | 1235.8 | | 1355.5 | | | 1587.3 | 19718.7 |
| 1933/34–1934/35[c] | 11,298.8 | | 2054.8 | 536.3 | 789.6 | 362.8 | 1640.8 | 925.5 | 1387.6 | 786.0 | 19782.0 |
| 1935/36–1938/39[b] | 9216.5 | 2291.0 | 1986.1 | 642.0 | 942.7 | 386.2 | 1791.5 | 1145.2 | 1176.9 | 679.7 | 20676.0 |
| 1939–1943[d] | 7505.1 | 1210.4 | 2200.6 | 836.2 | 1631.0 | 692.9 | 2827.7 | 1278.1 | 1268.2 | 1395.9 | 20846.1 |
| 1944–1948 (Budget) | 13543.4 | 5383.9 | 3823.6 | 1517.2 | 3164.0 | 966.8 | 5486.1 | 2695.5 | 1793.8 | 1892.8 | 40267.1 |

TABLE 10 (Continued)

| | Import duties | Export taxes | Liquor taxes | Stamp taxes | Direct taxes | Property-transfer taxes | Various taxes, fees, fines | Consular fees | Govt. enterprises | Other receipts | Total |
|---|---|---|---|---|---|---|---|---|---|---|---|
| *In per cent of total* | | | | | | | | | | | |
| 1900–1904 | 54.7 | 8.9 | 27.9 | 1.5[a] | ... | ... | 3.9 | | | 3.8 | 100.0 |
| 1905–1909 | 55.3 | 8.2 | 23.5 | 2.7 | ... | ... | 4.1 | | | 6.2 | 100.0 |
| 1910–1914 | 53.3 | 10.4 | 21.7 | 2.8 | ... | ... | 6.3 | | | 5.5 | 100.0 |
| 1915–1919 | 41.3 | 16.8 | 22.8 | 3.9 | | 4.1[b] | 5.5 | | | 6.5 | 100.0 |
| 1919/20–1923/24 | 45.4 | 14.8 | 18.3 | 4.1 | | 5.4 | 5.3 | | | 6.8 | 100.0 |
| 1924/25–1928/29 | 52.1 | 11.0 | 18.4 | 2.8 | | 4.0 | 6.7 | | | 4.9 | 100.0 |
| 1929/30–1932/33[b] | 44.9 | 16.8 | 14.2 | 2.9 | | 6.3 | 6.9 | | | 8.0 | 100.0 |
| 1933/34–1934/35[c] | 57.1 | | 10.4 | 2.7 | 4.0 | 1.8 | 8.3 | 4.7 | 7.0 | 4.0 | 100.0 |
| 1935/36–1938/39[b] | 44.6 | 11.1 | 9.6 | 3.1 | 4.6 | 1.9 | 8.7 | 5.5 | 5.7 | 3.3 | 100.0 |
| 1939–1943[d] | 36.0 | 5.8 | 10.6 | 4.0 | 7.8 | 3.3 | 13.5 | 6.1 | 6.1 | 6.7 | 100.0 |
| 1944–1948 (Budget) | 33.6 | 13.4 | 9.5 | 3.8 | 7.9 | 2.4 | 13.6 | 6.7 | 4.5 | 4.7 | 100.0 |

Note: Figures do not necessarily add up to total because of rounding.
[a] Three-year average.
[b] Four-year average.
[c] Two-year average.
[d] Four-and-one-half-year average (July 1939 to December 1943).

nues of El Salvador, and a survey of the development of the present revenue system over the last fifty years. This description will provide a factual basis for the analysis of the fiscal system in the subsequent chapters.

By far the greater part of the public revenues represents collections by the national government. Of the total of 60.2 million colones collected in 1947, 56.2 million, or 93 per cent (Table 9) were collected by the national government either directly or through the national lottery. The municipalities accounted for the remainder. There are at present no other public bodies that raise funds for public use.[1]

Like the revenue system of any other country, the Salvadorean system is not the result of a preconceived plan but the end product of a slow process of growth and adaptation to the changing economic structure of the country. In order to obtain a picture of the development of the present revenue structure, the revenue system of the national government during the last fifty years will be briefly described.

The revenues of the national government for the years 1900–1948 are summarized in Table 10. The figures include receipts of the General Fund as well as, since 1931–32, receipts of all special funds.[2] The data reveal the major changes in the structure of government revenues that took place during that period.[3]

[1] With the exception of certain charitable and welfare institutions which, in addition to government funds, obtain also small private donations. In previous years public funds accrued also to other administrative units, such as various departmental or special *juntas;* moreover, certain taxes and other charges were allocated to special funds. These institutions, however, never had the right to levy taxes directly, all taxes being levied for them by the fiscal administration of the government. They are therefore included in the figures of government receipts.

[2] The figures, as shown in Table 10 and subsequent tables, were taken from the official budget liquidation data as given in the annual *Memoria* of the Ministry of Finance or of the Court of Accounts. Data for the fiscal year 1935–36 and thereafter have been adjusted through the elimination of certain amounts that would otherwise have been counted twice (either in the same, or in consecutive years) as the result of the combination, in the statistics here developed, of the general and the special funds.

[3] Although the classification of receipts pertains to administrative aspects of revenues rather than to generic types. For instance, "stamp taxes" include certain taxes on liquor, collected through the affixing of stamps; consular fees are mainly fees for consular invoices which are tantamount to *ad valorem* import duties.

Total revenues increased in monetary terms almost sixfold. This seems to indicate that the functions of the government, so far as they find an expression in financial transactions, have substantially increased since the beginning of the century, although the increase in real terms (corrected for price changes) certainly has been substantially smaller than the absolute figures would suggest. The increase in total revenues is more or less in line with similar developments in other countries, and is partly accounted for by the rise in population and in national income and wealth experienced during the same period.

As to the respective contributions of the various classes of revenues to the total of government receipts, the outstanding development of the last fifty years has been the gradual and almost uninterrupted decline of the importance of import duties as the major revenue source. Import duties still form the most important single group of government revenues, but in the five years preceding this study they accounted for not more than 33 per cent of total receipts, while at the beginning of the century they amounted to 55 per cent. This substantial relative decline, which is in line with developments in many other countries, whether industrialized or not, is somewhat offset by the rising volume of collections of consular fees, the bulk of which represent another form of import duties.

The outstanding characteristic of export taxes seems to be the relative instability of this form of taxation as a source of government revenue, a fact that will be further explored below. Liquor taxes declined more than any other group of taxes, in terms of their significance to the Treasury. Between 1900 and 1904, more than one fourth of all government receipts was made up of liquor taxes; at present, their contribution is less than 10 per cent. Direct taxes and property-transfer taxes, both of which entered into the Salvadorean tax structure relatively early, have increased sharply in importance in the last three decades, although their contribution to total government receipts is at present less than in many other countries, including several Latin American republics. Since several other taxes, included in the table under export taxes or under "various" taxes, are collected in lieu of direct taxes, the Salvadorean achievement with respect to the development of direct taxes is not fully evident from the classifications of the accompanying tables.

Another outstanding characteristic of the composition of the Salvadorean government revenue system is the relative smallness of receipts from government services and enterprises as well as of "other receipts." Receipts of these types have played an increasingly important role in the revenue systems of several Latin American countries. The absence of such a development in El Salvador reflects the fact that the Salvadorean government has not engaged to any significant extent in industrial and commercial enterprise.

A reflection of the increasing diversification of the Salvadorean tax structure is the increase, in absolute and in relative terms, in receipts from the miscellaneous or "various" tax category. This group includes several internal consumption taxes on cotton, sugar, cigarettes, matches, etc., which have become more important in recent years.

### 3. The Revenue System since 1935

A more detailed and more systematic summary of Salvadorean revenues for the years 1935–36 to 1948 is presented in Table 11. Table 12 shows the percentage breakdown of revenues in this period. Tax receipts are further analyzed in Table 13.[4]

A scrutiny of the tables indicates that taxes, together with fees and fines, made up the bulk of government receipts. They

---

[4] As pointed out above, certain adjustments have been made in the original data for 1935–36 and subsequent years. These adjustments assure the comparability of the earlier with the later years when all receipts were allocated to the general fund. A reconciliation of the figures shown in Table 11 with the original data as presented in the *Memoria* is shown in Appendix E. It will be noted that in the case of the Mejoramiento Social, an institution of public law which has been engaged in the sale of government-owned land in family-size farm units to individuals, and in the operation of a textile factory, only tax receipts were included in the revenues of the government. "Other receipts," such as the proceeds from the sale of merchandise and receipts from the rent or sale of land, are excluded because they do not appear in the budget of the latest years, when taxes formerly received by the Mejoramiento Social flowed into the general fund and the agency's operations were supported through the payment of a government subsidy. Like other autonomous public bodies, the Mejoramiento Social maintains its own budget, which consists partly of receipts from sources other than the Treasury.

## TABLE 11
### GOVERNMENT REVENUES, 1935–1948
(*In thousands of colones*)

| | 1935/36 | 1936/37 | 1937/38 | 1938/39 | 1939[a] | 1940 | 1941 | 1942 | 1943 | 1944 | 1945 | 1946 | 1947 | 1948[b] |
|---|---|---|---|---|---|---|---|---|---|---|---|---|---|---|
| Taxes, fees, and fines, total.. | 17,555.5 | 20,462.2 | 19,522.8 | 18,186.7 | 8,904.7 | 17,428.2 | 17,640.5 | 18,497.8 | 21,865.5 | 26,143.9 | 26,708.9 | 36,723.1 | 50,368.7 | 47,429.4 |
| Direct taxes............. | 1,140.4 | 866.8 | 928.1 | 1,066.7 | 421.6 | 1,273.6 | 2,055.1 | 2,384.9 | 2,386.2 | 2,740.5 | 3,554.2 | 3,937.3 | 3,766.8 | 3,388.0 |
| Property and property-transfer taxes.......... | 482.4 | 469.3 | 423.1 | 480.0 | 224.4 | 497.9 | 536.8 | 652.5 | 777.2 | 600.3 | 864.1 | 958.9 | 993.8 | 835.0 |
| Taxes on exports......... | 1,400.9 | 4,107.4 | 2,067.8 | 1,588.1 | 208.6 | 1,515.9 | 892.4 | 1,374.9 | 1,471.5 | 4,423.7 | 1,775.6 | 4,498.9 | 7,221.3 | 9,000.0 |
| Transaction and business-license taxes......... | 925.6 | 779.6 | 936.4 | 935.6 | 453.0 | 1,110.7 | 1,133.7 | 1,290.6 | 1,454.7 | 1,510.6 | 1,539.9 | 1,912.6 | 2,165.9 | 1,766.7 |
| Taxes on imports......... | 10,196.4 | 10,640.9 | 11,664.2 | 10,540.8 | 5,518.4 | 9,212.8 | 9,214.3 | 7,779.0 | 9,700.2 | 9,719.8 | 11,242.7 | 15,028.1 | 24,531.7 | 22,292.2 |
| Consumption taxes....... | 2,643.2 | 2,885.2 | 2,942.3 | 3,041.0 | 1,697.7 | 3,342.6 | 3,348.1 | 4,047.6 | 5,048.7 | 6,414.3 | 7,053.6 | 8,644.1 | 10,663.4 | 9,170.9 |
| Beverage taxes....... | (1,923.0) | (1,988.6) | (2,133.3) | (2,147.1) | (1,079.8) | (2,033.8) | (1,953.6) | (2,384.7) | (2,896.3) | (3,658.4) | (3,824.6) | (4,571.1) | (5,227.9) | (4,285.9) |
| Tobacco taxes........ | (390.8) | (497.7) | (434.0) | (470.5) | (345.2) | (822.7) | (862.2) | (1,010.1) | (1,465.9) | (1,813.9) | (2,233.5) | (2,487.0) | (2,845.3) | (2,800.0) |
| Other consumption taxes | (329.4) | (398.9) | (374.1) | (424.4) | (272.7) | (468.1) | (541.3) | (643.8) | (686.5) | (930.0) | (1,095.5) | (1,586.0) | (2,590.2) | (2,085.0) |
| Other taxes............. | 535.6 | 514.8 | 362.4 | 298.9 | 275.6 | 239.6 | 221.7 | 711.0 | 716.1 | 479.0 | 384.1 | 1,305.0 | 594.9 | 652.0 |
| Fees................... | 100.4 | 112.1 | 116.4 | 123.5 | 49.1 | 118.6 | 157.5 | 165.6 | 202.1 | 187.1 | 204.9 | 262.3 | 243.5 | 198.1 |
| Fines.................. | 130.6 | 84.1 | 31.4 | 111.1 | 56.3 | 116.5 | 80.9 | 92.2 | 108.8 | 77.7 | 89.8 | 175.9 | 193.4 | 126.5 |
| Loans.................. | ... | ... | ... | ... | ... | ... | 1,660.0 | 1,460.0 | 1,260.0 | 1,000.0 | 50.0 | ... | ... | ... |
| Receipts from government enterprises, total...... | 1,335.0 | 1,269.8 | 1,333.6 | 1,285.9 | 661.0 | 1,448.7 | 1,283.9 | 1,376.7 | 1,820.8 | 1,608.1 | 1,742.2 | 2,084.3 | 2,225.5 | 2,141.3 |
| Postal system........... | 292.2 | 286.4 | 335.3 | 338.6 | 151.2 | 354.9 | 316.9 | 356.1 | 393.8 | 425.2 | 451.1 | 581.0 | 533.1 | 550.0 |
| Electric communications. | 619.7 | 691.2 | 688.5 | 682.6 | 350.7 | 695.8 | 719.3 | 777.5 | 852.2 | 949.4 | 999.4 | 1,182.3 | 1,155.0 | 1,206.0 |
| Other government enterprises.............. | 235.2 | 256.2 | 281.3 | 227.4 | 152.4 | 219.2 | 204.9 | 134.2 | 244.4 | 179.1 | 260.3 | 289.3 | 492.3 | 355.0 |
| Sale of government property.............. | 187.9 | 36.0 | 28.5 | 37.3 | 6.7 | 178.8 | 42.8 | 108.9 | 339.4 | 54.4 | 31.4 | 31.7 | 45.1 | 30.3 |
| Other receipts, total...... | 1,253.3 | 1,101.4 | 1,683.1 | 988.9 | 1,082.1 | 1,005.1 | 892.6 | 1,149.9 | 1,701.6 | 965.9 | 1,355.0 | 1,804.9 | 4,295.0 | 2,481.9 |
| Other receipts........... | 194.8 | 82.4 | 91.2 | 99.1 | 26.7 | 343.0 | 267.6 | 119.7 | 979.9 | 107.3 | 81.7 | 99.4 | 636.2 | 57.5 |
| Transitory items......... | 324.1 | 348.3 | 297.2 | 316.0 | 103.4 | 236.2 | 262.4 | 286.4 | 246.7 | 293.1 | 475.1 | 595.7 | 409.5 | 1,355.4 |
| Offset to expenditures and transfer of funds[c]...... | 322.2 | 487.0 | 1,143.7 | 202.3 | 801.5 | 157.3 | 23.1 | 265.5 | 98.4 | 15.9 | 18.3 | 24.2 | 28.7 | 719.0 |
| Funds in custody[c]........ | 412.2 | 183.7 | 151.0 | 371.5 | 150.5 | 268.6 | 339.5 | 478.3 | 376.6 | 549.6 | 779.9 | 1,085.6 | 3,220.6 | 350.0 |
| Grand total............. | 20,143.8 | 22,833.2 | 22,539.3 | 20,461.6 | 10,648.0 | 19,880.4 | 21,477.3 | 22,484.3 | 26,656.7 | 29,717.3 | 29,855.6 | 40,612.4 | 56,889.2 | 52,052.6 |
| Corrected total[d]......... | 19,409.4 | 22,162.5 | 21,244.6 | 19,887.8 | 9,696.0 | 19,454.5 | 21,114.7 | 21,740.5 | 26,181.7 | 29,151.8 | 29,057.4 | 39,502.6 | 53,639.9 | 50,983.6 |

[a] Second half of 1939 only.   [b] Budget.   [c] Excluded in corrected total.   [d] Excluding last two items under "Other receipts."

## TABLE 12

### PERCENTAGE COMPOSITION OF GOVERNMENT REVENUES, 1935–1948

| | 1935/36 | 1936/37 | 1937/38 | 1938/39 | 1939[a] | 1940 | 1941 | 1942 | 1943 | 1944 | 1945 | 1946 | 1947 | 1948[b] |
|---|---|---|---|---|---|---|---|---|---|---|---|---|---|---|
| Taxes, fees, and fines, total.. | 90.4 | 92.3 | 91.9 | 91.4 | 91.8 | 89.6 | 83.5 | 85.1 | 83.5 | 89.7 | 91.9 | 93.0 | 93.9 | 93.0 |
| Direct taxes.......... | -5.9 | 3.9 | 4.4 | 5.4 | 4.3 | 6.5 | 9.7 | 11.0 | 9.1 | 9.4 | 12.2 | 10.0 | 7.0 | 6.6 |
| Property and property-transfer taxes.. | 2.5 | 2.1 | 2.0 | 2.4 | 2.3 | 2.6 | 2.5 | 3.0 | 3.0 | 2.1 | 3.0 | 2.4 | 1.9 | 1.6 |
| Taxes on exports.......... | 7.2 | 18.5 | 9.7 | 8.0 | 2.2 | 7.8 | 4.2 | 6.3 | 5.6 | 15.2 | 6.1 | 11.4 | 13.5 | 17.7 |
| Transaction and business-license taxes.. | 4.8 | 3.5 | 4.4 | 4.7 | 4.7 | 5.7 | 5.4 | 5.9 | 5.6 | 5.2 | 5.3 | 4.8 | 4.0 | 3.5 |
| Taxes on imports.......... | 52.5 | 48.0 | 54.9 | 53.0 | 56.9 | 47.4 | 43.6 | 35.8 | 37.0 | 33.3 | 38.7 | 38.0 | 45.8 | 43.7 |
| Consumption taxes.......... | 13.6 | 13.0 | 13.8 | 15.3 | 17.5 | 17.2 | 15.9 | 18.6 | 19.3 | 22.0 | 24.3 | 21.9 | 19.9 | 18.0 |
| Beverage taxes.......... | (9.9) | (9.0) | (10.0) | (10.8) | (11.1) | (10.5) | (9.3) | (11.0) | (11.1) | (12.5) | (13.2) | (11.6) | (9.7) | (8.4) |
| Tobacco taxes.......... | (2.0) | (2.2) | (2.0) | (2.4) | (3.6) | (4.2) | (4.1) | (4.7) | (5.6) | (6.2) | (7.7) | (6.3) | (5.3) | (5.5) |
| Other consumption taxes | (1.7) | (1.8) | (1.8) | (2.1) | (2.8) | (2.4) | (2.6) | (3.0) | (2.6) | (3.2) | (3.5) | (4.0) | (4.8) | (4.1) |
| Other taxes.......... | 2.8 | 2.3 | 1.7 | 1.5 | 2.8 | 1.2 | 1.0 | 3.3 | 2.7 | 1.6 | 1.3 | 3.3 | 1.1 | 1.3 |
| Fees.......... | 0.5 | 0.5 | 0.5 | 0.6 | 0.5 | 0.7 | 0.7 | 0.8 | 0.8 | 0.6 | 0.7 | 0.7 | 0.5 | 0.4 |
| Fines.......... | 0.7 | 0.4 | 0.4 | 0.6 | 0.6 | 0.6 | 0.4 | 0.4 | 0.4 | 0.3 | 0.3 | 0.4 | 0.4 | 0.2 |
| Loans.......... | ... | ... | ... | ... | ... | ... | 7.9 | 6.7 | 4.8 | 3.4 | 0.2 | ... | ... | ... |
| Receipts from government enterprises, total.. | 6.9 | 5.7 | 6.3 | 6.5 | 6.8 | 7.4 | 6.1 | 6.3 | 7.0 | 5.5 | 6.0 | 5.3 | 4.2 | 4.2 |
| Postal system.......... | 1.5 | 1.3 | 1.6 | 1.7 | 1.6 | 1.8 | 1.5 | 1.6 | 1.5 | 1.5 | 1.6 | 1.5 | 1.0 | 1.1 |
| Electric communications.. | 3.2 | 3.1 | 3.2 | 3.4 | 3.6 | 3.6 | 3.4 | 3.6 | 3.3 | 3.3 | 3.4 | 3.0 | 2.2 | 2.4 |
| Other government enterprises.......... | 1.2 | 1.1 | 1.3 | 1.1 | 1.6 | 1.1 | 1.0 | 0.6 | 0.9 | 0.6 | 0.9 | 0.7 | 0.9 | 0.7 |
| Sale of government property.......... | 1.0 | 0.2 | 0.1 | 0.2 | 0.1 | 0.9 | 0.2 | 0.5 | 1.3 | 0.2 | 0.1 | 0.4 | 0.1 | 0.1 |
| Other receipts, total.......... | 2.7 | 1.9 | 1.8 | 2.1 | 1.4 | 3.0 | 2.5 | 1.9 | 4.7 | 1.4 | 1.9 | 1.8 | 2.0 | 2.8 |
| Other receipts.......... | 1.0 | 0.4 | 0.4 | 0.5 | 0.3 | 1.8 | 1.3 | 0.6 | 3.7 | 0.4 | 0.3 | 0.3 | 1.2 | 0.1 |
| Transitory items.......... | 1.7 | 1.6 | 1.4 | 1.6 | 1.1 | 1.2 | 1.2 | 1.3 | 0.9 | 1.0 | 1.6 | 1.5 | 0.8 | 2.7 |
| Corrected total.......... | 100.0 | 99.9 | 100.0 | 100.0 | 100.0 | 100.0 | 100.0 | 100.0 | 100.0 | 100.0 | 100.0 | 100.1 | 100.1 | 100.0 |

[a] Second half of 1939 only.
[b] Budget.

TABLE 13

PERCENTAGE COMPOSITION OF TAX RECEIPTS, 1935–1948

| | 1935/36 | 1936/37 | 1937/38 | 1938/39 | 1939[a] | 1940 | 1941 |
|---|---|---|---|---|---|---|---|
| Direct taxes............. | 6.5 | 4.2 | 4.8 | 5.9 | 4.7 | 7.3 | 11.6 |
| Property and property-transfer taxes.......... | 2.7 | 2.3 | 2.2 | 2.6 | 2.5 | 2.9 | 3.0 |
| Taxes on exports......... | 8.0 | 20.1 | 10.6 | 8.7 | 2.3 | 8.7 | 5.1 |
| Transaction and business-license taxes........... | 5.3 | 3.8 | 4.8 | 5.1 | 5.1 | 6.4 | 6.4 |
| Taxes on imports......... | 58.1 | 52.0 | 59.7 | 58.0 | 62.0 | 52.9 | 52.2 |
| Consumption taxes....... | 15.1 | 14.1 | 15.1 | 16.7 | 19.1 | 19.2 | 19.0 |
| Beverage taxes......... | (11.0) | (9.7) | (10.9) | (11.8) | (12.1) | (11.7) | (11.1) |
| Tobacco taxes......... | (2.2) | (2.4) | (2.2) | (2.6) | (3.9) | (4.7) | (4.9) |
| Other consumption taxes | (1.9) | (1.9) | (1.9) | (2.3) | (3.1) | (2.7) | (3.1) |
| Other taxes............. | 3.1 | 2.5 | 1.9 | 1.6 | 3.1 | 1.4 | 1.3 |
| Fees.................... | 0.6 | 0.5 | 0.6 | 0.7 | 0.6 | 0.7 | 0.9 |
| Fines.................. | 0.7 | 0.4 | 0.4 | 0.6 | 0.6 | 0.7 | 0.5 |
| Total taxes, fees, and fines.............. | 100.1 | 99.9 | 100.1 | 99.9 | 99.9 | 100.0 | 100.0 |

| | 1942 | 1943 | 1944 | 1945 | 1946 | 1947 | 1948[b] |
|---|---|---|---|---|---|---|---|
| Direct taxes............. | 12.9 | 10.9 | 10.5 | 13.3 | 10.7 | 7.5 | 7.1 |
| Property and property-transfer taxes.......... | 3.5 | 3.5 | 2.3 | 3.2 | 2.6 | 2.0 | 1.8 |
| Taxes on exports......... | 7.4 | 6.7 | 16.9 | 6.6 | 12.3 | 14.3 | 19.0 |
| Transaction and business-license taxes........... | 7.0 | 6.7 | 5.8 | 5.8 | 5.2 | 4.3 | 3.7 |
| Taxes on imports......... | 42.1 | 44.4 | 47.2 | 42.1 | 40.9 | 48.7 | 47.0 |
| Consumption taxes....... | 21.9 | 23.1 | 24.5 | 26.4 | 23.5 | 21.2 | 19.3 |
| Beverage taxes......... | (12.9) | (13.2) | (14.0) | (14.3) | (12.4) | (10.4) | (9.0) |
| Tobacco taxes......... | (5.5) | (6.7) | (6.9) | (8.3) | (6.8) | (5.7) | (5.9) |
| Other consumption taxes | (3.5) | (3.1) | (3.6) | (3.8) | (4.3) | (5.1) | (4.4) |
| Other taxes............. | 3.8 | 3.3 | 1.8 | 1.4 | 3.6 | 1.2 | 1.4 |
| Fees.................... | 0.9 | 0.9 | 0.7 | 0.8 | 0.7 | 0.5 | 0.4 |
| Fines.................. | 0.5 | 0.5 | 0.3 | 0.3 | 0.5 | 0.4 | 0.3 |
| Total taxes, fees, and fines.............. | 100.0 | 100.0 | 100.0 | 99.9 | 100.0 | 100.1 | 100.0 |

[a] Second half of 1939 only.
[b] Budget.

accounted for 90 per cent or more of all government revenues, except in those years in which the government obtained short-term loans from the central bank in accordance with the provisions of the Constitution and the Organic Budget Law.[5] Between 1935 and 1947, tax receipts almost tripled from 17.4 to 50.3 million colones. This increase, however, was not continuous: until 1942 tax revenues fluctuated between 17.4 and 20.5 million colones, but thereafter a gradual increase took place which gained momentum in the last two years for which performance figures (based on budget liquidations) are available. Receipts from government enterprises accounted for 4.2 to 7.4 per cent of total government receipts between 1935 and 1948. They have shown much greater stability than tax receipts but have followed the general upward trend, particularly in the latest years. "Other receipts" include so many divergent items that a year-to-year comparison is not very meaningful. If "offsets to expenditures and transfers of funds" and "funds in custody" [6] are excluded, "other receipts" dwindle to relatively insignificant proportions and do not in any way disturb the general picture.

## 4. Volume and Composition of Tax Receipts

In the period 1935 to 1948, taxes on imports showed the largest absolute increase, rising from 7.8 million colones in 1942 to a record level of 24.5 million colones, or by more than 200 per cent. The reasons for this sharp increase will be further explored below. The most stable tax groups were property and property-transfer taxes, and transaction and business-license taxes. Although in both groups substantial increases were recorded, they took the form of a gradual rise and did not exceed 130 per cent of the year with the lowest collections.

---

[5] Since these loans were repaid during the same year, they also appear under expenses.

[6] "Offsets to expenditures" are primarily receipts of overpayments (*devoluciones*) and of unauthorized expenditures; "transfers of funds" are receipts of the General Fund from special funds. For further discussion, cf. p. 320 in Appendix D.

"Funds in custody" were included in the official liquidations of general revenues only in the fiscal years 1935–36 and 1936–37. In order to make the data for these years comparable with the data for later years, these funds are included for all years in the uncorrected total and then excluded in the corrected total.

Of more interest and of greater significance for the analysis undertaken in later chapters is the fact that taxes on exports showed the widest fluctuations in the period under investigation, as well as the widest year-to-year fluctuations. This was almost exclusively due to the frequent and drastic changes that the price of coffee and the tax rates on coffee exports underwent during the period. Consumption taxes and direct taxes show the next widest fluctuations, although in both groups the year-to-year changes were much less pronounced than for export taxes. In both groups major increases took place only after 1943.

In terms of their relative contribution to total tax receipts (including fees and fines), the most important taxes were those on imports, including import duties, consular invoice charges, excise taxes levied on imported goods (such as taxes on pharmaceuticals and imported liquors), custom surcharges, etc. In all but one year (1944), this group accounted for more than 40 per cent of total tax receipts. Although their absolute volume has increased substantially, their relative importance as the most important source of government revenue has declined somewhat during the period of investigation. Prior to 1941 taxes on imports always accounted for more than 50 per cent of all taxes, but thereafter this percentage figure stayed significantly below 50. Consumption taxes, the second largest group of tax receipts, increased in relative significance, their percentage contribution to total tax receipts rising from a low of 14 per cent in the fiscal year 1936–37 to a high of 26.8 per cent in 1945. Taxes on exports, the major part of which is accounted for by the coffee tax, showed the largest percentage fluctuation of all tax groups, owing, as indicated above, to the highly volatile character of the coffee export tax.

The contribution of direct taxes to total tax receipts showed an upward trend during the period, which becomes quite pronounced when the coffee export tax, the sugar tax, and the cotton tax, which are paid in lieu of the income tax, are added. In the last two years, direct taxes, including gross receipt taxes, amounted to more than one fourth of total tax receipts; they accounted in the budget for 1948 for almost 30 per cent, a level previously reached only in 1944.

A detailed discussion of individual taxes, tax rates, schedules, and tax administration is contained in Appendix D. The information presented in that appendix serves as the factual basis for the analysis of the tax structure in the chapters that follow.

## 5. MUNICIPAL FINANCES

In view of the very limited importance of municipal finances, a few observations will suffice. The right of the municipalities to levy taxes or to assess charges against property under their geographical jurisdiction is severely limited. It is governed by the Municipal Rate Law (*Ley de Arbitrios Municipales*) of 1939, which permits the municipalities to administer their own real estate, movable property, and income therefrom, and to collect charges for public services such as light, water, sanitation, etc. As to the imposition of local taxes, the law provides that only such commodities or activities may be taxed as are "ordinarily" subject to municipal taxation, provided that such levies do not impede the free flow of commerce and are not harmful to the economy of the country.

Municipal taxes and fees are established by the municipal authorities. Before becoming effective, however, they must be approved by the Ministry of the Interior, which orders their publication. In order to assure equitability of municipal tax rates the Minister of the Interior may request information from the municipal authorities and from private persons.

The revenues of the municipalities, which, as indicated in Table 9, amounted to 4.3 million colones in 1947, consist primarily of an assortment of fees and charges for services such as street cleaning, garbage collection, maintenance of cemeteries, the issuance of certificates and permits, etc., and they therefore can be considered in part as payments for services rendered, not necessarily connected with the primary purposes and functions of government. No comprehensive statistical information is available for the financial activities of the municipalities except for the three years for which data are shown in Table 9. It is believed, however, that this omission is not of great significance.

## 6. THE NATIONAL LOTTERY

The third group of revenues shown in Table 9 are the receipts of the National Welfare Lottery (*Lotería Nacional de Beneficencia*), which is operated by a board of directors for the benefit of public welfare organizations. As Table 14 shows, the

TABLE 14

GROSS RECEIPTS OF THE NATIONAL LOTTERY, 1937–1947
(*In 1,000 colones*)

| | | | | | |
|---|---|---|---|---|---|
| 1937 | 1,126.1 | 1941 | 1,099.1 | 1945 | 1,844.7 |
| 1938 | 1,138.1 | 1942 | 1,108.2 | 1946 | 2,201.9 |
| 1939 | 1,153.9 | 1943 | 1,730.5 | 1947 | 2,610.1 |
| 1940 | 1,118.1 | 1944 | 1,467.1 | 1948[a] | 3,392.6 |

[a] Budget.

gross receipts of the lottery were quite substantial. However, net receipts, after deducting payments to lottery winners and commissions for the sale of lottery tickets (1948: 2.65 million colones) were relatively small (650,000 colones). The net receipts of the lottery (with the exception of some reserve funds) go to welfare institutions whose main financial support, however, is derived from subsidies paid by the national government from Treasury funds. There are no data available regarding the disbursements of the national lottery for public welfare purposes, and they therefore are not included in the discussion of Salvadorean public finances.

# CHAPTER V

## GOVERNMENT EXPENDITURES

FROM THE SURVEYS of the general administrative and legislative features of Salvadorean government finance and of government revenues in the two previous chapters, this study will now turn to a review of government expenditure. The economic significance of the figures here presented will be analyzed in detail in later chapters.

### 1. HISTORICAL BACKGROUND

The trend of expenditures of the Salvadorean government is shown in Table 15. The table indicates that in the last five dec-

TABLE 15

GOVERNMENT EXPENDITURES, 1900–1948

(*In thousands of colones*)

| Period | Expenditures | Period | Expenditures |
|---|---|---|---|
| *Five-Year Averages* | | *Annual Data* | |
| 1900–1904 | 7,725.3 | 1935/36 | 22,280.5 |
| 1905–1909 | 11,638.9 | 1936/37 | 22,250.2 |
| 1910–1914 | 14,684.9 | 1937/38 | 22,160.6 |
| 1915–1919 | 12,754.6 | 1938/39 | 19,958.4 |
| 1919/20–1923/24 | 15,680.3 | 1939[a] | 10,508.9 |
| 1924/25–1928/29 | 23,903.2 | 1940 | 22,173.5 |
| 1929/30–1933/34 | 21,810.5 | 1941 | 21,436.0 |
| 1934/35–1938/39 | 21,178.7 | 1942 | 21,843.0 |
| 1939[a]–1943 | 22,061.6 | 1943 | 23,315.7 |
| 1944–1948 | 41,597.4 | 1944 | 25,167.9 |
| | | 1945 | 29,135.5 |
| | | 1946 | 45,002.5 |
| | | 1947 | 51,847.2 |
| | | 1948[b] | 56,833.6 |

[a] Second half of 1939 only.
[b] Budget

ades expenditures have increased about fivefold. This increase is in line with the rise in government revenues, and is accounted for partly by the long-term increase of wealth and income of the country, partly by the increase in government functions, and partly by the decrease in the purchasing power of the currency. The latter was particularly pronounced in 1944–1948, and was largely responsible for the virtual threefold increase of government expenditures during the decade ending 1948.

The data shown in Table 15 are taken from the annual budget liquidations. Since the liquidations are prepared only a few months after the end of the fiscal year, not all data are final. This is made explicit by including in the liquidation figures an amount for unpaid obligations (*negocios pendientes*).[1]

## 2. EXPENDITURES SINCE 1935

A more detailed analysis, on an annual basis, of government expenditures has been made in Table 16 for the years 1935–1948. It should be noted that the figures used in this section are *unadjusted* data, that is, containing certain duplications that result from the combining of the general and all special funds (except trust funds).[2] In this period, total expenditures, as just defined, remained more or less stable at an annual level of 20 to 22 million colones until 1942. In subsequent years, an increase of expenditures, at first gradual and later rapid, took place, until the 1948 budget authorized expenditures of 57.5 million colones or almost two and one half times the amount expended only five years before. This increase is accounted for primarily by the inflationary price increases that took place during this period, and also by the fact that tax collections considerably above those in previous years permitted an expansion of expenditures.

---

[1] As is pointed out at the end of Appendix D, sums allocated in the budget liquidations for the payment of unpaid current obligations — obligations which subsequently proved to be over and above actual payment requirements and which, prior to 1940 only, were included as receipts in the following fiscal year — have been excluded from the so-called adjusted revenues for those fiscal years throughout this study.

[2] For a reconciliation of the official liquidation figures of government expenditures used in this section, with the totals shown elsewhere in this report, see Appendix F.

## TABLE 16

### GOVERNMENT EXPENDITURES BY TYPES, 1935–1948
#### (In thousands of colones and per cent of total)

| Year | Fixed expenditures (colones) | (per cent) | "Variable" expenditures excluding debt services (colones) | (per cent) | Debt service (colones) | (per cent) | Total expenditures[a] (colones) | (per cent) |
|---|---|---|---|---|---|---|---|---|
| 1935/36 | 12,003.8 | 53.8 | 5,935.3 | 26.6 | 4,360.0 | 19.6 | 22,299.1 | 100.0 |
| 1936/37 | 12,808.9 | 57.5 | 6,211.1 | 27.9 | 3,262.2 | 14.6 | 22,282.2 | 100.0 |
| 1937/38 | 13,249.2 | 59.6 | 6,614.8 | 29.7 | 2,373.4 | 10.7 | 22,237.4 | 100.0 |
| 1938/39 | 13,096.2 | 65.4 | 6,414.5 | 32.1 | 501.8 | 2.5 | 20,012.5 | 100.0 |
| 1939[b] | 6,876.8 | 65.0 | 3,588.1 | 33.9 | 117.5 | 1.1 | 10,582.4 | 100.0 |
| 1940 | 14,433.4 | 64.6 | 7,593.8 | 34.0 | 303.6 | 1.4 | 22,330.8 | 100.0 |
| 1941 | 14,405.0 | 67.1 | 5,332.6 | 24.9 | 1,721.5 | 8.0 | 21,459.1 | 100.0 |
| 1942 | 14,743.5 | 66.7 | 5,805.5 | 26.3 | 1,559.5 | 7.0 | 22,108.5 | 100.0 |
| 1943 | 15,018.2 | 64.1 | 6,984.7 | 29.9 | 1,411.2 | 6.0 | 23,414.1 | 100.0 |
| 1944 | 15,820.7 | 62.8 | 8,363.1 | 33.2 | 1,000.0 | 4.0 | 25,183.8 | 100.0 |
| 1945 | 17,608.8 | 60.4 | 8,919.3 | 30.6 | 2,625.9 | 9.0 | 29,153.8 | 100.0 |
| 1946 | 20,578.7 | 45.7 | 13,611.8 | 30.2 | 10,836.4 | 24.1 | 45,026.7 | 100.0 |
| 1947 | 25,389.6 | 48.9 | 23,950.2 | 46.2 | 2,536.2 | 4.9 | 51,875.9 | 100.0 |
| 1948[c] | 32,592.6 | 56.6 | 22,102.7 | 38.4 | 2,857.3 | 5.0 | 57,552.6 | 100.0 |

[a] These represent *unadjusted* totals, that is, without the elimination of certain duplications that result from the combining of the general and all special funds (except trust funds). For the adjustment of these figures to give the *adjusted* totals used elsewhere in this study, see Appendix F.
[b] Second half of 1939 only.
[c] Budget.

## FIXED AND "VARIABLE" EXPENDITURES

As was pointed out in Chapter III, the Budget Law and the control practices of the Court of Accounts distinguish fixed and "variable" expenditures. Basically, this distinction is based upon the regularity or nonregularity of expenditures. Fixed expenditures pertain almost exclusively to salary payments to government employees and to payments of subsidies to semipublic institutions (the main expenditures of which again are salaries), while "variable" expenditures represent disbursement for the purchase of materials, of real estate, the payment of wages in connection with public works, and the servicing of the public debt. If expenditures on the public debt are excluded from the category of "variable" expenditures, the breakdown of total expenditures in the categories under discussion takes the form shown in Table 16. The table indicates that fixed expenditures were somewhat more stable than "variable" expenditures and accounted for three fifths to two thirds of the total. Only in recent years has the proportion taken up by fixed expenditures fallen below 50 per cent. This was owing partly to the unusually large amounts spent on debt service in 1945 (after the resumption of the service on the foreign loan of 1922), and partly to the increased proportion of expenditures devoted to the purchase of materials and equipment. These changes are too recent to permit the identification of a definite trend in this connection.

## EXPENDITURES ON DEBT SERVICE

Expenditures on the public debt show wide fluctuations in absolute terms as well as percentage-wise. The great year-to-year differences in these expenditures have several causes. In the fiscal year 1935–36, the first year shown in the table, debt service was resumed after the 1931 suspension. Between 1939 and 1944 the servicing of the foreign loan of 1922 was again suspended, and the only payments incurred in this period were the repayment of short-term loans to the central bank and small interest and amortization payments for the Export-Import Bank loan of 1941. The large payment of 1946 represented the transfer of interest and amortization on the loan of 1922 in connection with the second resumption of the debt service.

It is worth noticing in this connection to what extent the relative importance of expenditures on the public debt has declined. These expenditures accounted for almost 40 per cent of the total budget at the beginning of the century. After the foreign loan of 1922 was obtained, they absorbed approximately one fourth of annual expenditures. Prior to 1940, the percentage declined to 10 per cent; in the last two years it amounted to only 5 per cent. This decline was due to the renegotiation of the terms of the loan of 1922 and to the general increase of prices and the ensuing increase of money income and accordingly of expenditures of the government. Thus, it appears that unless drastic changes in the revenue and expenditure system occur in the future, the fiscal problem posed by the foreign debt (as distinct from the transfer problem) has substantially declined.

### 3. GENERAL PATTERN OF GOVERNMENT EXPENDITURE DISTRIBUTION

Government expenditures are undertaken for a wide range of purposes, and any classification is bound to be arbitrary. The classification here presented, however, has the advantage not only of reflecting the main functions of a modern government, but also of facilitating international comparisons. The five categories distinguished are (1) general administration; (2) national defense; (3) cultural and social services; (4) economic development; (5) public debt service. This grouping underlies the subsequent discussion.

#### LONG-TERM EVOLUTION

The movement of expenditures since 1900 is summarized in Table 17. Under the heading of "general administration" have been included all expenditures not specifically allocated to national defense, cultural and social services, economic development, and public debt service. This group includes expenditures on all administrative functions of the government, as well as expenditures for the National Assembly and the judiciary system. Expenditures for general administrative purposes have increased more than tenfold in the last five decades and have

TABLE 17

FIVE-YEAR AVERAGES OF GOVERNMENT EXPENDITURES BY PURPOSE

| Period | General adminis- tration | National defense | Cultural and social services | Economic development | Public debt service | Total |
|---|---|---|---|---|---|---|
| *In thousands of colones* | | | | | | |
| 1900–1904 | 1,445.9 | 1,654.8 | 549.0 | 991.1 | 3,084.3 | 7,725.3 |
| 1905–1909 | 2,769.1 | 3,000.3 | 818.8 | 1,058.1 | 3,992.7 | 11,638.9 |
| 1910–1914 | 4,035.5 | 3,549.6 | 1,463.6 | 1,558.5 | 4,077.7 | 14,684.9 |
| 1915–1919 | 4,704.1 | 3,040.6 | 1,815.5 | 1,377.0 | 1,817.3 | 12,754.6 |
| 1919/20–1923/24 | 5,935.6 | 3,433.1 | 2,343.9 | 876.8 | 3,090.9 | 15,680.3 |
| 1924/25–1928/29 | 6,943.1 | 4,379.0 | 2,767.6 | 3,325.6 | 6,467.9 | 23,903.2 |
| 1929/30–1933/34 | 7,320.6 | 3,736.3 | 3,198.1 | 2,580.5 | 4,975.0 | 21,810.5 |
| 1934/35–1938/39 | 7,760.8 | 3,679.2 | 3,044.8 | 4,033.1 | 2,660.8 | 21,178.7 |
| 1939–1943[a] | 8,875.9 | 3,623.4 | 4,001.5 | 4,424.5 | 1,136.3 | 22,061.6 |
| 1944–1948[b] | 15,610.4 | 4,637.0 | 8,518.9 | 8,859.9 | 3,971.1 | 41,597.4 |
| *In per cent of total* | | | | | | |
| 1900–1904 | 18.7 | 21.4 | 7.1 | 12.8 | 39.9 | 100.0 |
| 1905–1909 | 23.8 | 25.8 | 7.0 | 9.1 | 34.3 | 100.0 |
| 1910–1914 | 27.4 | 24.2 | 10.0 | 10.6 | 27.8 | 100.0 |
| 1915–1919 | 36.9 | 23.8 | 14.2 | 10.8 | 14.2 | 100.0 |
| 1919/20–1923/24 | 37.9 | 21.9 | 14.9 | 5.6 | 19.7 | 100.0 |
| 1924/25–1928/29 | 29.0 | 18.3 | 11.6 | 13.9 | 27.1 | 100.0 |
| 1929/30–1933/34 | 33.6 | 17.1 | 14.7 | 11.8 | 22.8 | 100.0 |
| 1934/35–1938/39 | 36.6 | 17.4 | 14.4 | 10.0 | 12.6 | 100.0 |
| 1939–1943[a] | 40.2 | 16.4 | 18.1 | 20.1 | 5.2 | 100.0 |
| 1944–1948[b] | 37.5 | 11.1 | 20.5 | 21.3 | 9.5 | 100.0 |

[a] July 1939–December 1943.
[b] Budget data for fiscal year 1948.

approximately doubled in their relative position among total expenditures. It is difficult to find any specific reason for this disproportionate growth of administrative expenditures, unless it is that the functions of the government have become more complicated as a result of the greater diversification of the social and economic life in the last fifty years. On the other hand, it is notable that expenditures for national defense have increased relatively much less than total expenditures, and that they have accounted in 1944–1948 for not more than 11 per cent of total expenditures, compared with 20 to 25 per cent in the first two decades of the century.

Expenditures for cultural and social services include all government outlays for the educational system as well as for hospitals, orphan homes, etc., and also subsidy payments to semipublic institutions of the same character. Such expenditures have risen very substantially during the last fifty years, until at present about one fifth of the total budget is devoted to these purposes, compared with only 7 per cent in the period from 1900 to 1904. Expenditures for economic development, which include all disbursements for public works (with the exception of the purely administrative functions of the Ministry of Development) and the subsidies paid by the government to the Mejoramiento Social and to such public bodies as the Coffee Growers' Association (*Asociación Cafetalera*) and the Cattle Raisers' Association (*Asociación de Ganaderos*) have also increased considerably, though at a less rapid rate than those for cultural and social purposes. At present they account for another fifth of total expenditures, compared with approximately 10 per cent in the earlier years of this century.

### RECENT PATTERN OF EXPENDITURES

Annual figures on the distribution of government expenditures by objectives for the years 1935–1948 are shown in Tables 18 and 19, which reaffirm the tendencies shown for the longer period discussed above. Expenditures for national defense declined appreciably in relative significance, while the share of expenditures for cultural and social services and for economic development increased somewhat. If the debt service charges are excluded from the percentage distribution because of their highly erratic behavior, the over-all picture of the distribution of total expenditures among the various objectives remains largely unchanged. The fact that payment or nonpayment of debt services in the years under discussion did not particularly affect the distribution of expenditures among the other government objectives indicates that the burden of government debt was minimized by the policy of suspending debt service in those years in which

## TABLE 18

### ANNUAL GOVERNMENT EXPENDITURES BY PURPOSE, 1935–1948

*(In thousands of colones)*

|  | 1935/36 | 1936/37 | 1937/38 | 1938/39 | 1939[a] | 1940 | 1941 |
|---|---|---|---|---|---|---|---|
| General administration | 7,570.5 | 7,825.1 | 8,384.7 | 8,350.3 | 4,467.6 | 8,920.1 | 8,622.9 |
| National defense | 4,086.7 | 3,588.4 | 4,121.4 | 3,499.6 | 1,973.3 | 3,695.4 | 3,631.1 |
| Cultural and social services | 2,773.0 | 3,076.7 | 3,204.3 | 3,352.3 | 2,024.3 | 4,141.4 | 3,852.4 |
| Economic development | 3,507.7 | 4,529.5 | 4,153.4 | 4,308.4 | 1,999.2 | 5,270.8 | 3,631.4 |
| Debt service | 4,361.2 | 3,262.4 | 2,373.4 | 501.8 | 117.5 | 303.6 | 1,721.5 |
| Total | 22,299.1 | 22,282.2 | 22,237.4 | 20,012.5 | 10,582.4 | 22,330.8 | 21,459.1 |
| Adjustment | 18.6 | 32.0 | 76.8 | 54.1 | 73.5 | 157.3 | 23.1 |
| Adjusted total | 22,280.5 | 22,250.2 | 22,160.6 | 19,958.4 | 10,508.9 | 22,173.5 | 21,436.0 |

|  | 1942 | 1943 | 1944 | 1945 | 1946 | 1947 | 1948[b] |
|---|---|---|---|---|---|---|---|
| General administration | 9,231.9 | 9,317.2 | 10,098.8 | 11,681.3 | 13,716.8 | 20,684.1 | 22,676.4 |
| National defense | 3,618.8 | 3,386.6 | 3,619.3 | 3,814.6 | 4,460.2 | 5,857.0 | 5,434.1 |
| Cultural and social services | 4,001.5 | 3,987.2 | 4,685.3 | 5,238.3 | 7,401.0 | 10,692.3 | 14,577.8 |
| Economic development | 3,697.1 | 5,311.7 | 5,780.7 | 5,793.5 | 8,612.7 | 12,106.1 | 12,006.3 |
| Debt service | 1,559.5 | 1,411.2 | 1,000.0 | 2,625.7 | 10,836.3 | 2,536.2 | 2,857.3 |
| Total | 22,108.5 | 23,414.1 | 25,183.8 | 29,153.8 | 45,026.7 | 51,875.9 | 57,552.6 |
| Adjustment | 265.5 | 98.4 | 15.9 | 18.3 | 24.2 | 28.7 | 719.0 |
| Adjusted total | 21,843.0 | 23,315.7 | 25,167.9 | 29,135.5 | 45,002.5 | 51,847.2 | 56,833.6 |

[a] Second half of 1939 only.  [b] Budget.

## TABLE 19

### ANNUAL GOVERNMENT EXPENDITURES BY PURPOSE, 1935–1948

(In per cent of total expenditures)

| | 1935/36 | 1936/37 | 1937/38 | 1938/39 | 1939[a] | 1940 | 1941 | 1942 | 1943 | 1944 | 1945 | 1946 | 1947 | 1948[b] |
|---|---|---|---|---|---|---|---|---|---|---|---|---|---|---|
| **Including debt service** | | | | | | | | | | | | | | |
| General administration.... | 34.0 | 35.1 | 37.7 | 41.7 | 42.2 | 39.9 | 40.2 | 41.8 | 39.8 | 40.1 | 40.1 | 30.5 | 39.7 | 39.4 |
| National defense.......... | 18.3 | 16.1 | 18.5 | 17.5 | 18.6 | 16.5 | 16.9 | 16.4 | 14.5 | 14.4 | 13.1 | 9.9 | 11.3 | 9.4 |
| Cultural and social services | 12.4 | 13.8 | 14.4 | 16.8 | 19.1 | 18.5 | 18.0 | 18.1 | 17.0 | 18.6 | 18.0 | 16.4 | 20.6 | 25.3 |
| Economic development.... | 15.7 | 20.3 | 18.7 | 21.5 | 18.9 | 23.6 | 16.9 | 16.7 | 22.7 | 23.0 | 19.9 | 19.1 | 23.3 | 20.9 |
| Debt service............. | 19.6 | 14.6 | 10.7 | 2.5 | 1.1 | 1.4 | 8.0 | 7.1 | 6.0 | 4.0 | 9.0 | 24.1 | 4.9 | 5.0 |
| Total............... | 100.0 | 99.9 | 100.0 | 100.0 | 99.9 | 99.9 | 100.0 | 100.1 | 100.0 | 100.1 | 100.1 | 100.0 | 99.8 | 100.0 |
| **Excluding debt service** | | | | | | | | | | | | | | |
| General administration.... | 42.2 | 41.1 | 42.2 | 42.8 | 42.7 | 40.5 | 43.7 | 44.9 | 42.3 | 41.8 | 44.0 | 40.1 | 41.9 | 41.5 |
| National defense.......... | 22.8 | 18.9 | 20.7 | 17.9 | 18.9 | 16.8 | 16.8 | 17.6 | 15.4 | 15.0 | 14.4 | 13.0 | 11.9 | 9.9 |
| Cultural and social services | 15.4 | 16.2 | 16.1 | 17.2 | 19.3 | 18.8 | 19.5 | 19.5 | 18.1 | 19.4 | 19.7 | 21.6 | 21.7 | 26.7 |
| Economic development.... | 19.6 | 23.8 | 20.9 | 22.1 | 19.1 | 23.9 | 18.4 | 18.0 | 24.1 | 23.9 | 21.8 | 25.2 | 24.5 | 22.0 |
| Total............... | 100.0 | 100.0 | 99.9 | 100.0 | 100.0 | 100.0 | 100.0 | 100.0 | 99.9 | 100.1 | 99.9 | 99.9 | 100.0 | 100.1 |

[a] Second half of 1939 only.
[b] Budget.

the payment of interest and amortization charges would have infringed upon the availability of funds for other government objectives. This and the remarkable stability of the shares of the individual expenditure groups in total expenditures (aside from the long-term decline of national defense expenditures) are perhaps the most outstanding characteristics of the Salvadorean expenditure system since 1935.

It is quite surprising that the differences in economic conditions prevailing in, say, 1935, 1944, and 1947 should have left no noticeable mark on the composition of government expenditures. One of the major factors making for this stability is presumably the fact that the distribution of government expenditures among the various objectives has been well balanced in the sense that it has been suited best to the general political conditions prevailing in the country, with the result that the pressures on the Treasury for more funds for education, for economic development, and for general administrative purposes have more or less offset each other. On the other hand, the stability of the distribution of expenditures was perhaps also due to the lack of a conscious attempt to use the fiscal system to pursue specific economic objectives, and to the fact that preoccupation with certain immediate needs and policies (such as, for instance, the financing of the Mortgage Bank) overshadowed the conception and the enactment of long-run fiscal-policy of objectives.

Further light on the composition of government expenditures by objectives is thrown by the distinction between fixed and "variable" expenditures, as set forth in Table 20. If it is assumed that fixed expenditures are "unproductive" in the sense that they primarily assure the continuation of the functioning of existing government services, and if attention is focused on "variable" expenditures (excluding expenditures on debt service), which in most instances produce an increase in the quantity or quality of government services, it appears that the only pronounced change that occurred between 1935 and 1948, aside from the decline of the amount spent on national defense, was the constant rise of "variable" expenditures for cultural and social purposes. This seems to indicate that considerable additions were made in this period to the "plant facilities" for cul-

TABLE 20

GOVERNMENT EXPENDITURES, BY PURPOSES AND TYPES OF EXPENDITURES, 1935–1948

*In thousands of colones*

| | Fixed Expenditures | | | | | "Variable" Expenditures | | | | | | |
|---|---|---|---|---|---|---|---|---|---|---|---|---|
| | General administration | National defense | Cultural and social services | Economic development | Total Fixed | General administration | National defense | Cultural and social services | Economic development | Total "Variable" | Debt service | Grand total |
| 1935/36 | 5,480.3 | 2,632.5 | 2,595.8 | 1,295.1 | 12,003.8 | 2,091.4 | 1,454.2 | 177.2 | 2,212.6 | 5,935.3 | 4,360.0 | 22,299.1 |
| 1936/37 | 5,790.7 | 2,714.2 | 2,775.4 | 1,528.8 | 12,808.9 | 2,034.6 | 874.2 | 301.3 | 3,000.7 | 6,211.1 | 3,262.2 | 22,282.2 |
| 1937/38 | 6,171.1 | 2,747.2 | 2,967.6 | 1,363.4 | 13,249.2 | 2,213.6 | 1,374.2 | 236.7 | 2,790.0 | 6,614.8 | 2,373.4 | 22,237.4 |
| 1938/39 | 6,364.2 | 2,301.9 | 3,112.5 | 1,317.5 | 13,096.2 | 1,986.1 | 1,197.7 | 239.8 | 2,990.9 | 6,414.5 | 501.8 | 20,012.5 |
| 1939ᵃ | 3,354.8 | 1,415.2 | 1,641.4 | 465.1 | 6,876.8 | 1,112.8 | 558.1 | 382.9 | 1,534.1 | 3,588.1 | 117.5 | 10,582.4 |
| 1940 | 6,796.7 | 2,838.6 | 3,593.8 | 1,204.6 | 14,433.4 | 2,123.4 | 856.7 | 547.6 | 4,066.2 | 7,593.8 | 303.6 | 22,330.8 |
| 1941 | 6,931.4 | 2,874.2 | 3,396.3 | 1,197.6 | 14,405.0 | 1,691.5 | 756.9 | 456.1 | 2,433.8 | 5,332.6 | 1,721.5 | 21,459.1 |
| 1942 | 7,167.5 | 2,915.7 | 3,474.0 | 1,186.5 | 14,743.5 | 2,664.4 | 703.1 | 527.5 | 2,510.6 | 5,805.5 | 1,559.5 | 22,108.5 |
| 1943 | 7,260.6 | 2,932.5 | 3,490.9 | 1,333.9 | 15,018.2 | 2,056.6 | 454.1 | 496.3 | 3,977.8 | 6,984.7 | 1,411.2 | 23,414.1 |
| 1944 | 7,642.6 | 2,693.3 | 3,850.2 | 1,634.7 | 15,820.7 | 2,456.2 | 926.0 | 835.1 | 4,146.0 | 8,363.1 | 1,000.0 | 25,183.8 |
| 1945 | 8,557.9 | 3,341.2 | 4,349.2 | 1,360.3 | 17,608.8 | 3,123.4 | 473.4 | 889.1 | 4,433.2 | 8,919.3 | 2,625.7 | 29,153.8 |
| 1946 | 9,666.8 | 3,604.3 | 5,536.8 | 1,771.2 | 20,578.7 | 4,053.0 | 855.9 | 1,864.2 | 6,841.5 | 13,611.8 | 10,836.3 | 45,026.7 |
| 1947 | 11,842.8 | 3,884.9 | 7,046.6 | 2,615.3 | 25,389.6 | 8,841.3 | 1,972.1 | 3,645.8 | 9,490.8 | 23,950.0 | 2,536.2 | 51,875.9 |
| 1948 | 13,982.4 | 4,378.9 | 9,899.7 | 4,331.2 | 32,592.6 | 8,694.0 | 1,955.2 | 4,678.1 | 7,675.1 | 22,102.7 | 2,857.3 | 57,552.6 |

## TABLE 20 (Continued)

| | Fixed Expenditures | | | | | "Variable" Expenditures | | | | |
|---|---|---|---|---|---|---|---|---|---|---|
| | General administration | National defense | Cultural and social services | Economic development | Total Fixed | General administration | National defense | Cultural and social services | Economic development | Total "Variable" |
| *In per cent of total* | | | | | | | | | | |
| 1935/36 | 45.7 | 21.9 | 21.6 | 10.8 | 100.0 | 35.2 | 24.5 | 3.0 | 37.3 | 100.0 |
| 1936/37 | 45.2 | 21.2 | 21.7 | 11.9 | 100.0 | 32.8 | 14.1 | 4.8 | 48.3 | 100.0 |
| 1937/38 | 46.6 | 20.7 | 22.4 | 10.3 | 100.0 | 33.5 | 20.8 | 3.6 | 42.1 | 100.0 |
| 1938/39 | 48.6 | 17.6 | 23.8 | 10.0 | 100.0 | 31.0 | 18.7 | 3.7 | 46.6 | 100.0 |
| 1939ᵃ | 48.8 | 20.6 | 23.9 | 6.7 | 100.0 | 31.0 | 15.6 | 10.7 | 42.7 | 100.0 |
| 1940 | 47.1 | 19.7 | 24.9 | 8.3 | 100.0 | 28.0 | 11.3 | 7.2 | 53.5 | 100.0 |
| 1941 | 48.1 | 20.0 | 23.6 | 8.3 | 100.0 | 31.7 | 14.2 | 8.5 | 45.6 | 100.0 |
| 1942 | 48.6 | 19.8 | 23.6 | 8.0 | 100.0 | 35.6 | 12.1 | 9.1 | 43.2 | 100.0 |
| 1943 | 48.3 | 19.5 | 23.3 | 8.9 | 100.0 | 29.4 | 6.5 | 7.1 | 57.0 | 100.0 |
| 1944 | 48.3 | 17.1 | 24.3 | 10.3 | 100.0 | 29.4 | 11.1 | 9.9 | 49.6 | 100.0 |
| 1945 | 48.6 | 19.0 | 24.7 | 7.7 | 100.0 | 35.0 | 5.3 | 10.0 | 49.7 | 100.0 |
| 1946 | 47.0 | 17.5 | 26.9 | 8.6 | 100.0 | 29.8 | 6.3 | 13.7 | 50.2 | 100.0 |
| 1947 | 46.6 | 15.3 | 27.8 | 10.3 | 100.0 | 36.9 | 8.2 | 15.2 | 39.6 | 99.9 |
| 1948 | 42.9 | 13.4 | 30.4 | 13.3 | 100.0 | 39.3 | 4.8 | 21.2 | 34.7 | 100.0 |

ᵃ Second half of 1939 only.

tural and social services, or in other words that more and better equipped schools, hospitals, and similar institutions are available at present than seventeen years ago. "Variable" expenditures for economic development, which produce results in the form of better roads, more public buildings, and such less tangible but nevertheless real permanent improvements as better credit facilities (Mortgage Bank) and more small-scale farming (Mejoramiento Social), have not increased proportionately with the rise of all "variable" expenditures. As a matter of fact, in the last two years of this period "variable" expenditures for economic development declined in significance while "variable" expenditures for administrative purposes have shown a tendency to increase.

Neither fixed nor "variable" expenditures have shown a definite cyclical pattern in the period under discussion. This is more or less to be expected in the case of fixed expenditures. But it is surprising that the same situation has prevailed with respect to "variable" expenditures, the volume of which was apparently determined primarily by the availability of funds and not by fiscal-policy considerations, whether cyclical or developmental.[3]

## 4. Review of Three Major Expenditure Categories

So far, attention has been focused upon the general pattern of expenditures since 1900 and particularly since 1935–36. The three largest individual expenditure categories will now be surveyed: (1) general administration; (2) cultural and social development; and (3) economic development.

### EXPENDITURES FOR GENERAL ADMINISTRATION

A breakdown of administrative expenditures by government departments is shown in Table 21. Since within the period for which data are shown certain functions were shifted from one government department to another and new departments or offices within the departments were created, the original figures have been adjusted in order to make the annual figures comparable. The basis for the distribution by departments, as

[3] See, however, Chapter IX, page 165.

## TABLE 21

GENERAL ADMINISTRATIVE EXPENDITURES, BY DEPARTMENTS, 1935/36, AND 1940 TO 1948

*In thousands of colones*

| | 1935/36 | 1940 | 1941 | 1942 | 1943 | 1944 | 1945 | 1946 | 1947 | 1948 [a] |
|---|---|---|---|---|---|---|---|---|---|---|
| National Assembly | 225.7 | 224.1 | 198.8 | 193.1 | 192.3 | 372.3 | 554.0 | 365.5 | 373.8 | 363.8 |
| Office of the President | 243.6 | 252.4 | 263.4 | 250.1 | 244.2 | 272.7 | 351.9 | 462.2 | 552.4 | 596.7 |
| Ministry of the Interior | 1,631.3 | 1,798.1 | 1,706.2 | 1,811.0 | 1,938.6 | 1,943.9 | 2,019.9 | 2,362.6 | 3,155.8 | 4,157.6 |
| Ministry of Labor | 14.0 | 16.4 | 16.5 | 16.8 | 16.9 | 16.8 | 20.4 | 105.7 | 182.5 | 369.1 |
| Ministry of Development (administrative services only) | 45.0 | 55.7 | 56.2 | 58.5 | 59.0 | 65.0 | 83.5 | 93.1 | 145.1 | 199.4 |
| Ministry of Foreign Relations | 572.1 | 687.1 | 778.8 | 821.3 | 827.7 | 805.8 | 1,015.6 | 1,297.3 | 1,671.7 | 1,887.0 |
| Ministry of Justice | 416.1 | 538.3 | 542.0 | 515.5 | 491.3 | 573.3 | 606.4 | 870.4 | 993.8 | 1,601.4 |
| Ministry of the Economy | 1,063.2 | 1,719.9 | 1,732.9 | 1,925.6 | 2,151.5 | 2,432.0 | 2,122.8 | 3,087.3 | 4,215.8 | 5,255.1 |
| Ministry of Commerce | 5.5 | 5.7 | 6.0 | 21.3 | 21.1 | 5.8 | 21.3 | 23.1 | 24.1 | 24.4 |
| Ministry of Agriculture and Industry | 90.5 | 113.1 | 98.9 | 109.4 | 118.8 | 147.7 | 194.7 | 284.2 | 2,415.3 | 2,406.7 |
| Ministry of Public Safety | 1,050.0 | 1,245.0 | 1,203.7 | 1,168.3 | 1,187.7 | 1,175.0 | 1,316.3 | 1,582.5 | 1,716.7 | 1,977.1 |
| Court of Accounts | 229.2 | 341.8 | 347.5 | 349.9 | 346.7 | 354.8 | 377.0 | 429.4 | 658.2 | 730.7 |
| Judiciary Power | 510.7 | 640.2 | 642.9 | 652.6 | 655.4 | 643.5 | 708.5 | 789.8 | 905.2 | 1,131.4 |
| Pensions | 466.4 | 652.1 | 692.5 | 745.2 | 806.8 | 813.0 | 1,150.0 | 1,345.3 | 1,531.3 | 1,505.3 |
| "Automatic credits" | 1,007.2 | 630.2 | 336.6 | 593.3 | 259.2 | 477.2 | 1,139.0 | 618.4 | 2,142.4 | 410.7 |
| Total | 7,570.5 | 8,920.1 | 8,622.9 | 9,231.9 | 9,317.2 | 10,098.8 | 11,681.3 | 13,716.8 | 20,684.1 | 22,676.4 |

## TABLE 21 (Continued)

| | 1935/36 | 1940 | 1941 | 1942 | 1943 | 1944 | 1945 | 1946 | 1947 | 1948ᵃ |
|---|---|---|---|---|---|---|---|---|---|---|
| *In per cent of total* | | | | | | | | | | |
| National Assembly......... | 2.9 | 2.5 | 2.3 | 2.1 | 2.1 | 3.7 | 4.7 | 2.7 | 1.8 | 1.6 |
| Office of the President........ | 3.2 | 2.8 | 3.1 | 2.7 | 2.6 | 2.7 | 3.0 | 3.4 | 2.7 | 2.6 |
| Ministry of the Interior...... | 21.5 | 20.2 | 19.8 | 19.6 | 20.8 | 19.2 | 17.3 | 17.2 | 15.3 | 18.3 |
| Ministry of Labor.......... | 0.2 | 0.2 | 0.2 | 0.2 | 0.2 | 0.2 | 0.2 | 0.8 | 0.9 | 1.6 |
| Ministry of Development (administrative services only).. | 0.6 | 0.6 | 0.7 | 0.6 | 0.6 | 0.6 | 0.7 | 0.7 | 0.7 | 0.9 |
| Ministry of Foreign Relations. | 7.6 | 7.7 | 9.0 | 8.9 | 8.9 | 8.0 | 8.7 | 9.5 | 8.0 | 8.3 |
| Ministry of Justice.......... | 5.5 | 6.0 | 6.3 | 5.6 | 5.3 | 5.7 | 5.2 | 6.3 | 4.8 | 7.1 |
| Ministry of the Economy..... | 14.0 | 19.3 | 20.1 | 20.9 | 23.1 | 24.1 | 18.2 | 22.5 | 20.4 | 23.2 |
| Ministry of Commerce........ | 0.1 | 0.1 | 0.1 | 0.2 | 0.2 | 0.1 | 0.2 | 0.2 | 0.1 | 0.1 |
| Ministry of Agriculture and Industry.............. | 1.2 | 1.3 | 1.1 | 1.2 | 1.3 | 1.5 | 1.7 | 2.1 | 11.7 | 10.6 |
| Ministry of Public Safety..... | 13.9 | 14.0 | 14.0 | 12.7 | 12.7 | 11.6 | 11.3 | 11.5 | 8.3 | 8.7 |
| Court of Accounts........... | 3.0 | 3.8 | 4.0 | 3.8 | 3.7 | 3.5 | 3.2 | 3.1 | 3.2 | 3.2 |
| Judiciary Power............. | 6.7 | 7.2 | 7.5 | 7.1 | 7.0 | 6.4 | 6.1 | 5.8 | 4.4 | 5.0 |
| Pensions................... | 6.2 | 7.3 | 8.0 | 8.1 | 8.7 | 8.1 | 9.8 | 9.8 | 7.4 | 6.9 |
| "Automatic credits"......... | 13.3 | 7.1 | 3.9 | 6.4 | 2.8 | 4.7 | 9.8 | 4.5 | 10.4 | 1.8 |
| Total.................. | 99.9 | 100.1 | 100.1 | 100.1 | 100.0 | 100.1 | 100.1 | 100.1 | 100.1 | 99.9 |

ᵃ Budget.

presented in the table, is the organization of the government as it existed and was reflected in the budget for 1948.

The most noteworthy general observation with respect to the distribution of administrative expenditures by departments is the prevailing stability of the percentage distribution. In the period under consideration, expenditures of only five departments changed in relative significance. Expenditures for public safety, which include the cost of the state police, the finance police, and the customs guards, declined materially. This decline is the more noteworthy since, as indicated above, expenditures for the armed forces rose less than expenditures for any other purpose in absolute terms, and in relative terms declined to a fraction of their former share of total expenditures. Expenditures for pensions have behaved somewhat erratically in the last decade. Between 1940 and 1947 they increased two and one half times; during the same years, their relative share in total expenditures increased from 7 to almost 10 per cent. In the last two years of the period, however, the relative share of pension payments declined substantially, possibly owing to failure to adjust pension payments properly to the rising cost of living.

Expenditures for the judiciary system have not kept pace with the over-all increase in administrative expenditures, and the relative importance of the cost of the judiciary power has therefore declined — a phenomenon for which it is difficult to find an explanation.

The only branch of the government which in the last years has absorbed a much higher proportion of total administrative expenditures than ever before is the Ministry of Agriculture and Industry. This has been largely due to the assumption by the ministry of functions formerly allotted to other agencies of the government.[4]

EXPENDITURES FOR CULTURAL AND SOCIAL SERVICES

As pointed out above, the most important change in the distribution pattern of public expenditures has been the increase

---

[4] It proved to be impossible to adjust the expenditure data for previous years to take account of these administrative shifts. The increase must therefore be considered largely apparent only.

## TABLE 22

### Cultural and Social Expenditures, 1935/36, and 1940 to 1948

| | 1935/36 | 1940 | 1941 | 1942 | 1943 | 1944 | 1945 | 1946 | 1947 | 1948[a] |
|---|---|---|---|---|---|---|---|---|---|---|
| *In thousands of colones* | | | | | | | | | | |
| Ministry of Culture | 1,605.7 | 2,193.6 | 2,158.6 | 2,228.4 | 2,260.9 | 2,438.3 | 3,110.6 | 4,208.9 | 5,824.8 | 8,230.7 |
| Ministry of Social Assistance | 245.6 | 446.8 | 442.1 | 480.5 | 430.1 | 601.9 | 695.4 | 799.7 | 1,022.6 | 1,725.1 |
| Subsidies to cultural and social institutions | 597.9 | 1,501.0 | 1,251.7 | 1,292.6 | 1,296.2 | 1,645.1 | 1,432.3 | 2,392.4 | 3,844.9 | 4,622.0 |
| Expenditures of special funds | 323.9 | ... | ... | ... | ... | ... | ... | ... | ... | ... |
| Total | 2,773.0 | 4,141.4 | 3,852.4 | 4,001.5 | 3,987.2 | 4,685.3 | 5,238.3 | 7,401.0 | 10,692.3 | 14,577.8 |
| *In per cent of total* | | | | | | | | | | |
| Ministry of Culture | 57.9 | 53.0 | 56.0 | 55.7 | 56.7 | 52.0 | 59.4 | 56.9 | 54.5 | 56.5 |
| Ministry of Social Assistance | 8.9 | 10.8 | 11.5 | 12.0 | 10.8 | 12.8 | 13.3 | 10.8 | 9.6 | 11.8 |
| Subsidies to cultural and social institutions | 21.6 | 36.2 | 32.5 | 32.3 | 32.5 | 35.1 | 27.3 | 32.3 | 36.0 | 31.7 |
| Expenditures of special funds | 11.7 | ... | ... | ... | ... | ... | ... | ... | ... | ... |
| Total | 100.1 | 100.0 | 100.0 | 100.0 | 100.0 | 99.9 | 100.0 | 100.0 | 100.1 | 100.0 |

[a] Budget.

in the amounts devoted to cultural and social services. As Table 22 shows, the largest share of this increase has been devoted to an improvement of the educational system, the expenditures for which increased from 1.6 million to 8.2 million colones between 1935 and 1948, or approximately five times. As a scrutiny of the annual data for the final years indicates, the bulk of this increase was taken up by higher fixed expenditures, i.e., salary payments. A study of the "table of organization" of the educational system on the basis of the salary laws for earlier and later years reveals two important developments. In the first place, the number of positions for teachers in the school system has sharply increased since 1935. Secondly, the salaries paid to teachers, which were exceedingly low in the thirties compared with salaries paid to other government employees, have increased more than those of other employees, with the result that teaching in the Salvadorean school system became financially more attractive than a decade ago. It is to be assumed that as a result of this development, the quality of the teaching profession is also improving.

As to expenditures for social welfare purposes (hospitals, orphanages, free medical care, public hygiene, etc.), very substantial improvements have likewise been recorded since 1935. The most important development in recent years, however, has not been the increase in total expenditures for cultural and social services, but, as pointed out above, the continuous rise of "variable" expenditures, i.e., expenditures for new and improved physical facilities to provide such services. It is the increase in these expenditures that is most promising for a permanent rise in the social welfare and public health standards of the country.

Under the heading "subsidies to cultural and social institutions" are included payments by the government to those public educational and welfare institutions of which the financial transactions are not included in the annual budget of government expenditures but which operate their own budgets. With the exception of relatively small amounts received from the proceeds of the national lottery, the receipts of these institutions consist of subsidy payments from the General Fund. Therefore the subsidy payments, as shown in the annual budget liquidations

TABLE 23

EXPENDITURES FOR ECONOMIC DEVELOPMENT, 1935/36, AND 1940 TO 1948

| | 1935/36 | 1940 | 1941 | 1942 | 1943 | 1944 | 1945 | 1946 | 1947 | 1948[a] |
|---|---|---|---|---|---|---|---|---|---|---|
| *In thousands of colones* | | | | | | | | | | |
| Public works | 1,404.4 | 2,786.3 | 1,875.4 | 1,726.0 | 3,177.0 | 4,546.8 | 4,889.6 | 7,390.7 | 10,399.8 | 9,339.5[b] |
| Mejoramiento Social | 758.0 | 726.6 | 779.2 | 746.1 | 823.2 | 1,033.9 | 653.9 | 899.0 | 1,200.0 | 2,000.0 |
| Banco Hipotecario | 983.3 | 1,497.5 | 836.8 | 1,070.6 | 1,141.5 | ... | ... | ... | ... | ... |
| Subsidies to Coffee Growers' Association, etc. | ... | 260.4 | 140.0 | 154.4 | 170.0 | 200.0 | 250.0 | 323.0 | 506.3 | 666.8 |
| Expenditures of road and development funds | 362.0 | ... | ... | ... | ... | ... | ... | ... | ... | ... |
| Total | 3,507.7 | 5,270.8 | 3,631.4 | 3,697.1 | 5,311.7 | 5,780.7 | 5,793.5 | 8,612.7 | 12,106.1 | 12,006.3 |
| *In per cent of total* | | | | | | | | | | |
| Public works | 40.0 | 52.9 | 51.6 | 46.7 | 59.8 | 78.7 | 84.4 | 85.8 | 85.9 | 77.8[b] |
| Mejoramiento Social | 21.6 | 13.8 | 21.5 | 20.2 | 15.5 | 17.9 | 11.3 | 10.4 | 9.9 | 16.7 |
| Banco Hipotecario | 28.0 | 28.4 | 23.0 | 29.0 | 21.5 | ... | ... | ... | ... | ... |
| Subsidies to Coffee Growers' Association, etc. | ... | 4.9 | 3.9 | 4.2 | 3.2 | 3.5 | 4.3 | 3.8 | 4.2 | 5.6 |
| Expenditures of road and development funds | 10.3 | ... | ... | ... | ... | ... | ... | ... | ... | ... |
| Total | 99.9 | 100.0 | 100.0 | 100.1 | 100.0 | 100.1 | 100.0 | 100.0 | 100.0 | 100.1 |

[a] Budget.
[b] Includes 700,000 colones for purchases of the Proveeduría, to be reimbursed to the General Fund by the end of the year.

(and in Table 22), closely approximate the total disbursements of these institutions. It was not possible, however, to distinguish in this group between educational and social welfare expenditures. A scrutiny of annual budget figures indicates, nevertheless, that the expenditures of these institutions are approximately evenly divided between educational and social welfare purposes.

### EXPENDITURES FOR ECONOMIC DEVELOPMENT

Economic development expenditures, for which detailed figures are shown in Table 23, include a variety of disbursements having as a common denominator that they contribute more or less directly to the development of the Salvadorean economy. The development aspect is particularly apparent in the sharp expansion of expenditures for public works. Such expenditures primarily consisted during the period under consideration of a substantial volume of road construction and such projects as the construction of bridges and the improvement of docking facilities.[5]

Expenditures for the activities of Mejoramiento Social, an autonomous public-law organization established in 1932, pursue partly direct economic, and partly wider social, objectives. Originally, the primary purpose of the Mejoramiento Social was the surveying and distribution of public land in small farm units. Later the institution also acquired and operated a dairy and financed the development of low-cost urban housing projects. It also began the construction of a textile factory (which was to be operated as a "pilot" plant for the Salvadorean textile industry, and was to provide low-cost yarns for domestic weaving), but so far the plant has not been put into operation.[6]

[5] It should be noted that a certain portion of the expenditures for the largest single development project, namely the Inter-American Highway, is included not in the ordinary budget but in an extraordinary budget (of 1942) which has not been liquidated yet.

[6] Figures shown for the expenditures of the Mejoramiento Social include only the tax receipts allocated to the Mejoramiento Social and, since 1946, the subsidies paid by the General Fund to the institution. Actually the expenditures of the Mejoramiento Social are somewhat larger than such tax receipts and subsidies, because the Mejoramiento Social also obtains funds from other sources, primarily through the sale of goods and through installment payments on agricultural land sold to farmers. Since, however the nongovernment receipts of the Mejoramiento

Expenditures shown under the heading of *Banco Hipotecario* are amounts that the government has transferred annually to the Mortgage Bank in order to enable this institution to extend mortgage and corporation credits. Although the amounts expended by the government to provide funds for the Mortgage Bank did not, *per se*, have so distinctly the appearance of development expenditures as did expenditures for public works, they nevertheless must be classified as development expenditures since they unquestionably made a substantial contribution to the economic position of Salvadorean agriculture and had a lasting effect on the Salvadorean credit structure.

Subsidy payments by the government to the Coffee Growers' Association, the Cattle Raisers' Association, the Tourist Board (*Junta de Turismo*), and similar institutions were somewhat similar to those made to the Mortgage Bank, that is, they provided operating funds for the associations; in part, they defrayed the administrative expenses of these organizations.

The data given in Table 23 show that total expenditures for economic development increased by approximately 250 per cent between 1935 and 1948. This increase is more or less in line with the increase in total government expenditures. As to the distribution of economic development expenditures among the various objectives discussed above, the table indicates that expenditures for Mejoramiento Social maintained a stable relative position, while expenditures for public works absorbed, after 1944, that share of total economic development expenditures that had previously been used to provide funds for the Mortgage Bank.

Social were not included among the revenue figures discussed in the preceding chapter, they are likewise not included among expenditures. This omission somewhat understates the amount of public funds spent for economic development purposes, but in most years the difference between total expenditures and expenditures of public funds by the Mejoramiento Social is so small as to make the omission unimportant.

# CHAPTER VI

## INTERNATIONAL COMPARISONS

In Chapters IV and V, a description of the revenue and expenditure system of El Salvador has been presented. The purpose of the present chapter is to throw further light on the Salvadorean fiscal system by comparing it with those of other countries, and thus provide a convenient yardstick for appraising the fiscal sector of the economy relative to the other sectors, as well as the similarities and differences in the composition of government revenues and expenditures. Such comparison is of course only a rough indicator, especially since owing to the differences in size of the various economies, in the degree and direction of economic development, and in other factors peculiar to each country, one cannot arrive at simple and clearcut conclusions regarding the fiscal system of any particular country. If, however, the underlying differences are kept in mind, the comparison will serve to highlight certain important aspects of the fiscal structure of El Salvador.

The actual performance, rather than the budget data, of ten other countries has been selected for the comparison. So far as possible, data have been computed on a uniform basis, covering the activities of the national (central) governments[1] of Chile, Guatemala, Haiti, Mexico, Peru, Venezuela, the United States, Denmark, the United Kingdom, and New Zealand. The six Latin American republics were chosen for comparison because of their similarity of economic, political, and social institutions and general economic framework. The United States and the United Kingdom were selected to represent fully industrialized economies, while Denmark and New Zealand were included as examples of non-Latin American nations comparable in size and economic structure to most Latin American republics. The year

[1] See, however, footnote 3, p. 82.

TABLE 24

Total Government Receipts of Selected Countries[a]

(*In national currencies*)

| Type of receipt | EL SALVADOR Dec. 1946 (thousands of colones) | CHILE[b] Dec. 1946 (millions of pesos) | GUATEMALA[c] June 1946 As reported | GUATEMALA[c] "Intervened" income reallocated | HAITI Sept. 1946 (thousands of gourdes) | MEXICO Dec. 1946 (millions of pesos) | PERU Dec. 1946 (mil-of lions soles) |
|---|---|---|---|---|---|---|---|
| | | | (thousands of quetzales) | | | | |
| Taxes, fees, and fines...... | 36,723.1 | 4.730.6 | 20,930.3 | 20,930.3 | 42,217.0 | 1,580.6 | 451.7 |
| Direct taxes.............. | 3,937.1 | 1,592.8 | 2,957.2 | 2,957.2 | 4,416.4 | 374.0 | 148.9 |
| Property and property-transfer taxes........ | 958.9 | 457.6 | 517.9 | 517.9 | 909.9 | 171.4 | 28.0 |
| Taxes on exports.......... | 4,498.9 | 201.5 | 3,860.9 | 3,860.9 | 7,448.8 | 247.9 | 173.0 |
| Transaction and business-license taxes.......... | 1,912.6 | 383.4 | 1,693.5 | 1,693.5 | 790.9 | 19.1 | ... |
| Taxes on imports......... | 15,028.1 | 1,425.5 | 5,185.2 | 5,185.2 | 25,358.9 | 238.4 | 65.0 |
| Consumption taxes........ | 8,644.1 | 530.2 | 6,272.9 | 6,272.9 | 1,987.0 | 423.6 | 25.4 |
| Beverage taxes.......... | (4,571.1) | (173.3) | (4,559.1) | (4,559.1) | (450.8) | (55.1) | (19.5) |
| Tobacco taxes......... | (2,487.0) | (276.6) | (1,377.8) | (1,377.8) | (1,294.3) | (51.0) | ... |
| Other consumption taxes. | (1,586.0) | (80.3) | (336.0) | (336.0) | (241.9) | (317.5)[l] | (5.9) |
| Other taxes.............. | 1,305.0 | 36.7 | 201.1 | 201.1 | 20.8 | 58.6 | 6.0 |
| Fees..................... | 262.3 | 56.9 | 104.6 | 104.6 | 1,274.0 | 39.7 | 5.2 |
| Fines.................... | 175.9 | 46.0 | 137.0 | 137.0 | 10.3 | 7.9 | 0.2 |
| Loans (or budgetary deficit) | ... | 528.6 | ... | 4,870.0 | ... | ... | 8.0 |
| Receipts from government enterprises.......... | 2,084.3 | 378.1 | 6,531.7 | 1,661.7 | 1,555.5 | 177.2 | 131.6 |
| Postal system........... | 581.0 | 376.3 | 446.9 | 446.9 | 964.1 | 42.9 | 8.4 |
| Electric communications[k] | 1,182.3 | 376.3 | 478.6 | 478.6 | ... | 24.7 | 2.8 |
| Other government enterprises.............. | 289.3 | | 5,556.4 | 686.4 | 591.4 | 101.5[l] | 40.8 |
| Sale of government property................. | 31.7 | 0.8 | 49.8 | 49.8 | ... | 8.1 | 79.6 |
| Other receipts............ | 695.1 | 1,088.9 | 583.8 | 583.8 | 784.7 | 253.7 | 25.9 |
| Other receipts.......... | 99.4 | 1,088.9 | 504.9 | 504.9 | 784.7 | 253.7 | 25.9 |
| Transitory items........ | 595.4 | ... | 78.9 | 78.9 | ... | ... | ... |
| Total.............. | 39,502.6 | 6,726.2 | 28,045.8 | 28,045.8 | 44,557.2 | 2,011.5 | 617.2 |

[a] For fiscal year ending with month indicated. Budgetary receipts of national governments only. Combined United States federal and state data included for purposes of comparison.

[b] Ordinary and supplementary budgets only. Nonbudgetary revenues estimated at 23 per cent of these two items.

[c] Exclusive of lottery income. "As reported": as reported by government. "'Intervened' income reallocated": Unusual income received from "intervened" coffee estates, finally liquidated in 1945–46, arbitrarily allocated to "loan" receipts (thus signifying a government deficit) in order to adjust revenues to a more "normal" basis.

TABLE 24 (Continued)

| Type of receipt | VENEZUELA June 1946 (millions of bolivares) | UNITED STATES[d] June 1947 Federal only (millions of U.S. dollars) | Federal and state[e] | DENMARK[f] March 1947 (millions of kroner) | UNITED KINGDOM[g] March 1947 (millions of pounds) | NEW ZEALAND[h] March 1947 (millions of N.Z. pounds) |
|---|---|---|---|---|---|---|
| Taxes, fees, and fines...... | 384.2 | 39,958.7 | 47,340.7 | 1,896.4 | 3,020.2 | 113.0 |
| Direct taxes............. | 98.8 | 20,408.1 | 20,992.1 | 749.8 | 1,379.9 | 63.9 |
| Property and property-transfer taxes........ | ... | 49.1 | 356.1 | 45.6 | 39.0 | 10.4 |
| Taxes on exports......... | ... | ... | ... | ... | ... | ... |
| Transaction and business-license taxes......... | 21.2 | 9,676.5 | 11,017.5 | ... | 407.0 | ... |
| Taxes on imports........ | 161.9 | 494.1 | 494.1 | 140.1 | 620.7[j] | 15.7 |
| Consumption taxes........ | 98.0 | 7,221.1 | 10,477.1 | 905.7 | 573.6 | 22.8 |
| Beverage taxes.......... | (41.3) | (2,474.6) | (2,884.6) | (430.0) | (308.2) | (4.3) |
| Tobacco taxes.......... | (40.2) | (1,237.8) | (1,482.8) | (325.0) | (0.1)[j] | } (18.5) |
| Other consumption taxes. | (16.5) | (3,508.7) | (6,109.7) | (150.7) | (265.3) | |
| Other taxes............. | ... | 2,061.0 | 3,244.0 | } 45.4 | ... | 0.2 |
| Fees.................... | 2.9 | 23.7 | 734.7 | | ... | ... |
| Fines................... | 1.4 | 25.1 | 25.1 | 9.8 | ... | ... |
| Loans (or budgetary deficit) | 53.4 | ... | 717.0 | ... | 569.1 | 23.6 |
| Receipts from government enterprises.......... | 283.2 | 3,542.9 | 3,542.9 | 473.9 | 215 9 | 36.7 |
| Postal system.......... | } 282.3[m] | } 2,469.7 | } 2,469.7 | { 164.4 | ... | ... |
| Electric communications[k] | | | | | ... | ... |
| Other government enterprises............. | | | | 309.4[n] | 0.9 | ... |
| Sale of government property.............. | | 1,073.2 | 1,073.2 | ... | 215.0 | 36.7 |
| Other receipts........... | 33.9 | 1,216.7 | 2,369.7 | 139.9 | 105.1 | 9.7 |
| Other receipts......... | 33.9 | 1,216.7 | 2,369.7 | 139.9 | 105.1 | 9.7 |
| Transitory items........ | ... | ... | ... | ... | ... | ... |
| Total............. | 754.7 | 44,718.3 | 53,970.3 | 2,510.2 | 3,910.3 | 183.0 |

d Federal budget accounts, and net expenditures of trust accounts.

e Including also state budgetary incomes in order to include specific state income sources, which for most of the eleven countries in table were federal revenues.

f Closed budget, excluding lottery income, but including gross-revenues of some government enterprises as well as the "interest account."

g Excluding the "self-liquidating" budget.

h Ordinary budget, and Loan Development Account receipts.

i Of this, 88.6 million pesos consisted of consumption taxes on sugar.

j Of total taxes on imports, customs duties on tobacco amounted to 446.3 million pounds

k Including telephone, telegraph, and/or radio.

l Of this, returns from concessions amounted to 94.9 million pesos.

m Of this, returns from petroleum concessions amounted to 243.6 million bolivares.

n State railway income.

1946 was selected for the comparison as the most nearly representative postwar year for which data were available.[2]

In order to put the data into comparable form, numerous arbitrary classifications had to be made. Moreover, some of the data themselves, although taken from sources believed to be reliable, may in some cases be subject to correction, and in others are inherently subject to considerable margins of error. The resulting comparisons, in consequence, must be accepted with all due reservations, and in no case should be regarded as a value judgment as to the appropriateness or inappropriateness of any particular fiscal system or measure.

## 1. GOVERNMENT RECEIPTS

The first comparison to be made is of total government revenues, which are presented in local national currencies in Table 24. The data represent the realized gross income of the various governments, exclusive of government lottery income. In order to obtain comparability, the original data were so adjusted that the coverage of the other countries approximates that of the Salvadorean statistics analyzed in Chapter IV, although in some instances differences in institutional arrangements prevented complete adjustment.[3]

[2] For countries reporting on a fiscal year basis, the fiscal year ending June 1946 or the fiscal year containing the greater number of months in 1946 was used. In the case of the United States, the fiscal year ending June 1947 was substituted because war expenditures were still at their peak level in 1945–46.

[3] In the case of Chile, for instance, it is known that some semiautonomous institutions received tax income directly that was not recorded in the government's budget data. Since adjustment for this discrepancy was not possible, the compiled data must be understood as representing considerably less than the total receipts of the Chilean government. The Danish government's final "closed budget" included only *net* interest and the *net* income of government enterprises. The data were therefore adjusted upward by the addition of the "Interest Account" and of the gross receipts of major government enterprises, data for which were reported separately. Data for the United Kingdom are exclusive of the "self-liquidating" portion of the budget, which covered the revenue-liquidating post office expenditures and the excess-profits-tax reductions representing postwar tax refunds. In the case of Guatemala, two series were compiled: one covers revenues as reported, while in the other series the unusual income received by the government from the "intervened" coffee estates, finally liquidated in the fiscal year 1945–46, was arbitrarily allocated to "loan" receipts (thus signifying a government deficit) in order to adjust Guatemalan national revenues more nearly to the "normal" annual

## GENERAL COMPARISONS

Following the breakdown employed in Chapter IV, revenues have been divided into four categories: taxes, fees, and fines; loans (or deficits covered from Treasury funds, as the case may be); receipts from government enterprises; and other receipts, consisting both of "other" receipts and of nonregular sources of income. The relative importance of these various sources of government income is presented in percentage terms in Table 25.

It is striking, though not surprising, to find from Table 25 that, out of the eleven countries, El Salvador was one of only two (the other being Haiti) where taxes accounted for more than 90 per cent of total government revenues. In all the other Latin American countries shown, only about three fourths or less of total government revenues were derived from taxation, taxes in Venezuela actually accounting for little more than 50 per cent of the total. The primary reason for the large share of taxes in total Salvadorean revenue in comparison with the other Latin American countries was the fact that El Salvador derived little income from government enterprises, concessions, and exchange profits, which were of considerable importance as revenue sources in the others.

The fact that government enterprises were more important as a source of revenue in the other countries is reflected in the higher share of revenues from this source in Guatemala — where, as pointed out above, revenues from "intervened" coffee plantations were a major source of extraordinary income in 1946 — in Peru, Venezuela, Mexico, Denmark, and New Zealand.

That receipts from loans are shown for some of the other countries, but not for El Salvador, does not necessarily imply that the countries with which El Salvador is compared incurred budgetary deficits. In all countries except Chile and Venezuela,

---

level. To the New Zealand "Ordinary Revenue Account" was added the "Loan Development Account," reported separately. For the United States two series were compiled: the first presents the United States federal budget, including net expenditures of trust funds; in the second series, because the United States federal budget does not cover a number of activities (such as schools) included under the national budgets of the other governments in the comparison, the budget data of state governments were also included.

# TABLE 25

## PERCENTAGE DISTRIBUTION OF TOTAL GOVERNMENT RECEIPTS OF SELECTED COUNTRIES[a]

(In per cent of total receipts)

| Type of receipt | El Salvador Dec. 1946 | Chile Dec. 1946 | Guatemala June 1946 As reported | Guatemala June 1946 "Intervened" income reallocated | Haiti Sept. 1946 | Mexico Dec. 1946 | Peru Dec. 1946 | Venezuela June 1946 | United States June 1947 Federal only | United States June 1947 Federal and state | Denmark March 1947 | United Kingdom March 1947 | New Zealand March 1947 |
|---|---|---|---|---|---|---|---|---|---|---|---|---|---|
| Taxes, fees, and fines | 93.0 | 70.3 | 74.6 | 74.6 | 94.8 | 78.6 | 73.2 | 50.9 | 89.4 | 87.7 | 75.6 | 77.2 | 61.7 |
| Direct taxes | 10.0 | 23.6 | 10.6 | 10.6 | 9.9 | 18.6 | 24.2 | 13.1 | 45.8 | 38.9 | 29.9 | 35.3 | 34.8 |
| Property and property-transfer taxes | 2.4 | 6.8 | 1.9 | 1.9 | 2.0 | 8.5 | 4.5 | … | 0.1 | 0.7 | 1.8 | 1.0 | 5.7 |
| Taxes on exports | 11.4 | 3.0 | 13.8 | 13.8 | 16.7 | 12.3 | 26.1 | … | … | … | … | … | … |
| Transaction and business-license taxes | 4.8 | 5.7 | 6.0 | 6.0 | 1.8 | 0.9 | 0.5 | 2.8 | 21.7 | 20.4 | … | 10.4 | … |
| Taxes on imports | 38.0 | 21.3 | 18.4 | 18.4 | 56.9 | 11.9 | 10.5 | 21.5 | 1.1 | 0.9 | .6 | 15.9 | 8.6 |
| Consumption taxes | 21.9 | 7.9 | 22.3 | 22.3 | 4.5 | 21.1 | 4.1 | 13.0 | 16.1 | 19.4 | 36.1 | 14.6 | 12.5 |
| Beverage taxes | (11.6) | (2.6) | (16.2) | (16.2) | (1.1) | (2.7) | (3.2) | (5.5) | (5.5) | (5.4) | (17.1) | (7.9) | (2.3) |
| Tobacco taxes | (6.3) | (4.1) | (4.9) | (4.9) | (3.0) | (2.5) | … | (5.3) | (2.8) | (2.7) | (12.9) | … | … |
| Other consumption taxes | (4.0) | (1.2) | (1.2) | (1.2) | (0.4) | (15.9) | (1.3) | (2.2) | (7.8) | (11.3) | (6.1) | (16.7) | (10.2) |
| Other taxes | 3.3 | 0.5 | 0.7 | 0.7 | 0.04 | 2.9 | 1.0 | 0.4 | 4.6 | 6.0 | 1.8 | … | 0.1 |
| Fees | 0.7 | 0.8 | 0.4 | 0.4 | 2.9 | 2.0 | 0.8 | 0.4 | … | 1.4 | … | … | … |
| Fines | 0.4 | 0.7 | 0.5 | 0.5 | 0.02 | 0.4 | … | 0.1 | … | 1.3 | 0.4 | … | … |
| Loans (or budgetary deficit) | … | 7.9 | … | 17.4 | … | … | 1.3 | 7.1 | … | … | … | 14.6 | 12.9 |
| Receipts from government enterprises | 5.3 | 5.6 | 23.3 | 5.9 | 3.5 | 8.8 | 21.3 | 37.5 | 7.9 | 6.6 | 18.9 | 5.5 | 20.1 |
| Postal system | 1.5 | {5.6 | 1.6 | 1.6 | 2.2 | 2.1 | 1.4 | {37.5 | {5.5 | {4.6 | {18.8 | 5.5 | {20.1 |
| Electric communications | 3.0 | | 1.7 | 1.7 | … | 1.2 | 0.4 | | | | | … | |
| Other government enterprises | 0.7 | … | 19.8 | 2.4 | 1.3 | 5.5 | 8.4 | | 2.4 | 2.0 | 0.1 | 5.5 | 20.1 |
| Sale of government property | 0.4 | … | 0.2 | 0.2 | … | 0.4 | 12.9 | | … | … | … | … | … |
| Other receipts | 1.8 | 16.2 | 2.1 | 2.1 | 1.7 | 12.6 | 4.2 | 4.5 | 2.7 | 4.4 | 5.5 | 2.7 | 5.3 |
| Other receipts | 0.3 | 16.2 | 1.8 | 1.8 | 1.7 | 12.6 | 4.2 | 4.5 | 2.7 | 4.4 | 5.5 | 2.7 | 5.3 |
| Transitory items | 1.5 | … | 0.3 | 0.3 | … | … | … | … | … | … | … | … | … |
| Total | 100.0 | 100.0 | 100.0 | 100.0 | 100.0 | 100.0 | 100.0 | 100.0 | 100.0 | 100.0 | 100.0 | 100.0 | 100.0 |

[a] See footnotes to Table 24.

loan receipts were offset, or more than offset, by expenditures for amortization and interest on the public debt.[4]

Because of the wide variations between countries in the relative importance of taxes in total government receipts, the composition of the tax structure of the various countries is presented in Table 26 in terms of total tax receipts only, in place of over-all government receipts as in Table 25.

### DIRECT TAXES

In El Salvador receipts from direct taxes in 1946 were approximately 11 per cent of total tax receipts, while the average for the six other Latin American countries shown in the table was 25 per cent; for Denmark, 40 per cent; and for the United Kingdom, New Zealand, and the United States, about 50 per cent.

Such a difference is of course quite striking, and deserves some attention. On the basis of the discussion of the Salvadorean tax structure in Chapter IV, it might seem, prima facie, that one of the reasons for the relatively unimportant position of the direct tax in the Salvadorean revenue system is the fact that income received from coffee growing is not subject to the income tax, inasmuch as the coffee tax is collected in lieu of the income tax.[5] This explanation, however, is not satisfactory because export taxes have also played a major role in other Latin American revenue systems in the comparison, except in the case of Venezuela.[6] The discrepancy in the Salvadorean case thus cannot be explained as the result of an arbitrary statistical classification, but must rather be interpreted as a major characteristic of the Salvadorean tax structure, reflecting the peculiarities both of the structure of the Salvadorean economy and of the historical growth of the present tax system.

The Salvadorean economic structure is distinguished, among

[4] It has not been possible to separate amortization and interest payments.

[5] Salvadorean cotton and sugar taxes are likewise collected in lieu of the direct income tax. These may be disregarded in this connection, however, since they, though technically paid in lieu of income taxes, probably are shifted to the consumers.

[6] In Chile, export taxes are relatively unimportant. The income of producers of export commodities is affected, however, by the compulsory sale of the foreign exchange proceeds at special rates.

## TABLE 26

### Percentage Distribution of Government Tax Receipts of Selected Countries[a]

| Type of receipt | El Salvador Dec. 1946 | Chile[b] Dec. 1946 | Guatemala[c] June 1946 | Haiti Sept. 1946 | Mexico Dec. 1946 | Peru Dec. 1946 | Venezuela June 1946 | United States June 1947[d] Federal only | United States June 1947[d] Federal and state[e] | Denmark[f] Mar. 1947 | United Kingdom[g] Mar. 1947 | New Zealand[h] Mar. 1947 |
|---|---|---|---|---|---|---|---|---|---|---|---|---|
| Direct taxes | 10.7 | 33.6 | 14.1 | 10.5 | 23.7 | 33.0 | 25.7 | 51.1 | 44.3 | 39.5 | 45.7 | 56.5 |
| Property and property-transfer taxes | 2.6 | 9.7 | 2.5 | 2.1 | 10.8 | 6.2 | ... | 0.1 | 0.8 | 2.4 | 1.3 | 9.2 |
| Taxes on exports | 12.3 | 4.3 | 18.4 | 17.6 | 15.7 | 38.3 | ... | ... | ... | ... | ... | ... |
| Transaction and business-license taxes | 5.2 | 8.1 | 8.1 | 1.9 | 1.2 | ... | 5.5 | 24.2 | 23.3 | 7.4 | 13.4 | ... |
| Taxes on imports | 40.9 | 30.1 | 24.8 | 60.1 | 15.1 | 14.4 | 42.1 | 1.2 | 1.0 | 1.0 | 20.6 | 13.9 |
| Consumption taxes | 23.5 | 11.2 | 30.0 | 4.7 | 26.8 | 5.6 | 25.5 | 18.1 | 22.1 | 47.8 | 19.0 | 20.2 |
| Beverage taxes | (12.4) | (3.7) | (21.8) | (1.2) | (3.5) | (4.3) | (10.7) | (6.2) | (6.1) | (22.7) | (10.2) | (3.8) |
| Tobacco taxes | (6.8) | (5.8) | (6.6) | (3.1) | (3.2) | ... | (10.5) | (3.1) | (3.1) | (17.1) | ... | ... |
| Other consumption taxes | (4.3) | (1.7) | (1.6) | (0.4) | (20.1) | (1.3) | (4.3) | (8.8) | (12.9) | (18.0) | (8.8) | (16.4) |
| Other taxes | 3.6 | 0.8 | 1.0 | 0.05 | 3.7 | 1.3 | ... | 5.2 | 6.9 | } 2.4 | ... | 0.2 |
| Fees | 0.7 | 1.2 | 0.5 | 3.0 | 2.5 | 1.2 | 0.8 | 0.05 | 1.6 |  | ... | ... |
| Fines | 0.5 | 1.0 | 0.6 | 0.02 | 0.5 | ... | 0.4 | 0.05 | ... | 0.5 | ... | ... |
| **Total taxes, fees, and fines** | 100.0 | 100.0 | 100.0 | 100.0 | 100.0 | 100.0 | 100.0 | 100.0 | 100.0 | 100.0 | 100.0 | 100.0 |

a For fiscal year ending with month indicated. Budgetary receipts of national governments only. Combined United States federal and state data included for purposes of comparison.

b Ordinary and supplementary budgets only.

c Exclusive of lottery income.

d Federal budget accounts, and net expenditures of trust accounts.

e Including also state budgetary incomes in order to include specific state income sources, which for most of the eleven countries in table were federal revenues.

f Closed budget, excluding lottery income, but including gross revenues of some government enterprises as well as the "interest account."

g Excluding the "self-liquidating" budget.

h Ordinary budget, and Loan Development Account receipts.

other things, by the high proportion of nonmonetary income in the gross national product, which reflects both the prevalence of small-scale agricultural units producing largely for their own consumption requirements and the large number of small business units in general. These conditions, by discouraging the adoption of adequate bookkeeping and income accounting, have undoubtedly retarded the development of a more comprehensive system of direct taxes, such as would contribute a larger share of the total revenues.

As to the growth of the tax system, historically El Salvador never has experienced as drastic a curtailment of its foreign trade in times of depression as have most other Latin American countries. It has therefore been able to rely more heavily upon import duties, supplemented by export taxes, as the main source of governmental revenue, whereas in other countries decreases in foreign trade forced their governments to resort to other forms of taxes, particularly direct taxes, when revenues from import and export taxes fell off.

That the obstacles in the way of direct taxes, with their relatively higher yields, can be overcome is indicated, however, by the rapidly expanding importance of direct taxes in the revenue systems of the six other Latin American countries during recent years, as well as by the large contribution that such taxes have for many years made to total government revenue in most of these other countries. This lends weight to the expectation that ultimately the institutional and administrative impediments to the expansion of the system of direct taxes can and will be overcome in El Salvador.

### PROPERTY AND PROPERTY-TRANSFER TAXES

The very small contribution of property and property-transfer taxes to total Salvadorean tax revenues shown in Table 26 is not basically out of line with that in the six other Latin American countries, of which only Chile, Mexico, and Peru collected a higher proportion of total tax revenues from this source. The low United States and British percentages for property taxes is explained by the fact that in those countries such taxes are largely collected by the local (municipal and county) authorities, and therefore do not appear in Table 26.

## IMPORT AND EXPORT TAXES

The relatively light direct taxation in the Salvadorean tax structure is, as indicated above, made up for by a comparatively large contribution from taxes on exports and imports, which together accounted for 53 per cent of total Salvadorean tax revenue. This situation is paralleled in most Latin American countries, where a low yield from direct taxes is generally accompanied by high yields from taxes on imports and exports. Thus Peru derived 53 per cent of her tax revenues from export and import taxes — the same percentage as El Salvador — and Guatemala 43 per cent. In Chile, where the contribution of direct taxes to total government receipts is considerably larger (and where revenues from export and import taxes are supplemented by a system of multiple exchange rates through which the government derives exchange profits), export and import taxes yielded 34 per cent of the total tax revenues. In Mexico the share of these taxes was 31 per cent. In the non-Latin American countries shown in the table, export taxes are completely absent and taxes on imports are of minor significance, with the exception of the United Kingdom where they serve the purpose of restricting the consumption of imported goods and thus act as a corrective device for the prevailing balance-of-payment difficulties.

One important difference between export and import taxes should be noted. Export taxes tend not to be shifted forward to the foreign purchasers of exports. They are therefore borne largely by the producers of export commodities and accordingly are an addition to the burden of direct taxes,[7] to the extent that they cannot be shifted backwards to labor and to the economy as a whole. Compared with other Latin American countries, the 12 per cent share of export taxes in the Salvadorean tax structure was relatively small; in Guatemala and Haiti export taxes yielded 18 per cent of total tax revenues, in Mexico 16 per cent, and in Peru 38 per cent. In Venezuela, royalties for oil exports,

[7] For a more detailed discussion of this point see Chapters VII and VIII.

which as indicated above produced about one third of total government revenues, took the place of export taxes. In Chile, the low yield of export taxes (4 per cent) was supplemented by discriminatory exchange rates for certain exports.

Import taxes, on the other hand, although paid by importers, are generally shifted forward to the ultimate consumers of imported goods and therefore form an essential part of the taxation levied upon consumption. In El Salvador, import taxes yielded 40 per cent of the total tax revenue — the highest but one among the seven Latin American countries shown in the comparison. This conforms to the previous statement that the Salvadorean government relies heavily upon the yield of import taxes for revenues. It indicates also that the purpose of import taxes in Salvador is primarily the raising of revenue, while in some other Latin American countries and in the other countries shown in Table 26, the protection of domestic industries by import duties is at least as important a reason.[8]

## CONSUMPTION TAXES

In El Salvador consumption taxes were the second largest group of taxes, yielding 23.5 per cent of total tax revenues. In all the other countries consumption taxes yielded 20 to 30 per cent of total tax revenues except in Chile, Haiti, and Peru, where the yield was considerably smaller, and in Denmark where consumption taxes accounted for 48 per cent of total tax receipts.

In most countries a substantial proportion of the consumption taxes was derived from "nonessential" goods such as alcoholic beverages and tobacco. Combined revenues from the beverage and tobacco taxes represented about 20 per cent in Denmark. In the case of the United Kingdom the combined customs duties and consumption taxes on tobacco and beverages amounted to about 26 per cent of tax income. As already indicated, general sales or excise taxes, which are much more comprehensive, were not used in El Salvador, or for that matter in any of the other Latin American countries shown, except Mexico. In the United

---

[8] If protection is effective, the yield of import taxes is smaller than if duties are levied primarily for fiscal purposes, since under protection that is effective, imports, and with them import-tax yields, are curtailed more sharply.

Kingdom, New Zealand, Denmark, and the United States, on the other hand, such taxes were major components of the total taxes on consumption.

The consumption taxes of course did not reflect the entire burden of the taxes passed on to the consumer through higher prices, since most import duties and many business taxes likewise are so shifted. Together, these three groups of taxes may be regarded as representing those taxes that are principally shifted to the consumer; they accounted for the following proportions of total tax receipts:

| | | | |
|---|---|---|---|
| Venezuela | 73 per cent | Chile | 49 per cent |
| El Salvador | 70 per cent | United States[9] | 46 per cent |
| Haiti | 67 per cent | Mexico | 43 per cent |
| Guatemala | 63 per cent | New Zealand | 34 per cent |
| Denmark | 55 per cent | Peru | 20 per cent |
| United Kingdom | 53 per cent | | |

As this list shows, that proportion of the total tax revenues which in the broadest sense of the term reflects a burden upon consumption was in El Salvador second only to that in Venezuela; in all other countries this proportion was substantially smaller. This is, of course, not surprising, being merely another reflection of the relatively low level of direct taxation supplemented by export taxation that prevails in El Salvador. It may also be pointed out that, in absolute terms, the tax burden upon consumption is small in El Salvador because the total burden is small, as will be shown below.

### OTHER TAXES, FEES, AND FINES

The remainder of the Salvadorean tax structure is made up of the transaction and business-license taxes already mentioned, "other" taxes, and fees and fines, which altogether amounted to 10 per cent of total tax revenues. In most of the other Latin American countries shown, these taxes were likewise a relatively small proportion of the total. In the United States and the United Kingdom, on the other hand, this group was more important because in addition it includes corporate income taxes, with their heavy yields.

[9] Including state taxes.

## 2. Per Capita Income and Tax Burden

Of even greater significance and interest than the comparison of the tax structures is the comparison of per capita total taxes and per capita taxes on consumption, both in absolute terms and relative to per capita income, presented in Table 27. Receipts from total taxes and total taxes on consumption are given in United States dollars.[10] In view of the varying degrees of inflation in the various countries, and in some cases the not wholly realistic rates of exchange, dollar values probably do not reflect accurately the real burden of taxes borne by the nationals of

TABLE 27

Per Capita Income and Taxes of Selected Countries in 1946[a]
*(In United States dollars[b])*

| | Fiscal year ending with month indicated | Per capita income[c] | Total per capita taxes | Per capita taxes on consumption | Per cent to income of | |
| --- | --- | --- | --- | --- | --- | --- |
| | | | | | Total taxes | Taxes on consumption |
| El Salvador.... | Dec. 1946 | 87.13[d] | 7.35 | 5.12 | 8.4 | 5.9 |
| Chile.......... | Dec. 1946 | 247.03 | 28.12 | 13.90 | 11.4 | 5.6 |
| Guatemala..... | June 1946 | ...[e] | 5.90 | 3.70 | ...[e] | ...[e] |
| Haiti.......... | Sept. 1946 | ...[e] | 2.82 | 1.87 | ...[e] | ...[e] |
| Mexico........ | Dec. 1946 | 117.16 | 14.29 | 6.16 | 12.2 | 5.3 |
| Peru.......... | Dec. 1946 | ...[e] | 9.97 | 1.99 | ...[e] | ...[e] |
| Venezuela...... | June 1946 | ...[e] | 27.30 | 19.98 | ...[e] | ...[e] |
| United States Federal only.. | June 1947 | 1261.78 | 282.94 | 123.15 | 22.4 | 9.8 |
| Federal and state....... | June 1947 | 1261.78 | 335.21 | 155.70 | 26.6 | 12.3 |
| Denmark....... | Mar. 1947 | 675.74 | 96.36 | 53.14 | 14.3 | 7.9 |
| United Kingdom | Mar. 1947 | 662.02 | 246.85 | 130.89 | 37.3 | 19.8 |
| New Zealand... | Mar. 1947 | 688.38 | 205.79 | 70.14 | 29.9 | 10.2 |

[a] Or nearest fiscal year thereto.

[b] Conversions from national currencies made by using par values announced by the International Monetary Fund on December 18, 1946 (or non-member's par value or selling rate for 1946).

[c] Computed from data published in the United Nations *Monthly Bulletin of Statistics* for national income at current prices, and from estimates of total population present in area at midyear.

[d] Derived from the estimated gross national product. See Appendix B.

[e] Not available.

[10] Converted from local currency values at the prevailing rates of exchange for the period covered by the data.

each country. However, they will serve to measure the approxi-mate magnitudes of the respective individual tax liabilities.

The total per capita tax burden of $7.35 in El Salvador was exceeded by that of all other countries shown in the table except Guatemala and Haiti. Total per capita taxes in the other Latin American countries were considerably larger, particularly in Chile and Venezuela, where they reached $28.12 and $27.30, respectively. Furthermore, the Salvadorean per capita tax bur-den was only a fraction of that prevailing in countries outside Latin America.

Per capita taxes on consumption (which, in addition to direct consumption taxes, include import duties and business taxes) showed similarly wide differences. The per capita burden of consumption taxes amounted to $5.12 in El Salvador, compared with $155.70 in the United States and $130.89 in the United Kingdom. Among Latin American countries, such taxes were $19.98 in Venezuela, about $13.90 in Chile, $3.70 in Guatemala, and less than $2.00 in Peru and Haiti.

The per capita total taxes and per capita taxes on consump-tion in El Salvador and most of the Latin American republics may seem insignificant compared with those paid in the United States and the United Kingdom. To appraise the real tax bur-den, however, account must be taken of the level of per capita income. In El Salvador, 8 per cent of total per capita income of $87 was absorbed by taxes. In Mexico, where the per capita in-come was $117, 12 per cent was so absorbed. The data for the countries outside of Latin America reveal that, in general, the greater proportion of total income that was there taxed away — 37 per cent in the United Kingdom, 30 per cent in New Zealand, and 27 per cent in the United States — reflected the fact that the total per capita income was much higher in the first place.

It should be added that the rate of taxation does not indicate the full share of the government in the economy. If the govern-ment supplements its tax revenues by borrowing, as was done in several of the countries surveyed, it absorbs additional re-sources, whether by employing the people's voluntary savings or by means of inflation if its borrowings exceed voluntary sav-ings. This aspect of the government's participation in the economic life is best reflected in the ratio of per capita expenditures to per capita income.

### 3. GOVERNMENT EXPENDITURES

The preceding comparison of national government revenues has shown the tax burdens imposed upon the various economies by their respective fiscal systems. The following comparison of government expenditures is designed to point up the benefits derived from government activities, and incidentally provides in many respects a better measure of the importance of government activities in the economy, partly because this measure depends, not only upon the magnitude of the government's operations, but also to a high degree upon their nature and direction.

In Table 28, the government expenditures of the same eleven countries that were covered in the comparison of revenues are presented in terms of the respective national currency units. The percentage distribution is shown in Table 29.

Following the analytical divisions adopted in Chapter V, disbursements have been divided into five classes: administrative; national defense; cultural and social; economic development; and public debt. For some countries, a sixth class has been added in which are included various payments that do not fit into any of the regular categories.

#### ADMINISTRATIVE EXPENDITURES

The regular costs for the upkeep of government were the largest single category of government expenditure, not only in El Salvador, but in almost all the other countries. El Salvador devoted 30.5 per cent of its total government expenditures to the operation of administrative government agencies and the provision of general government services, or roughly the same as the average for the ten other countries.[11] Denmark, the United Kingdom, Peru, and Venezuela spent proportionately more than the ten-country average for administration; Guatemala and Haiti, about the same as the average; Chile, Mexico, and the

---

[11] Since payments on the public debt absorbed an unusually large share of total expenditures in 1946, the share of other types of expenditures was lower than in more "normal" years.

## TABLE 28

### GOVERNMENT EXPENDITURES OF SELECTED COUNTRIES[a]

(*In national currencies*)

| Kind of expenditure | El Salvador Dec. 1946 (thousands of colones) | Chile Dec. 1946 (millions of pesos) | Guatemala June 1946 (thousands of quetzales) | Haiti Sept. 1946 (thousands of gourdes) | Mexico Dec. 1946 (millions of pesos) | Peru Dec. 1946 (millions of soles) | Venezuela June 1946 (millions of bolivares) | United States June 1947 Federal only (millions of dollars) | United States June 1947 Federal and state (millions of dollars) | Denmark March 1947 (millions of kroner) | United Kingdom March 1947 (millions of pounds) | New Zealand March 1947 (millions of N.Z. pounds) |
|---|---|---|---|---|---|---|---|---|---|---|---|---|
| Administrative | 13,716.8 | 1,815.5 | 9,390.3 | 11,761.8 | 445.5 | 256.0 | 306.2 | 14,360.0 | 16,051.9 | 1,133.8 | 1,458.7 | 31.5 |
| National defense | 4,460.2 | 2,301.4 | 3,381.2 | 9,721.7 | 252.9 | 156.8 | 55.6 | 14,280.6 | 14,280.0 | 210.5 | 452.0 | 25.7 |
| Cultural and social | 7,401.0 | 1,685.8 | 5,304.6 | 7,710.0 | 259.5 | 128.9 | 82.7 | 2,283.2[c] | 7,155.0[c] | 680.2 | 1,356.4 | 58.8 |
| Economic development | 8,612.7 | 894.7 | 10,052.3 | 5,015.3 | 516.7 | 46.2 | 308.9 | 2,199.3 | 3,581.1 | 24.6 | 144.4 | 21.8 |
| Public debt | 10,836.3 | 28.8 | 1,106.0 | 6,168.4 | 295.8 | 29.3 | 1.3 | 16,093.7 | 16,302.7 | 445.6 | 498.8 | 26.0 |
| Other special expenditures | ... | ... | ... | ... | ... | ... | ... | 6,406.6[d] | 6,406.6[d] | ... | ... | 19.0[f] |
| Total | 45,026.7 | 6,726.2[b] | 29,234.4 | 40,377.2 | 1,770.4 | 617.2 | 754.7 | 55,632.4 | 63,777.9 | 2,494.8[e] | 3,910.3 | 182.8 |

a For fiscal year ending with month indicated. Budgetary expenditures of national governments only, so far as available data make this possible. Combined United States federal and state data included for purposes of comparison.

b Ordinary and supplementary budgets only. Excluding nonbudgetary expenditures (of Funds, Caja de Amortización, etc.) estimated at 23 per cent of the reported ordinary and supplementary budgets.

c Because expenditures for schools are not made by the federal government, expenditures of federal and state governments combined are also presented. Expenditures for schools amounted to 1,637.2 million dollars.

d Comprises foreign relief, international reconstruction and development (UNRRA), monetary stabilization (contributions to International Monetary Fund and International Bank), and payments for Philippine war damages and rehabilitation.

e Wherever data were available, gross expenditures have been substituted for the net figures reported in the "closed budget."

f Consists mainly of gifts to the United Kingdom as contributions to war costs.

## TABLE 29

### PERCENTAGE DISTRIBUTION OF GOVERNMENT EXPENDITURES OF SELECTED COUNTRIES[a]

| Kind of expenditure | El Salvador Dec. 1946 | Chile Dec. 1946 | Guatemala June 1946 | Haiti Sept. 1946 | Mexico Dec. 1946 | Peru Dec. 1946 | Venezuela June 1946 | United States June 1947 | | Denmark March 1947 | United Kingdom March 1947 | New Zealand March 1947 |
|---|---|---|---|---|---|---|---|---|---|---|---|---|
| | | | | | | | | Federal only | Federal and state | | | |
| Administrative........ | 30.5 | 27.0 | 32.1 | 29.1 | 25.2 | 41.5 | 40.6 | 25.8 | 25.2 | 45.4 | 37.3 | 17.2 |
| National defense........ | 9.9 | 34.2 | 11.5 | 24.1 | 14.3 | 25.4 | 7.4 | 25.7 | 22.4 | 8.3 | 11.6 | 14.1 |
| Cultural and social...... | 16.4 | 25.1 | 18.2 | 19.1 | 14.6 | 20.9 | 10.9 | 4.1 | 11.2 | 27.3 | 34.7 | 32.2 |
| Economic development... | 19.1 | 13.3 | 34.4 | 12.4 | 29.2 | 7.5 | 40.9 | 4.0 | 5.6 | 1.0 | 3.7 | 11.9 |
| Public debt............ | 24.1 | 0.4 | 3.8 | 15.3 | 16.7 | 4.7 | 0.2 | 28.9 | 25.6 | 17.9 | 12.7 | 14.2 |
| Other special expenditures | ... | ... | ... | ... | ... | ... | ... | 11.5 | 10.0 | ... | ... | 10.4 |
| Total............ | 100.0 | 100.0 | 100.0 | 100.0 | 100.0 | 100.0 | 100.0 | 100.0 | 100.0 | 100.0 | 100.0 | 100.0 |

[a] See notes to Table 28.

[ 95 ]

United States, somewhat less; and New Zealand, not much more than half as much. Although the share of the total represented by administrative expenditures thus varied considerably from country to country, it proved impossible to correlate such variations either with the extensiveness of government activity or with the efficiency (or its lack) of government operation. Nor did comparable levels of expenditure appear to be identifiable with the expenditure patterns characteristic of particular types of national economies.

### NATIONAL DEFENSE EXPENDITURES

Although the comparisons in Table 28 pertain to a postwar year, expenditures of many of the governments for defense purposes absorbed a relatively large portion of total disbursements. El Salvador, reporting only 10 per cent of total governmental expenses as for the national defense category, was in the lowest group. Chile spent the largest share (34 per cent) for this purpose; Haiti, Peru, and the United States allocated roughly one quarter of their budgets to this type of expenditure; while all the other countries shown in the table kept defense disbursements within 7 to 15 per cent of their total budgets.

### CULTURAL AND SOCIAL EXPENDITURES

The level of expenditures for cultural and social purposes varies according to national institutions and standards, as well as the attitudes of governments, which in turn reflect to some extent the social pressures operating in each country. The Salvadorean budget showed 16 per cent of total government expenses as devoted to cultural and social purposes, compared with the 15 to 25 per cent spent for these purposes in most of the Latin American countries surveyed. (In Venezuela expenditures for these purposes absorbed only 11 per cent of the total budget.)

The United Kingdom and New Zealand, which allocated one third of their budgets to cultural and social expenditures, were conspicuous as relatively the largest spenders in this category, owing to their extensive schemes for social insurance and pensions, in addition to their regular educational and social services. Denmark, whose activities of this kind included large-scale medical services and insurance plans, devoted 27 per cent of its budget to social and cultural purposes. The United States federal and state governments together spent a much smaller share of their funds for education, public health, recreation, and unemployment compensation; public expenditures for these purposes, however, are relegated in the United States to subordinate bodies of government, such as school districts and counties, and the actual amounts spent in this category were accordingly much larger than those shown in the combined federal and state data in Tables 28 and 29. Moreover, a large part of the United States expenditure for higher education comes from privately endowed institutions, and consequently does not appear in statistics pertaining to public funds.

### EXPENDITURES FOR ECONOMIC DEVELOPMENT

It was not surprising to find a relatively small proportion of total budgetary expenditures devoted to economic development in the economically more advanced countries, since in these countries where private capital formation is large, government expenditures for development amount to a relatively small proportion of total development activity.[12] It is therefore more appropriate to compare the development expenditures of El Salvador, which in 1946 amounted to 19 per cent of the budget, with those of the other Latin American countries. The Salvadorean percentage is roughly midway in a very wide range that extends from a high of 40 per cent for Venezuela to a low of 7 per cent for Haiti. For Guatemala, the share was 34 per cent; for Mexico, 30 per cent; for Chile, 13 per cent;[13] and for Peru, 12 per cent.

The development expenditure for a single year, however, cannot be taken as an indication of the intensity with which the objective of economic development is being pursued in the vari-

[12] The exceedingly low percentage figure shown for the United Kingdom was due to the fact that some of the investment expenditures of the central government are not included in the budget data, and that a large proportion of public investment activities (highway construction, public housing, etc.) is carried out by local government bodies whose financial activities are not included in the data shown in the tables. The latter also applies, with some modification, to the United States.

[13] Not including nonbudgetary expenditures of public funds.

ous countries, nor do the national budget figures necessarily tell the whole story. In some instances, the expenditures made in 1946 mark merely the beginning of a major development plan, the completion of which may take many years and may absorb many times the amount initially disbursed. In others, government development projects are financed through financial institutions especially created for that purpose, which obtain funds from the central bank or other financial institution, and expenditures for economic development therefore may not appear in the statistics of government expenditures.

### PUBLIC DEBT SERVICE

In any discussion of public debt service expenditures, it must be borne in mind that ordinary budget expenditures alone may not reflect the entire amount of the government's public debt payments since, in some instances, the governments have relegated debt retirement to institutions outside the ordinary budget. Furthermore, it is not strictly accurate to compare the expenditures on public debt service alone, since in many countries such payments were offset substantially by Treasury borrowing during the same period.

Comparability is further limited by the distinction that must be made between foreign and domestic debt servicing, inasmuch as the two types of payments have very different economic effects. Servicing of foreign debt represents an "exhaustive" national expenditure, reducing the supply of foreign exchange and curtailing the domestic demand for goods and services. Payment of a domestic public debt is rather an internal "transfer" of funds, resulting in a shifting of purchasing power from the taxpayer to the owner of government securities, and producing problems and burdens largely of a frictional character.[14]

In El Salvador, the servicing of the foreign debt in 1946 absorbed 24 per cent of the total budget. As pointed out above, the debt payment was unusually large, since in that year the debt service, suspended since 1938, was renewed with a substantial payment. In "normal" years, foreign debt servicing absorbs con-

[14] The situation is more involved in the case of services on public debts owed to the central bank or to the banking system.

siderably less than 10 per cent, compared with a total debt service of 4 per cent for Guatemala, 17 per cent for Mexico, 15 per cent for Haiti, and 18 per cent for Denmark; however, in Guatemala, Mexico, and Denmark, the major part of the debt service pertained to domestic debts. In the other countries in the table, expenditures on the public debt were offset to a greater or less extent by borrowing. The exceedingly low share of the debt service in Chile was due to the fact that the amortization of public debt in Chile is handled mainly by the *Caja de Amortización*, which receives nonbudgetary tax revenues earmarked specifically for debt payment, as well as revenues from other agencies for the servicing of specially authorized internal debts issued for them. It was estimated that debt service by this agency in 1946 was equal to approximately 10 per cent of total ordinary budget expenditures. At the same time the Chilean government obtained funds through internal loans. Debt payments of Peru, the United Kingdom, and New Zealand were likewise partly offset by borrowing. The high proportion of budgetary expenditures used for debt payments in the United States must be considered abnormal, resulting from the transition from war financing to postwar budgetary procedures and fiscal policies.

### 4. Per Capita Expenditures

In Table 30, government expenditures are shown on a per capita basis in terms of United States dollars. The table reveals, even more strikingly than the data on per capita tax payments, the wide discrepancies in the amounts disbursed by the governments of the various countries. The differences are of course the result of the differences in per capita income. Indirectly, they also indicate that in the underdeveloped countries the basic prerequisite for larger government expenditures, particularly for cultural and social purposes, is a rise in per capita income.

Total per capita government expenditures in El Salvador amounted to $9.02, compared with a high for the six other Latin American countries of $54 for Venezuela[15] and a low of $2.69 for

---

[15] In Venezuela, the dollar figure probably is misleading, because of the high price level.

## TABLE 30

### PER CAPITA GOVERNMENT EXPENDITURES BY PURPOSE OF EXPENDITURES, OF SELECTED COUNTRIES[a]
*(In United States dollars[b])*

| Kind of expenditure | El Salvador Dec. 1946 | Chile Dec. 1946 | Guatemala June 1946 | Haiti Sept. 1946 | Mexico Dec. 1946 | Peru Dec. 1946 | Venezuela June 1946 | United States June 1947 | | Denmark Mar. 1947 | United Kingdom Mar. 1947 | New Zealand Mar. 1947 |
|---|---|---|---|---|---|---|---|---|---|---|---|---|
| | | | | | | | | Federal only | Federal and state | | | |
| Administrative........ | 2.75 | 10.79 | 2.65 | 0.79 | 4.03 | 5.65 | 21.76 | 101.74 | 113.66 | 57.61 | 119.27 | 57.37 |
| National defense........ | 0.89 | 13.68 | 0.95 | 0.65 | 2.28 | 3.46 | 3.95 | 101.12 | 101.12 | 10.70 | 36.94 | 46.79 |
| Cultural and social...... | 1.48 | 10.02 | 1.50 | 0.51 | 2.35 | 2.84 | 5.88 | 16.17 | 50.66 | 34.56 | 110.85 | 107.08 |
| Economic development... | 1.73 | 5.32 | 2.83 | 0.33 | 4.67 | 1.02 | 21.95 | 15.57 | 25.36 | 1.25 | 11.81 | 39.70 |
| Public debt........... | 2.17 | 0.17 | 0.31 | 0.41 | 2.68 | 0.65 | 0.09 | 113.95 | 115.43 | 22.64 | 40.77 | 47.34 |
| Other special expenditures | ... | ... | ... | ... | ... | ... | ... | 45.36[c] | 45.36[c] | ... | ... | 34.60[c] |
| Total............. | 9.02 | 39.98 | 8.24 | 2.69 | 16.01 | 13.62 | 53.63 | 393.91 | 451.59 | 126.76 | 319.64 | 332.88 |

[a] For fiscal year ending with month indicated. Budgetary expenditures of national governments only, so far as available data make this possible. Combined United States federal and state data included for purposes of comparison.
[b] Conversions from national currencies made by using par values announced by the International Monetary Fund on December 18, 1946 (or nonmember's par value or selling rate for 1946).
[c] Expenditures for foreign aid and loans.

Haiti. Guatemala reported $8.24; Peru, $14; Mexico, $16; and Chile, $40. In the countries other than the Latin American, per capita government expenditures were so large as to make comparison meaningless: they exceeded even the total Salvadorean per capita income.

Considerable significance may be found, however, in a comparison of particular expenditure categories. Even if the differences in unit costs are taken into account, it is striking that in El Salvador only $1.48 was spent per capita for cultural and educational purposes, while in Chile and Mexico $5.32 and $4.67 were so spent. In the United States the corresponding figure (incomplete) was $50; in the United Kingdom, $111; and in New Zealand, $107. Similarly, per capita expenditures for economic development — which are of particular interest because they are important in determining the rate at which national income can grow — amounted to $1.73 in El Salvador. They were three times higher in Chile, two and one half times higher in Mexico, and 12 times higher in Venezuela.

# CHAPTER VII

## THE IMPACT OF THE FISCAL SYSTEM
## UPON BUSINESS

THE PURPOSE of this chapter is to analyze the manner in which the Salvadorean fiscal system, through the revenue structure and through the volume and direction of government expenditures, affects Salvadorean business enterprises.

On the tax side, the fiscal system affects enterprises mainly through the levying of indirect taxes upon different activities and products, through tariff protection to various industries, through the taxation of business profits, and through the general impact of taxation upon the willingness of businessmen to assume risks. On the side of government expenditures, enterprises are influenced by government purchases and by the effect that governmental development projects have upon demand, costs, and new investment opportunities in particular lines of business. Finally, there is the impact of the fiscal system upon aggregate national consumption and savings and hence upon the aggregate demand for the products of business and the sources of business capital. With these aggregative aspects we shall deal in Chapter X, on The Budget and the National Income. In the present chapter we shall be concerned with fiscal problems only as they affect individual enterprises and industries.

It is clear, of course, that taxes in the last analysis are borne by individuals and not by an impersonal entity, "business enterprise." This is to be borne in mind whenever reference is made to business taxes. But, as in the end all taxes come to rest upon individuals, so they all, directly or indirectly, affect business enterprises. In this sense, it is a somewhat arbitrary distinction to label certain taxes as business taxes, justified though this is for practical purposes. In the Salvadorean economy, the distinction tends to become further blurred because neither the structure of the revenue system nor that of the economy itself permits a clearcut distinction between business and nonbusiness income. There are, of course, in El Salvador a large number of business firms in which persons other than the owners are employed. But in the numerically and perhaps also economically most important sectors of the economy, namely in agriculture, handicraft production, and retail distribution, the distinction between business income and private income does not exist in most instances. The same person is affected by the fiscal system twice — as an entrepreneur, and again as an earner of wages, salaries, or profits paid to himself. Furthermore, in many instances where a clearcut distinction can be made, the tax system fails to take advantage of it. Thus, as indicated above, the income tax and the *vialidad* laws[1] do not distinguish between business and private income. Nonetheless, it is statistically possible to isolate the effects of the fiscal system upon business sufficiently to derive a number of interesting conclusions.

## 1. Effects of Taxes upon Business

### TAXES ON BUSINESS

The most direct, but by no means the most important, impact of the revenue system upon business enterprises obviously is that of the group of taxes referred to in Chapter IV as transaction and business-license taxes (Tables 11, 12, 13). This group of taxes embraces several specific taxes which have in common the fact that they are collected from business firms. Within this group two sets of distinctions can be drawn: (1) between taxes that do, and taxes that do not, vary with the volume of business; and (2) between taxes that are imposed on *all* business firms and taxes that are imposed on specific lines of business only. The stamp tax is largely a tax falling within the first category; it is imposed on the basis of the value of business invoices, and therefore becomes a cost of production to the business firm — a cost that can be allocated to each specific transaction. Business registration fees (*matrícula de comercio*), registration fees of motor vehicles belonging to business firms, and trade mark and patent registration fees, on the other hand, are taxes the payment of

[1] See Appendix D, pp. 276, 283.

which cannot be allocated directly to specific transactions. These are therefore paid out of the gross profits of business enterprises, although they are a business cost to the taxpayer. The liquor sales patents occupy an intermediate position between these two groups, since the amount of the patent fees varies within wide ranges with the volume of sales.

Examples of taxes paid by specific business firms include the license fees of pharmacies and drug stores, the gross receipts tax of electricity companies (abolished in 1944), and the registration fees of insurance companies. Within this group, too, the distinction noted can be introduced: some of the taxes can be allocated to each specific transaction (e.g., the tax on insurance premiums), while others are part of the overhead cost (e.g., pharmacy and drug-store licenses). Since these taxes are imposed upon specific branches of business only, they not only become a monetary cost to the firm but also put the affected branches of business at a financial disadvantage compared with other branches of business. This "discriminatory" disadvantage, however, is probably smaller than it might appear. In the first place, these special business taxes were introduced because the situation in the affected branches was presumably such as to enable them to bear the additional tax burden. Besides, the existence of the special tax may make the particular line of business more difficult to enter, particularly if the special tax takes the form of a substantial license fee which has to be paid irrespective of the volume of business. This may in some measure protect established firms against new competitors.

Although all business taxes are collected by the tax administration from business enterprises, it is not to be assumed that these taxes are actually paid by the enterprises themselves. Since they all are a cost from the viewpoint of the business firm, the firm will treat them like any other business cost and attempt to pass them on to the purchaser. This is obviously easiest in the case of those taxes which are imposed on the basis of the volume of sales. For purposes of the further analysis that is undertaken later in this chapter, it has been assumed that all business taxes are shifted to the consumer.

### TAXES ENTERING INTO BUSINESS COSTS

As indicated in Chapter IV, the Salvadorean revenue system includes a number of taxes levied on specific commodities, in particular the customs duties levied on many imported goods. These taxes are normally not thought of as entering into business transactions as costs. While this is true with respect to the bulk of those taxes and with respect to most of the commodities subject to import duties or internal consumption taxes, a closer examination of the Salvadorean taxation system and of the system of internal consumption taxes reveals that a certain proportion of these taxes is actually paid by business enterprises, although the burden may of course be shifted to the consumer. This is so because some of these commodities are "consumed" not by private individuals but by business firms. For instance, the import duty on a typewriter purchased and used by a business firm becomes in effect a business expense. Similarly, the purchase of cotton cloth used, for instance, for decoration purposes by a business firm is taxed either through the domestic cotton tax or by an import duty; again the tax has to be paid, in the first instance, by the business firm.

It is impossible to determine the exact amount of these "consumption taxes" which in effect become business costs. But a study of private consumption (as distinct from consumption by business), elaborated in more detail in the next chapter, indicates that in 1946 approximately 50 per cent of total import duty payments were imposed on commodities that were "consumed" by business enterprises. This is not particularly surprising when it is realized that the duty collections are very substantial on such articles as gasoline, lubricating oils, office equipment, etc., all of which primarily enter into business costs. In the case of other commodities, such as building materials (e.g., cement and steel), it cannot easily be determined whether such materials are actually used for private housing construction or for business construction purposes. In so far as they are used in business construction, they likewise become a business expense and the import duties imposed upon them become part of business costs.

Like business taxes proper, these taxes affecting business operations are presumably not borne in the end by business enterprises, but are largely shifted to the ultimate consumers. It has
been assumed in the computations shown below that this kind
of tax burden is shifted to the consumer in its entirety.

### DIRECT AND PROPERTY TAXES

As indicated above, Salvadorean tax statistics and tax laws do
not distinguish between the taxation of business income and
business property and the taxation of private income and property.[2] Income of individuals and corporations, from all sources,
is basically subject to the same income and *vialidad* taxes. Income from dividends is not subject to income tax, the income
having already been taxed to the corporation at personal income
tax rates. Since a corporation owned by more than one person
is likely to be in a higher income tax bracket than its shareholders, a special income tax is in fact levied upon corporate business.
The rate of this de facto tax, however, is indeterminate, depending upon the difference between the tax bracket of the corporation and those of its owners. Corporations, however, are few in
number in El Salvador, and their owners usually are men of
means who themselves are in high income tax brackets. The
aggregate of such "special taxation" levied against corporate
business therefore may not be substantial. In the computations
that follow no allowance for it has been made, owing to lack of
data. Apart from this "special taxation," the income of business
firms, as distinct from the income of business proprietors, is not
burdened by income taxes.

It has likewise been impossible to separate from the *vialidad*
property tax (Series A) and the special assessment pavement tax
the amount that falls upon business. No data are available that
would permit a distinction to be drawn between business and
nonbusiness property, although the volume of business property,
which includes agricultural land, is bound to be very substantial.

---

[2] The income tax law distinguishes between income of corporations and income
of unincorporated firms with regard to the amount of basic exemption. No information is available, however, regarding the amount of taxes levied on business
income and business property.

In the following analysis it has had to be assumed that the two taxes in question fall wholly upon nonbusiness property. For the purpose of analyzing the tax burden that falls upon business enterprises and consumers, respectively, this arbitrary procedure makes very little difference, because the part of the two taxes actually assessed against business properties is an element of overhead cost and as such probably tends to be shifted, in the long run, to the consumer.

Of the property-transfer tax, 50 per cent has been assumed, in the following computations, to fall upon business property transactions and is included among the "other" taxes falling upon business. Like the remaining taxes in this "other" category, it is assumed to be wholly shifted to the consumer.

There are several other taxes that in a certain sense must be considered as business taxes, since they affect the amount of income derived from business operations. The most important of these is the coffee export tax. As indicated in Chapter IV, this tax is paid by the exporter of coffee and must therefore be regarded as a tax upon the business of growing and exporting coffee. The burden of this "business tax" is offset, however, by the provision that income from the growing and exporting of coffee (after payment of the coffee export tax) is exempt from the income tax. In this case, the business tax thus takes the place of a "personal" tax.

If the coffee tax were largely shiftable, this would of course represent a considerable gain to the producer, since a personal tax is largely nonshiftable. The coffee tax, however, certainly cannot be shifted forward to the consumer. Since the price of coffee is dictated by the world market, which is influenced very little by the supply of coffee from El Salvador, the coffee producers must bear the burden of the coffee tax, unless they are able to shift backward at least a part of it to the agricultural workers employed in coffee production. To the extent that such shifting backwards does not take place, the coffee tax affects the producer in the same way as would the income tax that it replaces. It therefore does not put the industry as a whole at a disadvantage compared with other forms of investment, since the reduction in profits is made up by the exemption from income tax.

Since the tax varies with the price of coffee, and in the past has been removed altogether when the price fell very low, it resembles the income tax even in its tendency to vanish when net income vanishes. It does not, however, have the progressive character of the income tax, and therefore weighs more heavily upon the smaller producers than would an income tax. To that extent, it puts small-scale coffee production at a competitive disadvantage with other forms of enterprise, and thus may favor the concentration of coffee production in the hands of larger producers, although its burden probably is too small to make this effect important.

To the extent that the coffee tax can be shifted backwards, in the form of a reduction in wages, it may add a serious element of regressiveness to the tax structure. Downward pressure on coffee wages would tend to depress wages throughout the economy, since the coffee industry, as the largest employer of labor, tends to set the tone for wages in general. In that event, the additional inequality in the national distribution of income resulting from the shifting of the coffee tax would considerably exceed the amount of the tax actually shifted.

It is very difficult to make realistic estimates of the degree of backward shifting of this tax. Since the industry is subject to wide cyclical fluctuations, and the tax rate itself varies with prices, the degree of shifting probably is quite indeterminate and on the whole probably minor. In the case studies presented in the next section alternative assumptions have been made in which the consequences of a backward shift of 50 per cent of this tax are explored.

The situation is somewhat different in the case of the cotton and the sugar taxes. As will be recalled, these taxes are collected from the producers, that is, in the case of the cotton tax from the textile mills and in the case of the sugar tax from the sugar producers. Neither the textile mills nor the sugar producers are subject to taxation on income derived from their production, respectively, of cotton textiles and sugar. Since the textile mills are protected against foreign competition through high protective duties, they apparently pass on the entire tax, or at least a major part of it, to the ultimate consumer. Unlike coffee producers, the cotton textile producers therefore do not find their profits materially reduced by the tax, and their exemption from the income tax represents a net gain to them, at the expense of the consumer.[3] An almost identical situation prevails in the case of the sugar producers, who are liable to tax payment on sugar produced for domestic consumption but at the same time enjoy exemption from the income tax on the income thus derived. The textile and sugar industries thus enjoy a definite competitive advantage over other forms of investment.

### CASE STUDIES AS OF 1946

In order to obtain a picture of the taxes paid by business firms of various sizes and in various fields, including those taxes that are largely or wholly shifted to the consumer, the business tax liability and related data for a number of selected business cases have been computed and are presented in Table 31.[4] The first three cases pertain to small economic units; the second group shows medium-sized firms; in the third and fourth groups large business units are included. Within each group, the same amount of annual business income has been assumed, and, in addition, an amount of total capital (which includes both business and nonbusiness property) has been assumed at a level that reflects real conditions as closely as possible. This table also illustrates, on the basis of reasonable assumptions, the burden of taxation that the owner or owners of the business are forced to absorb in their character as entrepreneurs, and compares it with the burden they bear as "consumers" who enjoy a specified income. The importance of this comparison lies in the different burdens borne by coffee producers and by owners of other forms of business.

[3] When the tax on cotton yarns was introduced in 1944, however, cotton goods were subject to price controls. Therefore, originally, the tax could not be shifted to the consumer.

[4] The origin and computation of the figures shown in the table are explained and discussed in detail in Appendix G. It should be noted that the imputation of the tax burden to the various levels of business income is technically a rather complicated procedure and the results are at best approximations. The examples presented in the table must, therefore, be interpreted as indicative of the order of magnitude of the burden of business and other taxes rather than as statistically exact and reliable figures.

## TABLE 31

### BURDEN OF TAXES ON TYPICAL BUSINESS FIRMS IN 1946
#### (In colones)

| | Small units | | | Medium-size firms | | | | | Large business units | | |
|---|---|---|---|---|---|---|---|---|---|---|---|
| | Shop-keeper | Coffee producer | General agricultural producer | Shop-keeper | Coffee producer | General agricultural producer | Wholesale-retail importer | Coffee producer | Combination importer and coffee producer | Wholesale-retail importer | Coffee producer |
| Income.................... | 1,800 | 1,800 | 1,800 | 4,800 | 4,800 | 4,800 | 25,000 | 25,000 | 25,000 | 100,000 | 100,000 |
| Capital................... | 4,500 | 8,000 | 6,000 | 15,000 | 21,500 | 16,000 | 125,000 | 111,000 | 118,000 | 500,000 | 443,000 |
| Taxes paid by the business firm: | | | | | | | | | | | |
| Import duties on business goods......... | 47.8 | 50.8 | 63.6 | 130.4 | 139.0 | 173.8 | 1,786.0 | 1,143.0 | 1,464.6 | 6,556.0 | 3,671.4 |
| Business license and transaction taxes.... | 14.5 | 10.3 | 11.5 | 47.0 | 32.5 | 37.5 | 386.8 | 270.8 | 328.8 | 2,180.8 | 1,526.5 |
| Coffee export tax........ | 0.0 | 172.5 | 0.0 | 0.0 | 460.0 | 0.0 | 0.0 | 2,396.0 | 1,198.0 | 0 | 9,583.8 |
| Other taxes on business[a]..... | 10.4 | 8.7 | 8.7 | 33.7 | 28.1 | 28.1 | 276.4 | 230.4 | 253.4 | 1,014.4 | 840.4 |
| Total taxes paid by the business firm...... | 72.7 | 242.3 | 83.8 | 211.1 | 659.6 | 239.4 | 2,449.2 | 4,040.2 | 3,244.8 | 9,751.2 | 15,622.1 |
| Less taxes paid by the business firm, and shifted[b]........... | 72.7 | 69.8 | 83.8 | 211.1 | 199.6 | 239.4 | 2,449.2 | 1,644.2 | 2,046.8 | 9,751.2 | 6,038.3 |
| Taxes borne by owner of business as entrepreneur........... | 0.0 | 172.5 | 0.0 | 0.0 | 460.0 | 0.0 | 0.0 | 2,396.0 | 1,198.0 | 0.0 | 9,583.8 |
| Plus taxes borne by owner of business as consumer.......... | 132.5 | 119.4 | 125.7 | 480.5 | 399.1 | 467.2 | 3,355.5 | 1,579.9 | 2,034.6 | 21,247.1 | 5,209.1 |
| Total taxes borne by owner of business........ | 132.5 | 291.9 | 125.7 | 480.5 | 859.1 | 467.2 | 3,355.5 | 3,975.9 | 3,232.6 | 21,247.1 | 14,792.9 |
| Total taxes as per cent of income........... | 7.4% | 16.2% | 7.0% | 10.0% | 17.9% | 9.7% | 13.4% | 15.9% | 12.9% | 21.2% | 14.8% |
| *Alternative Assumption (coffee tax 50 per cent shifted)[c]* | | | | | | | | | | | |
| Total taxes paid by the business firm...... | 72.7 | 242.3 | 83.8 | 211.1 | 659.6 | 239.4 | 2,449.2 | 4,040.2 | 3,244.8 | 9,751.2 | 15,622.1 |
| Less taxes paid by the business firm, and shifted......... | 72.7 | 171.0 | 83.8 | 211.1 | 429.6 | 239.4 | 2,449.2 | 2,842.2 | 2,645.8 | 9,751.2 | 10,830.2 |
| Taxes borne by owner of business as entrepreneur........... | 0.0 | 71.3 | 0.0 | 0.0 | 230.0 | 0.0 | 0.0 | 1,198.0 | 599.0 | 0.0 | 4,791.9 |
| Plus taxes borne by owner of business as consumer.......... | 142.8 | 123.2 | 136.0 | 507.7 | 422.2 | 494.4 | 3,498.3 | 1,596.6 | 2,131.8 | 21,820.1 | 5,239.3 |
| Total taxes borne by owner of business........ | 142.8 | 194.5 | 136.0 | 507.7 | 652.2 | 494.4 | 3,498.3 | 2,794.6 | 2,730.8 | 21,820.1 | 10,031.2 |
| Total taxes as per cent of income........... | 7.9% | 10.8% | 7.6% | 10.6% | 13.6% | 10.3% | 14.0% | 11.2% | 10.9% | 21.8% | 10.0% |

a Includes those parts of fees, fines, property-transfer taxes, and other taxes that fall on business.

b Assuming that the coffee export tax is entirely borne by the coffee producer. All other taxes are shifted entirely to the consumer.

c Assuming that half of the coffee export tax is shifted to the worker. All other taxes are shifted entirely to the consumer.

"Taxes paid by the business firm" differ from those actually borne by the owner of the business in his role as an entrepreneur by the portion of taxes that can be shifted in the form of higher prices or lower wages. The taxes actually borne by the owner are shown here on two bases. That used in the body of the table assumes that the coffee export tax is borne entirely by the coffee producer.

These taxes are also shown under the alternative assumption that 50 per cent of the coffee tax is shifted back to the worker in the form of lower wages. The other taxes paid by the business firm are assumed, in line with earlier analysis, to be wholly shifted to the consumer in the form of higher prices. This assumption appears quite incontestible with regard to import duties and stamp taxes, which vary with the volume of transactions, but it may be less well founded with regard to those taxes that represent overhead rather than variable costs. Nevertheless it is likely, all circumstances considered, that a very high portion of these other taxes was also shifted. Since these doubtful taxes are relatively small compared with the total of the taxes paid by businessmen, the assumption that business taxes are shifted 100 per cent does not appear to be unrealistic. The last item in the compilation, "Taxes borne by owner of business as consumer," includes those taxes paid by the consumer directly and those shifted to him by business.[5]

A comparison of the total tax liabilities of the various cases reflects particularly the difference in the respective burdens under the income tax and under the coffee export tax. The result of the substitution of the flat-rate coffee export tax for the progressive income tax is that in the lowest business income brackets the tax burden upon incomes derived from coffee is substantially higher than that upon other incomes. This is so because in the low and middle income groups the income tax liability is either nil or very small. At a level of 25,000 colones income per year the impact of the coffee tax and of the income tax, at the rates prevailing in 1946, was about the same.[6] Only in the highest in-

[5] The tax liability of the consumer is discussed in detail in the next chapter.
[6] It should be noted that in the calendar year 1946 the coffee tax amounted to 4.50 and 5.18 colones per bag for the 1945–46 and for the 1946–47 crop respectively.

come groups did the coffee producers enjoy an advantage through the payment of the coffee export tax in lieu of income tax.

From the point of view of tax equity, a rather interesting case is that of the "combination importer and coffee producer" — a business enterprise that is engaged in part in the production of coffee and in part in other commercial pursuits. The fact that one part of the income is derived from the income tax exempt production of coffee leaves him in an income tax bracket with a lower rate than would prevail if his income were derived entirely from business other than coffee production. His total tax liability is smaller than that either of the coffee producer or of the entrepreneurs engaged exclusively in a "noncoffee" line of business.

Under the alternative assumption, where 50 per cent of the coffee export tax is assumed to be shifted, the total tax liability of the coffee producer becomes commensurately less. As a result of this, his total tax burden, in the lower and middle income brackets, now more nearly equals that of a noncoffee entrepreneur, but in the higher income brackets it is substantially less.

## 2. EFFECTS OF GOVERNMENT EXPENDITURES UPON BUSINESS

As indicated above, the government represents the largest "business unit" in the Salvadorean economy. In its expenditure of the revenues collected, it serves as a customer for the goods produced or traded by other business firms and, on the other hand, it competes with business in general for the factors of production, that is to say, for the services of wage earners and salaried employees and for raw material produced within the economy or imported from abroad. Only to a very minor degree does the government compete with private business in the sale of goods and services.

---

The coffee tax was raised considerably in the following year. If it is assumed that the price–cost relation in coffee production remained the same in the following year, the coffee tax at the new rate of 7.00 colones per quintal presumably imposed a heavier burden on income than the income tax, in brackets up to 50,000 colones of business income. It has been pointed out, however, that in the years after 1946, coffee prices advanced more rapidly than the cost of production. If this is correct, the position of the coffee producers relative to other producers should not have deteriorated as a result of the increase of the tax rate.

### THE GOVERNMENT AS A BUYER

In order to obtain an estimate of the volume of goods purchased from Salvadorean business firms, those amounts that are spent by the government directly on imports and on wages and salaries[7] have to be deducted from the government's annual "variable" expenditures. The remaining amounts represent the annual outlays of the government on the purchase of goods from Salvadorean business firms (see Table 32).

These expenditures are apparently distributed over a very wide range of business activities. The nature of government

TABLE 32

GOVERNMENT PURCHASES, 1937–1947
(*In thousands of colones*)

| Year | "Variable" Expenditures (excluding debt service) | Payment orders of government for purchase abroad | Domestic "variable" expenditures | Purchase of domestic commodities[a] |
|---|---|---|---|---|
| 1937 | 6,412.9 | 1,404.9 | 5,008.0 | 1,970 |
| 1938 | 6,514.6 | 1,434.5 | 5,080.1 | 1,990 |
| 1939 | 6,794.3 | 949.3 | 5,846.0 | 2,630 |
| 1940 | 7,593.8 | 2,191.0 | 5,402.8 | 1,800 |
| 1941 | 5,332.6 | 848.4 | 4,484.2 | 1,960 |
| 1942 | 5,805.5 | 1,286.3 | 4,519.2 | 1,770 |
| 1943 | 6,984.7 | 4,254.0 | 2,730.7 | 1,130 |
| 1944 | 8,363.1 | 4,123.9 | 4,240.2 | 1,760 |
| 1945 | 8,919.3 | 3,382.8 | 5,536.5 | 2,300 |
| 1946 | 13,611.8 | 2,733.7 | 10,878.1 | 4,430 |
| 1947 | 23,950.2 | 7,641.1 | 16,309.1 | 4,960 |

[a] Commodities include goods and business services, such as electricity, transportation, etc. Rental payments were not included since they appear in the original statistics under fixed expenditures. The figures shown in this column are rough estimates.

[7] As pointed out above, "variable" expenditures include purchases of goods as well as outlays for such wages and salaries as are paid in connection with public works, special activities of the government, etc. Since an exact breakdown of "variable" expenditures, which would permit a distinction between the purchase of goods and services from Salvadorean business firms and salaries and wage payments to individuals, is not available, the amounts disbursed for purchases from business firms have been estimated on the basis of budget figures. The budget figures have been adjusted to conform to liquidated expenditures.

operations makes it unavoidable, however, that the government purchases bulk very heavily in specific lines, of which the most important probably are building materials such as stone, sand, lime, and timber. As the annual budget data indicate, purchases of foodstuffs (for prisons, hospitals, and the armed forces) also represent a large proportion of the total business transactions in these branches of business.

It is difficult to determine whether business profits derived from sales to the government are larger or smaller than those derived from operations within the nongovernment sector. The rigid purchase regulations of the Purchasing Law (*Ley de Suministros*) would point in the direction of lower than average profits from such transactions. On the other hand, there may be other factors that would cause business with the government to yield more substantial profits. The significance of the government as a buyer in the economy is increased by the fact that for the performance of certain operations the government avails itself of the services of contracting firms.

### GOVERNMENT COMPETITION WITH BUSINESS

The government competes with private business in the labor market and, on occasion, in the market for raw materials. The government is the largest employer of professionals, white-collar workers, and skilled and unskilled labor. In times of full employment, which in El Salvador have been the norm, this competition is of some importance, and the same holds for periods of material shortages such as were experienced after the war. It is important to note, however, that owing to the absence of exchange control the government has never been forced to compete with business for a limited supply of foreign exchange.

As the largest single employer, the government exercises considerable influence in the labor market and contributes importantly to the setting of standards of salaries and wages and working conditions. The fact that there are hardly ever any openings in government service indicates that the government is considered a desirable employer. Since there are no statistics available for salaries paid in private employment, a comparison with government salaries is not possible. On the basis of information provided by government officials and by members of the business community, however, it would seem that the competition of the government in the market for white-collar workers is quite effective, not so much on account of salary differentials as because of the elimination of afternoon office hours and the resulting shorter work week. To the extent that the competition for white-collar workers raises salaries, or makes the employment of additional personnel in private business necessary, it results in an increase of business costs that to some extent may affect profits. But since the number of white-collar workers in private enterprises is relatively small, because of the small size of business units, the competition of the government as an employer in this field is not particularly felt.

The competition of the government for day labor employed in road and building construction is probably more important. The size of the labor force normally engaged in construction work is believed to be quite large, but migration to the United States and, in more recent years, to Panama and Venezuela has prevented an increase in the number of persons available for this kind of work. A rapid expansion of government activities in the construction field, or the expansion of private building activities at times when the volume of public construction is large, is therefore likely to result in temporary or seasonal shortages of labor and cause wage and cost increases.

This competition between government and private enterprise in the construction field could be avoided through the proper timing of government expenditures for public works. But, as indicated above, the government expands its investment activities primarily in times of large tax receipts, that is, in periods of business prosperity when the volume of private construction activity also is substantial.

The competition that at times prevails in the factors of production market seems to be felt also in the field of building materials, particularly of foreign origin. The conflicting demands of government and private enterprise for scarce imported materials such as structural steel and cement became quite apparent in the immediate postwar years. In order to resolve these difficulties, a system of price controls and rationing of imported building materials was established. This system was abolished, however, when the supply of imported materials became more ample.

While the competition that the government offers to private business as a buyer of services and materials is lively, the government does not compete actively as a seller. Unlike many other governments in Latin America, the Salvadorean government is not engaged in major industrial or commercial operations. The operation of government enterprises is confined, on the whole, to activities that do not compete with private business. The operation of postal, telegraph, and telephone services is considered in most countries a function that can be performed by the government most efficiently and economically. Other government enterprises, such as the operation of the printing office, the engraving shop, and the chemical laboratories, are closely associated with the special requirements of government operations and do not compete for business with the private sector of the economy. Moreover, operations of these enterprises are relatively small, with the result that even if it is assumed that functions performed by these enterprises could be performed equally well by private firms, the volume of business taken away from the private sector appears to be quite small.

The only government operations that may be considered in direct competition with private enterprise are some of the activities carried out by the Mejoramiento Social. Particularly after the completion of the textile mill of the Mejoramiento Social the government will be an effective competitor in this field. Against this aspect of the planned operations of the textile mill, however, it must be noted that the avowed purpose of the textile factory was to establish a "yardstick" plant, the operations of which would serve to obtain information and experience with respect to the kind and type of textile industry most suitable for the supply and demand situation prevailing in El Salvador.

Recently, plans have been made for the construction and the operation by the government, or with government participation, of a hydroelectric plant, the Lempa River project. The operation of this plant would, of course, compete with the existing private electric utility enterprises of the country. But since the purpose of the project is to establish through the sale of low-cost electrical power one of the prerequisites for the further industrialization of the country, and since the existing electric plants are working at full capacity, the threat of government competition with the private economy does not seem to arise here in serious form.

### 3. THE TARIFF AND THE STRUCTURE OF PRODUCTION

The influence of the tariff upon business is twofold. On the one hand it represents a tax upon some of the equipment and materials employed by business firms, and thereby increases costs. This aspect was discussed in section 1 of the present chapter. On the other hand, it gives protection to certain lines of business. To the extent that protection is the primary purpose of the tariff, its discussion belongs in the field of commercial policy rather than that of public finance with which we are here dealing. The protective features of the Salvadorean tariff, however, are not always clearly distinguishable from its revenue functions. For instance, the tariff on various types of textiles, which has strongly protective effects, is nevertheless a large revenue producer. The tariff on textiles undoubtedly is in part responsible for the growth of the textile industry in El Salvador. It compensates, or more than compensates, for the effects of the taxes levied upon the industry, which can therefore be passed on to the consumer. A similar situation prevails in the field of sugar production, where the producers are likewise both taxed and protected. Another instance in which the tariff is being used to promote a particular industry is given by the export tax of 0.25 centavos per bag on coffee shipped in bags made of other than domestic materials, which aids the henequen industry. A detailed examination of the effects of the protective tariff policy upon business would lead far into the field of commercial policy and cannot be undertaken here.

Somewhat different in character is the aid given to certain lines of business through tariff exemptions upon the raw materials, fuel, and particularly machinery, that they import for their use. This aid amounts to a direct subsidy at the expense of the budget, in contrast to the indirect subsidies involved in tariff protection. The industries that have benefited from such subsidies most frequently are coffee, sugar, mining, and transportation. The quantitative effect of such subsidies upon the expansion of these and other industries cannot, of course, be estimated. The principle of facilitating imports of capital goods into a country that needs them as much as El Salvador is undoubtedly a healthy one.

## 4. INFLUENCE OF THE FISCAL SYSTEM ON BUSINESS ORGANIZATION

The fiscal system plays a not inconsiderable role in molding the form of business organization in El Salvador. As indicated above, by far the largest proportion of production and distribution in the country is carried out by individuals and partnerships; with the exception of foreign-owned enterprises, the corporate form of organization is very little in use. It seems that while the relative absence of corporate enterprises is largely due to traditions and business customs, these traditions and customs have been strengthened by the discrimination of the income tax law as respects corporations.

Corporate income is taxed at the same rates as private income. From the tax angle, therefore, it is not advantageous to incorporate a partnership, because the income bracket of the corporation is normally higher than the brackets of the individual partners. Furthermore, corporate income enjoys no basic tax exemption, in contrast to the basic exemptions of 2,000–4,000 colones accorded to unincorporated enterprises (see Chapter IV). On the other hand, it should be pointed out that these handicaps are made up in part by the fact that there is no double taxation of dividends such as prevails in the United States. Dividend income is exempt from income tax.

The handicaps imposed by the income tax upon corporate business may quite possibly have retarded the development of certain lines of manufacturing production that require large investment of capital. In economically more advanced countries the corporate form of enterprise has made it possible to utilize the savings of a larger number of individuals in productive and profitable economic pursuits. It seems justifiable to assert that the opportunity to invest funds in profitable business organizations may in the long run raise the rate of savings and thereby accelerate the accumulation of productive capital. The power of corporations to retain some of their profits and plow them back into the business works in the same direction. Furthermore, the amount of bank credit that could be extended would probably be larger if, through the more widespread use of the corporate form, the size of business units could be made to increase.

The creation of a larger number of corporations probably would bring indirect benefits to the government. It would facilitate the assessment of income taxes, *Vialidad* A, and inheritance taxes, because bookkeeping and accounting methods employed by larger business organizations in which more than one person or a small group of persons have a financial interest are likely to be superior to those employed by smaller business units.

## 5. Capital Gains

Another influence that the fiscal system exerts upon business derives from the fact, mentioned previously, that capital gains from the sale of assets are not subject to income tax. The immediate effect of this tax exemption is to favor speculative transactions as against ordinary productive investment. Sometimes this form of speculation may be beneficial to the economic processes of production and distribution, even though investment aimed directly at these purposes would normally be more effective. At other times speculation may be downright harmful, as for instance during the war years, when it served to accentuate the inflationary pressures. At such times, some anti-inflationary effects might have been produced through the imposition of a capital gains tax. A capital gains tax, moreover, would help somewhat to redress the increasing inequality in the distribution of income and wealth that usually comes with inflation. On the other hand, it must be recognized that the capital gains tax is adverse to the formation of capital, and in an undercapitalized country like El Salvador it may be preferable to avoid interfering with the processes of capitalization even at some sacrifice in other respects.

The property-transfer tax (*alcabala*) in a small way takes the place of a capital gains tax. But its low rate and its limitation to real estate make it a very imperfect substitute. Moreover, the property-transfer tax may become a serious impediment to otherwise desirable transfers if in periods of low or falling prices the seller has to assume this tax liability in addition to a capital loss.

# CHAPTER VIII

## THE BUDGET AND THE CONSUMER

THE PRECEDING CHAPTER has presented a survey of the influence of the fiscal system upon business. This influence is important; as, however, has already been pointed out, the main effects and particularly the ultimate burden of taxation, as well as the benefits of government services, fall not upon impersonal business units but upon individuals in their roles as receivers and spenders of income. The present chapter therefore analyzes the impact of the fiscal system upon the consumer.

The form in which the consumer bears the ultimate burden of taxes depends upon the nature of each individual tax. Some taxes are paid directly out of income, others in the form of higher prices, still others in the form of reduced income.

The main task here is to find out what the over-all tax burden is for consumers at different income levels and in different occupations. An attempt also will be made to estimate the degree to which these different consumers benefit from the services provided by the government.

### 1. CLASSIFICATION OF TAXES

The tax structure will first be analyzed with regard to the following aspects of the various taxes: (1) their "shiftability" — the extent to which they can be shifted to other persons by the individual from whom they are collected; (2) their progressiveness — whether their ratio to the individual's income increases or decreases with higher income levels; and (3) their "avoidability" — the degree to which the individual person or firm may legally avoid a particular tax. With these data in hand, it will be possible to estimate the total tax burden on the consumer.

#### "SHIFTABILITY" OF TAXES

From the viewpoint of "shiftability," three groups of taxes can be distinguished, as shown in Table 33. The first group com-

TABLE 33

UNSHIFTED, SHIFTED, AND INTERMEDIATE TAXES FOR SELECTED YEARS
(*In thousands of colones*)

| | 1935/36 | 1942 | 1946 | 1948ᵃ |
|---|---|---|---|---|
| *Taxes mainly unshifted* | | | | |
| Income tax............. | 590.5 | 1,582.4 | 2,662.1 | 2,600.0 |
| Inheritance and gift tax... | 358.9 | 520.1 | 975.4 | 500.0 |
| Vialidad A............. | 158.7 | 258.6 | 341.8 | 250.0 |
| Vialidad B, C, D........ | 190.7 | 251.3 | 232.3 | 250.0 |
| Other unshifted taxesᵇ.... | 231.3 | 288.9 | 505.7 | 362.6 |
| Total unshifted taxes... | 1,530.1 | 2,901.3 | 4,717.3 | 3,962.6 |
| Per cent of total taxes.. | 8.7% | 15.7% | 12.8% | 8.4% |
| *Taxes mainly shifted* | | | | |
| Consumption taxes....... | 2,643.2 | 4,047.6 | 8,644.1 | 9,170.9 |
| Import duties........... | 10,196.4 | 7,779.0 | 15,028.1 | 22,292.0 |
| Transaction and business-license taxes........ | 925.6 | 1,290.6 | 1,912.6 | 1,766.7 |
| Total shifted taxes..... | 13,765.2 | 13,117.2 | 25,584.8 | 33,229.6 |
| Per cent of total taxes.. | 78.4% | 70.9% | 69.7% | 70.0% |
| *Intermediate taxes* | | | | |
| Coffee export tax........ | 1,394.5 | 1,353.0 | 4,414.3 | 9,000.0 |
| Pavement taxᶜ.......... | 134.1 | 258.6 | 121.2 | 150.0 |
| Property-transfer taxes... | 189.6 | 269.5 | 495.9 | 435.0 |
| Other taxesᵈ............ | 542.0 | 598.2 | 1,389.6 | 652.0 |
| Total intermediate taxes | 2,260.2 | 2,479.3 | 6,421.0 | 10,237.0 |
| Per cent of total taxes.. | 12.9% | 13.4% | 17.5% | 21.6% |
| Total taxes.............. | 17,555.5 | 18,497.8 | 35,723.1 | 47,429.4 |

ᵃ Budget.
ᵇ Includes Cédulas de Vecindad, dividend tax, bank profit tax, fees, and fines.
ᶜ The pavement tax is unshifted when a house is occupied by the owner, but is shifted at least in part where a house is rented.
ᵈ Alcabala and cattle-transfer tax.

prises "unshifted" taxes, i.e., those taxes that on the whole are unlikely to be shifted to any important extent from the individuals from whom they are actually collected; the second, those indirect taxes that probably are fully shifted; and the third, a miscellaneous but important group of taxes, largely indirect, the shifting of which is uncertain.

The taxes in the first group, which include among others the income tax, *vialidad*, and inheritance taxes,[1] are characterized by the fact that they are presumably paid out of the income (or capital) of the person from whom they are actually collected. In other words, the taxes are a deduction from the income received by the taxed individual, and the income disposable for other purposes (i.e., for consumption or saving) decreases proportionately. In most instances, the individual is fully aware of the payment of these taxes. In addition, the group of direct taxes includes the income tax paid by corporations, which cannot statistically be separated from the income tax paid by individuals. Quantitatively the income tax paid by corporations is not very important because of the small number of corporations. If its segregation were possible, it properly should be added to the group of "intermediate" taxes, since there is reason to believe that corporate income taxes may be shifted at least in part. It may be observed, however, that in El Salvador the likelihood of such shifting is relatively small because corporations must compete with partnerships where any shifting of the income tax is relatively unlikely.

More important in the aggregate to the consumer than the burden imposed by unshifted taxes upon him are the taxes of the second group, which are not collected from him but are shifted to him from the person or business firm from which the tax is collected. This group includes all consumption taxes specified in Chapter IV and all duty payments. As indicated above, these consumption taxes are treated as a business expense by the person or firm from which they are collected, and are therefore as a rule passed on to the consumer.

The fact that consumption taxes are normally shifted to the ultimate consumer does not mean that the firm engaged in the production or distribution of taxed commodities remains un-

---

[1] With the exception of income and *vialidad* taxes imposed upon business property, to the extent that such taxes exceed the amount of taxes that would be collected if personal income, rather than business income, were taxed. See above, Chapter VII, sections 1 and 4.

affected by such a tax. As indicated in the preceding chapter, the firm's volume of sales, and therefore its gross profits, are influenced by such taxes. Neither does shifting imply that the price will be increased by the exact amount of the tax. A reduction in the turnover of each firm, or a reduction in the number of firms, may affect unit costs, with the result that the price the consumer pays after all of these adjustments may be higher by either more or less than the amount of the tax. In the present study, however, it is assumed that the burden shifted to the consumer is the exact amount of the tax.[2]

Finally, there is an intermediate group of taxes with respect to which it is uncertain what part, if any, is at any given time passed on to the consumer. Business taxes that are not (or are only loosely) related to the volume of sales and import duties imposed upon commodities that enter business accounts as overhead expenses (machinery, office equipment, etc.) fall in this category. A business firm trying to maximize profits will, of course, endeavor to shift as much as possible of this tax burden to the consumer by charging higher prices. The extent to which its attempts in this direction will be successful, however, will depend, among other things, upon the competitive situation in which it finds itself (i.e., to what extent it is free to set its own prices) and on the kind of the commodity it sells. Moreover, the proportion of a business firm's tax burden that is shifted to the consumer undoubtedly varies from time to time. In a period of rising prices and rising money income the firm is likely to be able to pass on a larger proportion of such taxes than in a period of falling prices when it may be forced to reduce its prices and thereby absorb its tax burden fully or in part.

To determine with any degree of exactness the proportion of such taxes shifted to the consumer would require an investigation of cost accounting practices and of the competitive situation that would be far beyond the scope of this report and beyond the volume of information readily available from published sources. It is probable that in the long run the greater part, if not all, of

---

[2] The results of this assumption would remain unchanged if taxes affecting all business, instead of being shifted forward to the consumer, were shifted backward to labor. The possibility of such shifts is discussed on page 125.

these taxes are shifted to the consumer, and this assumption has been made throughout this report. Nevertheless, it is of course possible that part of the taxes in question actually are not shifted but are borne by the business firms who pay them in the first instance. In that case, the ultimate burden of the share of these taxes that is "borne" by business firms falls of course upon the owner of the business in his character as consumer, since his income is correspondingly reduced.

There is still another complication to be taken into account if the real burden of taxation is to be discovered. That is the fact that certain taxes can also be shifted backward. It is likely, for instance, that the imposition of the coffee tax has contributed to keep the wages paid to workers employed in the coffee plantations lower than they would otherwise be. In that way the real burden of the export tax is partly shifted to the agricultural workers.

Such shifting of the tax to labor, whether in the form of outright wage cuts or, in good times, of slower wage increases, is possible only if it occurs throughout a large sector of the economy. A single branch of industry or agriculture could not effect it, since labor would begin to move away into other fields. But the coffee industry represents so large a part of the Salvadorean economy that the labor force employed there probably would find it difficult to avoid having to bear the shifted tax, as there would not be enough employment opportunities outside the industry. Moreover, the coffee industry, because of its dominant position, importantly influences wage standards throughout the country. Pressure upon coffee wages tends to be reflected in similar pressure elsewhere. Hence the coffee industry is in a position, at least to some extent, to shift backward — upon labor — the special export tax to which the industry is subject.

This shifting backward of taxes, to the extent that it takes place, is obscured by the fact that in many instances production costs, particularly in the agricultural sector of the economy, do not exclusively take the form of wage payments but consist also of payments in kind, i.e., provisions for the feeding and housing of workers. In such instances, the shifting backward would not necessarily be limited to a lowering of wage payments (or slower wage increases), but might also involve a deterioration of working conditions through less ample provisions of food and shelter.

In order to show the effects that such a backward shift of the tax burden may have upon the distribution of the total tax burden, computations have been made in Table 36 with respect to the coffee tax under two alternative assumptions. Under the first assumption, the coffee export tax is borne entirely by the coffee producers.[3] Under the second assumption, 50 per cent of the tax is shifted backward to the agricultural population.

A breakdown of tax receipts into unshifted, shifted, and intermediate taxes is shown, for selected years, in Table 33. The data indicate that the bulk of Salvadorean tax receipts stems from taxes that can be shifted. Such taxes account for approximately two thirds of total tax collections. The percentage share of unshifted taxes fluctuated considerably in the years shown in the table, being highest in 1942 (15.7 per cent) and lowest in the budget figures for 1948 (8.4 per cent). If, however, it is assumed the coffee tax is not shifted backward, but is borne by the coffee producers, the share of unshifted taxes is considerably increased. More important, the percentage of unshifted taxes has shown, in the last decade, a tendency to rise. If the coffee export tax is included among unshifted taxes, their percentage shares show the following values: 1935–36, 16.6 per cent; 1942, 23.0 per cent; 1946, 24.9 per cent; and 1948, 27.3 per cent.

## PROGRESSIVENESS OF TAXES

Since all taxes ultimately become a burden upon the consumer, it is of interest to establish the relation of this burden to the consumer's income for different income levels. A tax is regarded as "proportional" if its proportion to income remains constant for different levels of income; it is "progressive" if this proportion rises for higher levels of income, "regressive" if the proportion declines. Table 34 shows a breakdown of the tax structure as of 1946 into progressive, proportional, and regressive taxes.

The "progressive" group includes the income tax, the inherit-

---

[3] It is assumed that the coffee tax cannot be shifted forward since coffee exports are sold in the world market where the volume of supplies forthcoming from El Salvador is too small to affect price determination.

TABLE 34

PROGRESSIVE, PROPORTIONAL, REGRESSIVE, AND MIXED TAXES IN 1946
(*In thousands of colones*)

| | |
|---|---:|
| *Progressive* | |
| Income tax.......................... | 2,662.1 |
| Inheritance and gift tax................ | 975.4 |
| Vialidad A........................... | 341.8 |
| Vialidad B, C, D..................... | 232.3 |
| *Cédula de Vecindad*................... | 41.5 |
| Total progressive taxes.............. | 4,253.1 |
| Per cent of total taxes............... | 11.6% |
| *Proportional* | |
| Coffee export tax..................... | 4,414.3 |
| Pavement tax........................ | 121.2 |
| Miscellaneous taxes................... | 2,414.5 |
| Total proportional taxes............. | 6,950.0 |
| Per cent of total taxes............... | 18.9% |
| *Regressive* | |
| Consumption taxes.................... | 8,446.7 |
| Import duties on business goods........ | 7,489.1 |
| Total regressive taxes................ | 15,935.8 |
| Per cent of total taxes............... | 43.4% |
| *Mixed* | |
| Import duties on consumers' goods....... | 7,539.0 |
| Shifted business taxes................. | 2,045.2 |
| Total mixed taxes................... | 9,584.2 |
| Per cent of total taxes............... | 26.1% |
| *Total taxes*........................... | 36,723.1 |

ance and gift tax, the *vialidad* taxes, and the fee for identification cards (*cédulas de vecindad*). The rates of all of these taxes are higher for the higher income brackets.

Most important in the group of "proportional" taxes is the coffee export tax, which is assessed per quintal of coffee, irrespective of the volume of coffee exported by each producer and therefore irrespective of the income derived from the production of coffee. The group includes in addition the pavement tax, which depends upon the physical size of the real property subject to special assessment; and a group of "miscellaneous taxes" with respect to which it has been assumed that their distribution by income groups is proportional to income.

The "regressive" group includes mainly consumption taxes. Since the amount spent on consumption normally forms a declining proportion of a rising income, consumption taxes are a heavier relative burden on lower than on higher income groups. The group of regressive taxes includes, in addition to the consumption taxes, the import duties imposed upon goods "consumed" by business firms, as well as the business taxes that are shifted to the consumer. The burden of these taxes is included in the price of the goods sold to the consumer and must therefore be treated like regular consumption taxes.

Table 34 also includes a fourth group of "mixed" taxes. Import duties on consumer goods and shifted business taxes shown in this group cannot be included in the three preceding groups because the expenditure patterns of various income groups show that these duties and business taxes burden the lowest and highest income groups more heavily than the middle groups. In other words, these taxes are regressive at the bottom of the income scale and progressive at the top.[4]

The breakdown of the tax structure into progressive, proportional, and regressive taxes indicates that progressive taxes yielded only 11.6 per cent of total tax collections in 1946. Proportional and regressive taxes accounted for one third of total tax collections each, while the rest was accounted for by "mixed" taxes.

## "AVOIDABILITY" OF TAXES

The third classification here presented is based upon the distinction of avoidable and unavoidable taxes. Avoidable taxes are,

---

[4] This is true of course only if import duties on consumer goods and shifted business taxes are considered as a whole. Within this group there are many taxes which are progressive in their impact; others are proportional to all levels of income; and some produce a heavier burden on low income groups than on higher ones.

generally speaking, taxes imposed upon commodities and services that are not necessities of life for the individual consumer, such as liquor, entertainment, and luxuries. If a person or family chooses to do without these commodities and services, payment of the taxes can be avoided. On the other hand, a person or family that purchases these commodities in larger quantities than the "average person" or "average family" incurs a correspondingly higher tax burden.

It is of course difficult to draw an exact line of demarcation between avoidable and unavoidable taxes. Clearly, such taxes as the income tax, the *vialidad* taxes, and the inheritance tax are

TABLE 35

BURDEN OF AVOIDABLE TAXES ON TYPICAL FAMILIES IN 1946[a]

(*In colones*)

| | 900 colones | | 1,800 colones | | 8,000 colones | |
|---|---|---|---|---|---|---|
| | *Heavy consumption* | *No consumption* | *Heavy consumption* | *No consumption* | *Heavy consumption* | *No consumption* |
| Avoidable taxes: | | | | | | |
| Cigarettes............. | 21.0 | 0.0 | 27.2 | 0.0 | 53.2 | 0.0 |
| Liquor................ | 20.4 | 0.0 | 24.2 | 0.0 | 11.4 | 0.0 |
| Beer.................. | 3.6 | 0.0 | 5.4 | 0.0 | 18.4 | 0.0 |
| Soft drinks........... | 1.6 | 0.0 | 2.0 | 0.0 | 4.6 | 0.0 |
| Shifted business taxes (Entertainment and liquor)............. | 1.2 | 0.0 | 2.2 | 0.0 | 9.0 | 0.0 |
| Imported luxury textiles | 4.8 | 0.0 | 11.2 | 0.0 | 64.6 | 0.0 |
| Imported beverages.... | 0.4 | 0.0 | 2.2 | 0.0 | 55.0 | 0.0 |
| Imported tobacco...... | 0.0 | 0.0 | 0.0 | 0.0 | 0.6 | 0.0 |
| Other imported luxuries. | 0.0 | 0.0 | 0.0 | 0.0 | 152.0 | 0.0 |
| Total avoidable taxes..... | 53.0 | 0.0 | 74.4 | 0.0 | 368.8 | 0.0 |
| Other personal taxes...... | 43.7 | 43.7 | 92.6 | 92.6 | 482.1 | 482.1 |
| Total personal taxes...... | 96.7 | 43.7 | 167.0 | 92.6 | 850.9 | 482.1 |
| Total personal taxes as per cent of income....... | 10.7% | 4.9% | 9.3% | 5.1% | 10.6% | 6.0% |

[a] By family income groups and consumption of commodities listed.

not avoidable, since the person receiving income or accepting an inheritance cannot legally avoid tax payment. Thus, the distinction applies merely to the limited range of consumption taxes and duties imposed upon consumer goods. But even there the distinction does not rest on objective criteria. Presumably it would be considered inappropriate to consider the sugar tax an avoidable tax, because sugar is considered an essential and necessary part of each person's diet; but one could argue that the "excessive" consumption of sugar over and above every person's "normal" or "minimum" requirements is avoidable, and to that extent, that the sugar tax is an avoidable tax.

The main purpose, then, of the distinction between avoidable and unavoidable taxes is to show that there is a relatively high degree of variability of the average tax burden in each income group. Table 35 shows for the year 1946 the tax burden imposed upon annual family incomes of 600, of 1,800, and of 8,000 colones, respectively, by a series of consumption taxes that at first glance appear avoidable. For each case, two alternatives are presented. One concerns a family with a "heavy" consumption of "unnecessary" commodities — "heavy" consumption being defined as twice the statistical-average consumption; the other pertains to a family in the same income bracket that does not consume any of the "unnecessary" goods or services. The difference in the total tax burden is quite striking. The tax burden of heavy consumers is two to three times as high as the tax burden of the "frugal" consumer. This is of course the result of the fact that a high proportion of the total tax burden consists of taxes on the consumption of commodities that are not necessities.

The examples presented in the table may be considered borderline cases. In reality, it is more likely that the majority of the population have a position somewhere between the limiting cases of no consumption and double consumption. It is likely that in many instances persons who avoid the payment of one consumption tax offset this advantage by consuming more of other taxed commodities. Thus, for instance, persons who do not purchase imported textiles become, through the purchase of domestic textiles, subject to the domestic cotton tax, with the result that at least part of their advantage from one tax is offset by the burden of the other.

## 2. The Consumer's Tax Burden by Income Brackets

The preceding section has thrown some light upon the impact of the tax system upon the consumer with regard to the shifting of taxes, their progressiveness, and their relative avoidability. With these data in hand, an attempt will now be made to estimate the total tax burden upon the consumer. The results are shown in Table 36.[5]

The tax burden consists of the levies that fall upon the consumer directly, such as income tax and *Vialidad* A, and of taxes shifted to him through higher prices, or lower wages or profits. With respect to the coffee tax, two alternative assumptions have been made, the reasons for which have been discussed above. Under the first assumption, the coffee export tax is borne entirely by the coffee producers; under the second assumption, 50 per cent of the tax is shifted backward to the plantation workers. The "consumer" whose tax burden is being studied is a family unit consisting of a married couple with three children. In so far as such units may have more than one income recipient, the study refers to the joint income of the group.

The consumption pattern of consumers at different income levels, upon which the tax burden study in good part depends, is presented in Appendix G, where the tax liabilities arrived at are *computed* liabilities for each level and are not based on taxes actually collected.

The most interesting result of the study is that the tax structure as a whole appears to be slightly progressive, as shown by the figures in the line "Total taxes as per cent of income" in Table 36. The main body of this table, it should be noted, assumes that the coffee export tax is not shifted, and the figures immediately following are based on this assumption. In the lowest income bracket, the total tax liability is somewhat more than 6 per cent. It rises to about 7.5 per cent in the group with an annual income of 1,800 colones, and to slightly less than 8 per

[5] A detailed explanation of the methods employed is given in Appendix G.

## TABLE 36

### BURDEN OF TAX SYSTEM ON TYPICAL FAMILIES IN 1946[a]
#### (In colones)

| | Rural worker | Unskilled urban worker | Skilled urban worker | Shopkeeper | Coffee producer | Government employee | Shopkeeper | General agricultural producer |
|---|---|---|---|---|---|---|---|---|
| Total income of family | 600.0 | 900.0 | 1,800.0 | 1,800.0 | 8,000.0 | 3,000.0 | 3,000.0 | 3,000.0 |
| Capital of family | 0.0 | 0.0 | 0.0 | 4,500.0 | 8,000.0 | 1,500.0 | 9,000.0 | 10,000.0 |
| Direct taxes and coffee export tax | | | | | | | | |
| Income tax and coffee export tax | 0.0 | 0.0 | 0.0 | 0.0 | 172.5 | 0.0 | 0.0 | 0.0 |
| Inheritance and gift tax | 0.0 | 0.0 | 0.0 | 0.9 | 7.0 | 0.0 | 8.9 | 10.8 |
| Vialidad | 1.0 | 1.5 | 3.0 | 3.0 | 5.0 | 6.0 | 5.0 | 5.0 |
| Cédula de vecindad | 0.1 | 0.2 | 0.3 | 0.5 | 0.5 | 0.3 | 0.5 | 1.0 |
| Other direct taxes, fees, fines[b] | 1.7 | 2.5 | 4.9 | 5.0 | 4.9 | 8.4 | 8.4 | 8.2 |
| Total direct taxes and coffee export tax | 2.8 | 4.2 | 8.2 | 9.4 | 189.0 | 14.7 | 22.8 | 25.0 |
| Direct taxes and coffee export tax as per cent of income | 0.5% | 0.5% | 0.5% | 0.5% | 10.6% | 0.5% | 0.8% | 0.8% |
| Consumption taxes[c] | | | | | | | | |
| Consumption taxes | 13.8 | 27.4 | 40.0 | 37.6 | 33.0 | 47.9 | 47.8 | 45.8 |
| Import duties on consumers' goods | 4.1 | 13.9 | 32.0 | 35.9 | 24.9 | 88.0 | 87.7 | 80.3 |
| Total consumption taxes | 17.9 | 41.3 | 72.0 | 73.5 | 57.9 | 135.9 | 135.5 | 126.1 |
| Consumption taxes as per cent of income | 3.0% | 4.6% | 4.0% | 4.1% | 3.2% | 4.5% | 4.5% | 4.2% |
| Other shifted taxes[d] | | | | | | | | |
| Shifted import duties on business goods | 11.2 | 18.2 | 35.6 | 35.6 | 32.0 | 58.3 | 58.1 | 58.1 |
| Shifted business-license and transaction taxes | 3.0 | 4.8 | 9.0 | 8.6 | 7.7 | 15.2 | 15.2 | 14.7 |
| Other shifted taxes | 1.6 | 2.4 | 4.9 | 5.4 | 4.4 | 8.9 | 8.9 | 8.1 |
| Total other shifted taxes | 15.8 | 25.4 | 49.5 | 49.6 | 44.1 | 82.4 | 82.2 | 80.9 |
| Other shifted taxes as per cent of income | 2.6% | 2.8% | 2.8% | 2.8% | 2.5% | 2.8% | 2.7% | 2.7% |
| Total taxes[e] | 36.5 | 70.9 | 129.7 | 132.5 | 201.0 | 233.0 | 240.5 | 232.0 |
| Total taxes as per cent of income | 6.1% | 7.9% | 7.2% | 7.4% | 16.2% | 7.8% | 8.0% | 7.7% |
| Alternative assumption (coffee tax 50 per cent shifted "backward") | | | | | | | | |
| Income tax and unshifted coffee export tax | 0.0 | 0.0 | 0.0 | 0.0 | 71.3 | 0.0 | 0.0 | 0.0 |
| Shifted coffee tax | 3.4 | 5.2 | 10.3 | 10.3 | 0.0 | 17.0 | 17.0 | 17.0 |
| All other taxes shown above[f] | 36.5 | 70.9 | 129.7 | 132.5 | 123.2 | 233.0 | 240.5 | 232.0 |
| Total tax | 39.9 | 76.1 | 140.0 | 142.8 | 194.5 | 250.0 | 257.5 | 249.0 |
| Total taxes as per cent of income | 6.7% | 8.5% | 7.8% | 7.9% | 10.8% | 8.3% | 8.6% | 8.3% |

[a] According to occupation of head of family.
[b] Includes fees and fines levied against individuals, the special pavement assessment on houses occupied by the owner, and the property-transfer tax on transactions in personal property.
[c] Based on disposable income, which is equal to total income minus direct taxes and coffee export tax.
[d] Includes fees and fines levied against business, the special pavement assessment on rented houses, and the property-transfer tax on transactions of business property.
[e] Equals sum of direct taxes and coffee export tax, consumption taxes, and other shifted taxes.
[f] Same as above except for coffee producer, who here has a larger disposable income.

TABLE 36 (Continued)

| | Private employee | Shopkeeper | General agricultural producer | Wholesale-retail importer | Coffee producer | Combination importer and coffee producer | Wholesale-retail importer | Coffee producer |
|---|---|---|---|---|---|---|---|---|
| Total income of family | 4,800.0 | 4,800.0 | 4,800.0 | 25,000.0 | 25,000.0 | 25,000.0 | 100,000.0 | 100,000.0 |
| Capital of family | 3,000.0 | 15,000.0 | 16,000.0 | 125,000.0 | 111,000.0 | 118,000.0 | 500,000.0 | 443,000.0 |
| Direct taxes and coffee export tax | | | | | | | | |
| Income tax and coffee export tax | 0.0 | 40.0 | 40.0 | 1,670.0 | 2,306.0 | 1,593.0 | 15,550.0 | 9,583.8 |
| Inheritance and gift tax | 0.0 | 20.8 | 23.1 | 513.6 | 428.2 | 470.9 | 3,201.1 | 2,800.2 |
| Vialidad | 10.0 | 7.5 | 8.0 | 68.8 | 58.3 | 63.5 | 400.0 | 343.0 |
| Cédula de vecindad | 0.5 | 1.0 | 1.0 | 1.5 | 1.5 | 1.5 | 1.5 | 1.5 |
| Other direct taxes, fees, fines[b] | 14.0 | 14.0 | 13.1 | 80.9 | 80.9 | 80.9 | 335.7 | 335.7 |
| Total direct taxes and coffee export tax | 64.5 | 83.3 | 85.2 | 2,334.8 | 2,064.9 | 2,209.8 | 19,578.3 | 13,064.9 |
| Direct taxes and coffee export tax as per cent of income | 1.3% | 1.7% | 1.8% | 9.3% | 11.9% | 8.8% | 19.6% | 13.1% |
| Consumption taxes[c] | | | | | | | | |
| Consumption taxes | 52.7 | 52.6 | 49.6 | 73.3 | 72.9 | 73.4 | 146.1 | 155.9 |
| Import duties on consumers' goods | 216.3 | 215.0 | 204.8 | 583.1 | 579.1 | 584.0 | 761.5 | 774.5 |
| Total consumption taxes | 269.0 | 267.6 | 254.4 | 656.4 | 652.0 | 657.4 | 907.6 | 930.4 |
| Consumption taxes as per cent of income | 5.6% | 5.6% | 5.3% | 2.6% | 2.6% | 2.6% | 0.9% | 0.9% |
| Other shifted taxes[d] | | | | | | | | |
| Shifted import duties on business goods | 80.5 | 90.1 | 90.1 | 228.8 | 226.1 | 229.4 | 401.5 | 414.5 |
| Shifted business-license and transaction taxes | 25.5 | 25.4 | 24.6 | 70.5 | 69.4 | 70.7 | 134.6 | 139.8 |
| Other shifted taxes[e] | 14.1 | 14.1 | 12.9 | 65.0 | 63.5 | 65.3 | 225.1 | 243.3 |
| Total other shifted taxes | 120.1 | 129.6 | 127.6 | 364.3 | 359.0 | 365.4 | 761.2 | 797.6 |
| Other shifted taxes as per cent of income | 2.7% | 2.7% | 2.7% | 1.5% | 1.4% | 1.5% | 0.8% | 0.8% |
| Total taxes[f] | 462.6 | 480.5 | 467.2 | 3,355.5 | 3,975.9 | 3,232.6 | 21,247.1 | 14,792.0 |
| Total taxes as per cent of income | 9.6% | 10.0% | 9.7% | 13.4% | 15.9% | 12.9% | 21.2% | 14.8% |
| *Alternative assumption (coffee tax 50 per cent shifted "backward")* | | | | | | | | |
| Income tax and unshifted coffee export tax | 40.0 | 40.0 | 40.0 | 1,670.0 | 1,198.0 | 994.0 | 15,550.0 | 4,791.9 |
| Shifted coffee tax | 27.2 | 27.2 | 27.2 | 142.8 | 0.0 | 71.4 | 573.0 | 0.0 |
| All other taxes shown above[g] | 422.6 | 440.5 | 427.2 | 1,685.5 | 1,596.6 | 1,665.4 | 5,697.1 | 5,239.3 |
| Total tax | 480.8 | 597.7 | 494.4 | 3,498.3 | 2,794.6 | 2,730.8 | 21,820.1 | 10,031.2 |
| Total taxes as per cent of income | 10.2% | 10.6% | 10.3% | 14.0% | 11.2% | 10.9% | 21.8% | 10.0% |

[ 133 ]

cent at an income of 3,000 colones. At an annual income of 25,000 colones it reaches 13 per cent; and at an income of 100,000 colones, 21 per cent. It will be noted that the total tax liability of coffee producers, in all income brackets below 25,000 colones and in the 100,000 colones bracket, is considerably out of line with the percentage figures shown for incomes derived from other sources. This phenomenon is due, as explained above, to the fact that the coffee export tax is a proportional tax, and this proportionality makes the percentage burden of the small-scale producer (annual income of 1,800 colones) more than twice the liability of other persons or families with the same level of income. On the other hand, the tax liability of the large coffee producer (annual income of 100,000 colones) is approximately one third smaller than that on income derived from other sources.[6]

The gradual progression of the tax structure is due to the unshifted direct taxes, mainly the income tax, which is highly progressive. The tax rates of the combined direct taxes rise from 0.5 to 19.6 per cent. However, they are of very little significance up to an income of 4,800 colones.

The burden of consumption taxes and other indirect taxes show the opposite trend. The burden rises very gradually from 3 per cent at the lowest income level to about 5.5 per cent at an income level of 4,800 colones. At an income of 25,000 colones, it falls to less than 3 per cent of total income; and at an income of 100,000 colones, declines to less than 1 per cent. The group of "other shifted taxes" absorbs a more or less stable proportion of about 2.7 per cent of all income groups up to 4,800 colones. This percentage figure declines thereafter and amounts to approximately 0.8 per cent only at an income of 100,000 colones.

If it is assumed that one half of the coffee export tax is shifted backward, the results are not materially changed, except for a flat increase of approximately 0.5 per cent in the tax liability of all persons (except coffee producers) shown in the table and a decrease of 4.5 to 5 per cent in the tax liability of the coffee producers themselves.

[6] It should be noted that the data shown in the table pertain to the year 1946. For the effect of the higher coffee tax rates in later years, see above, page 122.

It should be pointed out once more that the tax burden shown in the table reveals *computed* tax liabilities and not actual tax payments. For a calculation of actual per capita tax payments, it would be necessary to have reliable estimates of the number of taxpayers in each income bracket, so as to assess the per capita amount of each tax collected. Only very tentative estimates of the number of taxpayers, particularly in the upper brackets, are available, and calculations of actual per capita tax payments are correspondingly uncertain. They do not permit an exact comparison with the computed tax burden. For what they are worth, however, such comparisons convey the general impression that the tax burden actually paid is less progressive than the computed burden.

Finally, it is necessary to point out several qualifications to the preceding analysis, pertaining both to the correctness of the result and to its economic significance. The correctness of the result is subject to qualifications, in the first place, because of the uncertainty surrounding the basic statistical material, particularly the data on consumption patterns and income distribution. In the second place, there is considerable uncertainty as to the true degree and direction of tax shifting. Even under the most favorable conditions, economic theory can give no assured answers to these questions.

The uncertainties surrounding tax shifting are vividly illustrated if it is asked whether the tax burden is to be regarded as the reduction in real income resulting from the initial imposition of taxes or as the increase in real income that would result if existing taxes were suddenly removed. Neither case is realistic, except for small tax changes. It is quite clear, however, that the two possibilities would produce widely different results in the allocation of the tax burden, because of the different economic and political processes that would be set in motion. It may be added that from a purely statistical viewpoint the analysis of the tax burden here presented reflects more nearly the case of a removal of taxes than that of new imposition.

The economic significance of the results can be properly appraised only if it is borne in mind that the repercussions of the tax system go far beyond the mere shifting of taxes. The economy reacts to taxation in many different directions, including the level of national income, its distribution, the structure of production, and naturally also the grouping of political interests. A change in the tax structure that at first seems to increase the burden upon some particular group may nevertheless, through the changes that it calls forth in size and distribution of income, lead to an ultimate improvement in the position of that group. The reverse process is likewise possible, a reduction in the immediate tax burden leading ultimately to an economic loss for the seemingly favored group. These far-reaching consequences are hard to trace and no account has been taken of them in the preceding analysis of tax burdens.

One conclusion to be drawn from these observations is a reaffirmation of the old theorem of public finance that "old taxes are good taxes." This really means, of course, that whenever a change in the tax structure appears desirable, care must be taken to appraise not only the immediate tax effects of such a change but also the indirect results in terms of the structure of the economy, which has become adjusted to the prevailing "old taxes." It does not follow, however, that changes in the tax structure are undesirable in themselves and should be avoided at all costs. What is implied is merely that the "cost" (of disturbance and rearrangements in the economy) must be fully taken into account when the decision on reform is made.

One more technical qualification must be mentioned. Any tax structure embodying protective tariffs produces certain burdens that are equivalent to shifted taxes but nevertheless cannot be legitimately included in the tax burden. These are the "subsidies" that the consumer pays to the domestic producer who enjoys tariff protection. Economists have frequently suggested that it would be more appropriate if the producer received these "subsidies" from the government, which in turn would finance them out of taxation. In that case, the incidence of the burden of "subsidies" would, of course, be different. This is one of the points where the redistributory effects of the tax structure in their narrower sense border upon the wider effects in such a way that a quantitative appraisal becomes impossible.

### 3. Weight of Taxes upon Selected Commodities

In the preceding section, the total tax burden falling upon typical consumers was evaluated. Further light upon how the tax system affects the consumer can be obtained from an investigation of the total weight of taxes upon the consumption of specific commodities. Some information of this type is provided in Appendix D, which gives the rates of the more important taxes. In this section, however, the subject is approached by estimating the relation of the total taxes collected on certain commodities to the total value of these commodities (Table 37). This relation indicates the weight of each tax upon the respective commodity. No account is taken of taxes not directly levied upon specific commodities that nevertheless may enter into their price, such as taxes that form part of business overhead or taxes included in the price of materials.

To give a general idea of the significance of these taxes for different income brackets, the total consumed of the taxed commodities has been divided into consumption by families with annual incomes respectively below and above 3,600 colones. The commodities included in the table are divided into those subject to consumption taxes and those subject to import duties. The most important commodities in the first group are cotton textiles, sugar, and liquor; in the second group, imported clothing and foodstuffs. The commodities included in the two groups comprise all consumers' goods that are subject to consumption taxes or import duties.

It will be noted that the range of commodities subject to consumption taxes is quite limited, only two commodities being included that rank as necessities of life — sugar and cotton textiles. The taxes on these two articles are the lowest, in percentage terms, in the entire group. The weighted average for the group is only 19.4 per cent. The total weight of consumption taxes, therefore, is rather modest.

Duties on imported consumption goods affect, of course, a much wider range of articles than do the consumption taxes. In addition, they fall more heavily, on the whole, upon essential articles — food, clothing, medicines and drugs — except in so

## TABLE 37

### IMPACT OF "TAXES ON CONSUMPTION" ON CONSUMPTION EXPENDITURES IN 1946

| Consumption expenditures | Families with Annual Incomes of Less than 3,600 Colones | | | Families with Annual Incomes of 3,600 Colones or More | | | All Families | | |
|---|---|---|---|---|---|---|---|---|---|
| | Consumption[a] | Taxes | Tax/ Consumption | Consumption[b] | Taxes | Tax/ Consumption | Consumption[b] | Taxes | Tax/ Consumption |
| | (thousands of colones) | | (per cent) | (thousands of colones) | | (per cent) | (thousands of colones) | | (per cent) |
| *Commodities subject to consumption taxes* | | | | | | | | | |
| Sugar | 8,000 | 660 | 8.3 | 1,400 | 116 | 8.3 | 9,400 | 776 | 8.3 |
| Beer | 2,328 | 455 | 19.6 | 470 | 92 | 19.6 | 2,798 | 547 | 19.6 |
| Soft drinks | 2,116 | 215 | 10.2 | 230 | 23 | 10.2 | 2,346 | 238 | 10.2 |
| Liquor | 7,690 | 3,728 | 48.5 | 120 | 57 | 48.5 | 7,810 | 3,785 | 48.5 |
| Cotton | 16,020 | 276 | 1.7 | 600 | 10 | 1.7 | 16,620 | 286 | 1.7 |
| Cigarettes | 3,280 | 2,221 | 67.7 | 394 | 266 | 67.7 | 3,674 | 2,487 | 67.7 |
| Matches | 850 | 279 | 32.8 | 150 | 49 | 32.8 | 1,000 | 328 | 32.8 |
| Total | 40,284 | 7,834 | 19.4 | 3,364 | 613 | 19.4 | 43,648 | 8,447 | 19.4 |
| *Commodities subject to import duties* | | | | | | | | | |
| Food | 6,700 | 1,381 | 20.6 | 2,700 | 642 | 23.8 | 9,400 | 2,023 | 21.5 |
| Beverages | 610 | 131 | 21.5 | 1,225 | 275 | 22.5 | 1,835 | 406 | 22.1 |
| Clothing | 11,280 | 1,511 | 13.4 | 4,500 | 645 | 14.3 | 15,780 | 2,156 | 13.7 |
| Tobacco | ... | ... | ... | 6 | 3 | 50.0 | 6 | 3 | 50.0 |
| Gasoline | ... | ... | ... | 800 | 336 | 42.0 | 800 | 336 | 42.0 |
| Medicine and drugs | 3,900 | 502 | 12.9 | 1,100 | 144 | 13.1 | 5,000 | 646 | 12.9 |
| Other imported consumer goods[b] | 5,220 | 728 | 13.9 | 10,410 | 1,241 | 11.9 | 15,630 | 1,969 | 12.6 |
| Total | 27,710 | 4,253 | 15.4 | 20,741 | 3,286 | 15.9 | 48,451 | 7,539 | 15.6 |
| Total commodities subject to taxes on consumption | 67,994 | 12,087 | 17.8 | 24,105 | 3,899 | 16.2 | 92,099 | 15,986 | 17.4 |

a Including the taxes given in the adjoining column to the right.

b This group includes such items as soap, stationery, kitchen utensils, furniture, and (in the higher income groups) automobiles, electrical appliances, musical instruments, etc.

far as some of the imported products can be replaced by domestic items. Nevertheless, the average weight of these taxes, amounting to 15.6 per cent, cannot be called other than moderate.

### 4. Cyclical Variations in Tax Burden

The computation of the burden of taxes that was undertaken in the preceding sections of this chapter took as its basis the prices prevailing during a given period, that is, the prices of the year 1946. The inflationary price increase that has taken place in El Salvador in the war and postwar years makes it necessary to carry the investigation one step further and consider the effects of the price increases on the tax burden.

#### Impact of Inflation on "Real" Values

The effect of price changes may be treated in various ways. One way is to deflate the money amount of any given tax by the cost-of-living index. This reflects the viewpoint of the taxpayer, for to him the value of the money he pays to the government is determined largely by the cost of living. Another approach, which reflects the viewpoint of the government, is to deflate the money amount of taxes by the index of the cost of government services.

In this section a mixed approach will be adopted. The "real" value of taxes that are levied upon specific objects, primarily upon merchandise or property, will be appraised in relation to the changes in the prices of these objects; in other words, in *ad valorem* terms. This aspect of the "real" value of taxes will be referred to as their "weight." Taxes upon income, on the other hand, will be viewed in relation to changes in the cost of living and will therefore be deflated by the cost-of-living index. The "real" value of these taxes will be referred to as their "burden," since these taxes constitute a direct burden upon the taxed individual or firm.

Whether the weight or burden of a tax increases or decreases with price changes depends upon the basis on which the particular tax is levied. If the tax is a flat-rate tax based upon nonmonetary units (weight, area, etc.), the weight of the tax becomes lighter when the price of the taxed objects rises, i.e., its *ad valorem* value decreases. If the tax is levied on a money base at flat rates (a fixed percentage of a sum of money), the weight or burden of the tax remains unchanged. If the tax is levied on a money base with progressive rates, its weight or burden increases in a period of rising prices and falling value of money.

It follows from these general observations that in El Salvador the weight of consumption taxes, which consist mostly of specific taxes (sugar, taxed per quintal; liquor, taxed per liter; matches, taxed per box; etc.), decreases in a period of price inflation unless the effect of inflation is offset by an increase in rates.[7] An example of both aspects is the sugar tax, the weight of which was reduced by rising sugar prices; the rate of the tax was accordingly doubled in 1946.

A significant study of the impact of inflation upon the weight or burden of taxes cannot leave out of account the fact that the easing of these weights and burdens frequently becomes a reason to the government for raising rates. It would not be realistic to make comparisons of weights and burdens at different price levels with constant rates and treat the rate increases that have occurred as accidental phenomena, since these are usually a direct and inevitable consequence of the effects of inflation. This holds particularly true with respect to the coffee export tax, which although not a consumption tax is assessed on a specific basis. During the period under consideration the coffee tax has been raised on several occasions in accordance with the law providing for the adjustment of the rate to the coffee export prices. This adjustment is justified also on the grounds that the coffee export tax is collected in lieu of the income tax, the impact of which in "real" terms increases with a price rise.

### DECLINING WEIGHT OF IMPORT DUTIES

An example of the decline of the "real" value of a tax as a result of rising prices is provided by the prevailing system of specific import duties. In Table 38 the "real" burden of import duties levied upon imported goods consumed at various levels on income is shown for a number of years. In order to show the change in the "real" value of import duties, the money value of

---

[7] The pavement tax assessed per square meter of tax property also falls in this category.

TABLE 38

"Real" Weight of Import Duties on Consumers' Goods
by Income Groups, 1940–1946
(*In colones*)

| | 1940 | 1942 | 1943 | 1946 |
|---|---|---|---|---|
| *Income of 600 colones* | | | | |
| Money value of imports of consumers' goods[a] | 9.3 | 11.9 | 13.1 | 16.5 |
| Money import duties on consumers' goods... | 3.7 | 3.8 | 3.9 | 4.1 |
| Money import duties as per cent of value... | 39.8% | 31.9% | 29.8% | 24.9% |
| "Real" value of imports of consumers' goods[b] | 11.9 | 11.9 | 11.9 | 11.9 |
| "Real" import duties on consumers' goods[b].. | 3.7 | 3.8 | 3.0 | 2.2 |
| "Real" import duties as per cent of value... | 31.1% | 31.9% | 25.2% | 18.5% |
| *Income of 900 colones* | | | | |
| Money value of imports of consumers' goods[a] | 28.8 | 36.9 | 40.8 | 51.3 |
| Money import duties on consumers' goods... | 12.5 | 13.0 | 13.3 | 13.9 |
| Money import duties as per cent of value... | 43.4% | 35.2% | 32.6% | 27.1% |
| "Real" value of imports of consumers' goods[b] | 36.9 | 36.9 | 36.9 | 36.9 |
| "Real" import duties on consumers' goods[b].. | 12.6 | 13.0 | 10.1 | 7.6 |
| "Real" import duties as per cent of value... | 34.2% | 35.2% | 27.4% | 20.6% |
| *Income of 1800 colones* | | | | |
| Money value of imports of consumers' goods[a] | 75.1 | 96.3 | 106.5 | 133.8 |
| Money import duties on consumers' goods... | 32.4 | 33.7 | 34.3 | 35.9 |
| Money import duties as per cent of value... | 43.1% | 35.0% | 32.2% | 26.8% |
| "Real" value of imports of consumers' goods[b] | 96.3 | 96.3 | 96.3 | 96.3 |
| "Real" import duties on consumers' goods[b].. | 32.7 | 33.7 | 26.0 | 19.6 |
| "Real" import duties as per cent of value... | 34.0% | 35.0% | 27.0% | 20.4% |
| *Income of 3000 colones* | | | | |
| Money value of imports of consumers' goods[a] | 176.7 | 226.8 | 250.7 | 315.0 |
| Money import duties on consumers' goods... | 80.0 | 83.0 | 84.4 | 88.3 |
| Money import duties as per cent of tax..... | 45.3% | 36.6% | 33.7% | 28.0% |
| "Real" value of imports of consumers' goods[b] | 226.8 | 226.8 | 226.8 | 226.8 |
| "Real" import duties on consumers' goods[b].. | 80.8 | 83.0 | 63.9 | 48.3 |
| "Real" import duties as per cent of value... | 35.6% | 36.6% | 28.2% | 21.3% |

[a] Money value of imports is taken as consumers' budgetary expenditures on imports minus 75 per cent for domestic costs and importer's profit.
[b] At 1942 prices.

consumers' purchases of imports (which were assumed to consist of a fixed "bundle" of goods typical of the import purchases of consumers at various income levels in 1946) were deflated by the index of prices of imported goods.[8] Duty payments likewise were deflated by the index of retail prices to take account of the

[8] For an explanation of the construction of the index, see Appendix B.

changes in the purchasing power of money. The data so adjusted clearly indicate the effects on the real wieght of the duties that the price rises between 1940 and 1946 produced. For all income groups the "real" weight of duties (the "real" duty payments as a per cent of the "real" value of imports) declined from over 30 to approximately 20 per cent. The decline of the weight of import duties would have been even greater if the 6 per cent *ad valorem* consular invoice fee[9] had not mitigated the decline of the *ad valorem* equivalent of the specific duties.[10]

Taxes with a more or less constant "real" value include the most important types of business taxes (stamp taxes, stamped-paper taxes) since these taxes are mostly proportionate percentages of money values. There is nothing of special significance about these taxes that calls for comment.

### RISE OF "REAL" BURDEN OF INCOME TAX

In the cases of the income tax, the inheritance tax, and the property tax, the effects of price inflation are particularly pronounced. The reasons for this are twofold. In the first place, in a

TABLE 39

"REAL" VALUE OF EXEMPTIONS, 1940–1947[a]

| Year | Colones |
|------|---------|
| 1940 | 3,261 |
| 1941 | 3,125 |
| 1942 | 3,000 |
| 1943 | 2,655 |
| 1944 | 2,273 |
| 1945 | 2,069 |
| 1946 | 2,143 |
| 1947 | 1,936 |

[a] "Real" value of an income tax exemption of 3,000 colones, at 1942 prices.

[9] See Appendix D, Section 5.

[10] The addition of the consular invoice fees to the duties proper accounts for the differences in the "money import duties" shown for each year. Without the consular invoice fees, the money import duties that pertain to a fixed "bundle" of commodities would be constant.

period of rising prices the "real" value of the exemptions declines, with the result that more and more persons with smaller "real" incomes become subject to the tax. In the second place, the same amount of "real" income is moved up, so to speak, into higher tax brackets so that more and more taxpayers become subject to higher and higher rates.

The effects of the price rise from 1942 to 1947 upon the "real" value of a basic income tax exemption of 3,000 colones is shown in Table 39. The table shows that in 1947 the exemption was worth about one third less in "real" terms than in 1942.

How this phenomenon, combined with the shifting of money income into higher brackets, affects the incidence of the income tax is shown in Table 40. For this purpose the amounts of money income corresponding in each year to a fixed amount of "real" income were first computed. The tax liability, in "money" terms, for the money income of each year was then determined. This money tax liability was then deflated by the price index, in order to obtain the amount of the "real" tax liability. The computations show that, with some qualifications to be noted in the following paragraph, the "real" tax burden on a "real" income of 5,000 colones more than doubled between 1940 and 1947, and almost doubled on a "real" income of 10,000 colones. In higher income brackets, the effects of price inflation upon the "real" tax burden are less pronounced, because in those brackets the basic exemption, comprising a declining proportion of total money income, is relatively less important. Thus, the "real" tax burden upon a "real" income of 100,000 colones increased between 1940 and 1947 by only 13 per cent. It is interesting, however, to observe that, according to the present calculation, in 1947 the "real" tax burden upon a "real" income of 25,000 colones was almost as large as the "real" tax liability corresponding to a "real" income of 50,000 colones in 1940 (9.4 and 10.5 per cent, respectively).

In actual practice, the "real" burden of income, inheritance, and property taxes has increased, it is believed, considerably less than preceding figures suggest. In the first place, the income tax and the property tax (*Vialidad A*) are collected for the preceding year after a time-consuming procedure of filing returns, making

## TABLE 40

### EFFECTS OF PRICE CHANGES ON THE INCOME TAX BURDEN, 1940–1947

*(Values in colones; "real" income and income tax at 1942 prices)*

| | 1940 | 1941 | 1942 | 1943 | 1944 | 1945 | 1946 | 1947 |
|---|---|---|---|---|---|---|---|---|
| **"Real" income of 5,000 colones** | | | | | | | | |
| Money income.......................... | 4,600.0 | 4,800.0 | 5,000.0 | 5,650.0 | 6,600.0 | 7,250.0 | 7,000.0 | 7,750.0 |
| Money tax.............................. | 35.0 | 40.0 | 45.0 | 64.5 | 96.0 | 120.0 | 110.0 | 140.0 |
| "Real" tax............................. | 38.0 | 41.7 | 45.0 | 57.1 | 72.7 | 82.8 | 78.6 | 90.3 |
| "Real" tax as per cent of "real" income...... | 0.8% | 0.8% | 0.9% | 1.1% | 1.5% | 1.7% | 1.6% | 1.8% |
| **"Real" income of 10,000 colones** | | | | | | | | |
| Money income.......................... | 9,200.0 | 9,600.0 | 10,000.0 | 11,300.0 | 13,200.0 | 14,500.0 | 14,000.0 | 15,500.0 |
| Money tax.............................. | 205.0 | 225.0 | 245.0 | 318.0 | 448.0 | 550.0 | 510.0 | 635.0 |
| "Real" tax............................. | 222.8 | 234.4 | 245.0 | 281.4 | 339.4 | 379.3 | 364.3 | 499.7 |
| "Real" tax as per cent of "real" income...... | 2.2% | 2.3% | 2.5% | 2.8% | 3.4% | 3.8% | 3.6% | 4.1% |
| **"Real" income of 25,000 colones** | | | | | | | | |
| Money income.......................... | 23,000.0 | 24,000.0 | 25,000.0 | 28,250.0 | 33,000.0 | 36,250.0 | 35,000.0 | 38,750.0 |
| Money tax.............................. | 1,430.0 | 1,550.0 | 1,670.0 | 2,092.5 | 2,750.0 | 3,237.5 | 3,050.0 | 3,630.0 |
| "Real" tax............................. | 1,554.3 | 1,614.6 | 1,670.0 | 1,851.8 | 2,083.3 | 2,232.8 | 2,178.6 | 2,341.9 |
| "Real" tax as per cent of "real" income...... | 6.2% | 6.5% | 6.7% | 7.4% | 8.3% | 8.9% | 8.7% | 9.4% |
| **"Real" income of 50,000 colones** | | | | | | | | |
| Money income.......................... | 46,000.0 | 48,000.0 | 50,000.0 | 56,500.0 | 66,000.0 | 72,500.0 | 70,000.0 | 77,500.0 |
| Money tax.............................. | 4,850.0 | 5,210.0 | 5,580.0 | 6,850.0 | 8,750.0 | 10,050.0 | 9,550.0 | 11,050.0 |
| "Real" tax............................. | 5,271.7 | 5,427.1 | 5,580.0 | 6,062.0 | 6,628.8 | 6,931.0 | 6,821.4 | 7,129.0 |
| "Real" tax as per cent of "real" income...... | 10.5% | 10.9% | 11.2% | 12.1% | 13.3% | 13.9% | 13.6% | 14.3% |
| **"Real" income of 100,000 colones** | | | | | | | | |
| Money income.......................... | 92,000.0 | 96,000.0 | 100,000.0 | 113,000.0 | 132,000.0 | 145,000.0 | 140,000.0 | 155,000.0 |
| Money tax.............................. | 13,950.0 | 14,750.0 | 15,550.0 | 18,150.0 | 21,950.0 | 24,550.0 | 23,550.0 | 26,550.0 |
| "Real" tax............................. | 15,163.0 | 15,304.6 | 15,550.0 | 16,062.0 | 16,628.8 | 16,931.0 | 16,821.4 | 17,129.0 |
| "Real" tax as per cent of "real" income...... | 15.1% | 15.4% | 15.6% | 16.1% | 16.6% | 16.9% | 16.8% | 17.1% |

assessments, and issuance of payment orders — a procedure resulting in an average time lag of more than one year between the receipt of the income and the tax payment. This time lag affects the level of the "real" tax burden to the extent that the money tax liability is worth less in "real" terms at the time at which it becomes due than at the time when the income was obtained, since in a period of rising prices, money incomes are bound to rise. Thus the tax payment made, say, in 1947 on the money income of 1946 absorbs a smaller share of the (presumably higher) money income of 1947, out of which the tax is paid, than is shown in the preceding table. This compensating factor operates, at any rate, so long as prices continue to increase.

In the case of the inheritance and property taxes, which likewise are paid only after a considerable time lag, there is in addition the probability that the valuations upon which the tax assessments are based are likely to be out of date (i.e., too low in a period of rising prices), particularly when they are based in part upon the "objective criteria" (*datos reveladores*) as stipulated by the pertinent laws.

Since in the period of the fourteen years with which this report is primarily concerned a major price rise has taken place but no over-all price and money-income declines have occurred, no data are available as to the effects upon the "real" tax burden of declining prices. But what has been said and demonstrated with respect to rising prices may in good measure be expected to apply in reverse to a fall in the price level. In other words, in a period of falling prices the "real" burden of consumption taxes, based on specific rates, increases, while taxes with a progressive rate structure produce a lighter "real" tax burden. These conclusions naturally apply only if the rate structure remains unchanged.

# CHAPTER IX

## THE GOVERNMENT'S EXPERIENCE UNDER THE FISCAL SYSTEM

So FAR THIS STUDY has dealt with the interest of the businessmen and the consumer in the budget. There remains a third interested party, the government. In the present chapter an attempt is made to find out how the government fares under the Salvadorean fiscal system, not in its creative role as the originator and director of this system, but in its relatively passive role as collector of revenues and disburser of funds. The main points to be investigated are (1) the cost of collecting taxes and administering expenditures, (2) the cyclical "flexibility" of revenues, (3) the relation of rigid and "flexible" expenditures, (4) the "real" income of the government in times of inflation, (5) the potentialities of the tax system.

### 1. COST OF COLLECTING TAXES AND SEASONAL PATTERNS

The Salvadorean fiscal system, like that of other countries, consists of a multitude of sources from which revenues are derived and an even larger number of objectives for which funds are disbursed. One of the criteria (but by no means the only one) by which the efficiency of the fiscal system may be judged is the cost incurred in the collection and the disbursement of funds. Likewise, the cost incurred in collecting each individual tax provides a clue to the "profitability" of that tax; and analogous reasoning applies, with some qualifications, to the expenditure side.

#### COST OF COLLECTION

An analysis of the cost of tax collection for the year 1948 is presented in Table 41. As the table shows, the over-all cost of tax collection amounts to approximately 5 per cent of the total

TABLE 41

## COST OF TAX COLLECTION
### (In colones)

| Type of tax | Amount Collected | | Direct Costs | | | | Indirect costs[b] | Total Costs | |
|---|---|---|---|---|---|---|---|---|---|
| | Year[a] | Thousands of colones | Direct salaries | Other direct costs | Total direct costs Amount | Per cent of collections | | Amount | Per cent of collections |
| Income and vialidad taxes... | 1947 | 3,551.0[c] | 312,400 | 1,456 | 313,876 | 8.8 | 26,974 | 349,850 | 9.6 |
| | 1948 | 3,101.6[c] | | | | 10.1 | | | 11.0 |
| Inheritance and gift taxes... | 1947 | 477.2 | 81,000 | 924 | 81,924 | 17.2 | 3,950 | 85,874 | 18.0 |
| | 1948 | 500.0 | | | | 16.4 | | | 17.2 |
| Pavement tax.............. | 1947 | 161.1 | 20,340 | 720 | 21,060 | 13.1 | 1,279 | 22,339 | 13.9 |
| | 1948 | 150.0 | | | | 14.0 | | | 14.9 |
| Matrículas de comercio...... | 1947 | 37.0 | 23,580 | ... | 23,580 | 63.7 | 263 | 23,843 | 64.4 |
| | 1948 | 30.0 | | | | 78.6 | | | 79.5 |
| Stamp taxes.............. | 1947 | 2,045.9[d] | 34,980 | 37,000[e] | 71,980 | 3.5 | 14,860 | 86,840 | 4.2 |
| | 1948 | 1,615.0[d] | | | | 4.5 | | | 5.4 |
| Liquor taxes.............. | 1947 | 4,546.2[f] | 101,160 | 177,570[g] | 278,730 | 6.1 | 33,445 | 312,175 | 6.9 |
| | 1948 | 3,700.8[f] | | | | 7.5 | | | 8.4 |

[a] 1947, actual tax receipts; 1948 budget estimates.

[b] Including all direct salaries and other direct costs, not allocated to specific taxes; also 25 per cent of all Treasury expenditures not allocated either to cost of collections of specific taxes, or disbursement of expenditures; and 10 per cent of expenditures of Court of Accounts.

[c] Including receipts for tax fines and costs before the Tax Appeals Court.

[d] Including receipts for *matrículas* in lieu of stamp taxes; also stamp tax on imported liquor; beer stamp tax; soft drink stamp tax; and "other" stamp taxes.

[e] Remuneration of sales agent for tax stamps and stamped paper sold.

[f] Including liquor sales patents; and tax on denatured alcohol; but excluding stamp taxes on imported liquor.

[g] Expenditures for Finance Police are allocated as follows: liquor taxes 75 per cent; cigarette tax 15 per cent; sugar tax 10 per cent.

## TABLE 41 (Continued)

| Type of tax | Amount Collected | | Direct Costs | | | | Indirect costs[b] | Total Costs | |
|---|---|---|---|---|---|---|---|---|---|
| | Year[a] | Thousands of colones | Direct salaries | Other direct costs | Total direct costs | | | Amount | Per cent of collections |
| | | | | | Amount | Per cent of collections | | | |
| Sugar tax.............. | 1947 | 1,630.6 | 89,700 | 23,676[g] | 113,376 | 7.0 | 12,302 | 125,678 | 7.7 |
| | 1948 | 1,400.0 | | | | 8.1 | | | 9.0 |
| Beer and cigarette taxes..... | 1947 | 3,204.2 | 32,160 | 35,514[g] | 67,664 | 2.1 | 25,771 | 93,435 | 2.9 |
| | 1948 | 3,150.0 | | | | 2.1 | | | 4.0 |
| Entertainment tax.......... | 1947 | 137.7[h] | 16,200[i] | ... | 16,200 | 11.8 | 1,016 | 17,216 | 12.5 |
| | 1948 | 110.0[h] | | | | 14.7 | | | 15.6 |
| Export and import taxes.... | 1947 | 31,871.8[j] | 671,820 | 207,008[k] | 878,828 | 2.8 | 256,389 | 1,135,217 | 3.6 |
| | 1948 | 31,351.2[j] | | | | 2.8 | | | 3.6 |
| Other taxes.............. | 1947 | 2,396.5 | ...[l] | ...[l] | ...[l] | ... | 107,399 | 107,399 | 4.5 |
| | 1948 | 2,062.8 | | | | | | | 5.2 |
| Total taxes.......... | 1947 | 50,059.2[m] | 1,383,360 | 483,868 | 1,867,228 | 3.7 | 483,648 | 2,350,876 | 4.7 |
| | 1948 | 47,171.4[m] | | | | 4.0 | | | 5.0 |

h Including all taxes originally (prior to 1939) allocated to charitable institutions.

i Including 20 per cent of entertainment tax returned by collectors.

j Including consular invoice fees and other consular charges collected by the Customs Service; excise taxes on imported goods; customs warehouse fees; and customs fines.

k Including expenditures for Customs Police (154,980 colones).

l Not available.

m Including non-tax receipts included above.

amount of the taxes collected.[1] With the exception of the beer and cigarette taxes, the cost of collection of all internal revenues is found to be substantially higher than the cost of collection of export and import taxes by the customs service, which amounted to 3.6 per cent of the corresponding revenues. For internal revenues, the cost of collection varied from 2.9 per cent for beer and cigarette taxes to about 75 per cent for *matrículas de comercio*.[2] Of the other internal revenues, the stamp taxes appear to be the least expensive. The cost of collection of liquor taxes (6.9 per cent in 1947 and 8.4 per cent in 1948) probably is somewhat overstated because of the high proportion of the expenditures for the Finance Police that is allocated to liquor taxes. The most "expensive" consumption tax is the sugar tax, 8 per cent of which is absorbed through salaries and other collection costs. Among the direct taxes, both the inheritance and gift taxes and the pavement tax, which yield relatively small amounts, appear to involve surprisingly high costs of collection. The income and *vialidad* taxes cost about 10 per cent to collect.

The above comparisons do not *per se* permit any direct conclusions as to the efficiency of administration of the respective groups of taxes. It is not surprising that the collection cost of export and import taxes is proportionately the lowest, since ex-

[1] The table is based upon the budgetary appropriations for expenditures in the year 1948. Since the estimates of the taxes to be collected in that year are based upon adjusted five-year averages and are therefore believed to be somewhat low, the cost of collection has also been compared in the table with actual tax receipts of 1947. A direct comparison between actual receipts and actual costs is impossible since, contrary to the budgets themselves, the budget liquidations do not give an item-by-item breakdown of expenditures.

[2] The grouping of the taxes in the table is based upon the internal organization of the Bureau of Internal Revenue. The breakdown of salary expenditures by administrative sections was put at our disposal by the Bureau of Internal Revenue. To these data were added those salary expenditures of the local tax administrations that could be clearly allocated according to the table of organization contained in the annual salary law (*Ley de Salarios*). "Other direct costs" include expenditures for office equipment, utensils, etc., that could be allocated to a specific group of taxes. "Indirect costs" included all those expenditures of the Bureau of Internal Revenue and the local tax administrations that could not be allocated to a specific group of taxes, as well as 25 per cent of the expenditures of the Treasury, and 10 per cent of the expenditures of the Court of Accounts. The latter additions are believed to correspond to the proportion of the work involved in the administration of revenues by these two agencies. The indirect costs were allocated to the individual groups of taxes proportionately to the tax collections.

port and import transactions can be easily controlled at the small number of points at which Salvadorean products leave and foreign commodities enter the country. The low cost of collection of beer and cigarette taxes is undoubtedly due to the fact that the tax administration collects these taxes from a very small number of cigarette and beer manufacturers. On the other hand, the extremely high cost of collecting the *matrículas de comercio* by no means implies that this tax is not worth while, because the *matrículas* serve not only for the collection of the tax but also as a source of information for the collection of *vialidad* and income taxes.

Moreover, the breakdown presented in the table is not sufficiently detailed to warrant conclusions as to the profitability of various minor taxes. On the basis of nonquantitative information it appears, for instance, that the relative expense incurred in the collection of the comparatively low-yield *vialidad* taxes is considerably larger than in the collection of income taxes. The group "other taxes" includes numerous petty taxes with respect to which it is doubtful whether the cost of collection bears any reasonable relation to their yield. The information available suggests the following conclusions:

(1) The cost of collecting the pavement tax appears to be exceedingly high, particularly in view of the limitation of the tax to certain areas in San Salvador and Santa Ana.

(2) The cost of collecting the inheritance and gift taxes is extremely high. This seems to be due, not to heavy expenditures for this purpose *per se*, but to the low yields obtained.

(3) It appears that it would be possible to lower the cost of collecting the *vialidad* (series B, C, and D) and income taxes through partial collection at the source, by withholding by the employer. *Vialidad* A could be advantageously combined with the pavement tax, and certain types of *vialidad* D with a property tax limited to real and business property. In that case it might be advisable to discontinue annual valuation and replace it with periodic assessment every five or eight years, with flexible rates to take account of eventual cyclical inequities.

(4) The cost of collecting entertainment taxes and other taxes originally destined for charitable institutions (*instituciones de*

*beneficiencia*) appears excessive. It probably could be reduced if a system of spot checks could be substituted for the employment of controllers on a commission basis.

(5) Even in the low-cost category of export and import taxes, savings appear possible through the inclusion of certain excise taxes (on gasoline, pharmaceuticals, etc.) in the tariff schedule, and the combining of all payments for so-called consular services (consular invoice fee, bill of lading, manifest) in a flat *ad valorem* rate.

(6) Despite the incomplete character of the information now available, it appears that the cost of collection and administration of a large number of small taxes and fees is too expensive to warrant their continued collection unless the cost can be reduced by combining some of these small charges in a single tax.

### SEASONAL VARIATIONS IN TAX REVENUES

A thorough analysis of the seasonal variations of tax revenues is important for the effective control of expenditures during the course of the year and for the maintenance of an adequate but not excessive Treasury cash balance. Knowledge of the seasonal movement of revenues also makes it possible to determine to some extent whether any deviation of actually collected revenues is the result of seasonal factors or of a more basic change in economic conditions. The revenues of the Salvadorean government have in fact been subject to fairly pronounced seasonal fluctuations.

An index of the seasonal variation of tax receipts is shown in Table 42. The index reveals that considerable and fairly systematic seasonal variations have been the rule. Tax receipts normally have been substantially larger in the earlier part of the year than in later months. Thus, according to the index, the receipts in the first five months of the fiscal year are 11 per cent larger than if receipts had been distributed evenly throughout the year. Conversely, the receipts of the last five months of the year are considerably below the monthly average, Treasury receipts from taxes in this period being 10 per cent smaller than the monthly average.

These seasonal variations of Treasury receipts are caused pri-

TABLE 42

INDEX OF SEASONAL VARIATIONS OF TAX RECEIPTS[a]

| | |
|---|---|
| January | 119.9 |
| February | 111.9 |
| March | 117.5 |
| April | 105.1 |
| May | 103.2 |
| June | 89.6 |
| July | 101.7 |
| August | 88.0 |
| September | 84.1 |
| October | 98.1 |
| November | 84.2 |
| December | 97.2 |

[a] Based on tax receipts in 1940–1948.

marily by the concentration of coffee exports during the "coffee season," from December to March. This concentration, in the first place, produces heavy income from the coffee export tax. In the second place, however — and even more important — the concentration of coffee shipments enables coffee exporters, who are in many instances also general importers, to step up their purchases abroad. This results in large collections of import duties and other taxes on imports, which in the aggregate make up a very large proportion of total government revenues. Since there is a time lag between coffee exports and the resulting seasonal rise of imports, total tax collections expand somewhat later than the receipts from the coffee export tax and remain high for one or two months after the coffee export season has passed.

It should be pointed out that the seasonal variations in the last decade have been largely overshadowed by the gradual increase in tax revenues because of the rising price level and, in the last years, the increasing volume of imports and the consequent rise in import duty collections. The seasonal variations are likely to be more important in years when prices and business activity are stable or declining.

In order to avoid the undesirable effects of these seasonal variations on the government's cash position, and on the currency circulation of the private sector of the economy, it appears desirable to vary government expenditures with the seasonal pattern of government receipts, so that, for instance, government purchases of material and equipment, whenever possible, are concentrated in the early part of the fiscal year.

## 2. CYCLICAL FLEXIBILITY OF TAXES

It is of great importance to the government to know how its tax revenues react to fluctuations in national income. In a depression, revenues are of course bound to shrink, and in prosperity they are very likely to increase, but the magnitude of these fluctuations in revenues can be properly anticipated only on the basis of detailed analysis. Two separate aspects are involved: (1) the flexibility that consists in the capacity of revenues to fluctuate in response to a fluctuating national income at *existing* tax rates, which in technical language has come to be referred to as the "built-in flexibility" of the tax system;[3] and (2) the flexibility that consists in the capacity of existing tax rates to be modified, with greater or less ease, by the action of the administrative and legislative apparatus, within the generally stable framework of the revenue system. This second quality may be called "administrative flexibility." Both types of flexibility, which will now be discussed, are important in El Salvador.

### "BUILT-IN FLEXIBILITY"

To study the "built-in flexibility" of the tax system, it is necessary to observe actual fluctuations in revenues and, to the extent that they are the result of administrative or legislative changes in rates, to eliminate the effects of the changes. In that way it is possible to establish the relation between national income and revenues at *constant* tax rates. The period for which adequate data are available for studying the "built-in flexibility" of the Salvadorean tax system, covering the years 1939–1947, is one of almost constantly rising prices. The data therefore permit an analysis of only one phase of a cyclical movement, the phase

[3] It may also be referred to as the "elasticity" of revenues with respect to national income.

of expansion. It cannot be said with assurance that during a contraction precisely the same tendencies would make themselves felt in reverse, but it may reasonably be assumed that any differences would not be fundamental. A more serious obstacle to the analysis of normal relationships is the distortions produced by the war. As a result, the following discussion is predominantly an enumeration of special circumstances.

The flexibility of tax receipts may be measured both in terms of their relation to national income (or to gross national product) and in terms of their percentage fluctuations around a base period. In Table 43 the first "test" of the flexibility of the tax system is applied by comparing actual tax receipts, and those tax yields which would have prevailed if tax rates had remained unchanged, with estimates of the gross national product. As the data show, the proportion of actual tax receipts to gross national product amounted to 7.6 per cent from 1939 until 1941. During the war years the proportion declined quite sharply to a low of 6.1 per cent in 1943, despite a slight rise of revenues in absolute terms. In 1946, tax revenues recovered abruptly, absorbing what was probably a record share of the gross national product (8.4 per cent).

The comparison between actual tax receipts and gross national product gives an indication of the degree of what may be called "over-all flexibility." In order to arrive at a measurement of "built-in flexibility" proper, it is necessary to eliminate from the tax data those amounts which resulted from changes in tax rates. If the tax receipts which would have been obtained without changes in tax rates are compared with the gross national product, the "true" degree of built-in flexibility emerges. A comparison of the percentage figures of the last two columns of Table 43 shows that in the absence of rate adjustment tax receipts would have declined more in relation to the gross national product during the war years, and risen less in 1946, than they actually did as a result of rate adjustments.

The main reason for the low relative level of tax yields during the war was obviously the fact that import duty collections, which usually account for 40 per cent of total taxes,[4] did not in-

[4] Cf. Chapter IV, p. 55.

TABLE 43

TAX RECEIPTS[a] AND NATIONAL PRODUCT, 1939–1946

| | | | | Ratio to gross national product of | |
|---|---|---|---|---|---|
| Year | Total tax receipts | Total tax receipts at constant tax rates[b] | Estimated gross national product | Total tax receipts | Total tax receipts at constant tax rates |
| | *(millions of colones)* | | | *(per cent)* | |
| 1939 | 18.50 | 18.50 | 244 | 7.6 | 7.6 |
| 1940 | 17.43 | 17.43 | 229 | 7.6 | 7.6 |
| 1941 | 17.64 | 17.64 | 232 | 7.6 | 7.6 |
| 1942 | 18.50 | 18.23 | 279 | 6.6 | 6.5 |
| 1943 | 21.52 | 20.40 | 351 | 6.1 | 5.8 |
| 1944 | 26.14 | 21.95 | 367 | 7.1 | 6.0 |
| 1945 | 26.71 | 24.73 | 398 | 6.7 | 6.2 |
| 1946 | 36.72 | 31.08 | 435 | 8.4 | 7.1 |

[a] Including fees and fines.
[b] Constant tax rates are those prevailing in 1942. For derivation of tax yields at 1942 rates for taxes with important rate changes, see Table 45.

crease until 1945 because the level of imports was abnormally restricted by the limited availability of foreign goods. The physical volume of imports (which, as pointed out above, forms the basis of duty collections) was particularly low in 1942, when the weight of imports declined to 59 million kilograms from 79 million in 1941, although the gross national product rose during this period by about 10 per cent in money as well as in "real" terms.

The particularly pronounced decline in the proportion of total tax collections to the gross national product in 1943 may also reflect, to some extent, the political disturbances that took place in that year and that apparently had an adverse effect on the operation of the Bureau of Internal Revenue. The partial recovery in 1944 was accomplished largely by an increase in the rates of the coffee export tax and of various consumption taxes. Conversely, the renewed decline in the ratio in 1945 was caused by the suspension of the new coffee export tax rates, which more than offset the gains resulting from larger import duty collections. In 1946, all factors making for large tax yields were fully operative: the volume of imports was abnormally high, the coffee export tax rate had been adjusted upward, and the rates of certain consumption taxes had been increased.

The foregoing serves to explain the rather erratic year-to-year changes in the ratio of tax collections to the gross national product during the war period. These fluctuations do not as yet permit any general conclusions regarding the degree of built-in flexibility of the tax system as a whole. Further light, however, can be shed upon this flexibility of the tax structure and its sources by an investigation of the fluctuations in the composition of total tax receipts. In Table 44, the percentage changes of the

## TABLE 44

TAX RECEIPTS, 1940–1947, AS PERCENTAGES OF 1942 RECEIPTS

|  | 1940 | 1941 | 1942 | 1943 | 1944 | 1945 | 1946 | 1947 |
|---|---|---|---|---|---|---|---|---|
| Direct taxes........ | 53.4 | 86.2 | 100 | 100.1 | 114.9 | 149.0 | 165.1 | 157.7 |
| Property and property-transfer taxes. | 76.3 | 82.3 | 100 | 119.1 | 92.0 | 132.4 | 147.0 | 152.3 |
| Transaction and business-license taxes.. | 86.1 | 87.8 | 100 | 112.7 | 117.0 | 119.3 | 148.2 | 167.8 |
| Taxes on exports.... | 110.3 | 64.9 | 100 | 107.0 | 321.8 | 129.1 | 327.2 | 525.2 |
| Taxes on imports.... | 118.4 | 118.4 | 100 | 124.7 | 125.0 | 144.5 | 193.2 | 315.4 |
| Consumption taxes.. | 82.6 | 82.7 | 100 | 124.7 | 158.5 | 174.3 | 213.6 | 263.4 |
| All taxes, fees, fines[a]. | 94.2 | 95.4 | 100 | 116.3 | 141.3 | 144.4 | 198.5 | 272.3 |

[a] Including "other taxes," fees, and fines, not shown in this table.

major group of taxes since 1942 are compared. As the table indicates, total tax collections between 1942 and 1947 rose by over 170 per cent. But within this total, the respective yields of direct taxes, property taxes, and business taxes — three groups that together accounted in 1942 for 22 per cent of the total tax revenue — increased by only 50 to 60 per cent, while taxes on imports and exports rose, respectively, by more than 300 and 500 per cent. Consumption taxes showed approximately the same changes as the total tax yield, i.e., an increase of slightly more than 160 per cent.

The differences in the "built-in flexibility" of the various classes of taxes are due to the differences and nature of the bases upon which the taxes are levied and to the different ways in which cyclical changes in real income and prices affected the bases. Taxes that are levied on a flat fee basis (such as *vialidad* B, C, and D, the *matrículas de comercio*, and certain business-license taxes) are not directly affected by changes in prices and real income. They react only to an increase in the number of persons employed (*vialidad* D), or to an increase in the number of business establishments (*matrículas*, or business licenses). This explains in part the relatively small increases in the yields of business taxes, and of that portion of the *vialidad* taxes included in direct taxes (series B, C, D).

All other taxes are affected by changes either in real income, or in money income — the latter of course reflecting changes in prices, or real income, or both. Accordingly, we can distinguish two groups of taxes: the "real-income-elastic" taxes and the "money-income-elastic" taxes.

"Real-income-elastic" taxes are all those that are collected on a physical unit basis, such as the sugar tax, the cotton tax, the match tax, the liquor tax, and above all, the import duties. The yield of these taxes is affected only by changes in "real" income, that is to say, by changes in the physical magnitude of the tax base that are normally associated with changes in real national income. They do not respond to price changes, except in so far, of course, as the tax rates are changed under pressure of price changes. In the case of commodities of which the consumption is likely to change less than "real" income, such as sugar, matches, and tobacco, the tax yields are thus likely to remain more or less stable (at given rates). In other instances, physical quantities are likely to fluctuate widely with changes in real income. This is particularly true of import duties, which are based upon the physical quantities of imports — the latter fluctuating more widely than real income.[5]

The yield of "money-income-elastic" taxes depends, as the term implies, not only upon those fluctuations in real national income that are associated with changes in the physical magnitude of the tax base, but also upon fluctuations in income re-

[5] Cf. Chapters II and X.

flecting price changes solely. In this group belong the 6 per cent
consular invoice fees, which after the war rose even more than
revenue from import duties because these fees reflect both rising
volume and rising prices of imports. Stamp and stamped-paper
taxes also belong in this group.[6] The coffee export tax is a
"money-income-elastic" tax so long as it is assessed on a sliding
scale varying with the price of coffee, but not when it is assessed
simply upon the volume of coffee exported, as at present.

The income tax and the inheritance and gift taxes are levies
with a particularly high "money-income elasticity" because they
are assessed upon money income at progressive rates. The property and property-transfer taxes are likewise "money-income-
elastic." It is all the more surprising that this entire group of
taxes rose relatively less than the other groups, as shown in
Table 44. This was largely due to the fact that most of these
taxes are collected on the basis of assessments for the preceding
years. A contributory explanation probably may be found in the
time lag that occurs in the adjustment of tax assessments to
higher incomes and property values. Moreover, a breakdown of
the group of direct taxes[7] shows that the yield of the income tax
rose more than that of other direct taxes, of which part are in-
elastic (*vialidad* B, C, D) and part are subject to extraneous factors such as deaths of wealthy people (inheritance tax).

### ADMINISTRATIVE FLEXIBILITY

The preceding paragraphs have thrown some light upon the
"built-in flexibility" of the tax system by showing how different
taxes reacted to fluctuations in real income and in prices. The
spectacular rise in the yield of export taxes and the more moderate but nevertheless pronounced uptrend of consumption taxes,
however, are not to be explained primarily in these terms. The
explanation for the higher yield of these taxes is to be found in
the fact that the rates of these taxes were substantially increased
between 1942 and 1947.[8] The degree of ease or difficulty with

[6] Stamp taxes and stamped-paper taxes are included in Table 44 among business
taxes. In the business tax group as a whole, the higher yields of these taxes are
partly offset by the relative inflexibility of the business-license taxes.

[7] See Table 74 in Appendix D.

[8] For detailed information regarding the rates of individual taxes, see Appendix D.

which tax rates can be adjusted is what has been described above as administrative flexibility.[9] The practical importance of administrative flexibility is shown in Table 45, in which the yields of the most important taxes, the rates of which have been changed in the last five years, are compared with estimates of what the yields would have been if the old rates had been retained. As a result of the changes in the rates of the taxes shown in the table,[10] the yield of the tax structure was increased between 1942 and 1947 by 9 million colones. The increase accounts for 28 per cent of the total rise in tax revenue in that period.

This high degree of administrative flexibility is the combined result of speedy preparatory action by the Ministry of Finance, the Bureau of the Budget, and the Court of Accounts, and of prompt enactment of the recommended legislation by the National Assembly. Administrative flexibility has been increased by the occasional use of the sliding scale principle in connection with the coffee export tax and the sugar export tax.[11] According to this principle, the rate of the tax is to vary with the price of the taxed commodity, with the result that the yield varies more than merely in proportion to the price. If the application of this principle were fully automatic, one would have to speak of "built-in" rather than administrative flexibility. However, the application of the respective legislation still calls for some administrative decisions. Moreover, the coffee export tax has been modified frequently, and the sliding scale principle has not been fully adhered to with regard to that tax, and was completely abandoned in 1947. In general, it seems that the great importance which the coffee growers and the government attach to the coffee export tax has made this tax particularly susceptible to changes, that is to say, its administrative flexibility is very high.

[9] The term is used here to denote the responsiveness or "elasticity" of the tax system with respect to a given amount of legislative as well as administrative pressure, or, in the words employed above, the degree of ease or difficulty with which the tax system and the tax rates can be changed.

[10] The rates of some other taxes were also changed in the same period, but the changes were of minor significance.

[11] Cf. Appendix D, pages 291, 312.

## TABLE 45

### EFFECT OF RATE INCREASES ON YIELD OF SELECTED TAXES, 1940–1947

(In thousands of colones)

| | 1940 | 1941 | 1942 | 1943 | 1944 | 1945 | 1946 | 1947 |
|---|---|---|---|---|---|---|---|---|
| **Coffee export tax** | | | | | | | | |
| At actual rates | 1,472.2 | 864.6 | 1,353.0 | 1,388.8 | 4,392.9 | 1,751.9 | 4,414.3 | 7,221.3 |
| At 1942 rates | 1,472.2 | 864.6 | 1,353.0 | 1,282.8 | 1,601.2 | 1,447.3 | 1,207.8 | 1,626.0 |
| **Cigarette tax** | | | | | | | | |
| At actual rates | 822.7 | 863.2 | 1,019.1 | 1,465.9 | 1,813.9 | 2,223.5 | 2,487.0 | 2,845.3 |
| At 1942 rates | 822.7 | 863.2 | 754.1[a] | 453.0 | 558.1 | 684.1 | 765.2 | 875.5 |
| **Sugar tax** | | | | | | | | |
| At actual rates | 231.6 | 257.7 | 224.9 | 288.2 | 329.1 | 347.8 | 775.3 | 1,630.6 |
| At 1942 rates | 231.6 | 257.7 | 224.9 | 288.2 | 329.1 | 347.8 | 201.9 | 357.9 |
| **Cotton tax** | | | | | | | | |
| At actual rates | ... | ... | ... | ... | 288.2 | 265.4 | 286.4 | 373.4 |
| At 1942 rates | ... | ... | ... | ... | ... | ... | ... | ... |
| **Income tax**[b] | | | | | | | | |
| At actual rates | 803.8 | 1,238.0 | 1,700.4 | 1,718.3 | 2,163.4 | 2,971.0 | 2,662.1 | 2,964.9 |
| At 1942 rates | 803.8 | 1,238.0 | 1,700.4 | 1,718.3 | 2,307.5[c] | 3,103.7[c] | 2,805.3[c] | 3,151.6[c] |
| **Total selected taxes** | | | | | | | | |
| At actual rates | 3,330.3 | 3,223.5 | 4,297.4 | 4,861.2 | 8,986.9 | 7,559.6 | 10,625.1 | 15,035.5 |
| At 1942 rates | 3,330.3 | 3,223.5 | 4,032.4 | 3,742.3 | 4,393.1 | 5,582.9 | 4,980.2 | 6,011.0 |
| **Difference between yields at actual and 1942 rates** | ... | ... | 265.0 | 1,118.9 | 4,191.0 | 1,976.7 | 5,644.9 | 9,024.5 |

[a] The cigarette tax was changed in August 1942. The amount of 754,100 colones is the computed tax yield if the old rate had been maintained throughout the year.

[b] Including (until 1944) gross receipts tax of electric companies.

[c] Assuming that income tax yield of cotton manufacturing would have been one half of the proceeds of the cotton tax.

IS CYCLICAL FLEXIBILITY DESIRABLE?

If account is taken of the income elasticity of the specific duties, of the price and income elasticity of the direct and property taxes, and finally, of the existing administrative flexibility, the conclusion seems warranted that the Salvadorean tax system has a fairly high degree of cyclical flexibility. The flexibility of the system was sufficient, during the years 1939–1946, to allow the ratio of revenues to gross national product to fluctuate from 6.1 per cent to 8.4 per cent and to permit the more than doubling of revenues over the period. If it had been possible to include the years 1947 and 1948 in these calculations, the degree of flexibility probably would have been shown to be even greater. How desirable is this flexibility?

In the past, considerable emphasis has been placed upon the desirability of revenue *stability*, which denotes the relative absence of flexibility. The purpose was to protect governments against the consequences of sharp drops in revenues and perhaps also to protect taxpayers against the arbitrary imposition of high burdens. In recent years, however, a different concept has gained ground, particularly in industrialized countries, which favors built-in flexibility as a means of compensating fluctuations in national income. If expenditures are kept reasonably constant, a tax system with built-in flexibility will produce a surplus during prosperity, which serves to check the boom, and a deficit in depressions, which is expected to stimulate lagging activity. It must be pointed out that this reasoning is almost entirely inapplicable to El Salvador. Salvadorean experience shows that, for many reasons, expenditures tend to rise almost automatically whenever revenues increase. Under such circumstances, there is no deflationary effect that would help to curb the boom. A sharp drop of revenues, on the other hand, which would occur from time to time under a highly flexible tax system, would produce a large deficit unless heroic cuts were made in expenditures. Such a deficit in an economy like the Salvadorean might easily endanger monetary stability, while severe expenditure cuts might have grave social and political repercussions. The question of fiscal action against economic fluctuations will be discussed in detail in Chapter XI. For the moment, it is sufficient to conclude that a high degree of flexibility in the tax system does not seem desirable for El Salvador and that the present system probably goes, if anything, too far in the direction of flexibility.

### 3. Stable and Flexible Expenditures

Just as, among tax revenues, groups with various degrees of cyclical flexibility can be distinguished, a distinction can also be drawn between stable and flexible expenditures. While expenditures are to some extent dependent upon the deliberate activities of the government, it is nevertheless of value for the government to know what the inherent tendencies of various types of expenditures are in the course of cyclical fluctuations.

One may say that wholly stable expenditures are those that absorb approximately the same amounts of money irrespective of the prevailing level of either government revenues or the national income. Examples of such stable expenditures are annuity payments to a fixed number of persons, and the servicing of the public debt under a fixed debt retirement plan. Not quite so stable, but still not as flexible as other types of expenditures, are salary payments to the administrative personnel of the government for the maintenance of essential government services.

The group of flexible expenditures includes disbursements of public funds for such purposes as appear desirable and necessary under certain conditions only, as for instance if funds for such expenditures are available. More generally, expenditures can be classified as flexible if they can be postponed or advanced in time at will without interfering with the "normal" flow of government activities. Expenditures for public works (over and above expenditures for necessary maintenance) and the retirement of such debts as are not subject to firm contractual obligations clearly would belong in this category.

The statistics pertaining to government expenditures of El Salvador do not permit a clear distinction between stable and flexible expenditures. The only classification available is the breakdown of total expenditures into "fixed" and "variable" expenditures which, it must be remembered, represents in principle no more than an administrative classification.[12] Nevertheless the distinction is helpful for the purposes of the present analysis, subject to the appropriate adjustments.

If the series of "fixed" and "variable" expenditures are compared in their original form, it is true that the "fixed" expenditures appear to have been only slightly less unstable than the "variable" ones. This impression is misleading, however, because the rise of prices during the period under review affected differently the expenditures included in the respective series. To obtain a picture undistorted by divergent price movements, it is necessary to adjust the various series for these changes, that is, to "deflate" each by an appropriate price index. This is done in Table 46.

In the case of the gross national product series, with which the other two are compared in the table, a special price index has been used, the composition of which has been explained in Appendix B. For the deflation of the fixed expenditure data an index was used that measures changes in the level of salaries for a given number of government employees. This index was especially constructed for this purpose, and its derivation is explained in Appendix H. "Variable" expenditures were deflated by the index of wholesale prices, which is believed to reflect reasonably well the price changes of commodities and services purchased by the government.[13] Payments for debt service have been separated from the "variable" expenditures, among which they are administratively classified. Since the debt service of the government implies payment of a given sum of money irrespective of the prevailing price conditions, debt service expenditures did not require deflation.

If the various categories of the expenditures are thus adjusted for price changes, it appears that fixed expenditures actually fluctuated much less than the other components of total expenditures. This holds true both in terms of absolute amounts, which ranged from 13.84 million colones to 17.29 million in "real"

---

[12] Cf. Chapter V, especially Table 16.

[13] It should be noted that the adjustment is significant only if different deflators for the various time series are used. If the various series were deflated by the same price index, the relative magnitudes would remain the same.

## TABLE 46

### Government Expenditures and Gross National Product, 1939-1946

| Year | Estimated gross national product | Fixed expenditures | "Variable" expenditures | Debt service | Total expenditures | Fixed expenditures | "Variable" expenditures | Debt service | Total expenditures |
|---|---|---|---|---|---|---|---|---|---|
| | | (In millions of colones) | | | | (As per cent of gross national product) | | | |
| *In "Money" Terms* | | | | | | | | | |
| 1939 | 244 | 13.43 | 6.79 | 0.37 | 20.59 | 5.5 | 2.8 | 0.2 | 8.4 |
| 1940 | 229 | 14.43 | 7.59 | 0.30 | 22.33 | 6.3 | 3.3 | 0.1 | 9.7 |
| 1941 | 232 | 14.41 | 5.33 | 1.72 | 21.46 | 6.2 | 2.3 | 0.7 | 9.3 |
| 1942 | 279 | 14.74 | 5.81 | 1.56 | 22.11 | 5.3 | 2.1 | 0.6 | 7.9 |
| 1943 | 351 | 15.02 | 6.98 | 1.41 | 23.41 | 4.3 | 2.0 | 0.4 | 6.7 |
| 1944 | 367 | 15.82 | 8.36 | 1.00 | 25.18 | 4.3 | 2.3 | 0.3 | 6.9 |
| 1945 | 398 | 17.61 | 8.92 | 2.63 | 29.15 | 4.4 | 2.2 | 0.7 | 7.3 |
| 1946 | 435 | 20.58 | 13.61 | 10.84 | 45.03 | 4.7 | 3.1 | 2.5 | 10.3 |
| *In "Real" Terms*[a] | | | | | | | | | |
| 1939 | 266 | 13.84 | 8.83 | 0.37 | 23.03 | 5.2 | 3.3 | 0.1 | 8.6 |
| 1940 | 257 | 14.58 | 11.17 | 0.30 | 26.05 | 5.7 | 4.3 | 0.1 | 10.1 |
| 1941 | 251 | 14.55 | 6.24 | 1.72 | 22.51 | 5.8 | 2.5 | 0.7 | 9.0 |
| 1942 | 279 | 14.74 | 5.81 | 1.56 | 21.84 | 5.3 | 2.1 | 0.6 | 7.8 |
| 1943 | 312 | 14.87 | 5.82 | 1.41 | 22.10 | 4.8 | 1.9 | 0.5 | 7.1 |
| 1944 | 293 | 15.21 | 6.15 | 1.00 | 22.36 | 5.2 | 2.1 | 0.3 | 7.6 |
| 1945 | 289 | 16.01 | 5.72 | 2.63 | 24.35 | 5.5 | 2.0 | 0.9 | 8.4 |
| 1946 | 308 | 17.29 | 7.65 | 10.84 | 35.78 | 5.6 | 2.5 | 3.5 | 11.6 |

[a] At 1942 prices.

value, and in terms of their ratio to the gross national product. With the exception of 1943, when expenditures were apparently limited by abnormally low tax collections, "real" fixed expenditures absorbed regularly between 5.2 and 5.8 per cent of the "real" gross national product. "Real" variable expenditures fluctuated between 5.71 million colones and 11.17 million (in "real" value), and between 1.9 and 4.3 per cent of gross national product.

In interpreting these results, it must be remembered that in 1942 and the years following, "variable" expenditures additional to these shown in the table were incurred through disbursements in connection with the construction of the inter-American highway.[14] When "real" variable expenditures are compared with "real" gross national product, it is apparent that there was a tendency toward an inverse relationship, particularly at the beginning of the period. That is to say, "real" variable expenditures tended to be high in years of low gross national product, and vice versa. This conclusion is subject, of course, to considerable reservations, owing to the inadequacy of the statistical material and the abnormalities of the war period, and it is quite possible that a different picture would emerge if the years 1947 and 1948 could be included. But in so far as it may be permissible to draw conclusions, they appear to demonstrate the inadvisability of large-scale public works and developmental expenditures — the main content of "variable" expenditures — in periods of rising prices. As revenues increased during the years studied, the government increased "variable" expenditures rather more than "fixed" expenditures in terms of current prices. But the prices at which the "variable" expenditures were made, such as construction materials and wages, rose so much more that the "real" value of what was purchased actually declined. Vice versa, in periods of relatively low prices, a more modest volume of "variable" expenditures yielded larger "real" returns.

Applying the same reasoning to the trend of debt service payments, it will be noted that the sharp increase in debt payments in 1946 has proved a very fortunate and profitable move. When prices are high, money is worth less, and the best use that can

[14] As pointed out in Chapter V, these disbursements were approved in a special budget which has not been liquidated yet.

be made of it is to repay fixed obligations. This conclusion, of course, does not take into account the broader credit policy aspects of the suspension of the foreign debt service prior to 1946.

## 4. REAL INCOME OF GOVERNMENT AND REAL COST OF TAXES TO TAXPAYERS

In the preceding section it was shown how the "real" value of various government services is affected by differences in the movement of the prices of the goods and services the government buys. The outstanding fact observed was that the "real" value of services connected with "variable" expenditures was very adversely affected by the sharp rise in the wholesale price index that applies to that type of expenditure. The adverse effect of rising prices upon the services rendered by "fixed" expenditures was much less, because the government salaries that make up most of the fixed expenditures went up less.

Taking all expenditure types together, it becomes strikingly obvious that the great increase in the budget that took place between 1939 and 1946 was in large part an illusion. In monetary terms, the increase amounted to 119 per cent, but after the effect of rising prices is eliminated there remains a rise in total "real" expenditures of only 55 per cent, equal to 12,750,000 colones in 1942 prices. Of this sum, 10,470,000 colones were devoted to an increase in debt service (for the year 1946). The increase in "real" expenditures other than debt service from 1939 to 1946 was therefore only 2,270,000 colones in 1942 prices, or 10 per cent. The answer to the question why the great increase in revenues, in money terms, was not reflected in any striking increase in services rendered by the government is made very clear by these figures; in real terms, there was very little of an increase, after allowance is made for the renewal of debt service. And if disappointment is expressed over the failure of seemingly larger revenues to be reflected in greater public works, the answer is that the drop in the colón's purchasing power was particularly severe for that type of expenditure. A cut in public works in favor of still higher debt repayment would have been profitable, even though it might have been misinterpreted as neglect of some of the government's functions.

It is interesting to inquire how the rise in the cost per "unit" of government services compares with the rise in the general cost of living.[15] It appears, as shown in Table 47, that the cost of living in general increased even more in most years than the "unit" cost of government services. Expressed differently, the "real" value of a colón in the hands of a private individual, as measured by the cost of living, was declining more rapidly than the value of a colón in the hands of the government. If one assumes, as one must in a country with a democratic form of government, that government services on the whole are worth as much to the average taxpayer as the goods and services he can purchase privately for the same amount, it appears that, despite the rise in the cost of government services during the war, a colón paid to the government in taxes yielded more value to the taxpayer than a colón spent privately. In other words, the "purchase" of government services through the payment of taxes became for the taxpayer relatively a bargain.

This does not mean, of course, that an increase in the volume of government services would necessarily be desirable under such conditions, since the taxpayer might not want more services than he was getting. But in any case it is clear that the relative cheapening of these services, compared with the cost of living in general, is a gain to the taxpayer. An attempt is made to assess this gain in Table 47.

It is important to understand properly the nature of this gain. It represents the saving to taxpayers in the aggregate cost of all government services compared with what these services would have amounted to had their "unit" cost gone up in exact proportion to the cost of living. The saving is analogous to that which an individual would realize if one particular item in his expenditure budget, say rent, should rise less than the cost of other goods and services he buys. As the data of the table indicate, the gains in "real" income ranged up to 3.9 million colones, or up to 21.2 per cent of the aggregate "real" tax burden. In 1947 there were

---

[15] In the following discussion, the term "cost of government services" is used to denote cost per "unit" of such services, not the aggregate expenditure on all services. In that sense, the cost of government services is a price index exactly like the cost-of-living index.

## TABLE 47

### "Gains through Lowering of Costs of Government Services, 1939–1947"

| | 1939 | 1940 | 1941 | 1942 | 1943 | 1944 | 1945 | 1946 | 1947 |
|---|---|---|---|---|---|---|---|---|---|
| **"Real" gross national product[a]** | | | | | | | | | |
| In millions of colones | 266 | 257 | 251 | 279 | 312 | 293 | 289 | 308 | ...[d] |
| **"Real" tax burden[a]** | | | | | | | | | |
| In millions of colones | 19.3 | 18.9 | 18.4 | 18.5 | 19.0 | 19.8 | 18.4 | 26.2 | 32.5 |
| As per cent of gross national product | 7.3% | 7.4% | 7.3% | 6.6% | 6.1% | 6.8% | 6.4% | 8.5% | ...[d] |
| **"Real" costs of government services[b]** | | | | | | | | | |
| In millions of colones | 20.1 | 20.5 | 18.6 | 18.5 | 20.4 | 23.2 | 22.3 | 29.2 | 32.5 |
| As per cent of gross national product | 7.6% | 8.0% | 7.4% | 6.6% | 6.5% | 7.9% | 7.7% | 9.5% | ...[d] |
| **"Gain" from lowered costs of government services[c]** | | | | | | | | | |
| In millions of colones | 0.8 | 1.6 | 0.2 | 0.0 | 1.4 | 3.4 | 3.9 | 3.0 | 0.0 |
| As per cent of "real" tax burden | 4.2% | 8.5% | 1.1% | 0.0% | 7.4% | 17.2% | 21.2% | 11.5% | 0.0% |

[a] At 1942 prices.
[b] Adjusted so that expenditures (i.e., "costs of government services") and tax receipts (i.e., "tax burden") for each year are equal in money terms. Fixed expenditures were deflated by an index especially constructed for the purpose; for further explanation, see Appendix H. "Variable" expenditures were deflated by the wholesale price index. Expenditures for debt service were not deflated.
[c] "Cost of government services" less "tax burden."
[d] Not available.

no gains; in other words the rise in the cost of government services had caught up with the cost of living, because in that year the unit cost of "fixed" expenditures was raised substantially through salary increases.

The fact that gains and not losses for the taxpayer resulted from the divergent trends in the cost of living and the cost of government services is due to the predominance, among government expenditures, of "fixed" expenditures, which largely represent salaries of permanent employees, and to the heavy debt payments in 1946. If "variable" expenditures had predominated, there probably would have been a loss for the taxpayer, for the "unit" cost of "variable" expenditures is measured by the wholesale price index and this index rose more than the cost of living.

It also needs to be pointed out that the gains to the taxpayer were purchased at the expense of the average government employee. whose salary rose less than the cost of living. This, of course, is a typical inflation phenomenon. It is an interesting commentary on the prevailing state of Salvadorean "underemployment" that the government was able to increase the number of employees despite the fact that prior to the sharp rise in salaries in 1947 they were increasingly underpaid.

It further goes without saying that the preceding analysis presupposes that the output of services per government employee did not change as a result of variations either in the real income of employees or in their number. In practice, this condition cannot be expected to have been fully realized. There is, however, no strong reason to assume a pronounced deterioration of the output of government employees during the particular period under review. It is true that the hours of government employment in some services were curtailed during this period, although this was done in the expectation that the gain in efficiency would compensate for the hours lost. In general, however, it seems probable that the conditions typical of bureaucratic employment, in El Salvador as elsewhere, have led to some dilution of effort in recent years that may have undone to some extent the gains that the taxpayer should have realized from the lower cost of government services.

## 5. Capacity of Revenue System for Greater Yields

In an earlier section of this chapter, reference was made to the high degree of administrative flexibility of the Salvadorean tax system, i.e., the considerable scope for modifications of tax rates and yields that exists within the present administrative and legislative framework. A broader question of considerable importance to the government is the long-run capacity of the tax system for higher yields, should these become necessary.

To avoid misunderstandings, it should be made quite clear that the present observations are in no way to be interpreted as a suggestion that taxes should be increased. El Salvador is fortunate in having a lower cost of government, in proportion to the gross national product, than most other countries. There appears to be no urgent reason for changing this advantageous condition. But it is well known that historically the trend everywhere has been toward higher government expenditures. Whether or not El Salvador will be able to resist this trend remains to be seen. In any case it is necessary to know whether or not the tax system is capable of producing higher yields, so as to be able to meet whatever contingencies may arise.

There are, of course, several methods by which the tax system can be made to yield larger government receipts. In the first place, a concerted effort can be made to improve collections *at existing rates* through improvements of the tax administration.[16] In the second place, the rates of existing taxes can be adjusted upward. In the third place, new taxes can be introduced. Finally, a combination of these measures can be employed.

Experience in other countries shows that an effort to increase tax receipts through modernization of the tax administration, if pursued vigorously and with the backing of the entire executive branch of the government, would probably achieve considerable results. This assertion is in no way intended to reflect on the present tax administration. Revenue systems and administrative agencies everywhere are the products, not of exact planning and deliberate legislative action, but of more or less fortuitous

[16] Economies in the cost of collections, suggested on page 150 above, might be among these measures.

historic growth. There is room, therefore, in every tax administration for a certain amount of improvement. In preceding parts of this report, and in Appendices C and D, reference has been made to certain weaknesses and shortcomings of the tax administration; and it is likely that others could be discovered upon a closer inspection of administrative practices. It therefore appears quite certain that, wholly apart from changes in tax rates and the introduction of new taxes, the modernization of the tax administration would produce an increase in yields.

The possibility of raising receipts through changes in rates of existing taxes has been exploited by the Salvadorean government to a considerable extent[17] in recent years. Similar rate adjustments no doubt could be made in the future. An example of a tax that would have considerable potentialities is the property tax, which at present exists only in the rather rudimentary form of the *vialidad A* tax. But it is important to remember that changes in the rate structure of certain taxes are likely to have powerful direct and indirect repercussions on the economy, of the types discussed in Chapters VII and VIII. Under certain conditions, an increase in tax rates may actually reduce tax yields. An excessive rate increase in consumption taxes or import duties, for instance, may curtail the consumption of the taxed or dutiable commodities to such an extent that the yield at higher rates is smaller than at lower rates. Or, the economy as a whole, and particularly the rate of long-run economic development, may suffer. This would be the case if, for instance, the rate of the income tax were to be sharply increased with the result that the rate of private capital formation would decline;[18] or, if business-license taxes were to make the cost of starting new enterprises prohibitive.

There remains the possibility of introducing new taxes. The Salvadorean revenue system includes a fairly complete repertory of the various types of taxes employed in most countries, although many of the rates are quite low. It is noteworthy, how-

[17] Cf. page 158 above.
[18] Unless the government used for investment purposes a larger amount from the tax receipts than the private sector of the economy would have devoted to the same purpose if it had not been taxed by that amount.

ever, and fortunate, that some of the necessities of daily life are not taxed. Nor is there a general sales tax or turnover tax, such as many governments are currently employing. In view of the regressive character of these taxes, it is to be hoped that they will not need to be introduced, but their absence indicates that potentialities for new types of taxes exist if additional revenues should be needed and could not be raised otherwise. One may also draw attention to the relative absence of luxury taxes, which in the industrial countries have come increasingly into vogue, as well as of high import duties on luxuries. These examples are being mentioned, not because their introduction appears desirable, but to demonstrate that the present tax structure leaves a good deal of room for the introduction of new taxes if the need should arise.

In this connection it is necessary to emphasize once more as a general principle the desirability of avoiding unnecessary changes in the existing tax structure, because the economic structure of any country — and El Salvador is certainly no exception — is normally adjusted to the existing tax system and any change has certain effects and causes certain repercussions that are disturbing to the economy. By the same token, if changes are necessary, it usually is preferable to change the tax system gradually, through the introduction of new taxes or tax rates and the repeal of existing tax provisions, rather than to overhaul the entire tax structure at one time by one major reform.   The former policy gives the economic system time to adjust itself to new fiscal requirements and to new administrative procedures, with the result that the financial results for the government are likely to be better and the adverse effects on the private sector of the economy smaller than if several major revisions are made simultaneously.

## 6. Tax Consciousness

Closely connected with the yield capacity of the tax system is the question of tax consciousness — that is, the desirability of making taxpayers more or less aware of their own contributions and those of others to the financing of the government. Since only a relatively small proportion of the total tax receipts of the Salvadorean government are paid directly by the person upon whom the burden of the tax falls,[19] tax consciousness is probably not very highly developed in the country. It would be decidedly unfortunate if lack of awareness of the tax burden should lead to pressure upon the government for the expansion of government services without regard to the resulting budgetary and revenue problems. But there is no evidence in El Salvador of strong pressure in that direction. On the other hand, information provided by persons familiar with the habits and attitudes of persons subject to direct taxes makes it appear that the limited tax consciousness that results from predominantly indirect taxation is a pronounced advantage from the point of view of the Treasury and of the tax administration.

The desirability or undesirability of a high degree of tax consciousness is largely a question of what may be called tax morale. Without a certain amount of tax morale, tax consciousness is no advantage. It is exceedingly difficult to devise methods of raising tax morale, but there are certain factors that undoubtedly affect it, and with respect to these factors either administrative or legislative action, or both, can be taken. One is the elimination of discrimination among various classes of taxpayers, such as those between employees and self-employed, urban and rural, single and married. Another is the need for exact accounting of government expenditures, not only through the annual liquidation of the budget — which, as indicated earlier, is performed with considerable efficiency and speed by the Court of Accounts — but perhaps also through "proofs of real performance" in the form of annual reports on certain government activities such as the mileage of road construction and improvements, the progress of educational activities, and the like.[20] Finally, a more vigorous prosecution of tax evasion and tax delinquency would no doubt contribute to the gradual improvement of tax morale.

[19] The proportion of direct taxes is only 11 per cent. Cf. Table 33, in Chapter VIII.

[20] In recent years, the Ministry of Public Works (*Fomento*) has published such an account of its activities.

# CHAPTER X

## THE BUDGET AND THE NATIONAL INCOME

SO FAR THE FISCAL SYSTEM has been discussed as it affects the three principal interested parties — business, the consumer, and the government.[1] The study now turns to the broadest possible aspect: the effect of the budget upon the entire national income.[2]

Interest here centers upon the influence of the budget upon (1) the composition of the national income, (2) its distribution, and (3) its magnitude. In a subsequent chapter the role of the budget in maintaining the stability of the national income, commonly referred to as anticyclical fiscal policy, will be discussed.

### 1. THE BUDGET AND THE COMPOSITION OF THE NATIONAL INCOME

Government expenditures, in recent years, have equaled on the average about 9 per cent of the gross national product, ranging from a low of 7.3 per cent to a high of 10.3 per cent; the full data are given in Table 48. To help appraise these figures, a comparison is presented in Table 49 for a group of countries with widely differing economic characteristics. Except for Peru, the data refer to 1946 or in some cases fiscal 1946–47, the first postwar year in which "normal" peacetime conditions were to some extent being approached in the major countries. It will be noted that El Salvador shows the lowest figures of any of these countries for expenditures relative to national income.[3] El Salva-

---

[1] Needless to say, the sequence was dictated by analytical convenience and does not reflect an attempt at ranking the relative importance of these interests.

[2] The term "national income" is here used synonymously with "gross national product"; it is only for the latter that quantitative estimates are available.

[3] To some extent this may be due to the fact that the comparison is based, in the case of El Salvador, upon gross national product rather than the slightly lower national income figures. The latter have not been computed for El Salvador, but the difference probably is not so great as to destroy the value and approximate accuracy of the comparison.

TABLE 48

GOVERNMENT EXPENDITURES COMPARED WITH GROSS NATIONAL PRODUCT
AT CURRENT PRICES

(*In millions of colones at current prices*)

|  | Gross national product | Total government expenditures | Total government expenditures as per cent of gross national product |
|---|---|---|---|
| 1939............... | 244 | 10.5[a] | ...[b] |
| 1940............... | 229 | 22.2 | 9.7 |
| 1941............... | 232 | 21.4 | 9.2 |
| 1942............... | 279 | 21.8 | 7.8 |
| 1943............... | 251 | 23.3 | 9.3 |
| 1944............... | 267 | 25.2 | 9.4 |
| 1945............... | 398 | 29.1 | 7.3 |
| 1946............... | 435 | 45.0 | 10.3 |

[a] Second half of 1939 only.
[b] Not available.

dor, in other words, is fortunate in that only a relatively small part of its resources is absorbed by government activities. On the other hand, one may see some indication in the heavier expenditures of other countries — insofar as they are deliberate and not imposed by special circumstances — that their inhabitants have been sufficiently persuaded by the value of enlarged government services for them to give up to the government a higher proportion of private income than have the people of El Salvador.

In appraising the relatively low ratio of government expenditures to gross national product in El Salvador, however, it must be borne in mind that the Salvadorean budget contains only a negligible amount of transfer expenditures. Transfer expenditures are those expenditures of the government that do not absorb productive resources but merely cause the transfer of money from the taxpayer to the beneficiary. Examples of such expenditures are the service of the domestic public debt and pensions, which require no service by the beneficiary, in contrast to exhaustive expenditures, such as public works or administra-

# TABLE 49

## National Income Compared with Government Expenditures

| | Local currency unit | Year | Population[a] (in thousands) | National income[b] (in millions of local currency) | Per capita national income,[c] in U.S. dollars | Total government expenditures[c] (in millions of local currency) | Government expenditures as per cent of national income |
|---|---|---|---|---|---|---|---|
| El Salvador........... | Colón | 1946 | 1,997 | 435[d] | 87.13 | 45.0 | 10.3 |
| Chile................. | Peso | 1946 | 5,427 | 41,998[e] | 249.64 | 6,726.2 | 16.0 |
| Denmark............. | Krone | 1946 | 4,101 | 13,299 | 675.74 | 2,494.8[g] | 18.6 |
| Great Britain........ | Pound | 1946 | 49,335 | 8,100 | 662.02 | 3,910.3[g] | 48.3 |
| Mexico.............. | Peso | 1946 | 22,776 | 12,970 | 87.61 | 1,770.4 | 13.6 |
| New Zealand......... | N.Z. Pound | 1946 | 1,761 | 378 | 688.38 | 182.8[g] | 48.4 |
| Peru................. | Sol | 1942 | 6,457 | 2,043[f] | 48.69 | 409.0[h] | 20.0 |
| United States | | | | | | | |
| State and federal..... | Dollar | 1946 | 141,229 | 178,200 | 1,261.78 | 63,777.9[i] | 35.8 |
| Federal only......... | Dollar | 1946 | 141,229 | 178,200 | 1,261.78 | 55,632.4[i] | 31.2 |

[a] Mid-year population, from "Estimates of Total Population," *Monthly Bulletin of Statistics* (United Nations).

[b] National income in current prices at so-called factor cost (i.e., exclusive of taxes and depreciation), "Estimates of National Income," *Monthly Bulletin of Statistics* (United Nations). In the case of El Salvador, figures refer to gross national product.

[c] Reported expenditures of national governments, unless otherwise specified, as presented in Chapter VI.

[d] Estimate of gross national product. See Appendix B.

[e] Unpublished estimate of Corporación de Fomento de Chile; estimated on basis of disposable income.

[f] Estimate of Emilio G. Barreto in *Studies in Income and Wealth*, vol. X (National Bureau of Economic Research, New York).

[g] Fiscal year beginning April 1946.

[h] Total ordinary, extraordinary, and credit-operation expenditures, *Balance y Cuenta General de la República, 1942* (Lima, Peru).

[i] Fiscal year beginning July 1946.

tive services, which absorb manpower and materials. Transfer payments therefore do not constitute a burden upon the economy in the way that "exhaustive" expenditures do, although they do involve some burden because of the tax "friction" that they generate. Accordingly, to the extent that the higher proportion of government outlay to national income in other countries is accounted for by transfer payments, the true difference between them and El Salvador is less than it appears.

Of the various types of government expenditures that form part of the national income, two are of particular interest: amounts spent abroad; and amounts spent for permanent improvements, i.e., for the formation of physical capital. The first is important because it affects the balance of payments, the second because it increases the productivity of the country and thereby helps to raise the national income in future years. Both will be studied in some detail.

GOVERNMENT EXPENDITURES ABROAD

The government spends money abroad chiefly for three purposes: (1) service of the foreign public debt; (2) maintenance of the consular and diplomatic service; and (3) imports of goods and services for its own use, mainly for public works and military purposes. During 1939–1941, before El Salvador entered the war, imports were less on the average than consular and diplomatic outlays, but later this relation was reversed. Foreign public debt expenditure became important only in 1946 when service was resumed after the 1937 suspension. These data, for the period 1939–1946, are shown in Table 50. To eliminate so far as possible the distortion produced by wartime inflation, the data are presented in terms of both current and constant prices, each series being deflated by its appropriate index.

If the years 1943 and 1944 are disregarded, because of the extraordinary outlays on the inter-American Highway that they seem to reflect, it will be seen that the ratio of government expenditures abroad to total expenditures fluctuated between 11.9 and 19.7 per cent, with an average value of around 15 per cent. The ratio of imports of goods and services alone to total

## TABLE 50

### GOVERNMENT EXPENDITURES ABROAD COMPARED WITH TOTAL GOVERNMENT EXPENDITURES, 1939–1946[a]

*(In millions of colones)*

| Year | Total Government Expenditures | | Service of foreign debt | Consular and Diplomatic Services | | Government Imports of Goods and Services | | Total Government Expenditures Abroad | | Ratio to Total Government Expenditures, at Constant Prices, of | |
|---|---|---|---|---|---|---|---|---|---|---|---|
| | At current prices | At constant prices[b] | | At current prices | At constant prices[c] | At current prices | At constant prices[d] | At current prices | At constant prices | Government expenditures abroad | Government imports of goods and services |
| 1939 | 20.6 | 23.0 | 0.2 | 1.4 | 1.5 | 0.9 | 1.1 | 2.6 | 2.7 | 11.9% | 4.6% |
| 1940 | 22.3 | 26.1 | 0.3 | 2.0 | 2.1 | 2.2 | 2.8 | 4.5 | 5.1 | 19.7% | 10.8% |
| 1941 | 21.5 | 22.5 | 0.2 | 2.4 | 2.5 | 0.8 | 1.2 | 3.5 | 3.8 | 16.9% | 5.2% |
| 1942 | 21.8 | 21.8 | 0.2 | 1.6 | 1.6 | 1.3 | 1.3 | 3.1 | 3.1 | 14.2% | 5.9% |
| 1943 | 23.4 | 22.1 | 0.2 | 1.7 | 1.7 | 4.2 | 3.7 | 6.0 | 5.6 | 25.4% | 16.9% |
| 1944 | 25.2 | 22.4 | 0.2 | 1.9 | 1.9 | 4.1 | 4.1 | 6.3 | 6.2 | 27.7% | 18.4% |
| 1945 | 29.2 | 24.4 | 0.2 | 1.2 | 1.0 | 3.4 | 3.2 | 4.7 | 4.4 | 18.0% | 13.0% |
| 1946 | 45.0 | 35.8 | 1.0 | 1.9 | 1.6 | 2.7 | 2.0 | 5.7 | 4.6 | 12.9% | 5.5% |

[a] Figures may not add up exactly to totals, owing to rounding.
[b] At 1942 prices. Fixed government expenditures are deflated by an index especially designed for this purpose; for additional information, see Appendix H. "Variable" government expenditures are deflated by the index of wholesale prices. Expenditures for debt services are undeflated.
[c] Deflated by the special index used for deflating fixed government expenditures.
[d] Deflated by the index of cost of imports.

expenditures tended to be rather less than 10 per cent, fluctuating between 4.6 and 13.0 per cent.[4]

It is interesting to inquire how far the ratio of expenditures abroad to total expenditures tends to change with fluctuations in total government expenditure. To some extent, of course, this is subject to the arbitrary decision of the government. It is only in a qualified sense, therefore, that one may speak of a "propensity to import" on the part of the government, as it has become customary to do for the economy as a whole. Nevertheless, the fact that government expenditures abroad consist of three components, of which one (imports) tends to fluctuate sharply while the other two (debt and consular) tend to be less variable, permits the conclusion that with rising total budgets the proportion of expenditures abroad is not likely to rise, and may even fall. In technical terms, the "marginal propensity to import" of the government seems to be no higher than its "average propensity" and may even be lower, using these terms in the qualified sense in which they may be applied to the government.

It must be emphasized again that this conclusion is a very tentative one, and that the volume of expenditures abroad is in large measure subject to the desires of the government. If, for instance, a high level of revenues enables the government to plan for large public works, this may bring a substantial increase in government imports.

The government's expenditures abroad will now be compared with those of the private sector of the economy. Private imports of goods and services (the term being used to denote all current account liabilities in the balance of payments) during the period 1939–1946 ranged between 19.5 million colones and 56.6 million, as shown in Table 51. The years 1942 and 1943, when private buyers had great difficulty in obtaining goods, are probably quite unrepresentative, and so to some extent is the year 1946, when pent-up demand was being satisfied. If these years are excluded, the proportion of private imports of goods and services to gross private product (gross national product minus govern-

---

[4] The government, however, also purchases a small amount of imported goods in El Salvador, which would raise the ratio slightly.

## TABLE 51

### PRIVATE EXPENDITURES ABROAD COMPARED WITH
### GROSS PRIVATE PRODUCT,[a] 1939–1946
#### (*In millions of colones*)

| Year | Gross Private Product[a] | | Private Current-Account Expenditures Abroad | | Private Current-Account Expenditures Abroad as Per Cent of Gross Private Product, at Constant Prices |
|------|------------|-------------|------------|-------------|------|
| | At current prices | At constant prices[b] | At current prices | At constant prices[c] | |
| 1939 | 223 | 243 | 23.6 | 26.5 | 10.9% |
| 1940 | 207 | 231 | 19.5 | 25.0 | 10.8% |
| 1941 | 211 | 230 | 21.2 | 29.0 | 12.6% |
| 1942 | 258 | 258 | 22.3 | 22.3 | 8.6% |
| 1943 | 328 | 291 | 29.3 | 26.4 | 9.1% |
| 1944 | 343 | 272 | 30.0 | 30.0 | 11.0% |
| 1945 | 367 | 267 | 37.3 | 34.9 | 13.1% |
| 1946 | 390 | 283 | 56.6 | 40.7 | 14.4% |

[a] For the purposes of this analysis, gross private product is defined as the gross national product minus the government's fixed and variable expenditures.
[b] At 1942 prices.
[c] Deflated by the index of cost of imports (1942 = 100).

ment expenditures) fluctuated within the narrow range of 10.8 to 13.1 per cent, in terms of constant prices. Of course, this stability of the import ratio is not surprising since the gross national product series is itself built in part on import statistics. The order of magnitude of the ratio, however, seems to indicate that the import ratio of the private sector (average propensity to import) is somewhat lower than that of the government, which was found to average around 15 per cent. It is higher, however, than the government's ratio for imports of goods and services only (excluding debt services and diplomatic expenditures).

The import ratio of the private sector shows a fairly well defined tendency to vary with changes in the gross national product. Not only does the absolute amount of imports rise when national income goes up, but also the ratio of imports to national income. In technical terms, the marginal propensity to import of the private sector is greater than the average propensity. While the available data do not permit anything like an accurate calculation of the marginal propensity, they convey the impression that it lies somewhere between 20 and 30 per cent. That is to say, of every colón of additional income, 20 to 30 centavos tend to be spent on imports. This estimate is confirmed by an inspection of consumer budgets at various income levels. At levels above 600 colones per year, the marginal propensity to buy imported goods (at c.i.f. prices) is of the order of 25 per cent or more. The reason why the average propensity is so much lower is that the important consumer group with incomes of less than 600 colones (in 1946) consumes very few imported goods.

The marginal propensity to import of the private sector, of about 20 to 30 per cent, compares with a marginal propensity to import on the part of the government, including debt and consular service, of probably less than 15 per cent. This comparison is of course subject to a great many qualifications. Changing policies of the government may easily alter the government's marginal propensity to import inherent in the structure of the budget. The unknown volume of purchases of imported merchandise in El Salvador by the government adds further uncertainty. Nevertheless, an interesting conclusion can tentatively be drawn from the circumstance that the marginal propensity to import on the part of the private sector seems to be larger than that of the government. This conclusion concerns the effect upon *total* imports of a change in the relative sizes of private and public expenditures. Thus if, with a constant gross national product, the level of taxation and public expenditures is reduced and private income (after taxes) and private expenditure are correspondingly higher, there will be a net rise in total imports. If the budget, for instance, were cut by 5 million colones, the presumptive drop in government outlays abroad might be of the order of 750,000 colones or less, if past expenditure patterns continue to rule. The simultaneous increase in private incomes (after taxes) of 5 million would tend to raise private imports at the same time by 1.0 to 1.5 million, and there would therefore be a net increase in imports of 250,000 to 750,000 colones. Conversely, an increase in the budget, with a corresponding reduction in private incomes and expenditures, would probably bring about a reduction in total imports. The effects of such changes upon the balance of payments would be intensified, incidentally, if there should be a tendency for profits to be invested abroad. A higher or lower level of taxation would absorb a greater or smaller proportion of the funds otherwise going abroad. There can be little doubt that the coffee tax, which falls upon profits of the export sector of the economy, has had an effect of that kind.

The probable impact of changes in the relative sizes of the budget and of private income upon the balance of payments, as appears from the preceding estimates, is not very large, but it is worth noting. Under certain conditions, the impact upon the balance of payments may also bring about changes in the level of the gross national product itself. This will be discussed in a subsequent section.

### CAPITAL FORMATION

It is of considerable interest to inquire what proportion of government expenditures is devoted to capital formation, in view of the great importance of new investment for the growth of national income. Unfortunately, the data available are very scanty. In "real" terms, i.e., at constant prices, government capital formation in the form of roads, buildings, plant and

TABLE 52

GOVERNMENT GROSS CAPITAL FORMATION

(*In thousands of colones*)

| Year | Total Government Expenditures | | Government Gross Capital Formation | | Ratio of Government Capital Formation to Total Government Expenditures | |
|---|---|---|---|---|---|---|
| | At current prices | At constant prices[a] | At current prices[b] | At constant prices[c] | At current prices | At constant prices |
| 1940 | 22,330.8 | 26,050.9 | 3,026.2 | 4,450.3 | 13.6% | 17.1% |
| 1942 | 21,838.5 | 21,838.5 | 1,894.0 | 1,894.0 | 8.7% | 8.7% |
| 1946 | 45,026.7 | 35,766.2 | 5,470.3 | 3,073.2 | 12.2% | 8.6% |
| 1947 | 51,875.9 | 33,462.3 | 8,964.1 | 4,208.5 | 17.3% | 12.6% |

[a] At 1942 prices. "Fixed" government expenditures are deflated by an index especially designed for this purpose; for additional information, see Appendix E. "Variable" government expenditures are deflated by the index of wholesale prices. Expenditures for debt service are undeflated.

[b] Taken from the Annual Budget and adjusted to the "Liquidated Budget." The expenditures for the Pan-American Highway, which were budgeted separately, are excluded.

[c] At 1942 prices. Deflated by the index of wholesale prices.

equipment, and the like, ranged, during the years for which data are available, from a low of 8.6 per cent of total "real" expenditures in 1946, to 17.1 per cent in 1940, as shown in Table 52. In monetary terms, i.e., at current prices, government capital formation ranged from 8.7 per cent in 1942 to 17.3 per cent in 1947. It is of course the data in "real" terms that are of primary interest. These reveal that while governmental capital formation has fluctuated rather considerably, the ratio of capital formation to total expenditures has shown no pronounced tendency to rise with rising revenues.

An attempt has also been made to compare the government's ratio of capital formation with that of the private sector of the economy. Unfortunately, the data for capital formation in the private sector are extremely uncertain and can be regarded only as estimates of the order of magnitude involved. They are based primarily on data relating to building permits. Observers familiar with the Salvadorean economy estimate that building activity subject to such permits accounts for one quarter to one half of total capital formation[5] in the private sector of the economy. Table 53 presents estimates based on building permits, which seem to indicate that total private capital formation has ranged between 5 and 10 per cent of the income of the private sector. Studies of capital formation in other underdeveloped economies suggest that in El Salvador the ratio would normally tend to fall in the upper part of the indicated range. Although the Salvadorean data are extremely unprecise, they do seem to indicate that during cyclical fluctuations the capital formation ratio of the private sector tends to rise as income rises.

A comparison of the ratio of capital formation for the government and the private sectors, respectively, can only be made in extremely tentative terms. From such a comparison, it would appear that the ratio of governmental capital formation tends to be a little higher than that of the private sector. This does not necessarily mean, however, that an increase in taxation and government expenditures, accompanied by a corresponding reduc-

[5] The term "capital formation" is to be understood, of course, as relating to "physical capital." It does not relate to financial investment in securities, bank accounts, or currency in El Salvador or abroad.

TABLE 53

Private Gross Capital Formation

(*In millions of colones*)

| | | | Assumption I[c] | | Assumption II[d] | |
|---|---|---|---|---|---|---|
| Year | Gross private product at constant prices[a] | Gross private construction at constant prices[b] | Gross private capital formation at constant prices | Ratio of private capital formation to gross private product | Gross private capital formation at constant prices | Ratio of private capital formation to gross private product |
| 1939 | 243 | 4.6 | 9.2 | 3.8% | 18.4 | 7.6% |
| 1940 | 231 | 4.8 | 9.6 | 4.2% | 19.2 | 8.3% |
| 1941 | 230 | 6.0 | 12.0 | 5.2% | 24.0 | 10.4% |
| 1942 | 258 | 5.0 | 10.0 | 3.9% | 20.0 | 7.8% |
| 1943 | 291 | 6.5 | 13.0 | 4.5% | 26.0 | 8.9% |
| 1944 | 272 | 5.1 | 10.2 | 3.8% | 20.4 | 7.5% |
| 1945 | 267 | 7.8 | 15.6 | 5.8% | 31.2 | 11.7% |
| 1946 | 283 | 8.4 | 16.8 | 5.9% | 33.6 | 11.9% |

[a] At 1942 prices. For the purposes of this analysis, gross private product is defined as the gross national product minus the government's fixed and variable expenditures.

[b] The figures for 1942 and 1946 are taken from the direct estimates of the gross national product presented in Appendix A. Figures for the other years were interpolated on the basis of the series of building permits granted in San Salvador, which was furnished by the Bureau of Health. All figures were deflated to 1942 prices by the index of wholesale prices.

[c] Gross private construction assumed to be equal to 50 per cent of gross private capital formation.

[d] Gross private construction assumed to be equal to 25 per cent of gross private capital formation.

tion in the income and expenditures of the private sector, could be expected, on the basis of past expenditure patterns, to lead to a net increase in capital formation for the two sectors combined. The degree to which capital formation in the private sector would be reduced by an increase in taxation would probably depend, in good part, upon the particular incidence of the additional taxation. Additional taxes falling mainly upon the upper income groups who do most of the saving and investing might produce a reduction in saving and investment greater than the added capital formation to be expected from the government.

A net increase in the combined rate of capital formation of the two sectors could be expected, however, if the increase in taxation is effected in such a way as not to diminish drastically the investment incentives of the private sector, and if the yield of the additional taxation is fully or primarily used for purposes of capital formation by the government.

It goes without saying that these extremely tentative comparisons are based upon the assumption that past expenditure patterns will continue to rule. The pattern relating to the private sector appears to have been a fairly stable one. That of the government, on the other hand, has fluctuated more widely, and is of course subject in considerable measure to the economic policy decisions of the administration. It must be borne in mind, however, that these decisions are themselves determined by basic political, cultural, and economic considerations that are likely to produce similar expenditure patterns whenever special factors are absent.

### 2. Redistribution of National Income through the Budget

The burden that taxation imposes upon the economy is balanced, or should be, by the benefits that the economy derives from government services. But while it is possible to appraise with some degree of plausibility the tax burden at different income levels, it is much more difficult to estimate the value of the benefits that different income groups derive from government services. A comparison of the burden of taxation with the benefits derived is therefore a highly tentative and uncertain undertaking. Nevertheless, it is clear that in a country with a democratic form of government such a comparison is somehow constantly being made by the voters. The economist therefore has little excuse for not attempting it in analytical terms.

#### DISTRIBUTION OF BENEFITS

The difficulty of comparing burdens and benefits lies in the fact that the services of the government are largely of an "overhead" character — notably administration, security, and justice — and that the benefits flowing from them cannot be allocated convincingly to the various income groups. Moreover, the degree to which individuals with equal incomes avail themselves of particular services, such as highways, law courts, and statistics, varies widely. On the other hand, it has also been pointed out in this study that the tax burden of similar individuals varies considerably, according to whether or not, through smoking, drinking, or otherwise, they pay "avoidable" taxes. The lack of uniformity of incidence is therefore a problem that exists on both sides of the equation.

To attempt a comparison of tax burden and government benefits by no means implies the suggestion that the government ought to aim at equalizing burden and benefits. It has sometimes been urged that taxation should be made equal to benefits, but in the thinking of economists, the "benefit theory" of taxation has long played only a subordinate role. Moreover, the practice reflecting the "benefit theory" employed by some governments, of earmarking certain revenues for the benefit of the payers of the specific tax (as gasoline taxes for highways), is generally regarded as undesirable because it breaks up the unity of the budget. In El Salvador this practice has not been employed for some time.

For the purpose of estimating the distribution of benefits, the simplest but obviously least satisfactory assumption would be that all people share equally in the benefits of government services, irrespective of income or social status. The weakness of such an assumption is that many of the services that the government renders aim at the protection not only of the individual, but also of his income and wealth.

The value of the protection accorded to a person with a higher income or with more wealth is obviously larger than that rendered to a person with a lower income and little or no wealth. In order to arrive at a basis for a more adequate appraisal of the distribution of government benefits, it appears therefore useful to distinguish between the following three types of benefits: (1) the maintenance of order and protection against internal and external disturbances; (2) social and cultural services; and (3) economic benefits.

The services rendered by maintaining order and providing protection may reasonably be regarded as being distributed in direct proportion to each man's wealth and income.

The benefits of social and cultural services provided by the government seem to accrue predominantly to the poorer classes, which obtain education and medical care in hospitals free of charge or below cost. But it would be wrong to assume that the members of higher income groups do not benefit from these services. If, for instance, the government did not provide free education, the higher income groups would no doubt resort to private education; but since the government's educational facilities are available to them, their own expenses for this purpose are reduced. Moreover, the upper classes also derive indirect benefits from the social and cultural services rendered to the lower income groups, since an over-all improvement in education and health raises the productivity of the economy as a whole.

The benefits of economic development, finally, are probably distributed among the members of the community in proportion to their "stake" in the economic life of the country, i.e., in proportion to their income and wealth. This will certainly be true if developmental expenditures raise total national income without changing its distribution, which is in fact the most plausible assumption in the absence of special policies designed to aid specific social groups.

### REDISTRIBUTIVE EFFECTS OF BUDGET

The combined result of the tax burden imposed upon each income group and of the benefits derived by the same group[6] from the government services tends to be a redistribution of the national income. If tax burdens and government services were so adjusted that they roughly equaled each other for each income group, each group would receive back from the government, in the form of services, what it had paid in taxes. Even then there would be some redistribution among individuals, owing to the different degrees to which individuals in the same income bracket paid "avoidable" taxes and took advantage of government services. There is, however, no reason to assume that the burden of taxes and the benefits received equal one another even for each group. Given such inequality, some groups will therefore receive more in services than they pay in taxes, and vice versa. In such a case, the result clearly is a redistribution of income.

In the accompanying Table 54 the results of computations of the redistribution of the national income through the fiscal sys-

---

[6] It is assumed, as a pragmatic proposition, that the total of government services is worth what it costs.

## TABLE 54

### Redistribution of Income through Fiscal System in 1946

(*In thousands of colones*)

| | Family Income in Colones | | | | | |
| | Under 600 | 600–1200 | 1200–2400 | 2400–3600 | 3600 and over | Total |
|---|---|---|---|---|---|---|
| Number of families.............. | 249,000 | 120,000 | 20,000 | 10,000 | 10,000 | 400,000 |
| Income before impact of fiscal system.... | 140,303 | 105,305 | 34,998 | 29,114 | 125,280 | 435,000 |
| Taxes paid.............. | 10,932 | 9,474 | 2,943 | 2,583 | 11,691 | 36,723 |
| *Alternative A: Equal per capita benefits* | | | | | | |
| Benefits from government expenditures...... | 22,034 | 11,017 | 1,836 | 918 | 918 | 36,723 |
| Benefits received, as per cent of taxes paid... | 219.6% | 116.3% | 62.4% | 35.5% | 7.9% | 100.0% |
| *Alternative B: Benefits proportionate to income* | | | | | | |
| Benefits from government expenditures...... | 11,825 | 8,887 | 2,975 | 2,460 | 10,576 | 36,723 |
| Benefits received, as per cent of taxes paid... | 117.9% | 93.8% | 101.1% | 95.2% | 90.5% | 100.0% |
| *Alternative C: Benefits proportionate to income except cultural and social expenditures*[a] | | | | | | |
| Benefits from government expenditures...... | 12,211 | 9,177 | 3,005 | 2,539 | 9,731 | 36,723 |
| Benefits received, as per cent of taxes paid... | 121.7% | 96.9% | 102.1% | 98.3% | 83.2% | 100.0% |

[a] Benefits of cultural and social expenditures assumed to be distributed on basis of the groups with annual incomes of less than 3600 colones receiving 20 per cent more than their share on the basis of income alone, and of the upper income groups receiving proportionately less than their share.

tem are shown for the year 1946. Since it is impossible to allocate the benefits of government services with any degree of assurance, the results of computation under several alternative assumptions are presented.

If it is assumed that government services are distributed evenly among all inhabitants of El Salvador irrespective of their economic position (Alternative A in Table 54), the national income appears to be redistributed by the fiscal system in favor of the lowest income group, which would gain in benefits 119.6 per cent more than its "losses" through tax payments. This gain would amount to approximately 8.6 per cent of its original income. This results from the fact that its per capita contribution to the cost of government is less than the average contribution through assumption evenly distributed. Conversely, the tax burden of the upper income groups takes away more from them than the value of the benefits of government services received by them.

If it is alternatively assumed that benefits accruing to various income groups are divided in proportion to the income of each group (Alternative B), a somewhat more realistic picture is obtained. The result of the combination of the slightly progressive tax structure with the distribution of government benefits in proportion to income is still a redistribution in favor of lower income groups, but the transfer in favor of the lowest income group is substantially smaller, amounting to only 1.7 per cent of the taxes paid by it.

The third assumption (Alternative C) implies that all benefits are distributed proportionally to income except those derived from cultural and social services. Of the latter, it is assumed that groups with an annual income below 3,600 colones obtain 20 per cent more than their proportional share, while groups with annual incomes above 3,600 colones receive correspondingly less.[7]

[7] In the year 1946, for which the computations were made, government expenditures exceeded government receipts by several million colones. If total expenditures had been distributed among income groups in any of the ways indicated above, the apparent result would have been that all income groups benefited from the redistribution through the fiscal system. In order to avoid this obvious mistake (which, incidentally, would imply that a large government budgetary deficit would always benefit the economy as a whole), government expenditures were adjusted

The general conclusion to be drawn, under any set of reasonable assumptions, is therefore that the fiscal system as a whole so operates as to redistribute income in favor of the lower income groups.

No account has been taken in the preceding discussion of the possibility that the operations of the government may increase the national income. Such an increase, if realized, would require modifications in the analysis and might, in any case, be much more significant than the redistributive effect. This possibility is discussed in the next section.

It should be pointed out that the indicated degree of redistribution is not particularly high and can hardly be said to involve an excessive burden for the upper classes. A comparison with the more industrialized countries would probably show that the degree of redistribution there is considerably higher. A direct comparison is not possible because calculations of the type here presented for El Salvador are not available for the industrialized countries, but in view of the much more progressive tax structure of the latter, there is little doubt as to the validity of the general conclusion.

### 3. Influence of Budget upon Size of National Income

In the discussion of the various effects that the budget may have upon the national income, attention has so far been given to the composition and the redistribution of income. The information gathered in this connection will now be employed in analyzing the influence of the budget upon the level of national income.

Two separate types of influence that emanate from the budget must be distinguished: (1) those that affect national income by

to equal government receipts. As a matter of fact, the budget "deficit" of 1946 was due primarily to the resumption of the service on the government debt. The "deficit" was financed through Treasury surpluses accumulated in preceding years. The allocation of the benefits corresponding to the payment of a public debt owed to foreign bondholders was made on the principle that this expenditure represents a postponed payment for the goods and services on which the loan had been spent. Since the foreign loan was incurred primarily for the financing of economic development, debt payments were classified as expenditures for economic development.

increasing the aggregate demand for goods and services, as for instance, deficit spending; and (2) those that affect national income by stimulating economic development and by providing new incentives to produce and invest. The former are characterized by the fact that they call into play chiefly resources that previously existed but were idle or underemployed, while the latter involve predominantly the development of new resources.

In an economy where full employment prevails as a rule, it is the second set of influences — those involving the development of new resources — that are particularly promising. Nevertheless, it is important not to overlook the others which increase aggregate demand by drawing upon already existing resources. In the first place, in an economy like the Salvadorean there frequently exists what has been aptly called "underemployment," which means that while everybody has a job, his productive capacity is not utilized to the best advantage. Under such conditions, there is a possibility of the budget's contributing to an increase in national income. Furthermore, disregard by policy makers of the influence that *changes* in the budget can have upon income may produce dangerous inflationary or deflationary pressures. It is important to be aware of these influences in order to guard against them.

### THE BUDGET AND AGGREGATE DEMAND

An increase in aggregate demand via the budget occurs if the government sets money in motion within the economy that otherwise would not have been spent. Two major instances must be distinguished: (1) when the government runs a deficit which it finances with borrowed funds that otherwise would not have been spent; and (2) when the government, without running a deficit, absorbs through taxation some funds that otherwise either would have gone into idle savings[8] or would have been spent on imports. These two types of influence upon aggregate demand have been exhaustively investigated in industrial countries. In the Salvadorean environment, however, they take on rather different significance.

[8] Using the term "idle savings" in the qualified (financial) sense in which modern economics permits its use.

Significant deficit spending has not been practiced by the Salvadorean government since 1934. The experience of earlier years, however, as well as that of other Latin American countries, indicates what the probable results would be. If there were a tendency toward unemployment, government spending no doubt would help to counteract it. This action, however, would involve certain risks for the economy, which would be converted into definite harm if the action were overdone. More will be said on this subject later on.

The second possibility of an increase in aggregate demand — the taxing away of income that would otherwise have gone into idle savings or for imports — is probably realized in El Salvador at certain times. Any tax, whether paid directly out of income or in the form of higher prices, reduces the real income of the saver. At the lower income level, not only the consumption but also the saving of the taxpayer is lower. It is in this sense that one may speak of current savings being taxed away. To the extent that these savings would have gone into physical investment, directly or indirectly, their absorption and reëxpenditure by the government does not increase aggregate demand. It simply reduces demand by the private sector of the economy and increases government demand by an equal amount. But to the extent that some of these savings would have remained idle their absorption by the government would not reduce private demand, while their immediate expenditure by the government would increase government demand in the form of government contracts and salaries with the result that aggregate demand in the economy would be higher.

It is of course difficult to say how large a part of current savings tends at any time to remain idle. In such a country as the United States, it is believed that large amounts of current savings frequently remain idle for long periods. This would not immediately interfere with investment, because corporations and others who are planning physical investments can usually satisfy their needs from past accumulations of savings in the capital market, or through the banking system.

In El Salvador, on the other hand, savings probably are less likely to be idle, and taxation that reduces saving (as all taxation does to some extent) is much more likely to interfere with new investment. The connection between saving and investment is much closer than in the United States because of the relative lack of a capital market. A predominant part of physical investment is made by the saver himself and can only be made if he is given a chance to save.

Under these circumstances, taxation that reduces saving is certain to reduce private investment expenditure to some extent. To that extent, it not only fails to increase aggregate demand, but also impedes capital formation. In a country as much in need of capital as El Salvador, this is a serious disadvantage. On the other hand, there certainly is some portion of savings that remains idle, including the sometimes substantial volume of savings that goes abroad. To the extent that taxation curtails this type of saving, an increase in aggregate demand can be expected. The tax upon coffee exports, which cuts directly into profits of the export sector of the economy, probably has had some such effect.

The effectiveness of taxation in curtailing imports must also be considered. The lower income left after taxation means that the taxpayers' purchases of imported goods are reduced along with all other purchases. The government's expenditure of the tax revenues, on the other hand, to some extent goes for imports, as well as for debt service and diplomatic expenditures. The ratio of expenditures abroad to total expenditures, it was pointed out in an earlier section, actually has tended to be higher for the government than for the private sector. The increase in government expenditures abroad associated with an increase in revenues, however, was found to be probably less than the corresponding increase for the private sector. A given rise in government revenues and expenditures, matched by a corresponding decline in the private sector, therefore, would probably reduce the expenditures abroad of the two sectors combined, which would mean an increase in aggregate demand within the country. The calculations, however, rest upon estimates with a wide margin of error and do not permit definitive conclusions.

The foregoing discussion shows that the extent to which the budget affects aggregate demand depends upon two factors: (1)

the size of the budget in relation to the private sector of the economy; and (2) the degree to which the tax burden falls upon social groups whose saving and consumption of imported goods is large.

In El Salvador, the budget is small in relation to the private sector. The social groups with high savings are, of course, the upper income classes. The consumption of imported goods is less sharply concentrated than savings, but on the whole the proportion of imports consumed rises with income. Since the tax structure is mildly progressive, the tax burden does fall somewhat more heavily upon the high-saving and high-importing groups and, to that extent, intensifies the effect of the budget upon aggregate demand. But since the progressiveness of the tax structure is very mild, its effect in this direction cannot be great.

The conclusion to be drawn from the discussion thus far is that the budget probably brings about a moderate increase in aggregate demand. The really important question which must now be discussed is whether, by doing so, it increases national income. This depends on whether or not the private sector of the economy shows a tendency toward unemployment (or underemployment). The existence of such a tendency, if confirmed, would indicate that aggregate demand in the economy is too low to maintain full employment, despite the contribution made by the government. One might then conclude that in the absence of the govment's contribution to aggregate demand, employment and income would be still lower, and that the budget therefore does make a contribution to national income. In an economy, however, where no tendency toward unemployment or underemployment prevails, there is no particular reason to assume that the private sector of the economy could not by itself generate enough demand to maintain full employment even if the budget were materially reduced. In that case, it cannot be asserted that the budget constitutes a real addition to national income. All it does is to change the composition of such income by substituting a certain proportion of government services for privately produced goods and services.

On the whole, it seems reasonable to believe that conditions in the Salvadorean economy naturally tend toward full employment. There may indeed be underemployment in the sense that not all labor is utilized as steadily and effectively as it might be. It is conceivable that the added demand emanating from the government has helped somewhat to intensify the utilization of manpower and on the average may have increased the quality of employment. These beneficial effects, however, may well have been offset by the inevitable red tape and duplication of effort that are the familiar drawbacks of government operations everywhere.

It is important to note the relevance of this reasoning to changes in the level of the budget or in the degree of progressiveness of the tax structure. Either type of change will increase aggregate demand when the change is upwards and reduce it when the change is downward. Nevertheless, given Salvadorean full-employment conditions, the net effect upon national income will probably be nil after the economy has adjusted itself to these changes, no matter what the level and progressiveness of the budget. During the adjustment period, however, there may be considerable deflationary or inflationary pressures, such as have been noticeable during the recent inflation period experienced by El Salvador. It cannot be denied that the Salvadorean government, by increasing its budget, has added to aggregate demand and hence to the prevailing inflation, even though deficits have been avoided and at times surpluses have been achieved. It is an important and not sufficiently recognized fact that even a balanced budget may be inflationary and that consequently it is not enough, for the purpose of conducting an anti-inflationary policy, to avoid deficit spending. It may rather be found necessary to keep down the level of the entire budget, or to secure very sizable surpluses and sterilize the corresponding revenues through extraordinary repayments of foreign or bank-held debt or through accumulation in the Treasury.

### DEVELOPMENT AND INCENTIVES

The preceding section has dealt with the circumstances under which the budget may produce an increase in national income by increasing aggregate demand. It was found that the opportunities for raising national income in this manner are rather limited in the Salvadorean economy because the demand generated by the private sector would normally be sufficient to generate full employment. All the more importance therefore attaches to the opportunity that the government has of raising national income by stimulating economic development and by providing incentives to produce and invest. Expenditure as well as tax policy can be brought to bear upon these objectives. We shall first examine the former.

*Expenditures for Development.* It is notable that the Salvadorean government, unlike other Latin American governments, has not organized a "fomento" institute, i.e., a semi-independent organization charged exclusively with the execution of development projects, self-liquidating or otherwise. The Mejoramiento Social may be regarded as a small step in that direction, and some of the activities of the Mortgage Bank appear to have taken on "fomento" character during a certain period, but in general the responsibility for the creation of new industries has been left entirely to private enterprise.

This does not mean, however, that the government has been backward in developmental activities. The annual expenditures for development are shown in Table 55, from which it will be seen that rather considerable proportions of the total budget are normally devoted to this purpose. However, instead of going in

TABLE 55

RATIO OF BUDGETARY DEVELOPMENT EXPENDITURES
TO TOTAL GOVERNMENT EXPENDITURES

| Period | Total Government Expenditures in thousands of colones | Economic Development Expenditures | |
| | | Thousands of colones | Ratio to total government expenditures |
|---|---|---|---|
| 1929/30–1933/34 | 21,810.5 | 2,580.5 | 11.8% |
| 1934/35–1938/39 | 21,178.7 | 4,033.1 | 10.0% |
| 1939–1943[a] | 22,061.6 | 4,424.5 | 20.1% |
| 1944–1948[b] | 41,597.4 | 8,859.9 | 21.3% |

[a] July 1939–December 1943.
[b] Budgetary figures for fiscal year 1948.

directly for the creation of new enterprises, the government has directed its developmental expenditures toward the creation of facilities and conditions that will encourage private investment. During the late thirties, particular emphasis was placed on road construction. At the same time, monetary and credit conditions were being improved through the establishment of the Central Reserve Bank and the Mortgage Bank. At present, an ambitious electric power project is under discussion that would stimulate the use of power driven machinery.

It appears that the government's efforts to stimulate private initiative have met with only moderate success so far. It does not follow that the policy of relying upon private enterprise holds out no promise, but it may be suggested that in order to increase its effectiveness a more comprehensive and balanced approach would be desirable. Roads and electric power alone may not be sufficient to stimulate the creation and expansion of enterprises. Development of long-term credit, public and private instruction and training, storage and marketing facilities, and an appropriate social and political climate are important and perhaps essential parts of a balanced development program, the basis of which must be technical instructions and training.

*Effect of Taxation upon Development and Incentives.* The effects of taxation upon economic development and upon incentives to produce and invest are, on the whole, of a negative kind, discouraging rather than stimulating. The aim of tax policy therefore must be to minimize these adverse effects, and it will presently appear that in El Salvador such effects have indeed been kept low.

There is one major exception to the general statement that taxes *per se* hamper development — the tariff. A brief discussion of the protective aspects of the Salvadorean tariff has been given in Chapter VII, "The Impact of the Fiscal System upon Business." The subject really belongs in the field of commercial policy, and it must therefore suffice here to repeat that the tariff is essentially a revenue tariff but that it has had important protective effects in the fields of cotton textiles, sugar, and henequen. The industries that have developed behind this tariff are still in the initial stage of very high costs and high profits often characteristic of such ventures. It is therefore rather doubtful whether at present they are making a net addition to the real value of the national income or whether this value would not be higher if the country devoted more resources to increasing its exports in order to purchase goods abroad where they are cheaper. The low productivity of the nascent industries must be regarded, however, as a phase that will pass with the acquisition of greater skill, better equipment, and the emergence of more competition. The case for industrialization in a densely populated country like El Salvador is strong, and the high initial cost is a sacrifice that must be borne.

When the effects of taxation upon human effort are viewed in their broadest sense, several conflicting reactions become evident, the net result of which, as said above, tends to be on the negative side. Taxation reduces the reward for effort, be it by taking away part of income or by raising the price of the goods that can be bought out of income. The decision that a given additional effort is worth while or not is therefore biased in an unfavorable direction. This discouragement to marginal effort becomes particularly pronounced under a progressive rate structure, where each additional unit of income is taxed more heavily.

Counteracting to some extent the adverse effect of the reduction in marginal income is the effect that flows from the reduction in total income that taxation also brings about. The taxpayer, if he wants to achieve or maintain a given standard of living, must work harder than he would have to do without the tax burden. The truth of this has frequently been demonstrated in connection with wage increases, according to statements made by members of the Salvadorean business community; when wages were raised, workers put in fewer hours than before. A reduction, presumably, would induce them to work correspondingly more.

Once more, however, there is a counteracting factor to be considered — the effect of the free availability of government services upon the incentive to work. While most government services cannot be substituted for privately purchased goods and services, some of them can, as in the cases of medical care and education. To the extent that the taxpayer is able to get these things free from the government, the pressure to work is reduced.[9]

Whether the net result of these conflicting forces is an increase or a reduction in effort depends, of course, upon their respective magnitude. In El Salvador, the progressiveness of taxation is very mild, and the curtailment in marginal income brought about by taxation ought not to be unduly discouraging to effort. The total tax burden likewise is not heavy, but in so far as it has any influence, it tends to increase effort. The counteracting effect of free government services should be of a very small order, considering the volume and nature of these services. On the whole, it may therefore be concluded that the Salvadorean tax system minimizes the adverse impact of taxation upon the incentive to work.

The same appears to be true of the effect of taxation upon the willingness to bear risk, which in this sense may be regarded as simply another form of effort. High taxes upon the upper income brackets are particularly damaging to the willingness to bear risk, because the income of people who dispose of venture capital usually falls into these brackets. In El Salvador, however, taxation of even the highest brackets is moderate, and capital gains are not taxed at all.

Furthermore, the fiscal administration favors new investment by frequent, though apparently unsystematic, exemptions from customs duties granted to imported machinery. On the other hand, exemptions from income tax for the profits of new investments for a limited number of years (such as some countries have employed to stimulate investment) have not been granted in El Salvador. Taking all these factors together, it appears that taxation does not constitute a significant obstacle to new enterprise.

[9] An analogous case is that of unemployment benefits or old age pensions, both of which undoubtedly reduce the compulsion to work.

## CHAPTER XI

## FISCAL POLICY DURING ECONOMIC FLUCTUATIONS

IN RECENT YEARS there has been considerable discussion of the possibility of compensating fluctuations in business conditions and national income by fiscal and monetary means. From the Salvadorean point of view, the prospects of success in this direction must be viewed with considerable reserve. There is little that a small country, dependent largely upon foreign markets, can do to protect itself against disturbances in the world economy. Nevertheless, owing to several special circumstances, El Salvador is relatively well equipped to resist foreign booms and depressions. It is therefore worth while to survey in some detail the problem of cyclical stability as it presents itself in that country, and to discuss the courses of compensatory fiscal action that are open to the Salvadorean government.

### 1. CHARACTERISTICS OF ECONOMIC FLUCTUATIONS IN EL SALVADOR

During the last twenty years, the Salvadorean economy has gone through two major downswings, and likewise two major phases of expansion. The first cycle was that of the great depression of the early thirties and the recovery from it that ended in 1937; the second was the contraction that began in 1937 and continued, interrupted by only a partial recovery, through the initial stage of World War II, to be followed by the inflationary wartime and postwar boom. In both cycles the authorities adopted measures that had a compensatory character, although of a limited kind. Among these, there deserve to be mentioned, for instance, the facts that during the first depression the government established the Mejoramiento Social, protected debtors through a Moratorium Law (*Ley de Liquidaciones de Deudas Privadas*), and suspended the service of the external debt. During the second depression, the debt service, which meanwhile had been resumed, was again suspended, and the coffee export tax was likewise suspended when coffee prices reached extreme lows. The Department of Coffee Exports (*Departamento de Exportaciones de Café*) and, later, the Salvadorean Coffee Company (*Compañía Salvadoreña del Café, S.A.*), a semiofficial institution which took over the functions of the former, were established for the purpose of making crop loans, to stabilize domestic coffee prices and to make purchases to tide coffee producers over the period of low prices. The Central Reserve Bank expanded its credits in a modest way in 1938 in order to offset the contraction. During the following boom, on the other hand, the government devoted part of the increasing revenues to substantial debt repayments (in 1946), thereby counteracting, to some extent, the inflationary trend. The Central Reserve Bank pursued a policy of credit limitation during this period in order to avoid intensifying the rise in the volume of money. These measures undoubtedly helped in some small measure to counteract deflation and inflation respectively. It must be added, however, in connection with the suspension of debt payments, that the relief from this burden was achieved at so high a cost, in terms of the standing of government credit, that in the long run this action will probably prove to have done far more harm than good.

The actions taken in boom and depression demonstrate the possibility of anticyclical action even under the limiting conditions imposed by the nature of the Salvadorean economy. To appraise the potentialities of broader measures, it is necessary to investigate the causes of the fluctuations and the form in which they manifest themselves in the Salvadorean economy.

Although economic fluctuations may have diverse origins, historical evidence shows that in El Salvador they have usually been connected with conditions in the coffee industry. The state of the coffee business, in turn, has been governed predominantly by fluctuations in the world market, although crop conditions also may be important. The ups and downs experienced by the price of coffee in New York are shown in Table 56. They indicate a cyclical peak of 26.17 cents per pound in 1925, a low of 9.63 in 1932 and 1933, another peak of 11.20 in 1937, a low of 7.62 in

TABLE 56

AVERAGE ANNUAL SALVADOREAN WASHED HIGH-GROWN COFFEE PRICES
IN NEW YORK, 1913–1948[a]

*(Based on green coffee spot prices)*

| | U.S. cents per pound | | U.S. cents per pound | | U.S. cents per pound |
|---|---|---|---|---|---|
| 1913 | 15.25 | 1925 | 26.17 | 1937 | 11.20 |
| 1914 | 14.38 | 1926 | 24.84 | 1938 | 9.51 |
| 1915 | 11.84 | 1927 | 22.73 | 1939 | 9.22 |
| 1916 | 12.13 | 1928 | 23.71 | 1940 | 7.62 |
| 1917 | 11.34 | 1929 | 20.78 | 1941 | 14.57 |
| 1918 | 13.58 | 1930 | 14.29 | 1942[b] | 15.50 |
| 1919 | 25.43 | 1931 | 12.58 | 1943[b] | 15.50 |
| 1920 | 18.24 | 1932 | 9.63 | 1944[b] | 15.50 |
| 1921 | 12.70 | 1933 | 9.63 | 1945[b] | 15.50 |
| 1922 | 15.32 | 1934 | 12.33 | 1946 | 21.28 |
| 1923 | 15.25 | 1935 | 8.78 | 1947 | 29.86 |
| 1924 | 23.52 | 1936 | 9.66 | 1948 | 32.17 |

[a] Source: Pan-American Coffee Bureau.
[b] OPA ceiling prices 1942 through 1945.

1940, and a third cyclical peak of 32.17 in 1948.[1] In these figures is summarized, in brief form, the recent history of the Salvadorean economy.

The fact that cyclical developments in El Salvador are so strongly influenced by coffee prices is explained by the predominance of coffee in the economy, and particularly by the high proportion of exports represented by coffee. El Salvador's is an "export economy," and although it differs in important points from those of many other Latin American countries, which also are export economies, its processes of expansion and contraction are typical of all such economies.

In broadest terms, the typical pattern of the Salvadorean economic cycle may be summarized as follows: When demand in world markets rises, the price and total value of coffee exports go up. Higher profits and wages in the coffee industry are translated into greater domestic demand. The rise in the money sup-

[1] These quotations are yearly averages.

ply that results from the active turn in the balance of payments, together with the growing volume of credit, intensifies the domestic expansion. Government revenues increase, the value of real estate and other assets rises, and speculation contributes further to the general increase. The turn comes when the world market begins to contract. The value of exports then falls off, the balance of payments turns passive, the money supply shrinks, prices, wages, and profits go down, government revenues shrink, and unemployment may set in, until world demand once more increases.

The basic features of this process El Salvador has in common with other export economies, but there are some important differences that make El Salvador less vulnerable to economic fluctuations than many other countries. In the first place, Salvadorean coffee enjoys a market in the United States — the main customer country — unaffected by tariff restrictions or local competition, since coffee is not grown there. Furthermore, because of its superior quality Salvadorean coffee enjoys a competitive advantage over Brazilian coffee, which constitutes the bulk of United States imports. Even under very unfavorable conditions, therefore, El Salvador may expect to maintain the volume of its exports at a fair level, with prices at a premium above ordinary grades, without fear of being excluded from its chief market by tariff or other restrictions.

A second set of circumstances, relating to the domestic aspects of the coffee industry, helps to mitigate the impact of a depression, particularly as it affects the labor force. Most important is the fact that the preservation of the productivity of the coffee plantations calls for a certain amount of maintenance work each year, regardless of whether or not the prevailing price of coffee covers the costs. While this requirement makes it more difficult to bring about the restriction of output needed to restore prices, which El Salvador could not undertake alone in any case, it helps to stem the rise in unemployment among coffee workers. In addition, that part of the labor force which does not find employment can withdraw, to some extent, into the nonmonetary subsistence sector of the economy and can "sit out" the depression without extreme hardship, although this opportunity is not open to all workers. The important fact is that even in very bad times El Salvador will not have a large unemployed industrial population in need of public assistance.

Salvadorean imports in time of depression are capable of considerable contraction without great hardship. The country produces most of its basic foodstuffs, and a considerable proportion of its imports therefore consist of durable, semidurable, and luxury goods, the purchase of which can be postponed for some time or foregone altogether. If a wise monetary and fiscal policy is followed, the country is therefore unlikely to see itself confronted with an urgent demand for imports in excess of foreign exchange availabilities.

The nature of the present banking system, consisting of a small number of conservatively managed banks, also helps to avoid extreme fluctuations. The banking system has in general refrained from expanding its credits in proportion to the very sizable increase in its reserves that normally takes place during an upswing. This has held down speculation and curbed the intensity of the boom, and has helped to avoid extreme credit contraction during the downswing. The maintenance of large reserves in relation to the money supply has also helped to avoid exchange difficulties at such times.

The absence of exchange control likewise contributes to stability. During the upswing, it permits capital to flow out of the country and thus mitigates the rise in the prices of real estate and other forms of investment. During the downswing, the funds held abroad serve as an additional reserve for the economy to draw upon. Furthermore, the absence of exchange controls has helped to avoid that sharp expansion of imports during periods of easy availability of exchange which is a common phenomenon in countries operating under exchange control. It must be added that in other countries the absence of exchange control does not always have these favorable consequences, and frequently in fact has had the opposite results. In El Salvador, however, it seems fair to say that, so far as the effect upon cyclical fluctuations is concerned, the absence of exchange control has had beneficial results.

The foregoing factors all help to mitigate in some measure the instability that normally is a characteristic of an export economy, and they may be counted upon to reduce the amplitude of the fluctuations to which El Salvador might be subjected by changing world market conditions. There is one point in the domestic economy, however, where international fluctuations are likely to be reflected with considerable force — in the budget. The revenues of the government have proved quite sensitive to fluctuations in the national income, as was indicated in Chapter IX. This sensitivity probably was abnormally high during the immediate postwar period, owing to the very heavy imports during that period and the consequent abnormal increase in customs receipts. But granting that during some future economic cycle government revenues may fluctuate less sharply in response to a given national income change, the fact remains that during the present cycle there has been a considerable rise in revenues that may confront the government with a serious problem. In the event of a decline in national income, there is likely to be a severe drop in government revenues. The government will then have to devote a good deal of its effort to the task of avoiding a deficit of disastrous proportions by cutting all possible expenditures. To that extent, the scope for fiscal operations to relieve the crisis — through public works expenditures, surplus crop purchases, and credit expansion — will be curtailed. The finances of the government, instead of becoming the primary instrument for compensatory action, may prove to be the main center of difficulties.

## 2. Objectives for Salvadorean Anticyclical Policy

The discussion so far has dealt with the factors that are likely to shape the course of economic fluctuations in El Salvador. It now turns to a brief survey of some of the specific aims that may prove important for Salvadorean compensatory policy, and some of the measures that may be adopted to achieve them. Needless to say, the range of action open to the government goes far beyond the fiscal field. In fact, measures relating to international commercial policy, labor policy, and agricultural policy may under certain circumstances prove more feasible and also more effective than fiscal action. In this study, however, it will be

necessary to limit the discussion to the fiscal and the closely related monetary fields.

Interest in anticyclical policy has centered chiefly upon the
problems of the depression, although in recent years anti-inflation action also has received a good deal of attention. After a
number of years of rising income and prices in El Salvador, it
is possible that future anticyclical action will have to be directed not against further inflation, but against a contraction.
Nevertheless, since the character of a depression is to some extent determined by events during the preceding boom, and since
soundly conceived antidepression policy must start with measures taken during the boom, the problems of the inflation phase
need to be considered first.

The aim of anticyclical policy during times of rising prices and
incomes is twofold. The first and immediate objective is to minimize the hardships that inflation tends to create for some sections of the population, the second is to forestall so far as possible
the spread of maladjustments that would aggravate a subsequent depression. The first is a short-run objective, the second a
longer-run one. These two objectives, however, are not in conflict with each other; on the contrary, they both call for action
designed to restrain expansionary forces. The keynote of anticyclical fiscal policy during the boom must therefore be restraint
of budgetary and credit expansion.

The execution of such a policy will inevitably encounter numerous objections from business and political circles. Despite
the often prohibitive cost of public works during periods of inflation, it will be argued that the country needs many projects so
badly that delay is impossible. It will also be said that unless
public and private projects are carried out when the money is
easily available they will never be undertaken at all. Finally, the
economic authorities will be reminded that a government elected
for only a limited period cannot well afford politically to restrict
its expenditures and to leave large accumulated reserves to be
spent by its successor. None of these objections is altogether
without merit, but the fact remains that expansion of public and
private expenditures under conditions of full employment yields
relatively little in terms of additional investment, and does

aggravate in a dangerous fashion first the boom and later the depression. There can be little doubt that despite these objections economic logic favors restraint in public expenditure and private credit expansion during a boom.

The techniques for exerting monetary and fiscal restraint are familiar. They center, in the monetary field, in bank credit restriction; and in the fiscal field, in the reduction of government expenditures, the repayment of internal debt, the acceleration of external debt payments, the immediate execution of governmental purchases abroad that would otherwise have to be made at a later period, or the accumulation of a surplus in the Treasury. The most important aspect of a sound fiscal and monetary policy during a boom is the control of bank credit expansion, both to business and to the government. During such a period, the money supply tends to increase in any case, as a result of rising exports and an active balance of payments. If upon this monetary expansion of external origin there is superimposed an additional expansion of internal origin, the monetary system becomes highly vulnerable to the effects of an adverse balance of payments. For when the downswing sets in and the balance of payments turns passive, the means of payment of external origin, as well as those of internal origin, will convert themselves into demand for foreign exchange. This double demand may lead to an exhaustion of the reserves accumulated during the upswing. Even if credit expansion has been moderate, and therefore does not threaten the exhaustion of reserves, it has at least the effect of reducing the margin of safety within which the monetary and fiscal authorities can extend aid to the economy in the depression.

The nature and amount of this aid constitute, of course, the key question of all anticyclical policy. Generalization, however, is obviously impossible. According to the circumstances of the moment, anticyclical operations may have to be geared to aid producers unable to cover their costs, to support unemployed workers, or perhaps to relieve mortgage debtors in danger of losing their properties. Moreover, the range of possible measures obviously is not confined to credit expansion or government expenditures.

The Salvadorean economy, as pointed out in the beginning of this chapter, is probably better equipped to resist depressions than most other export economies. It is quite conceivable that the center of difficulties during a depression may be found, not in the private sector of the economy, but precisely in the state of the public finances. The government's main effort may have to be directed, not toward aiding the economy, but toward preserving the soundness of the monetary and fiscal structure. Unless this structure is adequately safeguarded, an attempt at aiding the economy through anticyclical expenditures carries with it the risk of serious fiscal and monetary disturbances.

In the depression phase there consequently exists a conflict between the short-run aim of alleviating economic pressures and the longer-run aim of maintaining the soundness of the fiscal and monetary structure. In this the situation differs from the inflation phase, when long-run and short-run objectives both counsel the same policy. Hence, in contrast to the inflation phase, no over-all policy guide exists in the depression, except perhaps the need to be on guard against pressures favoring an expansionary policy such as usually make themselves felt at such time, at the expense of long-term considerations.

### 3. Legislation for Anticyclical Policy

It may be suggested that anticyclical policy would be less exposed to short-run pressures from any side if its major principles were made part of the legislation that governs the planning, execution, and control of the budget. It is conceivable, for instance, that some general guidance for policy could be embodied in this legislation after the manner of a central bank law, which usually contains some policy guidance in the form of a limit upon credit expansion in relation to reserves. An analogous procedure for the budget law would certainly be feasible so far as the cyclical upswing is concerned, because during that period both short and long-term considerations point toward the same policy of monetary and fiscal restraint.

It might be stipulated, for instance, that, when prices or the money supply are rising at more than a certain rate, the government be required to avoid borrowing from the banking system, or perhaps to accelerate repayment of debt, or even to limit public works. Such provisions, if observed, would greatly fortify the economy against any contraction it might have to face. To increase the prospect that the rules would be observed, it would probably be advisable to include them in the national constitution, where a good part of the budgetary legislation of El Salvador is already anchored. It is true that no amount of legislation can guarantee adherence to correct principles. The principles here suggested, however, have at least the virtue of being in accord with economic logic, even though they may not be in accord with the frailties of human psychology.

For a policy to be followed during the downswing, on the other hand, it would be extremely difficult to set up any general guidance to be included in the law, owing to the conflict between short-run and long-run objectives. Any rules that were established not only would run the risk of proving inappropriate to the situation, but would also be in very great danger of being swept aside by the pressure of events.

# CHAPTER XII

## THE BUDGET AND THE CURRENCY

THE EFFECT OF GOVERNMENT finances upon the soundness of the currency is in most countries perhaps the most frequently discussed nonfiscal aspect of the budget. Government deficits probably have been responsible for more monetary disturbances throughout the world than any other factor; hence the cry of the hard-pressed central banker: "Give me sound finances and I will give you sound money." It is, therefore, particularly gratifying that in El Salvador there is little of importance to be said on this particular subject.

It is true that in earlier years the country had its share of fiscally induced monetary troubles. Since 1932, however, and particularly since the creation of the Central Reserve Bank in 1934, the budget has had very little influence upon the volume of money. The net effect of the budget upon the money supply has, if anything, been in the direction of contraction. Largely as a result of this restraint on the part of the government in "normal" years, as well as of a similar conservatism on the part of the Central Reserve Bank, the Salvadorean colón since 1934 has presented the spectacle, unusual in Latin America, of a currency not only completely stable in terms of gold, but also completely free from controls.

The observer is forced to ask himself what the benefits to El Salvador have been from the preservation of the stability and freedom of her foreign exchange market. This question will be discussed in the latter part of the chapter. First, however, the contribution of government finance to the money supply, modest as it was, will be traced.

### 1. FISCAL OPERATIONS AND THE MONEY SUPPLY

In order to show in proper perspective the impact of government finance upon the money supply, the three sources from which the money supply originates, in El Salvador as elsewhere, are set forth in Table 57. These three sources are, of course, (1) the balance of payments, whence is derived the "money of external origin"; (2) government financing, in the form of Treasury coin issues and borrowing from the banking system; and (3) business financing — the two last-named factors producing the "money of internal origin." To arrive at the net money supply in the hands of the public and government it is necessary to deduct from the aggregate means of payment created the amount that is neutralized in the banking system. The neutralizing factors are (1) the public's deposits, and other claims upon banks, in foreign currency; (2) the public's time and savings deposits, and (3) the capital and other nonmonetary liability accounts of the banking system. If money supply is defined as consisting only of money in the hands of the public, excluding money in the hands of the government, as is, for instance, the practice of the International Monetary Fund, then the government's deposits, too, must be regarded as a neutralizing factor. It may be said at once, however, that in the light of Salvadorean fiscal practice, the rise and fall of Treasury deposits cannot be regarded as results of deliberate monetary policy; the exclusion of Treasury deposits from the money-supply figures therefore does not appear altogether warranted.

This method of presentation makes immediately apparent the *gross* contributions made to the money supply by, respectively, the foreign trade sector, the government, and domestic business. It is not possible, of course, either practically or even conceptually, to define the *net* contribution of any one factor, since amounts neutralized can only be deducted from the aggregate of the means of payment created, and cannot be allocated to any single one of the three money-creating factors.

The impact of government finance upon the money supply has three main aspects: (1) the direct issuance of subsidiary currency by the government; (2) the various forms of financing of the government by the banking system; and (3) the movement in the government's balance in the Central Reserve Bank. As for the direct issues of subsidiary currency, only an approximation of the amount of coins in circulation is available for the

## TABLE 57

### SOURCES OF MONEY SUPPLY
#### (In millions of colones)

| End of | Creation of Means of Payment | | | | | | Neutralization of Means of Payment | | | | Total money supply (total "creation" less total "neutralization") |
|---|---|---|---|---|---|---|---|---|---|---|---|
| | Financing of government | | | | Financing of business[c] | Total | Deposit and other liabilities in foreign currency in banks | Time and savings deposits in banks | Banks' capital, reserves, and other nonmonetary accounts | Total | |
| | Balance of payments[a] | Treasury coin issues | Fiscal and nonfiscal borrowing[b] | Total | | | | | | | |
| 1934 | 15.0 | 3.9 | 9.8 | 13.7 | 21.4 | 50.1 | 3.8 | 0.7 | 21.5 | 26.0 | 24.1 |
| 1935 | 17.2 | 3.3 | 8.4 | 11.7 | 23.7 | 52.6 | 4.8 | 0.8 | 23.3 | 28.9 | 23.7 |
| 1936 | 16.2 | 3.3 | 8.0 | 11.3 | 25.5 | 53.0 | 3.7 | 1.1 | 23.1 | 27.9 | 25.1 |
| 1937 | 17.8 | 3.3 | 6.7 | 10.0 | 29.5 | 57.3 | 4.0 | 1.2 | 25.6 | 30.8 | 26.5 |
| 1938 | 18.7 | 3.3 | 6.0 | 9.3 | 27.6 | 55.6 | 2.5 | 1.5 | 26.5 | 30.5 | 25.1 |
| 1939 | 19.3 | 3.3 | 5.3 | 9.6 | 31.1 | 59.0 | 2.8 | 1.4 | 28.8 | 33.0 | 26.0 |
| 1940 | 18.7 | 3.3 | 6.2 | 9.5 | 33.0 | 61.2 | 6.4 | 1.2 | 31.5 | 39.1 | 22.1 |
| 1941 | 22.4 | 3.3 | 5.3 | 8.6 | 35.6 | 66.6 | 3.5 | 1.8 | 32.0 | 37.3 | 29.3 |
| 1942 | 44.0 | 1.6 | 5.5 | 7.1 | 39.4 | 90.5 | 9.1 | 4.8 | 33.2 | 47.1 | 43.4 |
| 1943 | 64.0 | 3.0 | 5.2 | 8.2 | 45.2 | 117.4 | 14.8 | 2.6 | 36.8 | 54.2 | 63.2 |
| 1944 | 70.7 | 4.5 | 4.4 | 8.9 | 48.1 | 127.7 | 15.7 | 1.3 | 38.0 | 55.0 | 72.7 |
| 1945 | 78.9 | 5.0 | 2.4 | 7.4 | 52.8 | 139.1 | 13.1 | 0.8 | 38.6 | 52.5 | 86.6 |
| 1946 | 79.8 | 5.0 | 1.5 | 6.5 | 67.8 | 154.1 | 18.1 | 0.9 | 45.5 | 64.5 | 89.6 |
| 1947 | 79.1 | 5.0 | 1.1 | 6.1 | 82.9 | 168.1 | 18.9 | 1.9 | 51.8 | 72.6 | 95.5 |
| 1948[d] | 92.6 | 5.1 | 0.9 | 6.0 | 64.4 | 163.0 | 18.9 | 1.3 | 45.3 | 65.5 | 97.5 |

[a] Gross gold, foreign exchange, and the banks' holdings of the government's External Debt Bonds (1922 Loan).

[b] A detailed breakdown of these government liabilities to the banking system is presented in Table 58.

[c] Consists of loans to the public, the central bank's loans to banks, holdings of the cédulas of the Mortgage Bank, portfolio investments, and various other nonmonetary assets of the banks.

[d] End of June, 1948.

period prior to 1943. Considerable hoarding of old silver coins occurred at various times, and other minor disturbances beyond the control of the government took place, all of which leave the amount actually in circulation prior to 1943 rather uncertain. For the rest of the period, the amounts of copper, nickel, and silver coin issued by the government are entered in the table, but they probably do not account for the full amount of coins in circulation. In any case, the government never made subsidiary issues for the purpose of benefiting from the seigniorage profit, and the issues that occurred are therefore of a nonfiscal character.

The government's liabilities to the banking system, as shown in Table 58, represent only in small part direct borrowings by the government from the banks (fiscal liabilities). By far the greater part represents contingent liabilities or other obligations that did not involve the financing of government expenditures; this part is summarized under the title of nonfiscal liabilities. A third type of obligation, which has no internal monetary significance whatever, is represented by the banks' holdings of external bonds purchased abroad with United States dollars; these are included, as far as data are available, in Table 57, among the external sources of money creation, since they are the equivalent of foreign exchange.

The fiscal obligations, representing short-term borrowings from the Central Reserve Bank as well as from the commercial banks, reached a high of 2.3 million colones in 1943 but have stood at zero from 1945 onward. The nonfiscal obligations, exclusive of the external bonds which have no significance for the money supply, reached a high of 8.1 million colones in 1934, and have since declined, with some fluctuations, to a level of 5.2 million in June 1948. They consist of various heterogeneous components. The government-guaranteed bonds held by the Central Reserve Bank, which together with unspecified but probably minor holdings of external bonds reached a maximum of 4.4 million colones in 1947, are *cédulas* of the Mortgage Bank that by law carry a government guarantee. Their purchase by the Central Reserve Bank constituted aid to the banking system, i.e., business financing, not aid to the government. The *Cuenta Espe-*

## TABLE 58

### LIABILITIES OF THE GOVERNMENT TO THE BANKING SYSTEM

*(In millions of colones)*

| End of | Fiscal[a] | | | Nonfiscal | | | | | | |
|---|---|---|---|---|---|---|---|---|---|---|
| | | | | | Central bank | | | | | |
| | Commercial banks | Central bank | Total | Commercial banks[b] | Government guaranteed bonds | 4% government bonds | Cuenta Especial Depositaria[c] | Total | Total | Total Fiscal and Nonfiscal |
| 1934 | 1.4 | 0.3 | 1.7 | 0.6 | ... | 0.5 | 7.6 | 8.1 | 8.7 | 10.4 |
| 1935 | 1.4 | ... | 1.4 | 0.6 | ... | 0.5 | 6.5 | 7.0 | 7.6 | 9.0 |
| 1936 | 1.4 | ... | 1.4 | 0.6 | ... | 0.5 | 6.1 | 6.6 | 7.2 | 8.6 |
| 1937 | 0.8 | ... | 0.8 | 0.6 | ... | 0.5 | 5.4 | 5.9 | 6.5 | 7.3 |
| 1938 | 0.5 | ... | 0.5 | 0.7 | ... | 0.5 | 5.0 | 5.5 | 6.2 | 6.7 |
| 1939 | 0.3 | ... | 0.3 | 0.8 | ... | 0.5 | 4.5 | 5.0 | 5.8 | 6.1 |
| 1940 | 0.5 | 1.3 | 1.8 | 0.8 | 1.1 | 0.5 | 3.9 | 5.5 | 6.3 | 8.1 |
| 1941 | ... | 1.3 | 1.3 | 0.8 | 1.6 | 0.5 | 3.7 | 5.8 | 6.6 | 7.9 |
| 1942 | 0.8 | 1.3 | 2.1 | 0.6 | 2.2 | 0.5 | 2.9 | 5.6 | 6.2 | 8.3 |
| 1943 | 1.0 | 1.3 | 2.3 | 0.6 | 2.5 | 0.5 | 2.4 | 5.4 | 6.0 | 8.3 |
| 1944 | 0.9 | 1.0 | 1.9 | 0.6 | 2.5 | 0.5 | 2.0 | 5.0 | 5.6 | 7.5 |
| 1945 | ... | ... | ... | 0.7 | 3.9 | 0.5 | 1.9 | 6.3 | 7.0 | 7.0 |
| 1946 | ... | ... | ... | 0.8 | 3.9 | ... | 1.5 | 5.4 | 6.2 | 6.2 |
| 1947 | ... | ... | ... | 1.1 | 4.4 | ... | 1.1 | 5.5 | 6.6 | 6.6 |
| June 1948 | ... | ... | ... | 1.1 | 4.3 | ... | 0.9 | 5.2 | 6.3 | 6.3 |

a Various short and longer-term loans.

b The holdings of the government's External Debt Bonds (1922 Loan) have been included, as far as data are available, among the banks' gross international assets in the computation of the sources of the money supply (Table 57).

c Consists of frozen credits which the Central Reserve Bank had to take over when it was created; see page 215.

*cial Depositaria* (Special Deposit Account), which started out at
8.4 million colones in July 1934 and has since been gradually reduced, represents private long-term credits, mostly secured by
mortgages, that the Central Reserve Bank had to take over when
it was created and for which the government gave a guarantee.
The reduction of this account to 900,000 colones in June 1948
took place through collection of credits and, to a lesser extent,
through transfers of sound credits to the Mortgage Bank. This,
too, represented a change in private credit rather than in government borrowing. The 4 per cent bonds were issued to compensate
the Central Reserve Bank for its assumption of liabilities at the
time it was established. In sum, it is evident that the totals that
the government has had to borrow from the banks at various
times to cover its own financial needs have been small. If, moreover, the aggregate trend of fiscal and nonfiscal government obligations in the hands of the banks is considered, these liabilities
are seen to have declined since 1934.

The cash balance of the government, i.e., the deposits of the
government in the Central Reserve Bank as of the end of each
calendar year, shown in Table 59, has fluctuated widely; from a
low of 700,000 in 1940 it rose to a high of 10.1 million at the end
of 1947. This sizable increase was the result of the rapid growth
of revenues in recent years, a process that almost inevitably
causes funds to accumulate as they pass through the Treasury.
The increase is reflected in the surplus of recent budgets on a
*cash basis*, as contrasted with the *accounting* surpluses and deficits
realized.

A rise in government balances means, of course, that the
money supply in the hands of the private sector of the economy
is correspondingly smaller than it would be otherwise. One is not
justified, however, in ascribing a positive deflationary significance to such increases in government deposits if simultaneously
there is a similar increase in the money supply held by the private sector, such as actually took place, since in that case the
rise in government balances merely constitutes a reflection of
the general inflationary process. To be considered a positive deflationary factor, government balances would have to increase
more than the money supply in the hands of the private sector.

## TABLE 59

### TREASURY AND PRIVATE BALANCES COMPARED WITH INDEXES OF CIRCULATORY REQUIREMENTS

| Period | Private Sector | | | | Government Sector | | | | | |
| --- | --- | --- | --- | --- | --- | --- | --- | --- | --- | --- |
| | Money supply exclusive of government deposits[a] | | Annual value of checks cleared[b] | | Gross national product[c] | | Value of government deposits in central banks[d] | | Total government expenditures[e] | |
| | Millions of colones | Index (1942 = 100) | Millions of colones | Index (1942 = 100) | Millions of colones | Index (1942 = 100) | Millions of colones | Index (1942 = 100) | Millions of colones | Index (1942 = 100) |
| 1934 | 23.3 | 57 | 16.6[f] | ... | ...[g] | ...[g] | 0.8 | 31 | 18.8 | 86 |
| 1935 | 21.2 | 52 | 38.4 | 53 | ...[g] | ...[g] | 2.5 | 96 | 20.8 | 95 |
| 1936 | 24.3 | 60 | 43.6 | 60 | ...[g] | ...[g] | 0.8 | 31 | 22.3 | 102 |
| 1937 | 23.9 | 59 | 58.5 | 81 | ...[g] | ...[g] | 2.6 | 100 | 22.2 | 102 |
| 1938 | 22.9 | 56 | 51.9 | 72 | ...[g] | ...[g] | 2.2 | 85 | 21.1 | 97 |
| 1939 | 23.2 | 57 | 56.2 | 78 | 229 | 87 | 2.8 | 108 | 20.5 | 94 |
| 1940 | 21.4 | 52 | 52.2 | 72 | 213 | 81 | 0.7 | 27 | 22.2 | 102 |
| 1941 | 28.3 | 69 | 60.0 | 83 | 216 | 82 | 1.0 | 38 | 21.4 | 98 |
| 1942 | 40.8 | 100 | 72.5 | 100 | 263 | 100 | 2.6 | 100 | 21.8 | 100 |
| 1943 | 60.5 | 148 | 95.7 | 132 | 334 | 127 | 2.7 | 104 | 23.3 | 107 |
| 1944 | 69.0 | 169 | 93.0 | 128 | 350 | 133 | 3.7 | 142 | 25.2 | 116 |
| 1945 | 81.7 | 200 | 98.5 | 136 | 379 | 144 | 4.9 | 188 | 29.1 | 133 |
| 1946 | 81.1 | 199 | 142.0 | 196 | 412 | 157 | 8.5 | 327 | 45.0 | 206 |
| 1947 | 85.4 | 209 | 205.6 | 284 | ...[g] | ...[g] | 10.1 | 388 | 51.8 | 238 |
| 1948[h] | 86.6 | 212 | ...[g] | ...[g] | ...[g] | ...[g] | 10.9 | 419 | ...[g] | |

[a] Coin and currency in hands of public plus sight deposits subject to check in all banks at the *end* of the calendar year.
[b] Clearings of the Oficina de Compensación, as reported in the *Revista Mensual* of the Central Reserve Bank of El Salvador.
[c] Estimated gross national product of private sector at current prices, as computed in Appendix B.
[d] Government sight deposits in the Central Reserve Bank of El Salvador at the *end* of the calendar year.
[e] Liquidated budget, as reported by the Court of Accounts. For years prior to fiscal accounting on a calendar year basis, expenditures have been prorated on a calendar year basis for purposes of comparison.   [f] Half year.   [g] Not available.   [h] June.

The increase in government deposits and private balances, respectively, might be measured and compared either in simple percentage terms or in terms of their relative adequacy for meeting the circulatory requirements that they served. Whether the existing circulating medium is adequate is indicated, of course, by the volume of transactions and by the level of prices — in other words, by the amount of money work to be done. The money work to be done by government balances may be measured, very roughly, by the annual total of government expenditures; and that to be done by the private money supply, by total check clearings or even by the level of the gross national product of the private sector.

From the inspection of these data in Table 59 it appears that there was no significant difference in the increase of the private money supply and of government deposits, respectively, in percentage terms from the late thirties to 1947–48. Both approximately quadrupled, although government deposits fluctuated rather erratically. Measured against the increase in the amount of money work to be done by each, the increase on the whole appears to have been slightly greater in the private sector than in the governmental. If, however, money work in the private sector is measured by the gross national product of that sector, the opposite impression is obtained. In sum, it may be said, therefore, that the growth in government balances, remarkable as it was, did not constitute a significant net deflationary force.

One further thread relating fiscal action with the money supply deserves to be traced, even though it leads to no evidence of direct influence. This is the contribution that the government made annually to the capital funds of the Mortgage Bank. The government devoted to this purpose part of the revenues from the coffee export tax. Assuming that even without such an annual contribution the government would have continued to levy the tax and would have spent the proceeds on something else, one must conclude that there was no direct monetary effect — the money would have gone into circulation in any case, either through the Mortgage Bank's lending or through government expenditure. If the alternative to the annual contribution had been a reduction in the coffee tax, part of the additional income

to coffee growers might have remained abroad, through nonre-
patriation of profits, in which case the money supply would have
been correspondingly lower.

Indirectly, the government's contributions to the capital funds
of the Mortgage Bank may have led to an increase in the money
supply, because the bank, thus strengthened, was able to increase
its loan operations more than in proportion to the increase in
capital, on the basis of the deposits that it received from the
public.

Further indirect effects of fiscal action upon the money supply
can be traced in the government's payments abroad and in its
tariff and import quota policy. Though undertaken for other
reasons, these actions may have monetary repercussions because
of their influence upon the balance of payments, but it is not
possible here to attempt their quantitative analysis.

## 2. Economic Effects of the Government's Monetary Neutrality

The investigation of the various channels through which the
government has influenced the money supply shows that on the
whole the government has exerted a major influence in the direction neither of expansion nor of contraction. It has, in fact, been
neutral. This conservative policy has been facilitated, of course,
by the absence of extreme deflationary pressures during the
period. The government's restraint, coupled with the conservative policy of the Central Reserve Bank, has in turn made possible the adherence to orthodox and quasi-gold-standard principles in the field of foreign exchange — stability and freedom
from exchange control.

The foregoing statement must be qualified by adding that, in
one respect, orthodox exchange policies were facilitated by a
distinctly unorthodox fiscal action — the default upon the foreign debt in 1932 and again in 1937. The elimination of these
payments relieved the balance of payments and helped to maintain free and stable exchanges. Whether in the long run the
damage resulting from the loss of confidence on the part of the
foreign, and also the domestic, investor has not been much

greater than the advantages gained is hard to assess. In every other respect, however, the exchange policies pursued were highly orthodox. What then have been the rewards of exchange stability and absence of exchange control?

Free and stable exchanges, according to common belief, help to increase the volume and efficiency of foreign trade, favor the accumulation of savings, encourage investment, and attract foreign capital. Some of these benefits can be clearly traced in El Salvador. There can be no doubt that the absence of exchange restrictions has been a great convenience to merchants, travelers, and investors. Furthermore, the absence of controls has given El Salvador the status of a "preferred market" among American exporters. This made it easier for Salvadorean importers to obtain merchandise during and after the war, when American traders gave preference to their best customers in the allocation of scarce supplies. The windfall profits that frequently accrue to importers under an exchange control regime at the expense of the consumer were probably absent in El Salvador, although importers' profit margins on the whole do not seem to have been conspicuously lower than elsewhere.

All this represents undeniable gains, but they are not gains of the first order. These one would expect to find in the form of the more rapid development of the economy, particularly along industrial lines. There is little evidence, however, that development in El Salvador has derived an unusual stimulus from orthodox exchange policies. The country has progressed, and new industries continue to be created and old ones to expand, but the rate of advancement has not been spectacularly different from that experienced by countries where exchange instability or exchange control, or both, have prevailed. Savings in El Salvador no doubt have been substantial during times of high coffee prices, but a good part have found their way to the United States as the balance of payments presented in Chapter II shows, instead of being invested locally. Foreign capital has entered only in very limited amounts. In sum, the gains from monetary orthodoxy do not seem to have been very striking.

Up to a certain point, the relatively modest character of the rate of development is the result of a conservatism which perhaps has gone beyond what may be regarded as "orthodoxy." It would have been possible to engage in some financing of public works for limited amounts through the use of the public credit, and it would likewise have been possible to expand somewhat the volume of long-term credit for purposes of private investment, without endangering the maintenance of free and stable exchanges. Nevertheless, it must be recognized that orthodox exchange policies do impose certain restrictions upon the means by which economic development expenditures may be financed.

The fact, on the other hand, that orthodox economic policies have produced no extraordinary results would not justify in any way the abandonment of these principles, for no kind of financial policy, whether liberal or conservative, could be expected to produce miracles. The forces that govern the rhythm of Salvadorean development spring from human and material factors that are much more fundamental than measures of fiscal or monetary policy. In a country where the supply of trained labor and managerial talent is limited and where the market is small, industrialization cannot be indefinitely accelerated. Since all nonagricultural labor normally is reasonably fully employed, there is frequently no outlet for all of the savings that the economy generates in times of high export prices. The potentialities for foreign capital, moreover, are further limited by the absence of readily exploitable mineral resources and of facilities for large-scale plantation operations, such as normally interest the foreign investor. Compared with these fundamental facts of economic life, monetary and fiscal policies in the short run can carry only minor weight.

The effectiveness of these policies may become greater, however, as time goes on and as these policies themselves become part of the economic facts of Salvadorean life. Confidence becomes more solidly established as the permanence of a conservative official attitude is demonstrated. The stimulating effects upon trade, saving, and investment then tend to become cumulative. In this sense the efforts and sacrifices at first required by a policy of conservatism must be regarded as a kind of investment that may be expected to bear increasing fruit with the passing of time, so long as conservative policy remains firmly established. The efforts of the past have thus given El Salvador a stake in the continuation of orthodox fiscal and monetary policies such as few other countries possess.

CHAPTER XIII

THE PUBLIC DEBT IN THE NATIONAL ECONOMY

THE PUBLIC DEBT and its management are of critical importance
in some countries for the stability and growth of the national
income, but in El Salvador the relatively small size of the public
debt has reduced its role to minor proportions. Only a short description will therefore be given of the history and present status
of the Salvadorean public debt operations, followed by a brief
analysis of three major economic aspects: the difficulty of tapping domestic savings; the avoidance of recourse to central bank
financing; and the small volume of government borrowing abroad
since the early twenties.

1. HISTORY AND PRESENT STATUS OF THE PUBLIC DEBT

On December 31, 1922, just prior to the Salvadorean government's most important borrowing operation, the internal debt
was 21.0 million colones, the largest until then, as contrasted
with an external debt of 13.3 million. Since 1923, when the securities authorized by the National Loan of 1922 were issued, the
internal debt has declined in importance and, as may be seen
from the data presented in Table 60, has in general been small
relative to the external debt.

The National Loan of 1922 authorized the issue of two series
of dollar bonds and one series of sterling bonds[1] for the purpose
of retiring certain foreign and internal indebtedness, financing
public works, and meeting subsidy payments due to the International Railways of Central America. There was pledged for the
service of this loan 70 per cent of the customs revenues, and the
Office of Fiscal Representative was created to see that the pledged

---

[1] The composition of the authorized loan was as follows: $6 million (U.S.) of
8 per cent Series "A" bonds, £1,050,000 of 6 per cent Series "B" bonds, and $10.5
million (U.S.) of 7 per cent Series "C" bonds.

TABLE 60

PUBLIC DEBT OUTSTANDING, 1910–1947

*(In thousands of colones)*

| Year Ended Dec. 31 | External | Internal | Total [a] |
|---|---|---|---|
| 1910 | 12,775.4 | 20,098.1 | 32,873.5 |
| 1911 | 18,807.0 | 14,211.3 | 33,018.3 |
| 1912 | 17,729.0 | 10,165.3 | 27,894.3 |
| 1913 | 16,648.8 | 11,165.5 | 27,814.3 |
| 1914 | 15,565.6 | 12,366.4 | 27,932.0 |
| 1915 | 15,002.6 | 12,557.7 | 27,560.3 |
| 1916 | 15,002.6 | 12,947.8 | 27,950.4 |
| 1917 | 15,581.0 | 12,924.3 | 28,505.3 |
| 1918 | 15,445.4 | 14,105.2 | 29,550.6 |
| 1919 | 12,292.6 | 13,588.6 | 25,881.2 |
| 1920 | 13,438.4 | 15,793.9 | 29,232.3 |
| 1921 | 13,296.8 | 20,271.4 | 33,568.2 |
| 1922 | 13,296.8 | 20,962.3 | 34,259.1 |
| 1923 | 35,122.5 | 12,156.6 | 47,279.1 |
| 1924 | 38,184.0 | 5,593.0 | 43,777.0 |
| 1925 | 37,261.2 | 10,965.8 | 48,227.0 |
| 1926 | 40,210.5 | 7,848.3 | 48,058.8 |
| 1927 | 43,046.8 | 5,453.2 | 48,500.0 |
| 1928 | 41,074.9 | 4,730.7 | 45,805.6 |
| 1929 | 38,987.7 | 3,733.2 | 42,720.9 |
| 1930 | 36,015.4 | 7,611.5 | 43,626.9 |
| 1931 | 34,786.6 | 11,941.1 | 46,727.7 |
| 1932 | 36,716.0 | 12,280.5 | 48,996.5 |
| 1933 | 37,136.7 | 9,797.4 | 46,934.1 |
| 1934 | 36,692.8 | 8,590.3 | 45,283.1 |
| 1935 | 37,313.4 | 5,813.6 | 43,127.0 |
| 1936 | 33,616.4 | 5,410.6 | 39,027.0 |
| 1937 [b] | 32,577.9 | 4,202.6 | 36,780.5 |
| 1938 | 33,203.5 | 3,511.5 | 36,715.0 |
| 1939 | 34,527.5 | 3,216.2 | 37,743.7 |
| 1940 | 35,813.6 | 5,610.0 | 41,423.6 |
| 1941 | 37,099.2 | 5,205.4 | 42,304.6 |
| 1942 | 34,745.2 | 7,439.7 | 42,184.9 |
| 1943 | 40,865.0 | 6,420.8 | 47,285.8 |
| 1944 | 42,204.3 | 1,591.2 | 43,795.5 |
| 1945 | 44,987.3 | 797.9 | 46,685.2 |
| 1946 | 39,140.4 | 1,559.6 | 40,700.0 |
| 1947 | 35,213.8 | 2,270.2 | 37,484.0 |

[a] Does not include lend-lease obligations to the United States, which amounted to 842,500 colones'
[b] November 30.

revenues were properly collected and were applied exclusively
to the debt service.

The interest rates of 6 to 8 per cent, which the loan contract
stipulated, constituted a heavy burden. In addition, as a result
of the great decline in world prices that occurred in the early
thirties, the burden of debt service in real terms increased appreciably. Interest payments on two series of bonds were suspended
in July 1932. As of May 5, 1933, interest was resumed for a time
under a temporary agreement, partly in cash and partly in 4
per cent deferred interest certificates,[2] but in July 1935 payments
on all three series of bonds were again suspended. Under the
Readjustment Agreement of April 27, 1936, the rates of interest
were permanently reduced, and annual service payments were
limited to $850,000.[3]

Payments were again suspended in January 1938, and were
not resumed until eight years later, when the Salvadorean government made its readjustment offer of June 27, 1946.[4] Under
the terms of this plan, which is still in effect, outstanding bonds
may be exchanged on a par for par basis for new bonds carrying
one half of the original interest rates, and the eight years of unpaid coupons may be exchanged at 50 per cent of face value for
new 3 per cent bonds and convertible certificates.[5] Total service
payments for the new bonds are to be limited to $800,000 annu-
ally; amounts remaining after interest are to be utilized for re-

[2] This readjusted interest payment applied only to Series "B" and "C" bonds.
Interest on Series "A" was paid in full. This temporary agreement was offered only
to those bondholders who deposited their bonds with the Bondholders Committee,
and only with respect to coupons due through January 1, 1935.

[3] Interest was reduced to 5½, 4, and 3½ per cent on Series "A," "B," and "C,"
respectively. After the payment of interest, 25 per cent of the balance of the service
funds was to be applied to the purchase (at not above 15 per cent of face value) of
the deferred interest certificates issued with respect to Series "C." The remainder
was to be transferred to a sinking fund to be used to purchase outstanding securities of all three series.

[4] The offer, which was made pursuant to Decree Law 296 of December 29, 1945,
as implemented by Executive Decree of April 26, 1946, was originally open to
January 1, 1949, but has since been extended to January 1, 1950.

[5] The convertible certificates may be exchanged for the new 3 per cent bonds
until July 1, 1950 (later extended to July 1, 1951). After that date, holders will be
entitled to a cash payment for their pro-rata portions of the proceeds (less expense)
from the public sale of the 3 per cent bonds underlying the certificates plus ma-
tured interest on these bonds.

tirement through purchases or drawings. Holders who accept
the offer agree to the annulment of the pledge of customs revenues and to the abolition of the Office of the Fiscal Representative. If, however, any future debt is secured by customs revenue,
these bonds are to share in such security with rights senior to
those of any other creditor.[6]

A detailed statement of the size and composition of the foreign
debt, as prepared by the Central Reserve Bank, which acts as
fiscal agent of the republic, is presented in Table 61. It will be
noted that on December 31, 1947, the total external debt was
the equivalent of 35.2 million colones,[7] a figure that is substantially below the total of 45.0 million on December 31, 1945, when
the accumulation of unpaid interest had raised the foreign debt
to the highest level in Salvadorean financial history. The internal debt, as of December 31, 1947, amounted to no more than
2.3 million colones, a relatively minor item compared with the
external debt, and far below the December 31, 1922 figure of
21.0 million. This amount consists mainly of transitory accounts
payable.

## 2. GENERAL ASPECTS OF PUBLIC DEBT OPERATIONS

Under the readjustment plan of 1946, the 2.4 million colones
of total service[8] on the external debt in 1946 amounted to 5.3
per cent of government expenditures, 3.7 per cent of exports,
and only 0.6 per cent of the gross national product, as shown in
Table 62. As these figures reveal, the service of the small past
public borrowing has probably not exerted important effects
upon the Salvadorean economy. However, the circumstances

---

[6] The offer also includes provisions for those bondholders who did not accept the
1933 and 1936 plans. Accumulated interest is to be paid as follows: $365 (U.S.)
for each $1,000 bond of Series "A"; £27 for each £100 bond of Series "B"; and
$213 (U.S.) for each $1,000 bond of Series "C."

[7] On December 31, 1947, the total dollar debt was $10.5 million (U.S.) and the
total sterling debt was £876,441.

[8] Service under the readjustment plan *per se* is 2 million colones while service on
the Export-Import Bank loan is 0.4 million. See Table 62, which shows what the
burden of external debt service would have been if the present contractual debt
service had been in effect during the forties. The internal debt is so small now (1947),
that the contractual obligation of 2.4 million colones with respect to the foreign
debt represents in effect the total debt service.

## TABLE 61

### DETAILED STATEMENT OF OUTSTANDING EXTERNAL DEBT, DECEMBER 31, 1947

| | Outstanding dollar debt[a] | Outstanding sterling debt | Total outstanding external debt in colón equivalent[b] |
|---|---|---|---|
| *National Loan of 1922 (bonds awaiting exchange)* | | | |
| Series "A": 5½% (formerly 8%) customs sinking fund gold loan, 1923... | 596,000.00 | | 1,490,000.00 |
| Series "B": 4% (formerly 6%) customs sterling loan, 1923... | | 117,050.00.00 | 1,182,205.00 |
| Series "C": 3½% (formerly 7%) customs gold loan, 1924... | 825,300.00 | | 2,063,250.00 |
| *Readjustment Plan of 1946* | | | |
| 4% external sinking fund dollar bonds... | 1,444,500.00 | | 3,611,250.00 |
| Interest past due... | 78,280.00 | | 195,700.00 |
| 3% external sinking fund sterling bonds... | | 708,280.00.00 | 7,153,628.00 |
| Interest past due... | | 19,510.16.11 | 197,059.54 |
| 3½% external sinking fund dollar bonds... | 4,078,300.00 | | 10,195,750.00 |
| Interest past due... | 132,536.25 | | 331,340.63 |
| 3% external sinking fund dollar bonds... | 1,611,500.00 | | 4,028,750.00 |
| Interest past due... | 52,243.08 | | 130,607.70 |
| Noninterest-bearing convertible certificates... | 26,464.00 | 1,431.12.00 | 80,619.16 |
| Interest due under Plans of 1933 and 1936: | | | |
| Series "A"... | 19,062.50 | | 47,656.25 |
| Series "B"... | | 2,076.12.00 | 20,973.66 |
| Series "C"... | 39,761.10 | | 99,402.75 |
| Interest due for eight years on bonds pending exchange: | | | |
| Series "A"... | 190,720.00 | | 476,800.00 |
| Series "B"... | | 28,092.00.00 | 283,729.20 |
| Series "C"... | 231,084.00 | | 577,710.00 |
| Certificates of deferred interest on Series "C"... | 16,398.11. | | 40,995.28 |
| *Export-Import Bank of Washington* | | | |
| 4% Inter-American Highway Bonds, 1941... | 317,094.35 | | 792,735.88 |
| 4% Public Works and Road Bonds, 1941... | 396,367.98 | | 990,919.94 |
| 4% Inter-American Highway Bonds, 1945... | 237,746.75 | | 594,366.80 |
| 4% Public Works and Road Bonds, 1945... | 251,332.27 | | 628,330.68 |
| Total Export-Import Bank... | 1,202,541.34 | | 3,006,353.38 |
| Total outstanding external debt... | 10,544,690.39 | 876,441.00.11 | 35,213,780.55 |

[a] Does not include lend-lease obligations to the United States, which amounted to $337,000 on December 31, 1947.
[b] Exchange rates: 2.50 colones per dollar; 10.10 colones per pound sterling.

TABLE 62

RELATION OF CONTRACTUAL EXTERNAL DEBT SERVICE TO SIGNIFICANT
ECONOMIC INDICATORS

(*Values in millions of colones*)

| Year | Contractual external debt service[a] | Gross national product | Relation of debt service to gross national product | Exports | Relation of debt service to exports | Government expenditures | Relation of debt service to government expenditures |
|---|---|---|---|---|---|---|---|
| 1940 | 2.4 | 229 | 1.1% | 30.6 | 7.8% | 22.3 | 10.8% |
| 1941 | 2.4 | 232 | 1.0% | 28.0 | 8.6% | 21.5 | 11.2% |
| 1942 | 2.4 | 279 | 0.9% | 46.2 | 5.2% | 22.1 | 10.9% |
| 1943 | 2.4 | 351 | 0.7% | 56.3 | 4.3% | 23.4 | 10.3% |
| 1944 | 2.4 | 367 | 0.7% | 57.5 | 4.2% | 25.2 | 9.5% |
| 1945 | 2.4 | 398 | 0.6% | 53.3 | 4.5% | 29.2 | 8.2% |
| 1946 | 2.4 | 435 | 0.6% | 65.4 | 3.7% | 45.0 | 5.3% |
| 1947 | 2.4 | ...[b] | ... | 100.2 | 2.4% | 51.9 | 4.6% |

[a] On the assumption that the present contractual external debt service was in effect throughout the forties. Debt service under the readjustment plan of 1946 is 2 million colones annually, while service on the Export-Import Bank loan is 0.4 million.
[b] Not available.

and policies that have kept the debt at such small proportions merit special comment. These are (1) the difficulty encountered in tapping domestic savings by borrowing in the internal capital market; (2) the avoidance of recourse to central bank financing: and (3) the virtual absence of government borrowing abroad since the early twenties.

## DIFFICULTY OF TAPPING DOMESTIC SAVINGS

It has been the policy of the government to finance public works not through borrowing, but out of taxes. This pay-as-you-go policy has kept down the burden of interest charges, but at the same time has limited the volume of public works that might have been undertaken during periods where inflation was not prevalent. Since such public works projects, if productive, increase the taxable capacity of the country, it is generally regarded as justifiable to finance part of their cost by borrowing from noninflationary sources, i.e., from domestic savers. The fact that the government has refrained from such financing has no doubt been determined in part by the absence of an adequate domestic capital market. The development of such a market would undoubtedly be of great benefit for the entire economy because it would permit more effective utilization of savings by both the government and the private sector.

### AVOIDANCE OF CENTRAL BANK BORROWING

The government has successfully avoided large-scale recourse to central bank financing of the kind that, as experience shows, may easily jeopardize stability of the currency. It has limited itself to modest seasonal borrowings authorized by the Budget Law and; in addition, to certain minor operations discussed in Chapter XII. It may be added, however, that purchases of government securities by central banks for the purpose of broadening the market are generally regarded as a justifiable practice. If undertaken in strictly limited amounts, on the bank's sole initiative and in the open market, such operations are normally innocuous so far as monetary stability is concerned.

### POSSIBILITIES OF BORROWING ABROAD

With the exception of small sums borrowed from the Export-Import Bank, the Salvadorean government has done no financing abroad since 1922. The lack of interest of American investors in Latin American securities would probably have precluded new borrowing in the private capital market if it had been attempted. However, since large-scale investment increases the need for imports, it is generally thought appropriate to finance part of the cost of these projects from external sources, if the projects themselves promise to improve the exchange position of the country. The country's very modest debt burden, with annual debt service in 1946 amounting, as already noted, to only 3.7 per cent of exports and 0.6 per cent of the gross national product, would allow it to assume some additional foreign indebtedness without fear of economic stress. This fact, plus the strength of the currency and the balanced state of the budget, should put the country in a favorable position if in the future it should desire to borrow from international or other foreign lending agencies.

PART THREE: APPENDICES

# APPENDIX A

## COMPOSITION OF ESTIMATES OF THE GROSS NATIONAL PRODUCT OF THE PRIVATE SECTOR OF THE ECONOMY, 1942 AND 1946

*(First appendix to Chapter II)*

THE FOLLOWING TECHNICAL DESCRIPTION and appended statistical data for estimating the gross product of the private sector of El Salvador for the years 1942 and 1946 are based on information furnished and computations made by a group of Salvadorean experts. The source of the data used, the methods of computation, and the resulting values for each item included in the estimates, as presented in Table 63, are discussed in detail below, the item numbers there given corresponding with those in Table 63.

*1. Agriculture.* (a) The computation of the value of the most important agricultural products is given in Tables 64 and 65. Production figures for these agricultural products were taken from data furnished by the Bureau of Statistics (*Dirección General de Estadística*). The prices of agricultural products reported by the central bank were used rather than those furnished by the Bureau of Statistics since the Salvadorean experts stated that they believed the former to be somewhat more accurate. The following prices were used for the valuation of agricultural production: (1) export prices for exports; (2) wholesale prices for rural consumption; (3) retail prices for urban consumption. The break-down between rural and urban consumption was estimated on the basis of rural and urban population components, which were approximated at 63 and 37 per cent, respectively, except as noted below. In the case of coffee consumption, it was assumed that 50 per cent was urban. In the case of sugar, it was believed that as much as 70 per cent was consumed in the towns. Both sugar loaf and unrefined brown sugar were considered to be entirely consumed in the rural areas.

(*b* and *c*) In addition to the major agricultural commodities, separate estimates were made for fruit and vegetable production as well as for "other agricultural products." Fruit and vegetable data were derived from consumption studies which indicated that daily per capita expenditures on these items amounted to three centavos in 1942 and four centavos in 1946. The value of "other agricultural products," which consisted of all other food-stuffs not covered in the other two agricultural categories, was estimated at 2 per cent of the combined agricultural production of the major agricultural products (*a*) plus fruits and vegetables (*b*).

(*d*) In order to correct for the under-reporting of agricultural production, an upward adjustment of 30 to 40 per cent in the case of corn, black beans, rice, and *maicillo* was estimated as approximately adequate. However, instead of making an adjustment of 30 per cent, which in 1942 would have amounted to 6,719,000 colones and in 1946 to 10,142,000 colones, it was decided to add 12 million colones to the total gross national product of the private sector in 1942 and 18 million colones in 1946. These adjustments were made to correct not only for under-reporting in agriculture but also for the omission of those small sectors of the economy that were not included in the general production estimates. Because it was felt that even these adjustments were quite moderate and did not fully correct for the under-reporting of agricultural production, no explicit deduction was made, in the estimates of *net* agricultural production, for the value of seed and foreign materials used in agricultural production or for the value of crops fed to cattle.[1]

2. *Poultry.* Production was estimated at 1,100,000 birds in

---

[1] A comprehensive statistical investigation by the Ministry of Agriculture disclosed that in 1948 — a year which can be considered "normal" — the production of corn amounted to 5,550,000 quintals, and that of *maicillo* to 3,598,000 quintals. Production figures of black beans (*frijoles*) and rice, as shown in statistics for earlier years, likewise proved to be distorted by under-reporting. Production of beans and rice in 1948 was 774,000 and 748,000 quintals, respectively. These figures show that the production data for earlier years were too small and indicate that the upward adjustments discussed above are justified. One quintal is equal to 101.41 pounds avoirdupois.

1942 and 1,200,000 in 1946, on the basis of average weekly poultry consumption.[2]

*3. Eggs.* Egg production, placed at 74 million in 1942 and 80 million in 1946, was estimated on the basis of the number of hens in the country.

*4. Fish.* On the basis of consumption estimates pertaining to the urban and coastal population, fish production was estimated at 9,000 quintals in 1942 and 10,000 quintals in 1946.[3]

*5. Livestock.* The estimates of the number of livestock and their value were provided by the Bureau of Statistics. The 1942 cattle slaughter was 86,661 animals, and the pig slaughter 207,937; in 1946, there were slaughtered 82,412 head of cattle and 177,460 pigs. The value of cattle as stated by the Bureau of Statistics was doubled in order to account for slaughtering, distribution costs, and retail profits.

*6. Wheat flour.* The estimate for 1942 was computed on the basis of an inquiry of mill owners. For 1946, the Bureau of Statistics supplied the data. Production was reported as 10,000 quintals in 1942 and 17,318 quintals in 1946. Since wheat production was already included in item 1 under Agriculture, only the value added is shown for this item in the table.

*7. Milk.* The Bureau of Statistics furnished data on the number of milch cows. Milk production was then computed on the basis of the cow population multiplied by an estimated 450 bottles of milk produced annually per cow. Production estimates for 1942 were 172 million bottles and for 1946 were 140 million bottles.[4]

*8. Dairy products.* It was estimated that 30 per cent of the milk was transformed into milk products. The value added in the processing of milk was estimated at 25 per cent of the value of the milk.

*9. Honey.* The Bureau of Statistics supplied a production esti-

---

[2] According to a later statistical investigation, poultry consumption amounted to 1,766,000 birds in 1946, and 1,889,000 birds in 1948.

[3] According to a later estimate, prepared by a representative of FAO, fish production in 1948 was valued at 1,600,000 colones.

[4] Later statistical investigation disclosed that this estimate of milk production used in the computation of the gross national product was somewhat too high.

mate of 232,000 liters for 1946. For 1942 production was estimated at 230,000 liters.

*10. Forestry production.* This category of production includes only the value of domestically consumed firewood and such wood as was used for furniture, tools, and household goods, which was estimated as equal to 50 per cent of domestic firewood consumption. Wood used in construction, and fuel wood consumed in industrial production and commercial services, were subsumed under construction and industrial production, respectively. The physical quantity of firewood was expressed in faggots about two feet in length by six inches in breadth. According to experts in the Ministry of Agriculture, a family of five members consumed about five faggots a day. The value of a faggot was estimated at $1\frac{1}{2}$ centavos in 1942 and 2 centavos in 1946.

*11. Mining.* Mining production and value figures were furnished by the Bureau of Statistics. In 1942, 30,323.58 ounces of gold and 283,157.09 ounces of silver were produced, while in 1946 production amounted to 21,808.95 ounces of gold and 213,000 ounces of silver.

*12. Seed and vegetable oils.* An inquiry by the Bureau of Internal Revenue revealed that 745,000 liters of seed oils were produced in 1942. The Bureau of Statistics reported production of 1,242,000 liters of seed oils in 1946. Vegetable oil production was considered insignificant in 1942 and was estimated at 3,949 quintals in 1946 by the Bureau of Statistics.

*13. Footwear.* Estimates were made from information supplied by the Bureau of Internal Revenue, the shoemakers' guild (*gremio de zapateros*), and the biggest producers. Since leather and other domestic raw materials used in shoe production were accounted for under another production category, only value added was shown in this group. Value added per pair of shoes was estimated at five colones in 1942 and seven colones in 1946. Production was 650,000 pairs in 1942 and 800,000 pairs in 1946.

*14. Cigarettes.* The Bureau of Statistics and Bureau of Internal Revenue supplied complete data. Production in 1942 amounted to 172.7 million cigarettes and in 1946 to 364.6 million cigarettes. The value added was found by adding wage payments and profits. Wage payments were computed on the basis of the number of employees and the annual average wage. Tobacco of national origin used in the production was excluded since it appears under agricultural production.

*15. Ice.* The Bureau of Internal Revenue reported 370,000 quintals produced in 1942 and 270,000 quintals in 1946. The reported unit value per quintal was reduced 10 per cent in order to correct for imported materials used in production.

*16. Salt.* The Bureau of Internal Revenue estimated that production amounted to 1,450,000 quintals in 1942 and 1,504,000 quintals in 1946.

*17. Wax.* Salvadorean producers estimated production in 1942 at 780 quintals and the Bureau of Statistics, reported that 844 quintals were produced in 1946.

*18. Henequen bags.* The estimates are based on producers' data and include only exports of empty henequen bags, since bags consumed in the coffee trade are included in the value of coffee exports. Production was valued at 617,000 colones in 1942 and at 315,000 colones in 1946.

*19. Other henequen products.* According to the Bureau of Statistics, production of henequen cord, textiles, rugs, etc., amounted to 531,000 physical units in 1942 and to 590,000 in 1946.

*20. Palm-tree products.* Production of rugs, mats, toys, hats, etc. amounted to 9,900,000 units in 1942 and 9,000,000 units in 1946, according to estimates of a special study and of the Bureau of Statistics, respectively.

*21. Hats.* The Bureau of Internal Revenue and the central organization of the credit cooperatives (*Federación de Cajas de Crédito*), the latter controlling part of the production, furnished data on the basis of which production was estimated at 1,360,000 in 1942. The Bureau of Statistics estimated production at 1,520,-000 in 1946.

*22. Soap.* Data for 1942 and 1946 were supplied by the Bureau of Internal Revenue. Production amounted to 22,000 quintals in 1942 and 29,000 quintals in 1946. The estimates assumed that value added was 30 per cent of the total value both in 1942 and in 1946. Domestic raw materials contributing to total value amounted to 20 per cent in 1942 and 30 per cent in 1946. However, only that part of the domestic raw materials not already covered under other production categories was used in the estimates.

*23. Rubber products.* The Bureau of Statistics reported production in 1942 at 130,000 units and in 1946 at 141,000 units. The estimates were computed on a value-added basis, the value of raw rubber used in production already having been included in item 1, Agriculture.

*24. Candles.* According to data of the Bureau of Statistics, production in 1942 amounted to 24,000 boxes of 20 pounds each, and 30,260 boxes in 1946. The value added was estimated at 30 per cent of total value.

*25. Hides.* The production estimate of the Bureau of Internal Revenue was 1,500,000 square feet in 1943 and 750,000 square feet in 1946. Total value was reduced 10 per cent to account for the value of foreign raw materials used.

*26. Sole leather.* The Bureau of Internal Revenue estimated, after an inquiry among producers, that production was 7,500 quintals in 1942 and 3,400 quintals in 1946. A 10 per cent deduction for foreign raw materials was made in the estimated total value of production.

*27. Beer and soft drinks.* The value added was estimated on the basis of information furnished by the Bureau of Internal Revenue. Production in 1942 amounted to 1,382,000 liters of beer and 5,404,000 bottles of soft drinks, while in 1946, totals of 3,211,000 liters of beer and 15,613,000 bottles of soft drinks were produced.

*28, 29, 30. Liquor ("Aguardiente"), Industrial Alcohol, and Denatured Alcohol.* Production data, as supplied by the Bureau of Statistics are as follows: *aguardiente,* 1,382,633 liters in 1942, and 2,185,657 liters in 1946; industrial alcohol, 37,364 liters in 1942, and 252,605 liters in 1946; denatured alcohol, 125,125 in 1942, and 148,827 in 1946. In the case of industrial alcohol, a 10 per cent deduction was made to correct for the value of foreign raw materials used, while a deduction of 3 per cent was made for the same purpose in the case of denatured alcohol production.

*31. Cotton textiles.* Production was estimated by the Bureau of Statistics at 14,374,000 meters in 1942 and 20,534,000 meters in 1946. Estimates for value added were computed by the Bureau of Internal Revenue, while the value of raw materials was included in item 1, Agriculture.

*32. Other industries.* In order to account for other industrial products, an addition of 10 per cent of the amounts shown under items 8, 9, 10, 12, 18, 19, 20, 21, 22, 23, 24, 25, 26, and 31 was made.

*33. New construction.* The Construction Office of the City of San Salvador (*Oficina de Construcciones de la Alcaldía Municipal de San Salvador*) estimated that the value of dwellings built in 1942 was on the average about 25 per cent lower than in 1946. On the basis of data from the city authorities and the Bureau of Health, reporting 412 houses as having been constructed in 1946 in the city of San Salvador, housing construction in 1942 was estimated at 300 units. Since the total number of houses of all types constructed in the entire country was reported at 3,942 in 1946, an estimate of 2,811 dwellings for 1942 was made. Because the reported valuation of houses in 1946 was believed to be too low, a 30 per cent upward adjustment was made in computing the value of construction both in 1942 and in 1946.

*34. Transportation.* The value added from this source was estimated on the basis of data of kilometers traveled and number of passengers transported, as reported by the Bureau of Statistics.

*35. Electric power industry.* Income was estimated on the basis of kilowatt hours consumed by domestic and industrial users.

*36. Commercial income.* This item does not include distribution of domestic products which, in so far as they pertained to urban consumption, were valued at retail prices and thus included the cost of distribution. The estimate includes only income derived from the distribution of imports, and was estimated at 75 per cent of the combined value of nongovernment imports plus customs duties. Imports, exclusive of those of the government, were valued at 18,400,000 colones in 1942 and at 48,800,000 colones in 1946. Customs duties amounted to 6,200,000 colones in 1942 and 11,800,000 colones in 1946.

*37. Domestic servants.* It was estimated that 35,000 domestic servants are employed in the country. The average income received, including meals furnished by the employer, was estimated at 192 colones in 1942 and 288 colones in 1946.

*38. Various professions.* On the basis of the census data of 1930 and other sources, an average of 1,000 professional people was estimated to have received in 1942 an average annual income of 4,800 colones and another 1,000 professionals were estimated to have received an average of 2,400 colones annually. The corresponding average annual income figures for 1946 were estimated at 7,200 colones and 3,600 colones respectively. The totals include, in addition, a sum of 700,000 colones representing the total annual income of the clergy.

*39. Craftsmen.* The group included only such workers as barbers, tailors, and carpenters not already included in the production figures given above. The number of persons in this category was estimated at 40,000, receiving an average annual income of 700 colones in 1942 and 875 colones in 1946.

*40. Residential rents.* The Bureau of Health reported in the city of San Salvador 10,375 dwellings in 1942 and 12,814 dwellings in 1946. These data were multiplied by five in order to approximate the total number of houses in the republic in both years. The total number of dwellings, thus estimated at 51,875 in 1942 and 64,074 in 1946, was multiplied by the annual average value to arrive at their total value. It was assumed that there was a return of 8 per cent on the total value; the latter amounted in 1942 to 147,843,000 colones and in 1946 to 243,466,000 colones. The 8 per cent return accounts for rental payments as well as imputed rent.

*41. Private interest payments.* Interest payments were estimated at 40 per cent on an annual private loan volume of 10 million colones in 1942 and of 15 million colones in 1946. Interest on commercial debts to banks or private individuals was not included in this category since it had already been subsumed in the cost of production.

*42. Various services.* This category includes income from hotel and restaurant services, public entertainments, noncommercial radio shows, and the like, with a total estimated income of 2,000,000 colones in 1942 and 3,000,000 colones in 1946.

TABLE 63

ESTIMATED GROSS NATIONAL PRODUCT OF THE PRIVATE SECTOR, 1942 AND 1946
(*In thousands of colones*)

|  | *1942* | *1946* |
|---|---|---|
| **I. General agricultural and pastoral** | | |
| 1. Agriculture | | |
| a. Major agricultural products (detail in Tables 64 and 65) | 78,682 | 115,177 |
| b. Fruits and vegetables | 20,367 | 29,200 |
| c. Other agricultural products | 1,980 | 2,887 |
| d. Adjustment | 12,000 | 18,000 |
| 2. Poultry | 825 | 1,320 |
| 3. Eggs | 2,200 | 3,200 |
| 4. Fish | 324 | 450 |
| 5. Livestock | 10,782 | 20,834 |
| 6. Wheat flour | 70 | 164 |
| 7. Milk | 6,075 | 8,019 |
| 8. Dairy products | 455 | 601 |
| 9. Honey | 69 | 121 |
| **II. General industrial** | | |
| 10. Forestry | | |
| a. Firewood | 10,180 | 14,200 |
| b. Lumber | 509 | 710 |
| 11. Mining | | |
| a. Gold | 2,636 | 1,906 |
| b. Silver | 213 | 600 |
| 12. Seed and vegetable oils | 1,043 | 2,338 |
| 13. Footwear | 3,250 | 5,600 |
| 14. Cigarettes | 509 | 1,350 |
| 15. Ice | 420 | 378 |
| 16. Salt | 2,580 | 3,032 |
| 17. Wax | 59 | 83 |
| 18. Henequen bags: exports | 617 | 315 |
| 19. Other henequen products | 276 | 479 |
| 20. Palm tree products | 630 | 986 |
| 21. Hats | 544 | 879 |
| 22. Soap | 2,750 | 5,315 |
| 23. Rubber products | 68 | 178 |
| 24. Candles | 120 | 133 |
| 25. Hides | 702 | 1,413 |
| 26. Sole leather | 675 | 1,008 |

TABLE 63 (Continued)

|  | 1942 | 1946 |
|---|---|---|
| 27. Beer and soft drinks..................... | 976 | 2,785 |
| 28. Aguardiente............................. | 4,166 | 7,103 |
| 29. Industrial alcohol....................... | 126 | 840 |
| 30. Denatured alcohol....................... | 307 | 435 |
| 31. Cotton textiles.......................... | 3,900 | 7,146 |
| 32. Other industries........................ | 1,550 | 2,716 |
| 33. New construction....................... | 8,199 | 14,979 |
| 34. Transportation.......................... | 1,900 | 3,000 |
| 35. Electric power industry.................. | 1,300 | 1,500 |
| *III. General business, professions, and services* | | |
| 36. Commercial income...................... | 18,450 | 45,450 |
| 37. Domestic servants....................... | 6,720 | 10,080 |
| 38. Various professions...................... | 7,900 | 11,500 |
| 39. Craftsmen.............................. | 28,000 | 35,000 |
| 40. Residential rents: including imputed rents... | 11,827 | 19,477 |
| 41. Private interest payments................. | 4,000 | 6,000 |
| 42. Various services......................... | 2,000 | 3,000 |
| GRAND TOTAL............................... | 262,931 | 411,887 |

## TABLE 64

### VALUE OF PRODUCTION OF MAJOR AGRICULTURAL PRODUCTS IN 1942

| | Production | | Domestic consumption | Retail price | Whole-sale price | Export price | Value of exports | Value of Consumption | | | Total value of production |
| --- | --- | --- | --- | --- | --- | --- | --- | --- | --- | --- | --- |
| | Total | Exports | | | | | | Rural | Urban | Total | |
| | *In quintals* | | | | | | *In colones* | | | | |
| Coffee | 1,407,008 | 1,154,315 | 252,693 | 24.53 | 19.00 | 32.15 | 37,111,227 | 2,400,583 | 3,099,279 | 5,499,862ª | 42,611,089 |
| Sugar | 412,000 | 68,560 | 343,440 | 13.00 | 9.67 | 8.87 | 608,127 | 996,319 | 3,125,304 | 4,121,623 | 4,729,750 |
| Sugar loaf | 30,000 | ... | 30,000 | 14.00 | ... | ... | ... | ... | ... | 420,000 | 420,000 |
| Unrefined brown sugar | 545,000 | ... | 545,000 | 4.00 | ... | ... | ... | ... | ... | 2,180,000 | 2,180,000 |
| Corn | 4,588,609 | 6,575 | 4,582,034 | 2.11 | 2.00 | 4.54 | 29,850 | 5,779,068 | 3,580,670 | 9,359,738 | 9,380,588 |
| Rice | 532,288 | 40,132 | 492,156 | 10.00 | 7.87 | 10.24 | 410,501 | 2,449,927 | 1,820,000 | 4,269,927 | 4,671,428 |
| Black beans | 538,655 | 273 | 538,382 | 10.00 | 8.54 | 8.08 | 2,205 | 2,894,906 | 1,994,000 | 4,888,906 | 4,891,111 |
| Maicillo | 2,068,618 | ... | 2,068,618 | 1.72 | 1.64 | 1.46 | ... | 2,136,040 | 1,317,784 | 3,453,824 | 3,453,824 |
| Wheat | 5,207 | ... | 5,207 | 17.00 | ... | ... | ... | ... | ... | 88,519 | 88,519 |
| Sesame | 1,040 | 427 | 613 | 13.00 | ... | 11.03 | 4,709 | ... | ... | 7,069 | 12,678 |
| Cocoa | 3,221 | ... | 3,221 | 41.00 | ... | 18.93 | ... | ... | ... | 132,061 | 132,061 |
| Potatoes | 17,896 | 295 | 17,601 | 10.00 | ... | 4.49 | 1,324 | ... | ... | 176,010 | 177,334 |
| Cotton | 45,993 | 8,361 | 37,632 | ... | 50.31 | 38.81 | 324,490 | ... | ... | 1,893,265 | 2,217,755 |
| Henequen | 93,123 | 13,023 | 80,100 | ... | 20.00 | 23.26 | 302,914 | ... | ... | 1,602,000 | 1,904,914 |
| Balsam | 5,995 | 2,196 | 3,799 | ... | 204.00 | 203.80 | 447,544 | ... | ... | 774,996 | 1,222,540 |
| Rubber | 2,151 | 7 | 2,144 | 43.00 | ... | 101.00 | 707 | ... | ... | 92,192 | 92,899 |
| Tobacco | 6,620 | 204 | 6,416 | 31.00 | ... | 31.74 | 6,474 | ... | ... | 198,896 | 205,370 |
| Blueing | 2,019 | 877 | 1,142 | 145.00 | 119.00 | 142.36 | 124,849 | ... | ... | 165,590 | 290,439 |
| Total (breakdown of Item 1a in Table 63) | | | | | | | | | | | 78,682,299 |

ª The volume and value of domestic coffee consumption was derived as a residual, by deducting exports from production. The figure therefore includes changes in the carry-over of stocks for export.

## TABLE 65

### VALUE OF PRODUCTION OF MAJOR AGRICULTURAL PRODUCTS IN 1946

| | Production (In quintals) | | Domestic consumption | Retail price | Wholesale price | Export price | Value of exports | Value of consumption (In colones) | | | Total value of production |
|---|---|---|---|---|---|---|---|---|---|---|---|
| | Total | Exports | | | | | | Rural | Urban | Total | |
| Coffee | 1,079,996 | 1,046,901 | 33,095 | 43.00 | 40.93 | 49.26 | 51,570,343 | 677,289 | 711,542 | 1,388,831a | 52,959,174 |
| Sugar | 570,000 | 32,036 | 537,964 | 25.00 | 23.75 | 36.27 | 1,611,945 | 3,832,988 | 9,414,375 | 13,247,363 | 14,859,308 |
| Sugar loaf | 26,930 | ... | 26,970 | 25.00 | ... | ... | ... | ... | ... | 673,250 | 673,250 |
| Unrefined brown sugar | ... | ... | ... | ... | ... | ... | ... | ... | ... | ... | ... |
| Corn | 302,930 | ... | 302,930 | 9.00 | 5.00 | 14.24 | ... | ... | ... | 2,726,370 | 2,726,370 |
| Rice | 3,026,753 | ... | 3,026,753 | 5.70 | ... | ... | ... | 9,528,670 | 6,389,808 | 15,918,478 | 15,918,478 |
| Black beans | 411,107 | 6,260 | 404,847 | 14.00 | 12.75 | 22.97 | 143,792 | 3,250,025 | 2,099,202 | 5,349,227 | 5,493,019 |
| Maicillo | 536,191 | 9,393 | 526,798 | 12.00 | 10.54 | 18.20 | 170,952 | 3,495,991 | 2,341,320 | 5,837,311 | 6,008,263 |
| Wheat | 1,641,263 | ... | 1,641,263 | 3.89 | ... | ... | ... | ... | ... | 6,384,513 | 6,384,513 |
| Sesame | 4,463 | ... | 4,463 | 20.00 | ... | ... | ... | ... | ... | 89,260 | 89,260 |
| Cocoa | 21,660 | ... | 21,660 | 24.00 | ... | ... | ... | ... | ... | 519,840 | 519,840 |
| — | 101 | ... | 101 | 49.00 | ... | ... | ... | ... | ... | 4,949 | 4,949 |
| Potatoes | 11,397 | 1,316 | 10,081 | 13.00 | 67.50 | 13.11 | 17,252 | ... | ... | 131,053 | 148,305 |
| Cotton | 71,497 | 22,302 | 49,195 | 85.00 | 25.83 | 51.62 | 1,151,229 | ... | ... | 4,181,575 | 5,333,804 |
| Henequen | 84,412 | 2,241 | 82,171 | ... | ... | 32.63 | 73,123 | ... | ... | 2,122,476 | 2,195,599 |
| Balsam | 5,464 | 1,978 | 3,486 | ... | 169.00 | 209.83 | 415,043 | ... | ... | 589,134 | 1,004,177 |
| Rubber | 120 | ... | 120 | ... | ... | 101.52 | ... | ... | ... | 12,182 | 12,182 |
| Tobacco | 9,243 | ... | 9,243 | 70.00 | ... | 30.67 | ... | ... | ... | 647,010 | 647,010 |
| Blueing | 1,518 | 1,079 | 439 | ... | 118.00 | 138.11 | 149,020 | ... | ... | 51,802 | 200,822 |

Total (break-down of Item 1a in Table 63)    115,177,323

a See footnote to Table 64.

# APPENDIX B

## ESTIMATED GROSS NATIONAL PRODUCT AND ESTIMATED "REAL" GROSS NATIONAL PRODUCT, 1939–1946

### (Second appendix to Chapter II)

THE ESTIMATED GROSS NATIONAL PRODUCT and "real" gross national product series are based on the direct estimates of the gross national product of the private sector for 1942 and 1946 presented in Appendix A.

### 1. ESTIMATED GROSS NATIONAL PRODUCT

An unweighted index of the value of imports, exports, check payments, and railroad shipments was first constructed for the years 1939 through 1946, with 1942 as a base, by the group of Salvadorean experts who had compiled the gross national product estimates for 1942 and 1946 shown in Appendix A. The experts were of the opinion that these four variables best reflect the significant movements in the economy. This preliminary index (column 1, Table 66) was then adjusted by interpolation

TABLE 66

ESTIMATED GROSS NATIONAL PRODUCT OF PRIVATE SECTOR

| Year | Preliminary index (1942 = 100) | Adjusted index (1942 = 100) | Gross national product of private sector (In millions of colones) |
|------|------|------|------|
| | (1) | (2) | (3) |
| 1939 | 83 | 87 | 229 |
| 1940 | 76 | 81 | 213 |
| 1941 | 77 | 82 | 216 |
| 1942 | 100 | 100 | 263 |
| 1943 | 135 | 127 | 334 |
| 1944 | 143 | 133 | 350 |
| 1945 | 158 | 144 | 379 |
| 1946 | 203 | 157 | 412 |

to the direct estimates of 263 million and 412 million colones for the gross national product of the private sector for the years 1942 and 1946 respectively. The adjusted index (column 2) was then converted to a series in millions of colones. The resulting series of the gross national product of the private sector is shown in column 3 of Table 66.

To these figures, repeated in column 1 of Table 67, were added the value (column 2, Table 67) of the services provided by both

TABLE 67

ESTIMATED TOTAL GROSS NATIONAL PRODUCT

*(In millions of colones)*

| Year | Gross national product of private sector | Gross national product of government sector | Total gross national product |
|------|------|------|------|
| | *1)* | *(2)* | *(3)* |
| 1939 | 229 | 15 | 244 |
| 1940 | 213 | 16 | 229 |
| 1941 | 216 | 16 | 232 |
| 1942 | 263 | 16 | 279 |
| 1943 | 334 | 17 | 351 |
| 1944 | 350 | 17 | 367 |
| 1945 | 379 | 19 | 398 |
| 1946 | 412 | 23 | 435 |

the national and local governments, which are approximated by "fixed" government expenses (*Gastos Fijos*), since these outlays almost entirely represent payments to individuals for services rendered. The sum of these series is the total gross national product series, which is shown in column 3 of Table 67.

## 2. ESTIMATED "REAL" GROSS NATIONAL PRODUCT

The "real" gross national product series shows the value, in terms of 1942 prices, of the goods and services produced for the years 1939 through 1946. The year 1942 was selected as the base year because it was the earliest one for which direct estimates of the gross national product of the private sector were available.[1]

[1] In selecting 1942 as the base year, no concept of "normality" for that year is implied.

For the deflating process, the gross national product was divided into three parts: the gross national product of the private sector net of exports; the value of exports; and the gross national product of the government sector. The three parts were then deflated by different indices.

A deflator for the gross national product of the private sector net of exports was constructed in the following manner. A simple arithmetic average of the retail food price and wholesale agricultural price indices was first computed because both types of prices were used in making the direct estimates of the gross national product of the private sector for 1942 and 1946. The rate of variation of the resulting index was then halved in order to adjust for sectors in the economy whose price indices had lagged behind those of food and agricultural prices.[2] This adjusted and combined retail and wholesale price index is shown in column 3 of Table 68.

TABLE 68

ADJUSTED COMBINED RETAIL-FOOD AND WHOLESALE-AGRICULTURAL PRICE INDEX
(1942 = 100)

| Year | Retail Price Index | Wholesale Price Index | Adjusted Combined Index |
|------|------|------|------|
|  | (1) | (2) | (3) |
| 1939 | 95 | 77 | 92 |
| 1940 | 99 | 68 | 90 |
| 1941 | 100 | 85 | 95 |
| 1942 | 100 | 100 | 100 |
| 1943 | 132 | 120 | 114 |
| 1944 | 192 | 136 | 133 |
| 1945 | 223 | 156 | 147 |
| 1946 | 183 | 178 | 143 |

[2] The prices of approximately 40 per cent of the goods and services included in the gross national product of the private sector are probably unrepresented in the retail and wholesale price indices because these are based primarily on food and agricultural prices. In 1946, out of a gross national product of the private sector of 412 million colones, a minimum of 165 million colones corresponded to activities that were clearly nonagricultural. Included in this sector are house rentals, professional services, pay of domestic servants, and interest payments, movements of which are relatively sticky during a period of rapid price changes.

The value of exports was deflated by the index of the unit cost of imports shown in Table 69. The purpose in using this index

TABLE 69

INDEX OF UNIT COST OF IMPORTS

| Year | Volume of Imports (In kilograms) | Value of Imports (In colones) | Unit Cost (Colones per kilo) | Index (1942 = 100) |
|---|---|---|---|---|
| | (1) | (2) | (3) | (4) |
| 1939 | 69,154,138 | 22,124,303 | 0.320 | 89 |
| 1940 | 72,241,050 | 20,270,110 | 0.281 | 78 |
| 1941 | 79,280,288 | 20,827,216 | 0.263 | 73 |
| 1942 | 59,363,625 | 21,431,078 | 0.361 | 100 |
| 1943 | 74,884,740 | 29,857,429 | 0.399 | 111 |
| 1944 | 84,696,074 | 30,682,655 | 0.362 | 100 |
| 1945 | 87,509,520 | 33,836,084 | 0.387 | 107 |
| 1946 | 105,434,220 | 52,890,000 | 0.501 | 139 |
| 1947 | 147,412,609 | 92,310,000 | 0.626 | 173 |

was to deflate export values to their "purchasing power," i.e., to their command over foreign goods. In other words, exports were considered as being produced as a means of obtaining imports, and the terms of trade had therefore to enter into the determination of the "real" value of these exports to the Salvadorean economy.

The gross national product of the government sector was deflated by a cost-of-government index that reflects the average salary of a broad, representative sample of government employees in all pay grades during the years 1939 through 1948. The derivation and construction of this index is presented in detail in Appendix H.

The deflating process and the resulting figures for the "real" gross national product are shown in Table 70. On the basis of these results, which, it must be pointed out, are not much more than an indication of the relative order of magnitude, it appears that the "real" gross national product of El Salvador increased by approximately 16 per cent between 1939 and 1946, as contrasted with an 80 per cent increase of the gross national product in money terms.

## TABLE 70

### CONSTRUCTION OF SERIES OF ESTIMATED "REAL" GROSS NATIONAL PRODUCT

*(In millions of colones; at 1942 prices)*

| | Private Sector, Net of Exports | | | | | Exports | | | Government Sector | | | |
| Year | Gross National Product of Sector | Exports | Gross National Product, Net of Exports | Adjusted Combined Price Index | "Real" Gross National Product of Sector, Net of Exports | Exports | Index of Cost of Imports | "Real" Value of Exports | Gross National Product of Sector | Unit Cost-of-Government Index | "Real" Gross National Product of Sector | Total "Real" Gross National Product |
| | $(1)$[a] | $(2)$ | $(3 = 1 - 2)$ | $(4)$[b] | $(5 = 3 \div 4)$ | $(6 = 2)$ | $(7)$[c] | $(8 = 6 \div 7)$ | $(9)$ | $(10)$[d] | $(11 = 9 \div 10)$ | $(12 = 5 + 8 + 11)$ |
| 1939 | 229 | 30 | 199 | 92 | 216 | 30 | 89 | 34 | 15 | 97 | 16 | 266 |
| 1940 | 213 | 26 | 187 | 90 | 208 | 26 | 78 | 33 | 16 | 99 | 16 | 257 |
| 1941 | 216 | 25 | 191 | 95 | 201 | 25 | 73 | 34 | 16 | 99 | 16 | 251 |
| 1942 | 263 | 44 | 219 | 100 | 219 | 44 | 100 | 44 | 16 | 100 | 16 | 279 |
| 1943 | 334 | 54 | 280 | 114 | 246 | 54 | 111 | 49 | 17 | 101 | 17 | 312 |
| 1944 | 350 | 56 | 294 | 133 | 221 | 56 | 100 | 56 | 17 | 104 | 16 | 293 |
| 1945 | 379 | 53 | 326 | 147 | 222 | 53 | 107 | 50 | 19 | 110 | 17 | 289 |
| 1946 | 412 | 64 | 348 | 143 | 243 | 64 | 139 | 46 | 23 | 119 | 19 | 308 |

a From column 3, Table 66.
b From column 3, Table 68.
c From column 4, Table 69.
d From Appendix H.

# APPENDIX C

## LEGAL AND ADMINISTRATIVE ASPECTS OF GOVERNMENT FINANCE

### (*Appendix to Chapter III*)

IN THIS APPENDIX detailed information is given regarding the general legal and administrative aspects of government finance in El Salvador, which were presented in summary form in Chapter III.

### 1. THE BUDGET

According to Article 90 of the Constitution of August 13, 1866 (as modified by Decree No. 251 of November 29, 1945), it is the duty of the executive power to

present to the legislative body through its ministers within eight days after the opening of its ordinary session, a complete report and a documented account of the public administration of funds in the past year, and the budget of the expenditures of the following year, indicating the means to cover them. If within the prescribed period this provision is not complied with, the derelict minister shall be suspended in his functions as of the same date; of this fact the executive power shall be immediately notified in order that in the following eight days the report of the budget referred to above may be presented through a minister who is assigned to this task; in case of noncompliance the President of the Republic is suspended and the executive power is assumed by the person authorized in accordance with this Constitution; and the new President shall comply within twenty days with such duty.

In that case the legislative power may extend its session for the same period.[1] No concrete situation appears to have arisen that

[1] In a declaratory decree of December 28, 1945 (No. 289), it is determined that, since in 1939 the budget year was shifted to coincide with the calendar year, the annual budget must be submitted to the National Assembly in the second period of its ordinary sessions in order that the budget may reach the Assembly not later than the fifteenth of December.

would have put the practicability of these extremely severe provisions to a test.

The Constitution further provides that

the general budget shall contain all receipts and expenditures of the nation for each year. However, the institutions and enterprises that are or shall become autonomous may be regulated by special budgets approved by the legislative power. In the budget law there shall be authorized the amount of floating debt that the government may incur during the year in question in order to offset temporary deficiencies of revenue; that debt must be covered in the same year and may not exceed 10 per cent of the estimated revenue for the year. A special law shall establish the preparation, the voting, the execution, and the liquidation of the budgets.

In execution of this constitutional provision the Budget Law was passed on December 22, 1945 (Decree No. 283).[2] According to this law, the Bureau of the Budget is directly responsible to the President. Prior to the enactment of the law, the Bureau of the Budget was an office of the Ministry of Finance. It has been pointed out that the transfer of the Bureau of the Budget from the Ministry of Finance to the Office of the President raises questions regarding the constitutional responsibility of the "minister in charge" in accordance with Article 90 of the Constitution. Since the Minister of Finance is obviously the minister in charge who is responsible for submitting the annual budget to the National Assembly within the time limit prescribed by the Constitution, he should have the right to speed up and supervise the preparation of the budget. This, however, is not possible under the present set up. It is not anticipated, though, that this conflict between administrative procedure and constitutional requirements will lead to any complications.[3]

The Budget Law defines as the major functions of the Bureau of the Budget the orientation, direction, supervision, preparation, and execution of the budgets, insofar as such supervision

[2] The date given is that of the latest version of the law, which existed in a slightly different form prior to 1945. In subsequent paragraphs, references to laws likewise pertain to the form now in force. Actually, the administration and control of the budget have been regulated by law for many years.

[3] After the above was written, the Bureau of the Budget was put under the administration of the Ministry of Finance by a government decree of March 3, 1949.

does not fall under the jurisdiction of the Court of Accounts. For the accomplishment of these tasks the Bureau of the Budget is required to (a) estimate government receipts, in cooperation with the Court of Accounts; (b) assemble the estimates of expenditures, examine them with a view to determining their necessity, and suggest the economies that are compatible with efficiency; (c) compare the estimates of receipts and expenditures and propose to the President and to the Ministry of Economy means for balancing them; (d) study systematically the organization and the functions of government services in order to assure economies of personnel and determine the adequacy of remunerations and the proper distribution of the functions among the various branches of the government; and (e) supervise the expenditure of public funds. According to the law, no funds may be obligated unless the Director General of the Bureau of the Budget gives his approval in advance. Only for those expenditures which the Director of the Bureau of the Budget exempts is it unnecessary to obtain advance approval.

The principle of budgetary comprehensiveness is safeguarded in the Budget Law by the provision that all receipts and expenditures of public funds must be accounted for in the annual budgets, in their liquidations, and in the reports regarding their execution. The law, however, permits a distinction between the General Fund and special funds. In practice, the annual budget laws include all receipts and expenditures in the budget of the General Fund, with the exception of funds taken in custody by the Treasury but belonging to autonomous public bodies (*quédanes*) and pension funds of the armed forces (*masitas*). In addition, the Budget Law also shows the budgets of autonomous bodies such as the Coffee Growers' Association, the Cattle Raisers' Association, the General Purchasing Office, and institutions that are supported by the government through subsidies but also obtain revenues through their own activities (e.g., hospitals, asylums, children's homes, etc.).

The inclusion of all receipts and expenditures in the General Fund constitutes a considerable improvement over previous practices, which were discontinued primarily as a result of a law providing for an administrative form in 1939. Prior to that date, various boards (*juntas*) and funds for special purposes, such as the fund for the construction of postal buildings, obtained certain taxes or a certain percentage of taxes directly without Treasury intervention. The rather unsatisfactory form in which the data on expenditures and receipts of these special funds used to be presented in the annual liquidations, as published in public documents, gives reason to believe that the method now followed of including all receipts and expenditures in the General Fund permits not only better and more uniform bookkeeping practices but also better controls.

### RECEIPTS

Regarding the preparation of estimates of government receipts, the Budget Law provides that the estimates of tax revenues for the ensuing fiscal year must not exceed the average of the revenues collected in the last five completed fiscal years. These average figures may be increased only to the extent of the estimated result of new taxes; they may be diminished by the deduction of the proceeds of taxes, of which the collection has been discontinued. The law permits, however, the taking account in the estimates of developments that are likely to change these mechanically-arrived-at figures.

The estimates of revenues are prepared by the Bureau of the Budget in cooperation with the Court of Accounts. If the Court of Accounts does not agree with the estimates of the bureau, the Director of the latter may submit his own estimates to the Ministry of Finance and the President. The Ministry of Finance has the right to depart from the estimates of revenues that the Bureau of the Budget submits but it must indicate the reasons for such changes in its message to the National Assembly.

In order to appraise the efficacy of the method by which estimates of government revenues have been prepared in recent years, budget and performance figures are compared in Table 71. A scrutiny of the table indicates that the performance figures showed excesses of up to 20 per cent over, and short-falls of up to 13 per cent under, the budget estimates. If government receipts are broken down by sources, it appears that the differences between the estimates and the actual receipts of taxes were

## TABLE 71

### COMPARISON OF BUDGET AND PERFORMANCE FIGURES OF GOVERNMENT EXPENDITURES AND RECEIPTS[a]

| Year | Original Budget | | | Performance | | | Budget vs. Performance[b] |
|------|---------|-------------|----------------------------|----------|-------------|----------------------------|----------------------------|
| | Revenues | Expenditures | Surplus (+) or Deficit (−) | Revenues | Expenditures | Surplus (+) or Deficit (−) | |
| 1935/36 | 16,620.3 | 21,073.3 | −4,453.0 | 20,191.3 | 22,993.9 | −2,802.6 | +1,650.4 |
| 1936/37 | 21,245.0 | 21,731.7 | −486.7 | 22,904.6 | 22,061.1 | +843.5 | +1,230.2 |
| 1937/38 | 22,487.6 | 23,105.6 | −618.0 | 22,506.8 | 22,126.5 | +380.3 | +998.3 |
| 1938/39 | 18,810.6 | 20,175.5 | −2,364.9 | 20,236.0 | 20,009.8 | +226.2 | +2,591.1 |
| 1939[c] | 10,994.7 | 11,731.4 | −736.7 | 10,575.5 | 11,120.3 | −544.8 | +191.9 |
| 1940 | 22,736.5 | 21,073.3 | +1,663.2 | 20,060.8 | 22,993.9 | −2,933.1 | −4,596.3 |
| 1941 | 21,797.2 | 21,843.9 | −46.7 | 21,289.5 | 21,342.2 | −52.7 | −6.0 |
| 1942 | 23,448.2 | 23,521.3 | −73.1 | 22,155.1 | 21,987.2 | +167.9 | +241.0 |
| 1943[d] | 21,744.0 | 21,738.8 | +5.2 | 24,308.6 | 21,449.4 | +2,859.2 | +2,854.0 |
| 1944[d] | 23,655.0 | 24,124.5 | −469.5 | 23,741.5 | 24,149.9 | −408.4 | +61.1 |
| 1945 | 29,866.8 | 31,361.3 | −1,494.5 | 29,476.1 | 29,281.2 | +194.9 | +1,689.4 |
| 1946 | 37,043.6 | 36,949.3 | +94.3 | 39,472.7 | 40,036.0 | −563.3 | −657.6 |
| 1947 | 45,323.3 | 46,174.2 | −850.9 | 53,668.7 | 51,875.9 | +1,792.8 | +2,643.7 |

[a] Data include general and special funds with the exception of trust funds. Data are taken from "Memoria de Hacienda" or from "Memoria de la Corte de Cuentas."
[b] (+) = performance better than budget (increased surplus or decreased deficit); (−) = performance worse than budget (increased deficit or decreased surplus).
[c] Second half of 1939 only.
[d] Data of General Fund only.

## TABLE 72

### COMPARISON OF BUDGET AND PERFORMANCE FIGURES OF GOVERNMENT REVENUE IN SELECTED YEARS, 1935-1947

#### (In thousands of colones)

| | Original Budget | Budget Changes | | Final Budget | Performance | Difference between Performance and | | Difference between Performance and (In % of budget) | |
|---|---|---|---|---|---|---|---|---|---|
| | | Increases | Decreases | | | Original Budget | Final Budget | Original Budget | Final Budget |
| **Fiscal Year 1935/36** | | | | | | | | | |
| Receipts from government property | 3.2 | .... | .... | 3.2 | 3.6 | +0.4 | +0.4 | +12.5 | +12.5 |
| Government enterprises | 1,089.5 | .... | 3.3 | 1,086.2 | 1,085.2 | −4.3 | −1.0 | −0.4 | −0.1 |
| Sale of goods | 375.6 | .... | .... | 375.6 | 509.8 | +134.2 | +134.2 | +35.7 | +35.7 |
| Administrative services | 675.6 | .... | .... | 675.6 | 983.0 | +307.4 | +307.4 | +45.5 | +45.5 |
| Taxes | 11,580.8 | 12.0 | .... | 11,592.8 | 12,920.9 | +1,340.1 | +1,328.1 | +11.5 | +11.5 |
| Fines, etc. | 126.0 | 1.1 | 1.0 | 126.1 | 129.8 | +3.8 | +3.7 | +3.0 | +2.9 |
| Various ordinary receipts | 622.3 | 208.3 | .... | 830.6 | 2,084.3 | +1,462.0 | +1,253.7 | +236.5 | +150.9 |
| Receipts of Mejoramiento Social | 615.9 | .... | .... | 615.9 | 805.6 | +189.7 | +189.7 | +30.8 | +30.8 |
| Receipts of autonomous institutions | 1,531.4 | 3.3 | .... | 1,534.7 | 1,669.1 | +137.7 | +134.4 | +9.0 | +8.8 |
| Total | 16,620.3 | 224.7 | 4.3 | 16,840.7 | 20,191.3 | +3,571.0 | +3,350.6 | +21.5 | +19.9 |
| **Fiscal Year 1940** | | | | | | | | | |
| Receipts from government property | 7.3 | .... | .... | 7.3 | 6.3 | −1.0 | −1.0 | −13.7 | −13.7 |
| Government enterprises | 1,329.8 | .... | .... | 1,329.8 | 1,221.3 | −108.5 | −108.5 | −8.2 | −8.2 |
| Sale of goods | 551.7 | .... | .... | 551.7 | 418.6 | −133.1 | −133.1 | −24.1 | −24.1 |
| Administrative services | 1,299.8 | .... | .... | 1,299.8 | 1,191.7 | −108.1 | −108.1 | −8.3 | −8.3 |
| Taxes | 17,106.2 | .... | .... | 17,106.2 | 14,028.3 | −3,077.9 | −3,077.9 | −18.0 | −18.0 |
| Fines, etc. | 99.5 | .... | .... | 99.5 | 116.5 | +17.0 | +17.0 | +17.1 | +17.1 |
| Various ordinary receipts | 387.4 | 0.3 | .... | 387.7 | 393.9 | +6.5 | +6.2 | +1.7 | +1.6 |
| Receipts of Mejoramiento Social | 867.7 | 366.3 | .... | 1,234.0 | 1,175.7 | +308.0 | −58.3 | +35.5 | −4.7 |
| Receipts of Banco Hipotecario | 1,087.2 | .... | .... | 1,087.2 | 1,508.4 | +421.2 | +421.2 | +38.7 | +38.7 |
| Total | 22,736.5 | 366.6 | .... | 23,103.2 | 20,060.8 | −2,675.7 | −3,042.4 | −11.8 | −13.2 |

TABLE 72 (Continued)

| | Original Budget | Budget Changes | | Final Budget | Performance | Difference between Performance and | | Difference between Performance and | |
| | | Increases | Decreases | | | Original Budget | Final Budget | Original Budget | Final Budget |
| --- | --- | --- | --- | --- | --- | --- | --- | --- | --- |
| | | | | | | | | (In % of budget) | |
| **Fiscal Year 1942** | | | | | | | | | |
| Receipts from government property | 5.5 | ... | ... | 5.5 | 6.1 | +0.6 | +0.6 | +10.9 | +10.9 |
| Government enterprises | 1,134.1 | ... | ... | 1,134.1 | 1,237.8 | +103.7 | +103.7 | +9.1 | +9.1 |
| Sale of goods | 304.4 | ... | ... | 304.4 | 392.5 | +88.1 | +88.1 | +28.9 | +28.9 |
| Administrative services | 1,280.8 | ... | ... | 1,280.8 | 1,218.9 | −61.9 | −61.9 | −4.8 | −4.8 |
| Taxes | 16,917.9 | ... | ... | 16,917.9 | 14,233.1 | −2,684.8 | −2,684.8 | −15.9 | −15.9 |
| Fines, etc. | 78.3 | ... | ... | 78.3 | 92.1 | +13.8 | +13.8 | +17.6 | +17.6 |
| Other ordinary receipts | 635.1 | ... | ... | 635.1 | 1,506.3 | +871.2 | +871.2 | +137.2 | +137.2 |
| Extraordinary receipts | 1,000.0 | ... | ... | 1,000.0 | 1,460.0 | +460.0 | +460.0 | +46.0 | +46.0 |
| Receipts of Mejoramiento Social | 1,092.0 | ... | ... | 1,092.0 | 895.1 | −196.9 | −196.9 | −18.0 | −18.0 |
| Receipts of Banco Hipotecario | 1,000.1 | ... | ... | 1,000.1 | 1,113.2 | +113.1 | +113.1 | +11.3 | +11.3 |
| Total | 23,448.2 | ... | ... | 23,448.2 | 22,155.1 | −1,293.1 | −1,293.1 | −5.5 | −5.5 |
| **Fiscal Year 1945** | | | | | | | | | |
| Receipts from government property | 6.6 | ... | ... | 6.6 | 5.6 | −1.0 | −1.0 | −15.2 | −15.2 |
| Government enterprises | 1,291.5 | ... | ... | 1,291.5 | 1,622.3 | +330.8 | +330.8 | +25.6 | +25.6 |
| Sale of goods | 354.1 | ... | ... | 354.1 | 392.0 | +37.9 | +37.9 | +10.7 | +10.7 |
| Administrative services | 1,360.1 | ... | ... | 1,360.1 | 1,925.3 | +565.2 | +565.2 | +41.6 | +41.6 |
| Taxes | 18,343.7 | ... | ... | 18,343.7 | 21,819.7 | +3,476.0 | +3,476.0 | +18.9 | +18.9 |
| Fines, etc. | 95.6 | ... | ... | 95.6 | 89.8 | −5.8 | −5.8 | −6.1 | −6.1 |
| Various ordinary receipts | 3,407.9 | ... | ... | 3,407.9 | 648.2 | −2,759.6 | −2,759.6 | −81.0 | −81.0 |
| Receipts of Mejoramiento Social | 1,341.7 | ... | ... | 1,341.7 | 1,221.3 | −120.4 | −120.4 | −9.0 | −9.0 |
| Receipts of public debts fund | 3,665.6 | ... | ... | 3,665.6 | 1,751.9 | −1,913.7 | −1,913.7 | −52.2 | −52.2 |
| Total | 29,866.8 | ... | ... | 29,866.8 | 29,476.1 | −390.6 | −390.6 | −1.3 | −1.3 |

TABLE 72 (Continued)

| | Budget Changes | | | | Performance | Difference between Performance and | | Difference between Performance and | |
|---|---|---|---|---|---|---|---|---|---|
| | Original Budget | In-creases | De-creases | Final Budget | | Original Budget | Final Budget | Original Budget | Final Budget |
| | | | | | | | | (In % of budget) | |
| *Fiscal Year 1947* | | | | | | | | | |
| Receipts from government property | 6.0 | ... | ... | 6.0 | 2.7 | −3.3 | −3.3 | −55.0 | −55.0 |
| Government enterprises............. | 1,680.0 | ... | ... | 1,680.0 | 1,938.8 | +258.8 | +258.8 | +15.4 | +15.4 |
| Sale of goods.................... | 1,451.1 | ... | ... | 1,451.1 | 500.7 | −950.4 | −950.4 | −65.5 | −65.5 |
| Administrative services............ | 2,080.6 | ... | ... | 2,080.6 | 5,330.4 | +3,249.8 | +3,249.8 | +156.2 | +156.2 |
| Taxes............................ | 38,652.8 | ... | ... | 38,652.8 | 43,742.0 | +5,089.2 | +5,089.2 | +13.2 | +13.2 |
| Fines............................ | 101.5 | ... | ... | 101.5 | 193.4 | +91.9 | +91.9 | +90.5 | +90.5 |
| Various ordinary receipts.......... | 813.8 | ... | ... | 813.8 | 1,425.7 | +611.9 | +611.9 | +75.2 | +75.2 |
| Social assistance fund............. | 537.5 | ... | ... | 537.5 | 535.0 | −2.5 | −2.5 | −0.5 | −0.5 |
| Total...................... | 45,323.3 | ... | ... | 45,323.3 | 53,668.7 | +8,345.4 | +8,345.4 | +18.4 | +18.4 |

approximately of the same order of magnitude in all categories of receipts (Table 72). The greatest discrepancies in most years occurred in the item "various ordinary receipts." This is not surprising, since this category of receipts includes, among other entries, usually one item of "unforeseen receipts," which by definition is nearly impossible to forecast. In general, it appears that the more or less mechanical basis for making revenue estimates was quite adequate in periods when neither rapid expansions nor contractions of business activity, and neither significant price movements nor significant changes in the volume and value of exports and imports, occurred (e.g. 1942, 1945). In other periods the simple mechanical basis of the revenue estimates proved inadequate; or else the authority granted to the Bureau of the Budget to take account, in the estimates, of changes in economic conditions that might make inadequate the mechanically-arrived-at estimates, was not sufficiently utilized.

In the budget figures, account is also taken of the cash balance in the Treasury, from which deductions are made to provide for the anticipated Treasury obligations for the current fiscal year.[4]

## EXPENDITURES

As to the budget of the expenditures, the law provides that the Director General of the Bureau of the Budget must set at least one month in advance the date when the various department heads must submit the estimates of their requirements for the next fiscal year. If no estimates are obtained from department heads by the date set, the Bureau of the Budget is authorized to assume that the figures of the current budget year are to be reapplied in the next year. The Bureau of the Budget then prepares and presents to the Assembly, through the Ministry of Finance, a detailed budget of government expenditures to-

[4] The budget figures for government revenues shown in Table 72 do not include the cash carry-over from the previous year. The carry-over was excluded in the table because the revenue-performance figures pertain to current receipts of revenues only. Besides, budget figures as shown in Table 72 include special funds, as well as the General Fund. As a result of the elimination of cash balances, budgeted expenditures of special funds likewise occasionally exceed the budgeted expenditures. The omission of the cash balances thus accounts for the deficit as shown in Table 72.

gether with recommendations regarding the means by which expenditures and receipts are to be balanced. That is to say, if the Bureau of the Budget finds that anticipated government revenues are insufficient to cover anticipated expenditures, it must propose measures for the increase of government revenues, or recommend authorization of a loan. As in the case of the revenue budget, the Bureau of the Budget must obtain the consent of the Court of Accounts for its budget of expenditures. Likewise, the Ministry of Finance has the right to change the budget as submitted by the Bureau of the Budget.

A comparison between the original budget figures[5] and performance data, as given in Table 73, indicates that the over-all expenditure figures stay reasonably well within the orders of magnitude of the original budgets. If the item "automatic credits," which is for expenditures for such items as paper for tax forms and similar expenses associated with changes in revenues, is disregarded, we find that in "good" years when revenues exceeded budgetary expenditures the Ministry of Public Works (*Ministerio de Fomento*) and the armed forces benefited primarily from the availability of additional funds, while in "bad" years expenditures for public credits and expenditures of special funds (Mejoramiento Social) suffered most from the curtailment of revenues.

## LEGISLATIVE ENACTMENT

As to the legislative enactment of the budget, the Budget Law provides that in addition to the budget for the ensuing year the National Assembly may, but need not, require reports regarding (a) the performance of the budget currently in force; (b) the expected financial situation at the beginning of the next fiscal year; (c) the "economic situation of the country and its influence on the budget in force and on the preparation of the budget for the following year"; (d) the reasons for modifications of budget figures for particular items in the budget; and (e) proposals for changes in the tax laws. The legislative authority of the National Assembly is restricted by the provision of the Budget

[5] The differences between the original and the final budget (see Table 73) caused by budget changes during the fiscal year are discussed below.

## TABLE 73

### COMPARISON OF BUDGET AND PERFORMANCE FIGURES OF GOVERNMENT EXPENDITURES IN SELECTED YEARS, 1935–1947[a]

*(In thousands of colones)*

| | Original Budget | Budget Changes | | Final Budget | Performance | Difference between Performance and | | Difference between Performance and (In % of Budget) | |
|---|---|---|---|---|---|---|---|---|---|
| | | Increases | Decreases | | | Original Budget | Final Budget | Original Budget | Final Budget |
| *Fiscal Year 1935/36* | | | | | | | | | |
| National Assembly | 135.0 | 167.1 | 70.9 | 231.2 | 225.7 | +90.7 | −5.5 | +67.2 | −2.4 |
| Presidency | 180.0 | 96.0 | 24.7 | 251.3 | 243.6 | +63.6 | −7.7 | +35.3 | −3.1 |
| Ministry of Interior | 2,502.0 | 196.1 | 129.0 | 2,569.1 | 2,531.3 | +29.3 | −37.9 | +1.2 | −1.5 |
| Ministry of Labor | 14.0 | 0.6 | … | 14.6 | 14.0 | … | −0.6 | … | −4.1 |
| Ministry of Development | 1,275.0 | 520.2 | 337.8 | 1,457.4 | 1,449.4 | +174.4 | −8.0 | +13.7 | −0.5 |
| Ministry of Agriculture | 88.0 | 46.0 | 19.7 | 114.3 | 90.5 | +2.5 | −23.8 | +2.8 | −20.8 |
| Ministry of Public Health | 210.0 | 81.5 | 36.1 | 255.4 | 245.6 | +35.6 | −9.9 | +17.0 | −3.9 |
| Ministry of Welfare | 553.0 | 47.0 | 2.1 | 597.9 | 597.9 | +44.9 | … | +8.1 | … |
| Ministry of Foreign Relations | 522.0 | 95.5 | 39.2 | 578.3 | 572.1 | +50.1 | −6.2 | +9.6 | −1.1 |
| Ministry of Justice | 430.0 | 11.9 | 16.8 | 425.1 | 416.1 | −13.9 | −9.0 | −3.2 | −2.1 |
| Ministry of Public Education | 1,625.0 | 53.4 | 33.9 | 1,644.5 | 1,605.7 | −19.3 | −38.8 | −1.2 | −2.4 |
| Ministry of Finance | 1,210.0 | 323.3 | 214.3 | 1,319.0 | 1,213.2 | +3.2 | −105.8 | +0.3 | −8.0 |
| Automatic credits | 254.0 | 753.2 | … | 1,007.2 | 1,007.2 | +753.2 | … | +296.5 | … |
| Ministry of Industry and Commerce | 6.0 | … | … | 6.0 | 5.5 | −0.5 | −0.5 | −8.3 | −8.3 |
| Ministry of Public Credit | 3,989.0 | 2,103.4 | 1,143.4 | 4,949.0 | 4,361.2 | +372.2 | −587.8 | +9.3 | −11.9 |
| Ministry of War, Navy, Airforce | 3,480.0 | 762.5 | 124.9 | 4,117.6 | 4,086.7 | +606.7 | −30.9 | +17.4 | −0.8 |
| Court of Accounts | 75.0 | 2.6 | 2.1 | 75.5 | 74.7 | −0.3 | −0.8 | −0.4 | −1.1 |
| General Accounting Office | 155.0 | 1.5 | 1.5 | 155.0 | 154.5 | −0.5 | −0.5 | −0.3 | −0.3 |
| Judiciary Power | 510.0 | 14.8 | 11.7 | 513.1 | 510.7 | +0.7 | −2.4 | +0.1 | −0.5 |
| Pensions | 462.0 | 17.6 | 9.2 | 470.4 | 466.4 | +4.4 | −4.0 | +1.0 | −0.9 |
| Expenditures of Mejoramiento Social | 898.9 | 255.4 | 55.4 | 1,098.9 | 622.6 | −276.3 | −476.3 | −30.7 | −43.3 |
| Expenditures of autonomous institutions | 2,499.4 | … | … | 2,499.4 | (2,499.4)[b] | … | … | … | … |
| Total | 21,073.3 | 5,549.6 | 2,272.7 | 24,350.2 | 22,993.9 | +1,920.6 | −1,356.3 | +9.1 | −5.6 |

[ 258 ]

TABLE 73 (Continued)

| | Original Budget | Budget Changes | | Final Budget | Performance | Difference between Performance and | | Difference between Performance and | |
|---|---|---|---|---|---|---|---|---|---|
| | | Increases | Decreases | | | Original Budget | Final Budget | Original Budget | Final Budget |
| | | | | | | | | (In % of Budget) | |
| *Fiscal Year 1942* | | | | | | | | | |
| National Assembly.............. | 179.9 | 19.4 | 0.3 | 199.0 | 193.1 | +13.2 | −5.9 | +7.3 | −3.0 |
| Presidency.................... | 230.5 | 0.5 | 0.5 | 230.5 | 207.8 | −22.6 | −22.6 | −9.8 | −9.8 |
| Ministry of Interior........... | 2,853.1 | 115.2 | 61.1 | 2,907.1 | 2,837.8 | −15.3 | −69.3 | −0.5 | −2.4 |
| Ministry of Labor............. | 17.9 | ... | ... | 17.9 | 16.1 | −1.1 | −1.1 | −6.1 | −6.1 |
| Ministry of Development........ | 1,951.0 | 630.6 | 480.0 | 2,101.6 | 1,784.3 | −166.7 | −317.2 | −8.5 | −15.1 |
| Ministry of Agriculture......... | 116.1 | 25.3 | 25.3 | 116.1 | 109.4 | −6.7 | −6.7 | −5.8 | −5.8 |
| Ministry of Welfare............ | 460.8 | 54.2 | 13.1 | 501.9 | 480.5 | +20.3 | −21.4 | +4.4 | −4.3 |
| Ministry of Foreign Relations.... | 783.8 | 67.0 | 37.7 | 813.1 | 797.5 | +13.7 | −15.6 | +1.7 | −1.9 |
| Ministry of Justice............ | 560.6 | 52.8 | 52.8 | 560.6 | 515.5 | −45.1 | −45.1 | −8.0 | −8.0 |
| Ministry of Public Education.... | 2,211.3 | 60.3 | 60.3 | 2,211.3 | 2,224.4 | +13.1 | +13.1 | +0.6 | +0.6 |
| Ministry of Finance............ | 2,549.9 | 95.8 | 400.0 | 2,245.8 | 2,152.6 | −397.3 | −93.2 | −15.6 | −4.1 |
| Automatic credit.............. | 221.2 | ... | ... | 221.2 | 593.3 | +372.1 | +372.1 | +168.2 | +168.2 |
| Ministry of Industry and Commerce | 6.0 | ... | ... | 6.0 | 5.8 | −0.2 | −0.2 | −3.3 | −3.3 |
| Ministry of Public Credit....... | 2,208.8 | 0.2 | 0.2 | 2,208.8 | 1,559.5 | −649.3 | −649.3 | −29.4 | −29.4 |
| Ministry of War, Navy, Airforce.. | 3,878.0 | 70.2 | 31.0 | 3,917.2 | 3,618.7 | −259.3 | −298.4 | −6.7 | −7.6 |
| Court of Accounts............. | 355.5 | 16.8 | 16.1 | 356.1 | 349.9 | −5.6 | −6.3 | −1.6 | −1.8 |
| Judiciary Power............... | 667.2 | 4.1 | 4.1 | 667.2 | 652.6 | −14.6 | −14.6 | −2.2 | −2.2 |
| Subsidies.................... | 1,378.8 | 96.8 | ... | 1,475.5 | 1,447.0 | +68.2 | −28.5 | +4.9 | −1.9 |
| Pensions..................... | 724.0 | 23.3 | ... | 747.3 | 745.2 | +21.2 | −2.0 | +2.9 | −0.3 |
| Expenditures of Mejoramiento Social | 1,167.0 | ... | ... | 1,167.0 | 624.8 | −542.1 | −542.1 | −46.5 | −46.5 |
| Expenditures of Banco Hipotecario | 1,000.1 | ... | ... | 1,000.1 | 1,070.6 | +70.5 | +70.5 | +7.0 | +7.0 |
| Total....................... | 23,521.3 | 1,332.5 | 1,182.5 | 23,671.3 | 21,987.2 | −1,534.0 | −1,684.0 | −6.5 | −7.1 |

# TABLE 73 (Continued)

| Fiscal Year 1945 | Original Budget | Budget Changes | | Final Budget | Performance | Difference between Performance and | | Difference between Performance and (In % of Budget) | |
| --- | --- | --- | --- | --- | --- | --- | --- | --- | --- |
| | | Increases | Decreases | | | Original Budget | Final Budget | Original Budget | Final Budget |
| National Assembly.............. | 211.8 | 345.8 | 3.1 | 554.6 | 554.0 | +342.2 | −0.6 | +161.6 | −0.1 |
| Presidency...................... | 312.1 | 58.8 | 14.7 | 356.3 | 351.9 | +39.7 | −4.4 | +12.7 | −1.2 |
| Ministry of Interior............. | 1,322.0 | 111.6 | 10.3 | 1,423.3 | 1,403.2 | +81.2 | −20.1 | +6.1 | −1.4 |
| Ministry of Labor............... | 22.5 | 1.3 | 1.9 | 21.9 | 20.4 | −2.1 | −1.5 | −9.3 | −6.8 |
| Ministry of Development......... | 5,712.2 | 870.7 | 591.8 | 5,991.1 | 5,979.7 | +267.5 | −11.4 | +4.7 | −0.2 |
| Ministry of Agriculture.......... | 177.7 | 68.4 | 4.8 | 241.5 | 194.7 | +17.0 | −46.8 | +9.6 | −19.4 |
| Ministry of Welfare............. | 729.9 | 3.3 | 11.3 | 721.9 | 695.4 | −34.5 | −26.6 | −4.7 | −3.7 |
| Ministry of Foreign Relations.... | 963.9 | 233.5 | 145.9 | 1,051.5 | 1,008.3 | +44.4 | −43.2 | +4.6 | −4.1 |
| Ministry of Justice.............. | 615.0 | 369.9 | 356.7 | 628.1 | 606.4 | −8.6 | −21.7 | −1.4 | −3.5 |
| Ministry of Public Education..... | 2,760.0 | 502.3 | 136.0 | 3,126.4 | 3,109.6 | +349.6 | −16.8 | +12.7 | −0.5 |
| Ministry of Finance............. | 2,585.1 | 161.7 | 498.8 | 2,248.0 | 2,195.0 | −390.1 | −53.0 | −15.1 | −2.4 |
| Automatic credits............... | 207.0 | 932.0 | ... | 1,139.0 | 1,139.0 | +932.0 | −0.4 | +450.2 | ... |
| Ministry of Industry and Commerce | 16.7 | ... | ... | 16.7 | 16.3 | −0.4 | −0.4 | −2.4 | −2.4 |
| Ministry of Public Credit........ | 274.7 | ... | 267.5 | 274.7 | 240.0 | −34.7 | −34.7 | −12.6 | −12.6 |
| Ministry of National Defense..... | 4,080.2 | 120.9 | ... | 3,933.7 | 3,814.7 | −265.5 | −119.0 | −6.5 | −3.0 |
| Ministry of Public Safety........ | 837.4 | 23.6 | ... | 861.0 | 867.8 | +30.4 | +6.8 | +3.6 | +0.8 |
| Court of Accounts............... | 384.5 | 8.8 | 8.8 | 384.5 | 377.0 | −7.5 | −7.5 | −2.0 | −2.0 |
| Judiciary Power................. | 711.9 | 7.4 | 4.2 | 715.1 | 708.6 | −3.3 | −6.5 | −0.5 | −0.9 |
| Subsidies....................... | 1,920.7 | 75.2 | 301.4 | 1,694.6 | 1,682.3 | −238.4 | −12.3 | −12.4 | −0.7 |
| Pensions........................ | 1,100.0 | 50.0 | ... | 1,150.0 | 1,150.0 | +50.0 | ... | +4.5 | ... |
| Expenditures of Mejoramiento Social | 1,000.1 | 391.6 | ... | 1,391.7 | 781.3 | −218.8 | −610.4 | −21.9 | −43.9 |
| Expenditures of public debt fund.... | 5,415.6 | ... | ... | 5,415.6 | 2,385.7 | −3,029.9 | −3,029.9 | −55.9 | −55.9 |
| Total.................. | 31,361.3 | 4,336.8 | 2,357.0 | 33,341.1 | 29,281.2 | −2,080.1 | −4,059.9 | −6.6 | −12.2 |

TABLE 73 (Continued)

| | Budget Changes | | | | Performance | Difference between Performance and | | Difference between Performance and | |
|---|---|---|---|---|---|---|---|---|---|
| | Original Budget | Increases | Decreases | Final Budget | Performance | Original Budget | Final Budget | Original Budget | Final Budget |
| | | | | | | | | (In % of Budget) | |
| *Fiscal Year 1947* | | | | | | | | | |
| National Assembly............ | 345.0 | 40.0 | 6.1 | 378.9 | 373.8 | +28.8 | -5.1 | +8.3 | -1.3 |
| Presidency................. | 505.9 | 55.1 | 1.5 | 559.5 | 552.4 | +46.5 | -7.1 | +9.2 | -1.3 |
| Ministry of Interior......... | 3,348.9 | 36.7 | 33.1 | 3,352.4 | 3,155.8 | -193.1 | -196.6 | -5.8 | -5.9 |
| Ministry of Labor........... | 173.2 | 44.7 | 8.1 | 209.8 | 182.5 | +9.3 | -27.4 | +5.4 | -13.1 |
| Ministry of Development..... | 7,953.5 | 3,821.7 | 961.8 | 10,813.3 | 10,545.1 | +2,591.6 | -268.2 | +31.7 | -2.5 |
| Ministry of Foreign Relations..... | 1,548.9 | 260.5 | 79.4 | 1,730.0 | 1,671.7 | +122.8 | -58.3 | +7.9 | -3.4 |
| Ministry of Justice.......... | 1,037.8 | 83.2 | 72.0 | 1,049.0 | 993.8 | -44.0 | -55.2 | -4.2 | -5.3 |
| Ministry of Public Education... | 5,353.1 | 889.3 | 243.3 | 5,999.1 | 5,824.8 | +471.7 | -174.3 | +8.8 | -2.9 |
| Ministry of Welfare.......... | 863.1 | 307.7 | 22.7 | 1,148.2 | 1,022.6 | +159.5 | -125.5 | +18.5 | -10.9 |
| Ministry of Finance.......... | 5,471.2 | 2,137.0 | 873.0 | 6,735.1 | 6,358.3 | +887.1 | -376.8 | +16.2 | -5.6 |
| Ministry of Public Credit..... | 2,600.0 | ... | ... | 2,600.0 | 2,536.2 | -63.8 | -63.8 | -2.5 | -2.5 |
| Ministry of Commerce....... | 24.4 | ... | ... | 24.4 | 24.0 | -0.4 | -0.4 | -1.6 | -1.6 |
| Agriculture and Industry..... | 1,561.3 | 1,078.9 | 42.7 | 2,597.6 | 2,415.3 | +854.0 | -182.3 | +54.7 | -7.0 |
| Ministry of National Defense... | 5,251.1 | 912.7 | 193.8 | 5,970.0 | 5,857.0 | +605.9 | -113.0 | +11.5 | -1.9 |
| Ministry of Public Safety..... | 1,633.3 | 195.2 | 90.6 | 1,737.9 | 1,716.7 | +83.4 | -21.2 | +5.1 | -1.2 |
| Court of Accounts........... | 606.7 | 67.6 | 0.1 | 674.2 | 658.2 | +51.5 | -16.0 | +8.5 | -2.4 |
| Judiciary Power............. | 912.7 | 27.4 | 8.7 | 931.5 | 905.2 | -7.5 | -26.3 | -0.8 | -2.8 |
| Subsidies.................. | 4,931.4 | 1,106.4 | 105.3 | 5,932.5 | 5,551.2 | +619.8 | -381.3 | +12.6 | -6.4 |
| Pensions.................. | 1,515.3 | 16.0 | ... | 1,531.3 | 1,531.3 | +16.0 | ... | +1.1 | ... |
| Social assistance fund....... | 537.5 | ... | ... | 537.5 | ... | -537.5 | -537.5 | -100.0 | -100.0 |
| Total.................. | 46,174.2 | 11,080.2 | 2,742.1 | 54,512.3 | 51,875.9 | +5,701.7 | -2,636.3 | +12.3 | -4.8 |

ᵃ Data are those given in the "Memoria de Hacienda." They pertain to the General Fund only.

Law that the budget cannot be changed before or after its enactment without according a hearing to the Ministry of Finance. Moreover, the Assembly cannot reduce or eliminate revenues included in the budget without obtaining the views of the Ministry of Finance, which in turn must obtain the opinion of the Court of Accounts and of the Bureau of the Budget regarding the effects that such a reduction or elimination would have upon the execution of the budget. The Assembly cannot approve a budget that is not balanced, in the sense that sufficient means, including loan proceeds, must be available to cover the proposed volume of expenditures. The Constitution (but not the Budget Law) provides (Article 134) that the Assembly cannot increase appropriations without a request to that effect from the Administration.

### FORM OF BUDGET

The budget of expenditures is divided into titles and chapters. Titles pertain to various government departments; chapters refer to offices within the individual departments. Thus, the budget for 1948 of the Ministry of Finance has the following chapters: (1) Office of the Minister; (2) Treasury Service; (3) Customs Service; (4) Bureau of Internal Revenue; (5) Court of Tax Appeals; (6) Bureau of Statistics; (7) Legal Office of the Ministry; (8) Administration of Inheritance and Gift Taxes; (9) National Engraving Office; (10) Automatic Credits; (11) Various Expenses of the Department.[6] The 1948 budget contains seventeen titles with 152 chapters.

The subdivision of the budget into so many chapters is of practical significance, since the Administration may transfer appropriations without legislative approval only within a chapter. The basis for the establishment (or discontinuance) of individual chapters, however, is not quite clear. It appears that in the preparation of the budget an attempt is made to assure continuity by maintaining the same breakdown as that used in previous years. Since the functions of some administrative bodies, which in previous years were considered worthy of a special

[6] The chapter on "Various Expenditures" includes all items that can not be allocated to any particular subdivision of the department.

chapter, have considerably shrunk, and functions of other divisions have expanded, the result of this procedure is that the budget consists of chapters of very uneven size. Thus, the annual budget of the Salvadorean consulate in Puerto Barrios, Guatemala, presented as a special chapter, is 9,000 colones, while the chapter "Bureau of Public Works" of the Ministry of Public Works amounts to 3,418,880 colones.

Regarding the breakdown of the chapters of the budget into individual items, the Budget Law provides (Articles 28 and 29) that each item must clearly indicate the purpose of the proposed expenditure. Global and undetermined assignment of funds, from which the purpose of the proposed expenditure cannot be clearly recognized, are prohibited. An inspection of the budgets of the last years indicates that, in general, these provisions of the Budget Law are adhered to, and sufficiently detailed information is given to enable interested persons, such as the members of the National Assembly, to recognize the purpose of the proposed expenditures. In certain instances, however, this clause of the law is by-passed. For instance, the above-mentioned budget of 3.4 million colones of the Bureau of Public Works includes, in addition to various exactly defined construction projects, one item for "the construction of national buildings and accessory works" of 1 million colones.

In the annual budgets, and in their liquidations, expenditures are divided into two categories, fixed and "variable." The main purpose of this distinction is to simplify the control of government expenditures. Fixed expenditures are allocated by the Treasury and approved by the Court of Accounts on an "installment" basis, i.e., one twelfth of the amount budgeted for the entire year is made available for the particular budgetary purpose each month. Fixed expenditures include primarily the salaries of government employees, recurrent payments for rents and office supplies, and subsidies granted to autonomous public bodies (which likewise are expended largely on salaries). All other expenditures are considered "variable." The main objectives of "variable" expenditures therefore are the acquisition of goods, the payment of wages for public works and such lump-sum payments as the servicing of the public debt and contributions to international organizations. The distinction between "variable" and fixed costs, aside from its control functions, is a useful basis for a critical appraisal of the discharge of government functions. Several parts of the analysis that follows are based upon it.

### DEBT PROVISIONS

The Budget Law implements the constitutional provisions regarding the limitation of the floating public debt by the provision that credit operations without special legislative approval must be strictly transient and must be terminated by repayments before the end of the fiscal year. In recent years the limit has been fixed in the "general dispositions" appended to every annual budget, at 10 per cent of the budgeted revenues, the constitutional maximum. All other credit operations of the government must be specifically authorized by the National Assembly. Legislative action is not required, however, if the Minister of Finance engages in refunding operations through which the amount of public debt does not increase.

## 2. CHANGES IN THE BUDGET

The Budget Law distinguishes three legal forms through which the budget can be amended: credit transfers, supplementary credits, and exceptional credits. The Administration has the right to authorize, through an announcement (*acuerdo*) published in the official gazette, transfers of expenditures of the same "type" (fixed or "variable") within the same chapter of the budget. This right of the Administration to make transfers is restricted in several important respects. Transfers of appropriations for salaries are not permitted unless the appropriations have been saved as a result of the positions in question having been vacant. Credits for other fixed expenditures can be transferred only if the services that were to have been financed by such credits have been abolished or provisions have been made to obtain such services free of charge. Credits allocated for the servicing of the public debt cannot be transferred unless a formal arrangement with the creditors is made. Transfers from ordinary to exceptional appropriations and shifts from the general to special funds and vice versa are prohibited.

Supplementary appropriations can be requested only in the second half of the fiscal year. They are permitted if the appropriations of the original budget prove insufficient or if new services are to be established. Departments desirous of obtaining supplementary appropriations must make applications to that effect to the Ministry of Finance, substantiate them by citing reasons why existing appropriations are insufficient, and prove the impossibility of postponing the proposed expenditures or of meeting them through credit transfers. For favorable action upon requests for supplementary credits, the consent of the Court of Accounts is required. The Court of Accounts must determine whether sufficient funds are available in the form of cash balances, savings on other appropriations, or expected revenues. It must certify the probability that the granting of supplementary credits will not cause a deficit at the end of the fiscal year. If the report of the Court of Accounts is favorable, the Bureau of the Budget prepares a supplementary budget and submits it for legislative action to the National Assembly. If, however, the Court of Accounts or the Bureau of the Budget, which likewise must render an opinion on the advisability of supplementary appropriations, raises objections, the Ministry of Finance can reject the requests. Such a rejection can be overruled only by a unanimous vote of the President and all the cabinet ministers with the exception of the Minister of Finance.

Exceptional credits can be resorted to only in the case of war, revolts, epidemics, earthquakes, and "other similar catastrophes," and must be limited to the amounts absolutely necessary to meet expenditures of immediate urgency. They must be appropriated by the National Assembly. If the legislature is not in session, however, the executive power can appropriate funds provisionally, but it must seek legislative approval of such action within the first eight days of the next ordinary or extraordinary session of the National Assembly. In general, exceptional appropriations are to be covered by ordinary revenues. If this is impossible, the Administration has the right to suspend such government services as are dispensable. If funds at the disposal of the government are still insufficient, it can contract loans up to 500,000 colones beyond the general limits set for short-term credit operations of the government.

An inspection of Table 73 indicates that credit transfers and supplementary credits were resorted to every year, the final budget of expenditures being larger in all years than the original budget. The increase, however, varied considerably, from a record increase of more than 8 million colones in 1947 to 150,000 colones in 1942. Shifts in the budget were in the same directions as those appearing in the comparison between performance and original budget figures presented above. That is to say, most supplementary appropriations accrued to the Ministry of Public Works and to the armed forces. One of the results of transfers and supplementary appropriations is that performance figures are consistently smaller than the final appropriations, although as indicated above, in several years actual expenditures exceeded the appropriations of the original budget. This performance record suggests that, generally speaking, public finances of El Salvador have been well managed, in the sense that expenditures have remained within the limits of appropriated funds. On the other hand, the impression is conveyed that rather liberal use is made of transfers and supplementary credits.

Adjustments of the budget to rapidly changing needs are in themselves appropriate and, in instances when the government is faced with rapid price increases such as those experienced in 1947, necessary. It seems, however, that the resistance of the Ministry of Finance, of the Bureau of the Budget, and of the Court of Accounts, to supplementary appropriations decreases with an increase in revenues. If it is assumed that the original budget was organically balanced in the sense that it divided available funds and revenues equitably among the various departments and the functions that they perform, transfers and supplementary appropriations may disturb that balance. In order to curtail the use of supplementary credits and transfers within the chapters of the budget, it might be appropriate to limit the amount of supplementary credits allocated to any one chapter of the budget, or to any department, to a fixed percentage of the original budget. Such a limitation would bring about a more exact scrutiny of original budget requests on the one hand, and on the other would prevent too much reliance on supplementary appropriations and the uneconomical use of appropriated funds.

### 3. COLLECTION OF PUBLIC REVENUES

Revenues of the Salvadorean government are collected through three distinct administrative organizations: the Treasury, which controls the fourteen local tax administrations (*Administraciones de Rentas*), the Bureau of Internal Revenue, and the Customs Service. Various government enterprises (the Postal, Telegraph, and Telephone Administration, and such lesser enterprises as the National Printing Office) and several other agencies, such as police offices, consular offices, and other administrative agencies are authorized by law to accept fees for services rendered and to impose fines, likewise obtain revenues directly. The Treasury, whose primary duties consist of the administration of public funds and their disbursements, obtains directly only such payments to the government as are not collected by the Bureau of Internal Revenue, the Customs Service, or other administrative agencies authorized to accept payments for the government. Thus, the Treasury collects the proceeds of loans and contributions to public funds from other governments, such as the contribution of the United States government for the construction of the inter-American highway in El Salvador.

#### TAX ADMINISTRATION

Since about 90 per cent of all government revenues are derived from taxation, the Bureau of Internal Revenue, together with the local tax administration and the Customs Service, is the most important source, from an administrative point of view, of government receipts. The Bureau of Internal Revenue is headed by a Director General and a Subdirector General, and is organized in thirteen sections, five of which serve such purely administrative purposes as the keeping of archives and correspondence. The remaining eight sections are in charge of the following classes of taxes:

1. Sanitation and pavement taxes
2. Liquor taxes

3. Stamp taxes
4. Entertainment taxes
5. Transfer, inheritance and gift taxes
6. Business registrations (*matrículas de comercio*)
7. Various taxes (including cigarette, beer, soft drink, and sugar taxes)
8. Income and *vialidad* taxes

In the local tax administration offices the administration of various types of taxes is frequently combined in order to save personnel; in the larger offices, however, the administrative division prevailing in the Bureau of Internal Revenue is maintained through the allocation of all tasks pertaining to one type of taxes to one person or one group of persons. Most of the indirect taxes, such as liquor taxes, the cigarette tax, the sugar tax, and certain business taxes, are collected at the source, that is to say, at the place of production (liquor tax, cigarette tax), or through the sale of tax stamps (beer tax, soft drink tax).

Direct taxes are assessed on the basis of tax returns, and payment is requested through the issuance of a payment order (income tax, property-transfer tax) or against the "sale" of a printed receipt (*vialidad* taxes).

The local tax administration offices serve several purposes. In the first place they act as local agents of the Bureau of Internal Revenue, accepting tax returns from taxpayers and forwarding tax assessments from the Bureau of Internal Revenue to taxpayers. In addition, they act as receiving offices to which taxes are paid. Finally, they act as pay offices for the disbursement of public funds for the Treasury.

All funds received by the local tax administration offices are turned over to the Treasury. Funds necessary for the making of payments by the local tax offices are received from the Treasury. In the case of certain taxes the municipal offices (*Alcaldías*) take care of the notification of taxpayers and the collection.

### CUSTOMS SERVICE

The Customs Service is responsible for the assessment and collection of all taxes levied on imports and exports. It consists of a Bureau of Customs headed by a Director General and a Subdirector, five customs offices, and a postal customs office. The five customs offices are supplemented by seven customs "delegations," which exercise limited jurisdiction at border points and at other points of entry into and departure from the country (airports).

Receipts of the Customs Service, which consist of export and import duties, consular invoice fees, storage fees, and similar charges, are turned over to the Treasury.

## 4. ADMINISTRATION AND DISBURSEMENTS OF PUBLIC FUNDS

The administration and the disbursement of public funds are the responsibility of the Treasury. Its internal organization and its functions are regulated by the provisions of the Treasury Law (*Ley de Tesorería*) of 1936. The law contains numerous detailed provisions (208 articles) regarding the operations of Treasury accounts, the disposition of public funds, and their control.

### COLLECTIONS

For the purposes of internal control and better administration, two distinct services are maintained. All funds flowing to the Treasury go through the channels of "collectors." There are several collectors in charge of receiving funds from local tax administrations and from the Customs Service. Other collectors control receipts of the government enterprises and of the police. All revenues are consolidated in a General Fund which is maintained by the Treasury with the Central Reserve Bank or in depositories selected by the central bank

In order to control the flow of funds paid to the government, control stamps are issued to all collectors, who must affix the stamps, in the amount of the sums paid to them, on official receipt blanks. Copies of the receipts accompany the transfer of all funds from the individual collectors to the Treasury. Collectors are also responsible for the receipt on time of all payments due to the government. For that purpose they receive copies of payment orders issued to individuals by other government authorities. If payment is not received at the end of the period within which the payment is due, the collector must notify the Director General of the Treasury, who in turn is authorized by law to extend a period of grace of ten days to the delinquent debtor. If payment is not received within this additional period the case is turned over to the Legal Department (*Fiscalía*) to levy execution.

### DISBURSEMENTS

The disbursement of public funds is the duty of the Paymaster General (*Pagador General*), who controls a staff of "career paymasters" in the Treasury and various other government departments and enterprises and also controls the activities of "honorary paymasters" who disburse the salaries of government employees and are elected for that purpose by them. In order to obtain funds, each department must submit to the Finance Minister every second month a statement of the fixed and "variable" expenditures that the budget provides for the particular department, and request the allocation of funds. The law provides (Article 67) that if the Finance Minister finds that the requests for the allocation of funds is likely to exceed the funds available to the Treasury and endanger the budgetary equilibrium, it can request the department heads to lower their estimates. If his advice is not heeded, the Minister of Finance must submit the dispute for decision to the cabinet. The Director General of the Treasury is likewise required by law to notify the Minister of Finance of an existing or anticipated shortage of funds and, if such a deficiency is considered transient, to request authorization to obtain a short-term loan from the Central Reserve Bank, within the limits laid down in the Budget Law.[7] The Minister of Finance must obtain the approval of the Court of Accounts prior to consenting to the contraction of a loan. Short-term loans must be repaid with interest within the same fiscal year, from unobligated funds of the Treasury. If no unobligated funds are available, the Director General of the Treasury or the President of the Court of Accounts is required by law (Article 145) to call the attention of the Minister of Finance to this situation. It is then the obligation of the Minister of Finance to find means

[7] Cf. above, p. 264.

for the reduction of expenditures, and to propose economies to the cabinet, which if approved form the basis for the future allocation of public funds.

## PURCHASES

The purchase of goods and of services other than those rendered by government employees is regulated in the Purchasing Law of 1945, which defines the functions of the General Purchasing Office. All purchases with the exception of real estate and certain kinds of merchandise, including locally produced building materials, must be made for all government departments by the General Purchasing Office. Exempted are purchases amounting to less than 200 colones for government agencies and less than 1,000 colones for autonomous public bodies. The General Purchasing Office also negotiates all rental contracts for the government that involve payment of more than 75 colones, with the exception of rentals outside of El Salvador. The General Purchasing Office maintains a warehouse of merchandise (such as office supplies, gasoline, etc.) generally needed by the government departments. The law requires that the General Purchasing Office must make all purchases only after publicly announcing its purchase intentions and obtaining bids from all interested parties. It is then required to accept that offer which is "best suited for the interests of the service."

If a government department wants to purchase merchandise or services of persons not employed by the government, it has to submit a request for approval to the Court of Accounts or submit an order to the purchasing office. In both instances, the department desiring to make the purchase must certify that credits for the purchase in question are available in the budget. This certification must be approved by the Fiscal Accounting Office (*Contaduría Fiscal*) of the Court of Accounts. In order to make payment for goods delivered or services rendered to the government, the department requesting payment must issue a payment order which must show title, chapter, and article of the budget under which the purchase falls. The Fiscal Accounting Office must approve the payment order prior to the transfer of funds to the paymaster who is to effect payment. If merchandise is purchased for a government department by the General Purchasing Office, or is transferred from the warehouse of the General Purchasing Office to the government department, funds appropriated for that purchase are transferred from the department to the General Purchasing Office. The administrative expenses of the General Purchasing Office are covered by an addition of 15 per cent to the purchase price, which addition is also charged against the appropriation.

The payment of salaries of government employees is regulated by a Salary Law which determines the monthly salaries paid to all government employees. Since all positions are enumerated in the law, it serves at the same time as a table of organization of the public administration. In the last few years, several general salary increases have taken place, the functions of several departments have been expanded, and personnel has been added to their staff, with the result that the implied permanent character of the Salary Law has been considerably weakened. As a matter of fact, three new salary laws have been passed in the last three years prior to the passing of the annual budget. The "general dispositions" attached to each salary law provide that employees in every position established by the law shall be classified in four categories, the salaries for which range from 70 to 100 per cent of the "full" salary provided in the law. The appointment of each employee, which is published in the Official Gazette, determines in which category he is included. A comparison between the salaries allocated to each position in the Salary Law and the amount of money appropriated in the annual budget for the salaries of each government office indicates that sufficient funds are customarily made available to pay the highest salary category to all employees. This, and the fact that in a number of departments the classifying of employees in lower than the first category is not permitted, indicates that in most instances employees obtain the full salaries allocated in the Salary Law to their positions.

# APPENDIX D

## DESCRIPTION OF THE MORE IMPORTANT TAXES

### (*First appendix to Chapter IV*)

As INDICATED IN CHAPTER IV, the purpose of this appendix is to familiarize the reader with the fiscal and administrative aspects of the more important taxes of the Salvadorean tax system. In particular, those characteristics of individual taxes that serve as a basis for the analytical investigations presented in the second part of the report have been fully presented.

### 1. DIRECT TAXES

As indicated in Chapter IV and confirmed by Tables 74 and 75, the contribution of direct taxes to total government revenues is only moderately significant. At present, six different kinds of direct taxes are levied: the income tax; series B, C, and D of *vialidad*; inheritance and gift taxes; fees for the extension of the *cédulas de vecindad*; a 2 per cent tax on dividends of corporations; and a 1 per cent tax on profits of commercial banks.

The total yield of these taxes during 1940 to 1947 fluctuated between 2.4 and 3.8 million colones or between 7.3 and 13.3 per cent of total tax receipts.

In addition to the direct taxes proper, however, the government collects three gross-revenue taxes — the coffee export tax, the sugar tax, and the cotton tax[1] — which are paid in lieu of the income tax. That is to say, no income tax is levied on the income derived from the production of coffee, sugar, or cotton textiles. If the amounts collected on these taxes are added to the yield of direct taxes proper, the share of the combined group of direct taxes and taxes in lieu of the income tax, increases to more than one fourth of total tax receipts.

---

[1] The henequen tax and the gross receipts tax on electric companies also shown in Tables 74 and 75 were discontinued in 1943 and 1944, respectively.

## TABLE 74

### DIRECT TAXES AND TAXES PAID IN LIEU OF INCOME TAX, 1935/36 AND 1940 TO 1948

*(In thousands of colones)*

| | 1935/36 | 1940 | 1941 | 1942 | 1943 | 1944 | 1945 | 1946 | 1947 | 1948a |
|---|---|---|---|---|---|---|---|---|---|---|
| **Direct Taxes** | | | | | | | | | | |
| Income tax | 590.5 | 692.8 | 1,125.7 | 1,582.4 | 1,602.4 | 2,023.3 | 2,971.0 | 2,662.1 | 2,964.9 | 2,600.0 |
| Vialidad B, C, D | 190.7b | 225.1 | 224.5 | 251.3 | 254.1b | 205.5 | 241.6 | 232.3 | 242.4 | 250.0 |
| Inheritance and gift taxes | 358.9 | 335.1 | 560.5 | 520.1 | 491.5 | 463.5 | 244.7 | 975.4 | 477.2 | 500.0 |
| Cédulas de Vecindad | 0.3 | 3.4 | 126.0 | 14.2 | 14.5 | 24.9 | 73.8 | 41.5 | 34.3 | 20.0 |
| Dividend tax | ... | 16.1 | 17.4 | 15.5 | 21.9 | 21.1 | 20.5 | 22.7 | 37.0 | 16.0 |
| Tax on bank profits | ... | 1.1 | 1.0 | 1.4 | 1.8 | 2.2 | 2.6 | 3.3 | 5.0 | 2.0 |
| Total | 1,140.4 | 1,273.6 | 2,055.1 | 2,384.9 | 2,386.2 | 2,740.5 | 3,554.2 | 3,937.3 | 3,760.8 | 3,388.0 |
| **Taxes in lieu of income tax** | | | | | | | | | | |
| Coffee tax | 1,394.5 | 1,472.2 | 864.6 | 1,353.0 | 1,388.8 | 4,392.3 | 1,751.9 | 4,414.3 | 7,200.0 | 9,000.0 |
| Sugar tax | 233.7 | 231.6 | 257.7 | 224.9 | 288.2b | 329.1 | 347.8 | 775.3 | 1,630.6 | 1,400.0 |
| Cotton tax | ... | ... | ... | 158.8 | ... | 288.2 | 265.4 | 286.4 | 373.4 | 300.0 |
| Henequen tax | 26.6 | 82.1 | 75.8 | ... | 76.4 | ... | ... | ... | ... | ... |
| Gross receipts tax on electric companies | ... | 111.0 | 112.3 | 118.0 | 115.9 | 140.1 | ... | ... | ... | ... |
| Total | 1,854.8 | 1,896.9 | 1,310.4 | 1,834.7 | 1,869.3 | 5,149.7 | 2,365.1 | 5,476.0 | 9,204.0 | 10,700.0 |
| Grand Total | 2,995.2 | 3,160.5 | 3,365.5 | 4,216.6 | 4,255.5 | 7,890.2 | 5,919.3 | 9,413.3 | 12,964.8 | 14,088.0 |

a Budget.
b Estimated.

## TABLE 75

### RATIO OF DIRECT TAXES AND TAXES PAID IN LIEU OF INCOME TAX TO TOTAL TAXES, 1935/36 AND 1940 TO 1948

(*In per cent*)

| | 1935/36 | 1940 | 1941 | 1942 | 1943 | 1944 | 1945 | 1946 | 1947 | 1948 [a] |
|---|---|---|---|---|---|---|---|---|---|---|
| Income tax, to total taxes | 3.4 | 4.0 | 6.4 | 8.6 | 7.4 | 7.7 | 11.1 | 7.2 | 5.9 | 5.5 |
| Total direct taxes, to total taxes | 6.5 | 7.3 | 11.6 | 12.9 | 11.1 | 10.5 | 13.3 | 10.7 | 7.5 | 7.1 |
| Total taxes in lieu of income taxes, to total taxes | 10.6 | 10.9 | 7.4 | 9.9 | 8.7 | 19.7 | 8.9 | 14.9 | 18.3 | 22.6 |
| Income tax, and taxes in lieu of income tax, to total taxes | 13.9 | 14.9 | 13.8 | 18.5 | 16.1 | 27.4 | 20.0 | 22.2 | 24.2 | 28.0 |
| Total direct taxes, and taxes in lieu of income tax, to total taxes | 17.1 | 18.1 | 19.1 | 22.8 | 19.8 | 30.2 | 22.2 | 25.6 | 25.8 | 29.7 |

[a] Budget.

### INCOME TAX

The income tax is a progressive tax on the net income of individuals and corporations. It is one of the oldest in Latin America, having been enacted in 1917, when the rates were as follows;

| Income (colones) | Rate (per cent) |
|---|---|
| 2,000– 3,000 | 2 |
| 3,000– 4,000 | 2½ |
| 4,000– 5,000 | 3 |
| 5,000– 6,000 | 3½ |
| 6,000– 7,000 | 4 |
| 7,000– 8,000 | 4½ |
| 8,000– 9,000 | 5 |
| 9,000–10,000 | 5½ |
| 10,000 and above | 6 |

In 1919 the tax base was redefined through more specific provisions regarding the basic exemption of 2,000 colones, with the result that thenceforth the highest rate of 6 per cent was reached at a *taxable* annual income of 8,000 colones. The present rate structure was established by an amendment of December 1940. The rates prevailing since then are as follows:

| Taxable income (colones) | Rate (per cent) |
|---|---|
| Up to   1,000 | 2 |
| 1,000– 2,000 | 2½ |
| 2,000– 3,000 | 3 |
| 3,000– 4,000 | 3½ |
| 4,000– 5,000 | 4 |
| 5,000– 6,000 | 4½ |
| 6,000– 7,000 | 5 |
| 7,000– 8,000 | 5½ |
| 8,000– 9,000 | 6 |
| 9,000–10,000 | 7 |
| 10,000–12,000 | 8 |
| 12,000–14,000 | 9 |
| 14,000–16,000 | 10 |
| 16,000–18,000 | 11 |
| 18,000–22,000 | 12 |
| 22,000–26,000 | 13 |
| 26,000–30,000 | 14 |
| 30,000–34,000 | 15 |
| 34,000–38,000 | 16 |

| Taxable income (*colones*) | Rate (*per cent*) |
|---|---|
| 38,000–42,000 | 17 |
| 42,000–46,000 | 18 |
| 46,000–50,000 | 19 |
| 50,000 and above | 20 |

The law defines net income as income from all sources minus all expenses, excluding the distribution of profits of corporations. Since income on which income tax has been paid once is not subject to further taxation, there is no double taxation of corporate profits. Capital gains are not taxed.

The law provides for a basic exemption of 2,000 colones on income from capital. On income derived at least 80 per cent from work a further exemption of 2,000 colones is permitted. If the income is "mixed," i.e., derived from work (to the extent of less than 80 per cent) and from capital, the additional deduction is reduced to 1,000 colones. The basic exemption of 2,000 colones applies irrespective of the number of persons dependent on the income. If, however, more than five minors depend on the income, an additional exemption of 1,000 colones is allowed. Partnerships (*sociedades colectivas*) and limited partnerships (*sociedades en comandita simple*) obtain the basic exemption of 2,000 colones only. No exemption is accorded to corporations (*sociedades anónimas*, and *sociedades en comandita por acciones*). It has been pointed out by various members of the Salvadorean business community that the absence of a basic exemption for corporate profits, and the taxation of such profits at rates applicable to the entire amount (instead of at the rates — presumably lower — applicable to the income of individual shareholders) has retarded the development of the corporate form of enterprise and has contributed to the prevailing absence of a distinction between private and business capital. The results of the gradation of exemptions according to the form of business organization and the differentiation between income from capital and from work are shown in the schedule of effective rates given in Table 76.

The determination of net taxable income is regulated, in great detail, in the income tax law and in an administrative order (*reglamento*). The *reglamento* permits the application of flat per-

TABLE 76

EFFECTIVE INCOME TAX RATES, BY SOURCES OF INCOME
(*In per cent*)

| Income in Colones | Corporate Income | Income from Noncorporate Capital | Income from both Work and Capital | Income from Work[a] |
|---|---|---|---|---|
| 1,000 | 2.0 | 0.0 | 0.0 | 0.0 |
| 2,000 | 2.3 | 0.0 | 0.0 | 0.0 |
| 3,000 | 2.5 | 0.7 | 0.0 | 0.0 |
| 4,000 | 2.8 | 1.1 | 0.5 | 0.0 |
| 5,000 | 3.0 | 1.5 | 0.9 | 0.4 |
| 6,000 | 3.3 | 1.8 | 1.3 | 0.8 |
| 7,000 | 3.5 | 2.1 | 1.6 | 1.1 |
| 8,000 | 3.8 | 2.4 | 1.9 | 1.4 |
| 9,000 | 4.0 | 2.7 | 2.2 | 1.7 |
| 10,000 | 4.3 | 3.0 | 2.5 | 2.0 |
| 12,000 | 4.9 | 3.6 | 3.0 | 2.5 |
| 14,000 | 5.5 | 4.2 | 3.6 | 3.1 |
| 16,000 | 6.1 | 4.8 | 4.3 | 3.7 |
| 18,000 | 6.6 | 5.4 | 4.8 | 4.3 |
| 22,000 | 7.6 | 6.5 | 6.0 | 5.4 |
| 26,000 | 8.4 | 7.4 | 6.9 | 6.4 |
| 30,000 | 9.2 | 8.2 | 7.8 | 7.3 |
| 34,000 | 9.9 | 9.0 | 8.5 | 8.1 |
| 38,000 | 10.5 | 9.7 | 9.2 | 8.8 |
| 42,000 | 11.1 | 10.3 | 9.9 | 9.5 |
| 46,000 | 11.7 | 10.9 | 10.5 | 10.2 |
| 50,000 | 12.3 | 11.5 | 11.2 | 10.8 |
| 75,000 | 14.9 | 14.3 | 14.1 | 13.8 |
| 100,000 | 16.2 | 15.8 | 15.6 | 15.4 |

[a] To the extent of at least 80 per cent.

centage deductions from gross receipts in lieu of exact figures. Amortization allowances for real property and equipment are limited to a percentage of the value of the property.

Persons and business organizations subject to the income tax must submit an income declaration. For that purpose the Bureau of Internal Revenue sends declaration blanks to all persons presumed to be subject to the income tax; if the person liable to tax does not receive a blank, he is responsible for requesting one.

The declaration must be submitted in the first three months of each year for the income of the preceding year. The declaration distinguishes twenty-seven different sources of income, including imputed income from a house occupied by the owner. All income declarations are checked by an Expert Court (*Tribunal Pericial*) of the Bureau of Internal Revenue.

### INCOME TAX ADMINISTRATION

The Bureau of Internal Revenue is responsible for the maintenance of lists of income taxpayers. These lists also contain "general information" (*datos reveladores*) regarding the taxpayers' income and capital. These lists are kept up to date by the Information Court (*Tribunal de Información*). The "general information" includes, among other things, reports on salaries paid to government and private employees submitted annually by the employers, copies of property registers maintained by the courts, etc.

If a declaration of the taxpayers appears to be in accordance with the "general information" of the Information Court, the Bureau of Internal Revenue assesses the tax and notifies the taxpayer, who has the right to contest, within fifteen days, the correctness of the assessment. His appeal is directed to the Bureau of Internal Revenue which itself forms a Tax Court (*Tribunal Tasador*), consisting of the bureau's director, assistant director, and secretary.

If, on the basis of the information available at the Information Court, the income declaration is not considered adequate, the Expert Court is charged with the investigation of the tax liability of the taxpayer. This investigation may simply involve the nonrecognition of deductions made in the declaration, or the substitution of data in the hands of the Information Court; or experts of the Expert Court may audit the books of the taxpayer. The findings of the tax experts are communicated to the taxpayer, who again has the right to appeal to the Tax Court of the Bureau of Internal Revenue. If the appeal is fully or partly rejected, the taxpayer can carry his appeal to the Court of Appeals (*Tribunal de Apelaciones*), which is the highest authority on tax matters.

If the taxpayer does not appeal the assessment, the Bureau of Internal Revenue issues a payment order to the appropriate tax administration office, which in turn notifies the taxpayer through the municipal authorities and requests payment. Payment must be made within fifteen days after the taxpayer is notified; if payment is not made, the payment order is collected by execution of judgment.

The income tax law provides that, if requested by the government, private and public employers are obliged to collect the income tax of their employees through payroll deductions. So far no use has been made of this provision.

It would be misleading to appraise the income tax and the position that it holds in the tax structure without first describing and discussing the other important component parts of the tax structure. Certain legal and administrative aspects of the tax, however, may be commented upon at once. On the basis of Table 77 it appears that the number of persons subject to the income

TABLE 77

NUMBER OF INCOME TAXPAYERS, BY AMOUNT OF TAXABLE INCOME, 1942 AND 1946

| Taxable Income (in colones) | Number of Taxpayers | |
|---|---|---|
| | 1942 | 1946 |
| Up to 2,000 | 1,087 | 1,094 |
| 2,001– 4,000 | 428 | 488 |
| 4,001– 6,000 | 192 | 236 |
| 6,001– 8,000 | 110 | 152 |
| 8,001– 10,000 | 70 | 102 |
| 10,001– 15,000 | 92 | 128 |
| 15,001– 20,000 | 50 | 54 |
| 20,001– 30,000 | 60 | 64 |
| 30,001– 50,000 | 33 | 55 |
| 50,001– 100,000 | 17 | 35 |
| 100,001– 200,000 | 8 | 16 |
| 200,001– 500,000 | 3 | 5 |
| 500,001–1,000,000 | 1 | 6 |
| Total | 2,151 | 2,435 |

tax is relatively small. The small number of income taxpayers is to some extent offset, however, by the collection of the Series B, C, and D of the *vialidad* tax, which as is indicated in subsequent paragraphs, is a continuation of the income tax below the level of basic exemptions applying to the income tax.

As to the effectiveness of assessments and collections, it seems that the "general information" collected and applied by the Information Court is of limited value as a basis for tax assessments. This seems to be particularly true at times when business conditions change rapidly, as during a period of expansion of business activity and large continuous price increases. Thus, in the last three years for which complete collection data are available (1945–1947), the level of income tax collections remained more or less stable although the national income figures reveal a considerable expansion of business and personal incomes. Since collection of the *vialidad* tax (B, C, and D) likewise showed only minor changes, it cannot be argued that the bulk of income increases took place in those income brackets that are not subject to income taxation.

One of the major factors contributing to the discrepancy between the increase in national income and the relative stability of tax collections may well be the exemption of capital gains from income taxation. The real estate and building boom that began at the end of the war undoubtedly led to substantial capital gains which were not taxed. Some of these gains, however, were presumably speculative in character and would have lent themselves readily to income taxation without seriously impeding orderly capital formation. It has been pointed out by members of the Salvadorean business community that the exemption of capital gains from income taxation leads to a perpetuation of the investment of savings in land and real estate, a form of investment that is one of the least productive of all potential investment outlets.

One of the major handicaps that the Bureau of Internal Revenue faces in its task of assessing and collecting income taxes is the fact that the bulk of business transactions on the wholesale and retail level takes the form of cash transactions, with the consequence that one of the basic sources of information of countries where payment by check is more prevalent, is not available. This situation is aggravated by the fact that bookkeeping and auditing methods are inadequately developed in El Salvador. The latter can be partly attributed to the almost complete lack of a distinction between business and private funds, which in turn has allegedly been caused in part by the discrimination of the income tax law against corporations.[2]

In the last few years the number of tax experts (*peritos*), who in the main are responsible for the adequacy of tax assessments, has substantially increased (from nineteen in 1942 to sixty in 1948), and their salaries also have been increased. Given, however, the lack of adequate bookkeeping on the part of a large segment of the business community, the effectiveness of the tax experts' operations is of necessity limited. It is probable, nevertheless, that the methods applied by the experts in the investigation of tax liabilities could be further improved through specialized training, particularly in accounting and auditing. In particular, the limited size of the Salvadorean business community should make it possible to develop a general scheme of cross-checking of business expenses that necessarily appear as receipts in the accounts of other firms or as income of other persons. The development of orderly accounting practices by business firms could be encouraged, for instance, by a more stringent application of the provisions of the income tax *reglamento* that pertain to the documentation of deductions of business expenses.

As to the efficiency and completeness of collections, the experience of other countries indicates that, generally speaking, collections are improved if the period that elapses between the receipt of income and the payment of taxes thereon is curtailed. Salvadorean regulations and administrative practices permit a considerable delay in the discharge of tax liabilities. Although income tax declarations have to be submitted three months after the end of the year for which taxes are due, the actual assessment is normally delayed by several months — a period that may easily be extended to a year or more if the Expert Court and the taxpayer disagree regarding the amount of the tax liability. The present situation could be considerably improved if partial pay-

[2] See above, page 277.

ments were required at the time of the submission of the tax declaration. Besides, tax delinquencies could be partly avoided if the authority, provided in the law, to collect income taxes of government and private employees by payroll deductions were applied.

A minor weakness of the tax administration, the elimination of which presumably would not be opposed, is the present low level of fines levied for the failure to submit a tax declaration, for making false declarations, and for not paying taxes on time. In the face of the higher incomes caused by the general price increase, the present upper limit of 200 colones for tax fines seems inadequate.

### VIALIDAD TAX

The *vialidad* tax is partly a general property tax (Series A), and partly a composite of poll tax, income tax, and business-property tax (Series B, C, and D). The tax derives its name from the fact that originally its proceeds were reserved for road construction purposes; in addition, in 1926 it replaced road fund tax assessments which had been collected until then.

Series A, the proceeds of which do not appear in the accompanying tables but in the section on property and property-transfer taxes, is a progressive tax levied on all "liquid capital" in excess of 10,000 colones. The tax rates of Series A are:

| *Liquid capital (colones)* | *Tax rate (per mil)* |
|---|---|
| 10,000 – 100,000 | ½ |
| 100,000 – 300,000 | ¾ |
| 300,000 – 600,000 | 1 |
| 600,000 – 1,000,000 | 1½ |
| Over 1,000,000 | 2 |

The *vialidad* law does not contain any definition of "liquid capital." The *vialidad* tax declaration blank, however, lists the following assets as forming the tax base: real estate (residential buildings, urban lots, landed property, and estates, including buildings, processing machinery, and cattle); financial assets (mortgages, accounts receivable, loans outstanding, participations in ownership, cash, bank deposits, savings bank deposits); and business investments (agriculture, mining, industry, profes-

sional offices, shops, movable property, including private automobiles). Mortgage debts, loans, and other debts can be deducted from the value of the assets. The administration of the
*vialidad* tax (Series A) is similar to that of the income tax, and
is under the jurisdiction of the Bureau of Internal Revenue which
issues, after assessments, a tax list (*matrícula*) to the tax administration office, which collects the tax.

Neither the *vialidad* tax law nor the *reglamento* implementing
it contain detailed provisions regarding the assessment of property values. The Bureau of Internal Revenue uses in actual practice the same administrative apparatus and personnel as are in
charge of the income tax administration. The information available at the Information Court is used in the determination of the
correctness and completeness of the *vialidad* tax declarations
submitted by the taxpayers. In most instances the *vialidad*
Series A and the income tax are assessed by the same experts.

*Vialidad* Series B is a flat rate of 10 colones, assessed annually
on all persons following liberal professions (doctors, lawyers,
ministers, etc.) with the exception of regular army officers.

*Vialidad* Series C is a tax on salaries and wages of government
and private employees. The tax is based on the monthly income
on the basis of the following rates:

| Monthly earnings (colones) | Annual tax (colones) |
|---|---|
| Up to 50 | 1.50 |
| 50– 100 | 2 |
| 100– 200 | 3 |
| 200– 300 | 6 |
| 300– 400 | 10 |
| 400– 600 | 15 |
| 600– 800 | 20 |
| 800–1,000 | 25 |
| Over 1,000 | 30 |

Series C is also assessed on business enterprises ("capitalists,
farmers, and merchants") with capital of less than 10,000 colones,
at the following rates:

| Capital (colones) | Annual tax (colones) |
|---|---|
| Up to 2,000 | 1.50 |
| 2,000– 5,000 | 3 |
| 5,000–10,000 | 5 |

Persons with assets in excess of 10,000 colones are subject to *vialidad* Series A.

*Vialidad* Series D is levied on artisans and workers. Artisans who own a "first category." shop with an assessed value from 5,000 to 10,000 colones pay 5 colones; artisans with a "second category" shop (1,000 to 5,000 colones) pay 3 colones; artisans with a "third category" shop (100 to 1,000 colones) pay 2 colones; craftsmen (artisans without shop) pay 1.50 colones; unskilled workers pay 1.00 colón.

The four series of the *vialidad* taxes are mutually exclusive, a taxpayer liable under two or more types of *vialidad* taxes finding his liability limited to that category in which he pays the highest tax. As pointed out above, the *vialidad* tax Series B, C, and D are in effect downward extensions of the income tax, and counteract to some extent the progressive rate structure of the income tax.[3] Tax statistics do not distinguish between collections of Series B, C, and D, because all three series are collected by the same method.

Municipal governments maintain lists of *vialidad* taxpayers. Each year they request the Bureau of Internal Revenue to issue the necessary number of tax receipts (*boletos-recibos*) which are issued to persons subject to the taxes upon payment. The lists maintained by the municipalities are periodically revised and brought up to date.

The tax collections are enforced by making the *vialidad* receipts serve as personal identification papers (since nearly everybody pays this tax),[4] which must be carried by all persons subject to the tax and shown upon request to police and government officials. Table 74 indicates that the collection of *vialidad* taxes Series B, C, and D has remained practically unchanged in the last eight years. This perhaps indicates the effectiveness of the collection system through the issuance of *boletos-recibos*, but it may also be taken as an indication of the reluctance of persons liable to the *vialidad* tax to volunteer information regarding their transfer from one bracket into another. It is probably also due

[3] Parts of Series C and D are at the same time a downward extension of the *vialidad* property tax (Series A).

[4] Minors, persons over sixty years of age, members of the armed forces, school teachers, and married women are exempt, unless they own property.

to the fáct that the municipal authorities are slow in making corrections in the tax lists.

## INHERITANCE AND GIFT TAX

The inheritance and gift tax has been in force in its present form since 1936. It is levied on all inheritances and gifts valued at 4,000 colones or more. The tax is progressive in two directions: one progression is determined by the value of the estate; the other by the proximity of the relationship between the deceased or donor and the beneficiary or beneficiaries. The law distinguishes five classes of beneficiaries. The first class (with the lowest tax rates) includes all descendants and ascendants. The fifth class includes all persons beyond the fourth grade of blood relation. The result of the twofold progression is a highly progressive rate structure, which extends in the first class from 1.4 to 20 per cent (for estates valued at from 4,000 to 6,000 colones, and at more than 1,000,000 colones respectively); in the second beneficiary class, from 2.4 to 23 per cent; in the third, from 6.4 to 38 per cent; in the fourth, from 9.4 to 41 per cent; and in the fifth, from 12.4 to 50 per cent. For estates valued at less than 10,000 colones the law provides a reduction of one half of the tax if such estates are acquired by minors, widows, or invalids, whose property does not exceed 10,000 colones. As a result of the relatively large size of the average family, the prevalence of strong family ties, and the small number of estates valued at more than 100,000 colones, the effective rates in most instances do not exceed 8 per cent.

The administration of the inheritance and gift tax is independent of that of other taxes. In each department a Fiscal Delegate (*Delegado Fiscal*), appointed by the government, is charged with the administration of the inheritance tax. He submits the inheritance declarations to the local Fiscal Representative (*Representante del Fisco*), who together with two experts appointed either by the Bureau of Internal Revenue or by the Fiscal Delegate, determines the tax liability of the heirs. If the Fiscal Representative disagrees with the assessment proposed by the experts, the case is submitted to the Bureau of Internal Revenue, which has the right to set aside the assessment of experts appointed by the Fiscal Delegate. The laws pertaining to the inheritance and gift tax do not contain any provisions regarding the valuation to be applied to the estates, and it is therefore difficult to appraise the effectiveness of administration. Since the law permits inheritance and gift taxes to be paid in installments over a period of up to two years, and since no time limit is set for the determination of the tax liability, the collection figures shown in Table 74 likewise give no indication of the effectiveness of administration. The considerable year-to-year fluctuations in the collection of the inheritance and gift taxes that appear in the table may also be due to changes in the mortality rate of persons whose estates are liable to inheritance tax.

## CÉDULAS DE VECINDAD

The primary purpose of the *cédulas de vecindad* is the identification of residents of El Salvador. The *cédulas* are identification papers which were issued for the first time in 1936 to all persons eighteen years old or more. They contain personal data regarding the holder, a photograph, and fingerprints. The reason for the inclusion of the *cédulas* in the group of direct taxes is that in 1940 a tariff of fees for the issuance of the *cédulas* was created, which in effect transformed the issue fee into a graduated poll tax. The rate begins at 15 centavos (for students, workers, and women who are not subject to the *vialidad* tax or who earn less than 30 colones per month), and rises to 5.50 colones for persons with property of more than 25,000 colones. The *cédulas* have to be renewed every four years. Since the largest number of *cédulas* were issued for the first time in 1937, the collections of 1941 and 1945 exceeded those of all other years.

## OTHER DIRECT TAXES

The 2 per cent tax on corporate dividends was originally paid to a special fund. Its proceeds were transferred to the General Fund in 1940. The small amount of taxes collected is indicative of the relative unimportance of corporate enterprises in El Salvador. The 1 per cent tax on bank profits is even less important.

## 2. Property and Property-Transfer Taxes

As pointed out above, property and property-transfer taxes have accounted for only a small percentage of total tax collections; in recent years the significance of property and property transfer tax collections has declined.

### VIALIDAD SERIES A

The general property tax (*vialidad* A) has been described in the preceding section. As to the amount of general property tax collected, Table 78 indicates that, unlike collections of *vialidad* income taxes (Series B, C, and D), the yield of Series A has considerably increased in the last two years. This increase in collections is presumably due to some extent to the large volume of building, which has resulted in an increase in the tax base; but it also seems that the valuation of old property has been adjusted upward.

### SANITATION AND PAVEMENT TAX

The sanitation and pavement tax is a special assessment for the pavement and construction of sewer systems in certain sections of San Salvador and of Santa Ana. The special assessment for San Salvador was originally introduced in 1925, and the present rates in 1933. The tax is assessed per square meter of property located in the improved zones. There are three tax zones in San Salvador. In the first, the tax rate is 1 centavo per month; in the second, which embraces the largest area, 0.4 centavos; and in the third, 0.25 centavos. In Santa Ana the special assessment was introduced in 1941. There the rates are 0.5 centavos per month in the first, and 0.2 centavos in the second zone. The special assessment is collected through the issuance of payment orders to the local tax administrations. The tax is of particular interest because it is the only type of property tax for which the assessment is based on an objective criterion, i.e., the size and location of the property. The tax yield has fluctuated considerably in the last years, which is surprising since the rates as well as the tax basis have remained unchanged since 1941.

## TABLE 78

### PROPERTY AND PROPERTY-TRANSFER TAXES, 1935/36 AND 1940 TO 1948

*(In thousands of colones)*

| | 1935/36 | 1940 | 1941 | 1942 | 1943 | 1944 | 1945 | 1946 | 1947 | 1948[a] |
|---|---|---|---|---|---|---|---|---|---|---|
| Vialidad A............ | 158.7[b] | 208.1 | 200.3 | 258.6 | 254.1[b] | 196.8 | 299.4 | 341.8 | 339.2 | 250.0 |
| Pavement special assessment............ | 134.1 | 95.8 | 114.6 | 124.4 | 136.3 | 81.9 | 136.9 | 121.2 | 161.1 | 150.0 |
| Real Estate transfer tax (*Alcabala*)............ | 166.9 | 165.2 | 190.6 | 222.2 | 336.4 | 280.7 | 382.6 | 453.7 | 453.6 | 400.0 |
| Cattle transfer tax...... | 22.7 | 28.8 | 31.3 | 47.3 | 50.4 | 40.9 | 45.2 | 42.2 | 39.9 | 35.0 |
| Total............ | 482.4 | 497.9 | 536.8 | 652.5 | 777.2 | 600.3 | 864.1 | 958.9 | 993.8 | 835.0 |

[a] Budget.
[b] Estimated.

This seems to indicate that considerable delay is experienced in both the assessment and the payment of the tax.

## REAL ESTATE TRANSFER TAX

The real estate transfer tax was introduced in 1928. Originally the rate was 1 per cent of the "real value" of the transferred property, but in 1940 it was raised to 1.5 per cent. It is collected on all real estate transfers with the exception of those subject to inheritance or gift taxes. Since capital gains are not subject to income taxation, the tax is, in effect, a minor equivalent, with limited applicability, of a capital gains tax.

The law governing the assessment of the administration of the transfer tax does not provide a definition of the term "real value" but it establishes certain minimum bases for the valuation. The law establishes the presumption that the "real value" of real estate cannot be less than eight times the rent of rented property, or eight times the value of the crop in the case of agricultural property, but an amendment (in 1941) permits a deduction of 20 per cent of this presumed value. An alternative legal presumption is that the value cannot be less than the mortgage on it. The tax is assessed by the local rent offices, and payment is made against the issuance of a receipt, without which the property transfer cannot be entered in the property registers of the courts. The Bureau of Internal Revenue is charged by law with reviewing the valuation put on the transferred property and with collecting additional taxes, and is authorized to impose a 25 per cent fine if it finds that the property has been undervalued. This automatic review can be avoided if the seller requests the Bureau of Internal Revenue, prior to the sale of real estate, to appoint experts to value the property. In the course of the last years the collections of real estate transfer tax has substantially increased. This increased yield undoubtedly reflects the larger volume of real estate transactions in connection with the expanded building activity and higher valuation of real property.

The cattle transfer tax and the tax on the transfer of cattle brands (which is included in the same item in Table 78) are paid in connection with the registration of the sale of cattle.

## 3. TAXES ON EXPORTS

### COFFEE EXPORT TAX

The coffee export tax is by far the most important levy imposed on the exportation of goods from El Salvador. The present tax rate, which was established at the end of 1947, is 7.00 colones per 46 kilograms of coffee.

Prior to this rate, the tax was governed by a 1943 law which had established a sliding-scale export duty. The base for the progressive rate structure under this law was the New York spot

| *New York quotation per 46 kilograms of No. 4 Santos Coffee* | *Tax per 46 kilograms (in colones)* |
|---|---|
| $ 9.00–$ 9.24 | 0.13 |
| 9.25– 9.49 | 0.23 |
| 9.50– 9.74 | 0.33 |
| 9.75– 9.99 | 0.44 |
| 10.00– 10.24 | 0.56 |
| 10.25– 10.49 | 0.69 |
| 10.50– 10.74 | 0.81 |
| 10.75– 10.99 | 0.95 |
| 11.00– 11.24 | 1.10 |
| 11.25– 11.49 | 1.26 |
| 11.50– 11.74 | 1.41 |
| 11.75– 11.99 | 1.58 |
| 12.00– 12.24 | 1.75 |
| 12.25– 12.49 | 1.94 |
| 12.50– 12.74 | 2.12 |
| 12.75– 12.99 | 2.31 |
| 13.00– 13.24 | 2.52 |
| 13.25– 13.49 | 2.73 |
| 13.50– 13.74 | 2.94 |
| 13.75– 13.99 | 3.16 |
| 14.00– 14.24 | 3.39 |
| 14.25– 14.49 | 3.63 |
| 14.50– 14.74 | 3.87 |
| 14.75– 14.99 | 4.12 |
| 15.00– 15.24 | 4.38 |
| 15.25– 15.49 | 4.65 |
| 15.50– 15.74 | 4.91 |
| 15.75– 15.99 | 5.19 |

quotation for No. 4 Santos coffee that prevailed in October of each year. The law provided that the tax rate was to be established annually by decree in that month, in which export shipments normally begin. The old rate structure, as shown in the tabulation on page 291, was highly progressive.

The 1943 law further authorized the government to decree, under certain conditions, a tax reduction or the imposition of a surtax. It also provided that no other national or municipal taxes could be imposed upon the income derived from the growing or processing of coffee; this provision was retained in the 1947 tax law.

In accordance with the 1943 law the tax rate for the crop year 1943–44 was set at 3.16 colones,[5] a rate that also prevailed initially in the following year. In January 1945, the tax was reduced to 1.20 colones, the reduction being made retroactive to November 1944. According to the executive order announcing the tax reduction, the purpose of the reduction was to compensate producers for the small volume of the crop. For the 1945–46 crop, when the New York quotation rose over $14.50, the corresponding rate of 3.67 colones was introduced by executive order in accordance with the tax law. In addition, a surcharge of 0.63 colones was introduced by a special act of the National Assembly. For 1946–47 the rate was set at 5.19 colones. For the crop year 1947–48, legal and administrative difficulties arose because the New York quotation had risen substantially above the uppermost price quotation of $15.99 given in the rate table. At first, an amendment to the law was passed extending the progressive rate structure beyond the base of $15.99, and setting the rate for the crop year at 7.00 colones. Later, the progressive tax schedule was repealed and a commission was appointed and charged with the preparation of recommendations regarding the future level and structure of the coffee export tax.[6]

[5] Prior to 1943, coffee exports were subject to several taxes, one in favor of the General Fund, another in favor of the Mortgage Bank Fund, as well as a departmental tax of 10 to 20 centavos in favor of departmental road funds. The total tax burden amounted to 2.475 or 2.575 colones respectively per 100 kilograms, or 1.13 and 1.17 colones respectively for 46 kilograms.

[6] In October 1948, the continuation of the prevailing rate of 7 colones for the crop year 1948–49 was announced by executive decree.

When the tax of 7.00 colones was introduced in 1947, coffee growers and coffee merchants objected to what they considered an undue increase of the tax burden. They pointed out that the high tax rate was equivalent to the imposition of the income tax at the highest rate, i.e., 20 per cent. Since a considerable part of the coffee crop is produced by a large number of small coffee growers whose income tax liability would be substantially smaller than that corresponding to the highest tax bracket, it was felt that tax relief should be given to the coffee growers and processors. On the other hand, it has been pointed out that the present coffee tax has great advantages from the point of view of the fiscal administration. It is exceedingly easy to administer (being collected by the Customs Service), compared with the administration of direct taxes, and evasion or delinquency is almost impossible.

As to the volume of the tax yield, Table 79 indicates that re-

TABLE 79

TAXES ON EXPORTS, 1935/36 AND 1940 TO 1948
(*In thousands of colones*)

|  | Coffee Export Tax | Other Export Duties | Total |
|---|---|---|---|
| 1935–36 | 1,394.5 | 6.4 | 1,400.9 |
| 1940 | 1,472.2 | 43.7 | 1,515.9 |
| 1941 | 864.6 | 27.8 | 892.4 |
| 1942 | 1,353.0 | 21.9 | 1,374.9 |
| 1943 | 1,388.8 | 82.7 | 1,471.5 |
| 1944 | 4,392.3 | 31.4 | 4,423.7 |
| 1945 | 1,751.9 | 23.7 | 1,775.6 |
| 1946 | 4,414.3 | 84.6 | 4,498.9 |
| 1947 | 7,221.3 | | 7,221.3 |
| 1948 (Budget) | 9,000.0 | | 9,000.0 |

ceipts of coffee taxes, although highly fluctuating, were very substantial in the last few years. Several factors seem to account for the high amplitude of the year-to-year fluctuations of the tax yield. One is the fact that in some years the bulk of export shipments took place in October or November, and in others much later, in January or February. The result is that if a crop year with late shipments is followed by a year with early shipments, taxes for more than one crop are collected in a single calendar year. If, however, a crop year with early shipments is followed by one with late shipments, less than one crop year's taxes are collected in the calendar year. Other reasons for the fluctuations are the rises in the tax rates since 1943, and the fluctuating volume of the coffee crop.

OTHER EXPORT TAXES

Export duties are also levied on the exportation of gold and silver (3 per cent *ad valorem*) and on bags (25 centavos per bag) that are not produced of domestic raw materials, i.e., henequen or cotton, the latter duty thus affording protection to the henequen and cotton producers. All other exports are duty free except for the payment of an export declaration fee (2.75 colones per declaration).[7]

4. TRANSACTION AND BUSINESS-LICENSE TAXES

This group of taxes includes a set of levies with the common characteristic that they are imposed upon business enterprises or business transactions or both. In most instances the amounts collected are not directly related to any particular commodity, or to the income or turnover of the enterprise or person subject to the tax. In some cases "business" taxes are also paid by private individuals for nonbusiness pursuits. The bulk of the levies segregated under the above heading, however, appear to fall upon business transactions and are paid by business firms. Table 80 gives an indication of the multiplicity of the system of transaction and business-license taxes. Actually the individual types of taxes listed in the table are, in turn, imposed upon a variety of activities and for a variety of reasons, and the range of impact of this type of taxes therefore is much larger than the table suggests. In view of the complexity of the tax base it is not surprising that the yield from these taxes has been relatively stable in the last years, and has followed the general upward trend of

---

[7] Between 1945 and 1947 an export tax was levied on sugar. See Section 6, page 312, on consumption taxes.

## TABLE 80

### TRANSACTION AND BUSINESS-LICENSE TAXES, 1935/36 AND 1940 TO 1948

(*In thousands of colones*)

| | 1935/36 | 1940 | 1941 | 1942 | 1943 | 1944 | 1945 | 1946 | 1947 | 1948 [a] |
|---|---|---|---|---|---|---|---|---|---|---|
| Stamp tax......................... | 524.8 | 390.3 | 399.5 | 433.3 | 531.4 | 536.0 | 604.9 | 812.3 | 958.1 | 700.0 |
| Stamped paper tax.............. | 180.9 | 196.1 | 209.0 | 226.7 | 269.3 | 241.2 | 298.9 | 367.2 | 377.2 | 350.0 |
| *Matriculas* in lieu of stamp tax...... | 27.2 | 43.6 | 85.0 | 41.8 | 44.8 | 41.8 | 50.5 | 53.8 | 60.3 | 50.0 |
| *Matriculas de comercio*........... | 14.7 | 27.5 | 25.9 | 25.5 | 27.2 | 26.3 | 28.3 | 31.5 | 37.0 | 30.0 |
| Trade-mark and patent registration.. | 9.6 | 8.3 | 13.0 | 10.4 | 12.0 | 19.3 | 23.1 | 29.2 | 28.4 | 20.0 |
| Business registration............. | 1.4 | 1.5 | 1.1 | 1.3 | 1.7 | 1.0 | 2.4 | 4.5 | 13.8 | 10.0 |
| Liquor sales patents.............. | 116.6 | 133.5 | 125.7 | 132.5 | 141.8 | 167.3 | 197.1 | 232.6 | 260.0 | 220.0 |
| Gross receipts tax of electric companies...................... | ... | 110.0 | 112.3 | 118.0 | 115.9 | 140.1 | ... | ... | ... | ... |
| *Matriculas* of insurance companies... | 8.0 | 10.0 | 11.0 | 9.0 | 10.0 | 10.0 | 10.0 | 11.0 | 14.0 | 13.0 |
| Tax on life and fire insurance premiums | ... | 20.0 | 21.9 | 27.0 | 30.1 | 35.9 | 40.4 | 45.1 | 52.3 | 40.0 |
| Pharmacy and drug store licenses.. | 9.2 | 10.5 | 8.5 | 10.6 | 9.5 | 10.8 | 26.2 | 27.0 | 19.2 | 13.1 |
| Registration of motor vehicles...... | 30.6 | 151.7 | 115.9 | 151.7 | 142.1 | 145.2 | 144.9 | 160.4 | 218.5 | 200.0 |
| Registration of wagons........... | ... | ... | ... | 100.1 | 107.6 | 123.7 | 108.4 | 122.2 | 114.6 | 110.0 |
| Other stamp and license taxes....... | 1.7 | 6.7 | 4.9 | 8.7 | 11.3 | 12.0 | 9.8 | 10.5 | 12.5 | 9.6 |
| Total................. | 925.6 | 1110.7 | 1133.7 | 1290.6 | 1454.7 | 1510.6 | 1539.9 | 1912.6 | 2165.9 | 1766.7 |

[a] Budget.

business conditions and prices. As to the share of transaction and business-license taxes in total tax receipts, Table 13 in Chapter IV indicates that it declined to 4.3 per cent in 1947, after it had exceeded 5 per cent in the preceding ten years.

### STAMP TAX

The stamp tax was introduced in 1902, its rate structure being revised for the last time in 1939 when a new tariff for stamps on invoices was established. The present stamp rates for invoices amount to one per mil for the invoiced amount for all invoices exceeding two colones. For invoices amounting to more than 20 colones the law establishes a detailed tariff which is divided into thirty tax brackets. Invoices falling within a particular bracket are subject to a tax of one per mil of the upper limit of the bracket, as in the following examples:

| Tax bracket (*colones*) | Tax (*colones*) |
|---|---|
| 20– 100 | 0.10 |
| 900– 1,000 | 1.00 |
| 10,000– 15,000 | 15.00 |
| 90,000–100,000 | 100.00 |

In addition, the tax stamp is collected on numerous other documents such as corporate shares, bills of exchange, checks, rental agreements, permits for public performances of theaters, movie houses, circuses, etc., as well as inventories of estates, savings deposit books, etc. Furthermore, the stamp tax is imposed upon certain types of enterprises, thus performing in effect the functions of business-license taxes. Soap factories, for instance, pay 25 to 150 colones monthly in stamp taxes, depending upon the volume of their production; ice factories pay 12 to 100 colones per year; soft drink factories, 15 to 200 colones per month. Persons appointed to government positions are liable to a stamp tax of 2 to 25 colones, depending upon their salary.

As the name of the tax implies, it is collected through the affixation of tax stamps to documents and their simultaneous invalidation. The stamps are disbursed by the local tax administration offices and sold in stores. In instances where the tax does not pertain to a specific document, it is collected periodically (monthly or annually) by the tax offices against the issuance of a *matrícula*.

### STAMPED-PAPER TAX

The stamped-paper tax is a corollary to the stamp tax, and its imposition is governed by the same law. The law provides that stamped paper is to be used for the drawing up of contracts, agreements, petitions to courts, and to administrative offices, applications for administrative actions, etc. The stamped-paper tariff is similar to that of the stamp tax, but exceeds it slightly. Examples follow:

| *Tax bracket (colones)* | *Tax (colones)* |
|---|---|
| 10– 100 | 0.15 |
| 900– 1,000 | 1.15 |
| 10,000– 15,000 | 15.85 |
| 90,000–100,000 | 105.10 |

Stamped paper is sold through the same channels as tax stamps.

### MATRÍCULA DE COMERCIO

The *matrícula de comercio* is the fee for a license plate which is issued annually to business firms by the Bureau of Internal Revenue. The license plate is issued free of charge to firms whose capital does not exceed 1,000 colones. Firms with a capital of 1,000 to 5,000 colones pay 10 colones; firms whose capital exceeds 5,000 colones, 20 colones. A business registration fee of 5 colones is paid by all business firms requesting the entry of their names in the business register maintained by the courts. The trade marks and patents registration fee amounts to 25 colones for each application.

### LIQUOR-SALES PATENTS

Liquor-sales patents are governed by the provisions of the liquor law, which is the codification of all regulations pertaining to the production, distribution, and consumption of hard liquor and alcohol, and by the Fiscal Code of 1942. At present, the laws distinguish six different types of liquor-sales patents which authorize their holders to engage in wholesale or retail trade in liquor, or both. The patents for the sale of *aguardiente* and alcohol are assessed and collected by the Bureau of Internal Revenue. Prior to 1940, the bureau was authorized by law to determine the patent fees themselves. In 1940, a tariff was introduced that established monthly patent fees for the sale of *aguardiente* of from 5 to 50 colones, depending upon the sales quota of each sales outlet.[8] For the sale of other domestic liquor (*licores confeccionados*) and for imported liquor, the monthly business patent fee is 77 colones for wholesalers, and an amount equivalent to the patent fees for the sale of *aguardiente* for retailers. For a combined retail and wholesale patent, both fees minus a reduction of 30 per cent have to be paid.

### OTHER BUSINESS LICENSES

Other business-license fees are collected for the operation of pharmacies and drug stores. In addition to ordinary license fees, pharmacies and drug stores also pay a special license for the distribution of packaged drugs ("pharmaceutical specialties"). Another special license fee is imposed on the sale of narcotics. Insurance companies are subject to a matriculation fee of 300 colones per year. In addition, premium payments on life insurance are subject to a 2 per cent and on fire insurance to a 5 per cent tax. These taxes are collected from the insurance companies against the issuance of payment orders.

Prior to 1945, electric companies were subject to a tax of 5 per cent on their gross receipts. This tax was collected in lieu of income taxes, but was abolished when an investigation disclosed that the tax liability of the electric companies under the gross-receipts tax was smaller than their tax liability under the income tax would have been.

### MOTOR VEHICLE TAXES

The operation of motor vehicles is subject to an annual registration fee, the amount of which depends upon the type and tonnage of the vehicle. The license fee for a passenger car, for instance, amounts to 40 colones per year; for a three-ton diesel truck, 150 colones; for a bus with 31 seats or more, 200 colones.

---

[8] For an explanation of the sales quota system, see under Liquor Tax in Section 6, page 309.

# TABLE 81

## Taxes on Imports, 1935/36 and 1940 to 1948
### (In thousands of colones)

| | 1935/36 | 1940 | 1941 | 1942 | 1943 | 1944 | 1945 | 1946 | 1947 | 1948[a] |
|---|---|---|---|---|---|---|---|---|---|---|
| Import duties........... | 8,390.8 | 7,819.8[b] | 7,559.3 | 5,871.0 | 7,190.2 | 7,224.8 | 8,886.9 | 11,933.0 | 18,622.6 | 19,591.2 |
| Surcharges............. | 44.0 | 78.3 | 76.8 | 109.0 | 153.9 | 155.3 | 183.0 | 248.5 | 377.9 | 250.0 |
| Gasoline taxes.......... | 123.7 | 134.5 | 126.1 | 103.9 | 65.4 | 88.9 | 94.9 | 173.0 | 273.2 | 200.0 |
| Tax on pharmaceutical specialties.......... | 33.2 | 43.6 | 45.0 | 49.4 | 53.0 | 53.2 | 44.5 | 90.2 | 81.4 | 60.0 |
| Tax on imported cigarettes | ... | 3.9 | 3.1 | 2.5 | 7.4 | 4.9 | 4.9 | 5.6 | 31.6 | 5.0 |
| Consular invoices......... | 802.6 | 1,011.1 | 1,056.4 | 1,023.0 | 1,454.6 | 1,532.7 | 1,649.6 | 2,358.3 | 4,862.1 | 2,000.0 |
| Bills of lading.......... | 36.2 | 47.0 | 46.2 | 36.5 | 49.4 | 48.4 | 54.8 | 84.4 | 140.6 | 100.0 |
| Certificates of origin..... | 49.4 | 54.9 | 55.2 | 41.1 | 58.9 | 55.0 | 58.5 | 92.0 | 125.2 | 70.0 |
| Shipping manifests....... | 13.6 | 8.4 | 5.8 | 3.2 | 4.7 | 4.4 | 3.4 | 5.0 | 4.5 | 5.0 |
| Blanks for consular invoices | 10.2 | 11.3 | 12.0 | 8.3 | 11.5 | 8.4 | 4.5 | 3.0 | 4.1 | 6.0 |
| Exchange difference....... | 692.7 | ... | 228.4 | 531.1 | 651.2 | 543.8 | 257.7 | 35.1 | 8.5 | 5.0 |
| Total............. | 10,196.4 | 9,212.8 | 9,214.3 | 7,779.0 | 9,700.2 | 9,719.8 | 11,242.7 | 15,028.1 | 24,531.7 | 22,292.2 |

[a] Budget.
[b] Including 9,100 colones of departmental taxes.

The transfer of vehicles is likewise subject to a license fee. For bicycles an annual fee of 5 colones must be paid. The vehicle taxes[9] are collected by the Police Administration, which issues the license plates. Horse and ox-drawn vehicles are also subject to license fees (*matrículas de carretas*). Prior to 1941 these fees were collected by the municipal authorities, but since then, the proceeds have accrued to the General Fund of the national government.

Other business and stamp taxes are imposed upon the slaughtering of cattle and the sale of firearms.

## 5. TAXES ON IMPORTS

Taxes on imports are, as pointed out above, the most important single source of government revenue (see Table 81). With the exception of one year (1944), they have always accounted for more than 40 per cent of all tax collections of the national government (see Table 13 in Chapter IV): prior to 1942, they produced more than one half of the total tax revenue. The amounts of import taxes collected each year depend largely on the volume of imports. Since the volume declined during the war, taxes also declined. After 1945 imports expanded rapidly, and import tax receipts therefore rose too, although at a considerably smaller rate (see Table 82).

### IMPORT DUTIES

Import duties accounted for the bulk of import taxes. The levying of import duties is governed by the tariff law of 1918, in which the nomenclature of the Brussels convention was introduced. The duty schedules were modified in 1926, after the Customs Service had been put under the supervision of the fiscal representative of the Foreign Loan,[10] and reorganized. In 1934

---

[9] Motor vehicles operated by private persons not in connection with their business are, of course, also subject to the vehicle tax. That part of the tax yield accruing from nonbusiness vehicles should not be included in the list of business taxes. However, since the tax statistics do not distinguish between business and private vehicles and since it is believed that the major part of the vehicle tax is actually collected on business vehicles, the tax has been classified as a business tax.

[10] The full title of the fiscal representative is Representative of the Fiscal Agent under the Loan Agreement of 1922.

TABLE 82

BURDEN OF IMPORT TAXES, 1935/36 TO 1947

*(Values and amounts in thousands of colones)*

| Year | Value of Imports, c.i.f. | Total Import Taxes | | Import Duties Only | |
|---|---|---|---|---|---|
| | | Amount | Ad valorem rate | Amount | Ad valorem rate |
| | | | % | | % |
| 1935/36 | 20,846.3 | 10,196.4 | 48.9 | 8,390.8 | 40.3 |
| 1936/37 | 21,910.3 | 10,640.9 | 48.6 | 9,362.6 | 42.7 |
| 1937/38 | 26,673.0 | 11,664.2 | 43.7 | 10,057.4 | 37.7 |
| 1938/39 | 21,893.2 | 10,540.8 | 48.1 | 9,055.1 | 41.4 |
| 1939[a] | 10,610.8 | 5,518.4 | 52.0 | 4,740.8 | 44.7 |
| 1940 | 20,270.1 | 9,212.8 | 45.5 | 7,810.7 | 38.5 |
| 1941 | 20,827.2 | 9,214.3 | 44.2 | 7,559.3 | 36.3 |
| 1942 | 21,431.1 | 7,779.0 | 36.3 | 5,871.0 | 27.4 |
| 1943 | 29,857.4 | 9,700.2 | 32.5 | 7,190.2 | 24.1 |
| 1944 | 30,682.7 | 9,719.8 | 31.7 | 7,224.8 | 23.5 |
| 1945 | 33,836.1 | 11,242.7 | 33.2 | 8,886.9 | 26.3 |
| 1946 | 52,840.2 | 15,028.1 | 28.4 | 11,933.0 | 22.6 |
| 1947 | 92,310.0 | 24,531.7 | 26.6 | 18,622.6 | 20.2 |

[a] Second half of 1939 only.

another edition of the tariff was published which incorporated approximately 2,000 schedule changes that had been made in the preceding years. At present, the assessment of import duties is governed by the revised (tenth) issue of the tariff of 1941.

The tariff is, in effect, a two-column tariff. The minimum tariff, which was established in 1934 and which is identical with the one-column schedule that prevailed at that time, was originally applicable to imports from all countries with which El Salvador had either a favorable trade balance or at least an approximately balanced position. The minimum rates were also extended, regardless of trade balances, to products of countries with which El Salvador had most-favored-nation agreements, as well as to the member countries of the Pan-American Union. The minimum tariff also applies to a number of products irrespective of their origin, including all petroleum products. The minimum tariff is modified through agreement rates contained in trade agreements with France, Italy, and the United States. The most important changes in the minimum tariff were effected by the trade agreement with the United States, in which substantial concessions were made on the duties for manufactured foods and other manufactured products, particularly automobile tires. All countries with which El Salvador has most-favored-nation agreements benefit from the agreement rates, with the exception of the Netherlands to which the rates of the agreement with the United States do not apply.

Between 1934 and 1948, the tariff also contained a column of maximum rates. These were introduced in 1934 on imports from countries whose purchases of Salvadorean exports were less than one fourth of Salvadorean imports therefrom. The maximum tariff was equivalent to 300 per cent of the basic rates,[11] and was applicable to imports from sixteen countries, including Japan, India, and Portugal. It was introduced as a measure of commercial policy at a time when the international financial position of El Salvador was believed to be threatened by adverse trade balances with many countries, particularly Japan. Since, however, imports from Japan were curtailed and later eliminated as a result of the war, and imports from other countries in the maximum tariff list had always been negligible, the maximum tariff was abolished in September 1948.

What is now the second column, covering preferential duties, pertains to certain imports from Central American countries. In several instances imports from these countries are duty free (e.g., cut timber, plants, flowers, tortoise shell, woolen blankets); in others they enjoy tariff reductions of from 10 to 90 per cent (e.g., wheat, 20 per cent; wheat flour, 10 per cent; beans, 10 per cent; cocoa, 80 per cent; and spices, 90 per cent). Imports from Honduras, except coffee,[12] hides, and cigarettes, are duty free under the provisions of a special free trade agreement in effect since 1918.

[11] Originally, the law provided also for an intermediate tariff on imports from those countries with which El Salvador had an unfavorable balance of trade but whose purchases of Salvadorean exports were equal to at least one fourth of the value of Salvadorean imports.

[12] In 1949, a government decree authorized the free importation of coffee from Honduras.

## DUTY STRUCTURE AND TARIFF POLICY

Rates of duty in the Salvadorean tariff are predominately specific, based usually on gross weight. *Ad valorem* rates are employed for articles made of precious metals and for automobiles, and are based on net market values at the point of origin. The specific rates of duty are stated in terms of United States dollars per 100 kilograms. The result of using weights as the basis for the assessment of specific duties is that the *ad valorem* equivalent of the duties declines with an increase in the price of the dutiable commodities (see Tables 82 and 83). Since import duties account, as indicated above, for the major part of import taxes, the result of the system of specific duties is that in times of business prosperity, when the demand of El Salvador for imports is likely to be ample, imports are relatively less burdened by duties than in times of depressed business activity, low prices and, presumably, low foreign exchange earnings through exports. The main argument for the imposition for specific duties, however, is the ease of assessment and the corollary difficulty of duty evasion through false value declarations.

The primary purpose of the import tariff is the raising of revenue, the granting of protection to domestic industry and agriculture being a secondary and minor objective. The only industries that have enjoyed protection through high import duties are cotton growing, the manufacture of cotton textiles,[13] and the production of wheat and sugar (which is subject to a relatively high internal tax). The fiscal character of the tariff schedule is revealed in Table 83, which indicates (1) the wide range of coverage of the duty schedule; and (2) the concentration of high duties on consumers' goods, and on commodities for which the demand does not vary greatly with the price (e.g., sulphuric acid, plate glass). The table likewise indicates that in the composition of the duty schedule, an effort has been made to minimize the

---

[13] In 1948, the duty rates on a large number of cotton textiles were substantially raised, the increases amounting in some instances to more than 100 per cent. The purpose of these increases was to grant additional protection to the domestic textile industry.

TABLE 83

COMPUTED AD VALOREM RATES ON IMPORT TAXES ON SELECTED COMMODITIES[a]
1938, 1940, 1944, AND 1946

| Commodity | 1938 | 1940 | 1944 | 1946 |
|---|---|---|---|---|
| Ham, not specified............ | 27.0 | 28.9 | 25.7 | 23.5 |
| Wheat flour.................. | 136.1 | 160.3 | 130.3 | 121.0 |
| Tea, not specified............ | 63.0 | 59.1 | 54.0 | 45.2 |
| Portland cement.............. | 37.7 | 29.6 | 30.0 | 31.1 |
| Sulphuric acid................ | 31.8 | 36.6 | 49.6 | 44.8 |
| Cigarettes................... | 284.5 | 273.7 | 290.0 | 277.1 |
| Leather belts................. | 54.4 | 42.9 | 28.1 | 27.4 |
| Rayon yarn.................. | 117.2 | 115.3 | 113.5 | 86.4 |
| Bleached cotton cloth.......... | 47.2 | 51.3 | 33.2 | 28.9 |
| Wool and felt hats............ | 47.7 | 33.7 | 22.2 | 21.8 |
| Rayon underwear.............. | 103.6 | 99.7 | 48.9 | 42.7 |
| Cotton shirts................. | 70.9 | 67.3 | 43.0 | 39.4 |
| Cotton clothing for men........ | 122.5 | 126.3 | 80.7 | 60.1 |
| Rayon dresses................ | 54.5 | 61.2 | 40.4 | 31.9 |
| Automobile tires.............. | 20.0 | 18.7 | 15.9 | 15.4 |
| Bottle corks................. | 73.5 | 81.3 | 52.5 | 62.4 |
| Newsprint, in sheets........... | 25.8 | 29.0 | 18.6 | 23.6 |
| Cellophane.................. | 12.4 | 12.7 | 12.8 | 13.1 |
| Cardboards, not specified....... | 88.0 | 100.6 | 97.3 | 71.9 |
| Plate glass.................. | 174.9 | 118.2 | 133.2 | 143.3 |
| Electric motors............... | 10.7 | 12.1 | 10.9 | 11.1 |
| Electric generators............ | 10.6 | 8.9 | 10.6 | 9.5 |
| Combustion engines........... | 12.5 | 10.4 | 9.2 | 10.5 |
| Typewriters................. | 24.6 | 23.7 | 26.8 | 22.9 |
| Pickaxes.................... | 62.2 | 53.6 | 46.7 | 42.3 |
| Files, not specified............ | 21.7 | 18.3 | 17.0 | 14.8 |
| Trucks...................... | 21.5 | 25.2 | 23.0 | 21.0 |
| Musical instruments........... | 28.1 | 21.6 | 15.5 | 11.2 |
| Watches.................... | 19.4 | 24.5 | 8.3 | 9.2 |
| Machetes................... | 59.9 | 56.8 | 48.3 | 46.0 |

[a] The *ad valorem* rates shown in this table were computed on the basis of the tariff schedule and the rates of other import taxes. The *ad valorem* import duties were derived from import statistics by tariff positions, from the archives of the now defunct Office of the Fiscal Representative of the Foreign Loan (for 1938 and 1940), and from import statistics made available by the Bureau of Customs (for 1944 and 1946). The statistics provide data on the quantity and the value of imports. To the quantity figures the specific-duty rates of the tariff were applied. To the figures thus obtained were added: (a) the surcharge of 1 or 2 per cent of the duty computed; (b) charges for the consular invoice fee (6 per cent of the value of imports); and (c) a charge for the bill-of-lading fee ($1.00 for $500 of the value of the import, up to a maximum of $10.00 for imports of $5,000 colones and above). The computed import duties are somewhat, though not significantly, lower than the actual duty collections since the computed rates do not allow for payment for certificates of origin, shipping manifests, and consular invoice blanks. Besides, the computed surcharge is smaller than the actual surcharge since the surcharge is levied upon import duties as well as warehousing fees. Since warehousing fees are not included in the computation of import taxes, the surcharge on these fees could not be included either.

burden of import duties upon commodities used in agricultural and industrial production (e.g., motors, combustion engines).

The tendency to avoid the taxation of producers' goods is further strengthened by the practice of exempting industries, particularly new ones, from the payment of duties on imports of essential supplies and equipment. For instance, the importation of machinery used in coffee processing is duty free. Besides, the National Assembly has periodically granted duty exemptions (*franquicias*) to enterprises producing alcohol, flour, cotton textiles, and certain other manufactured articles.

The tariff schedule is divided into titles, chapters, divisions, and subdivisions. The result of this elaborate scheme is the creation of several thousand tariff positions. Since in many instances several positions in one subdivision or division have the same duty rate, the schedule appears unnecessarily voluminous and complex. As to the equity of the tariff structure, its complexity and the fact that the prices which prevailed at the time when the specific duties were originally established have undergone many divergent changes, have produced a system of rates that bears little resemblance to the original schedule. Duties on goods which only a limited number of persons can afford to purchase are in many instances much lower than the average *ad valorem* rates on all imports. The duties on automobiles, for instance, amount to 21 per cent; on watches, 9.2 per cent; on musical instruments, 11.2 per cent.[14] On the other hand, the tax burden on imports of commodities widely used and needed by low income groups is substantial. The *ad valorem* equivalent of duties (and other charges) on pickaxes amounts to 42.3 per cent, on machetes 46 per cent. Textiles, even if they do not compete with domestically produced commodities, are subject to particularly heavy duties (rayon yarns 86 per cent, cotton shirts 39 per cent). There does not seem to be any particular reason except the obsolescence of the rate structure why, for instance, the *ad valorem* rate of cardboard should be 72 per cent while that on cellophane amounts to only 13 per cent.

[14] These percentages include consular invoice fees and other charges on imports.

## TARIFF REVISION

The inadequacy and partial obsolescence of the tariff now in force have been recognized by the Salvadorean government. In 1947 a committee composed of representatives of the interested government agencies and of business interests was created and charged with the task of preparing recommendations for the revision of the tariff. So far the committee has not made any specific recommendations, but it is known that it has given thought and consideration to the elimination of technical deficiencies of the present tariff and to the development of a rational basis for a general overhauling of the existing tariff structure. As to the technical inequities, it seems that the gross weight basis of the specific duties has caused considerable difficulties. The unfortunate result of the gross weight basis of the specific duties is that importers prefer to keep the weight of packing material to a minimum. Inadequate packing frequently causes damage to the imported merchandise. A change to a net weight basis seems desirable also because the present gross weight basis distorts the relationship between duty rates and value, since it depends upon the physical characteristics on the imports in question (especially on whether or not heavy packing is necessary). A change presupposes, however, a thorough investigation of the average weight of packing used in various lines of merchandise if the new net weight duties are to produce the same revenue as the present gross weight rates.

Another technical question to be considered by the committee is the present classification system. Many of the tariff positions contained in the present schedule are useless, since no transactions in the specified commodities take place. On the other hand, it has become necessary to supplement the schedule by an index that determines the tariff classification of commodities not specifically mentioned in the schedule. It appears that the Brussels classification, which forms the basis of the nomenclature, is not too well adapted to the specific requirements of Salvadorean foreign trade. The substitution of a new classification conforming more closely to the composition of Salvadorean imports therefore appears desirable.

The main problem confronting the committee working on the revision of the tariff, however, is undoubtedly a reconstruction of the rate structure itself. It appears that the first step in this direction would have to be a decision in principle as to the level of the *ad valorem* duty burden on the various categories of imports. The establishment of such categories should take account of the type and use of the commodities in question (e.g., consumers' as against producers' goods, necessities as against luxuries, the existence as against the absence of domestic substitutes). Once the basic *ad valorem* rate structure is established it should not be too difficult to convert the *ad valorem* rate of duties into a set of specific rates that would not change the revenue yield of customs collections.

### SURCHARGE

The surcharge on import duties was originally levied in favor of a special fund, and it amounted to one per cent of the duty charged and of the warehousing fee collected by the Customs Service. In 1942, when duty collections fell off as a result of a temporary sharp curtailment of imports, the surcharge was raised to 2 per cent.

### OTHER IMPORT TAXES

The gasoline taxes, the tax on pharmaceutical specialties, and the tax on imported cigarettes are technically not import duties, but since they pertain explicitly or implicitly to imported goods, they are merely another form of import duty. There are actually two gasoline taxes in effect: one, of 2 cents per gallon, was originally collected for a special fund in favor of physical education; the other, of 30 cents per hundred kilograms, was imposed and collected in favor of the National University fund. There is no reason why these special taxes should not be incorporated into the tariff schedule, thus eliminating the necessity of separate accounts and complicated assessment procedures.

### CONSULAR INVOICE FEE

The consular invoice fees form a major part of the total taxation of imports, amounting to 6 per cent of the c.i.f. value of imports. The effect of this additional *ad valorem* taxation of imports is the conversion of the specific duty system of the tariff into a system of mixed duties. The fiscal result of this combination is that the fluctuations in the effective *ad valorem* equivalent of the total taxes on imports are somewhat mitigated by the inclusion of the value of imports in the tax base through the consular invoice fee. This is particularly true with respect to commodities that are subject to low rates of specific duties. There the consular fee actually forms the larger part of the total tax burden (e.g., motors, combustion engines, watches). In 1948, the requirement of consular invoices was abolished, but the "invoice fee" was retained. Henceforth, commercial invoices can be submitted to the Salvadorean customs authorities, but they must be visaed by consular authorities.

### OTHER CONSULAR FEES

Other "consular" fees that are actually collected by the Customs Service, are the fees for the bill of lading and the certificate of origin. The fee for the bill of lading amounts to $1.00 (U.S.) for each $500 c.i.f. value of imports, up to a maximum of $10.00 for imports valued at more than $5,000. A fee of $2.00 for the issuance of certificates of origin was formerly collected, but in 1948 it was replaced by a fee, also of $2.00, for the visaing of commercial invoices. The fees are collected by the Customs Service.

The payment of shipping manifests has been included among the taxes on imports because the payment for the issuance of the manifests forms part of the c.i.f. value of imported goods. These fees are collected by the offices issuing the manifests.

The table on import taxes and duties (Table 81) includes also an item referred to in the official revenue statistics as "exchange difference." The reason for the inclusion of this item among the taxes on imports is as follows: Originally the conversion rate for the import duties was set at 2 colones for one dollar, but in 1932 it was changed to 2.25 colones, and in 1935 to 2.50. Until 1945, however, all tax collections of the Customs Service (gasoline taxes, consular invoice fees, etc.) except duties were collected at the rate of 2.50 colones to the dollar, but were accounted for at the rate of 2 colones. The difference of 50 centavos per dollar was accounted for and shown in the revenue statistics as the "exchange difference."[15]

## 6. CONSUMPTION TAXES

Consumption taxes comprise the second largest group of taxes in the Salvadorean revenue system, accounting in the last ten years for one fifth to one fourth of total tax receipts.

In absolute figures they have shown substantial increases, as is shown in Table 84. Between 1940 and 1947 they increased more than threefold. This was due partly to the increase in the level of consumption of most of the commodities upon which taxes are imposed, and partly to an increase in the tax rates on some of the commodities.

### LIQUOR TAXES

Approximately one half of all consumption-tax collections stem from taxes imposed upon beverages. Among those, the liquor tax (*impuesto sobre el aguardiente*) is by far the most important, the tax yields doubling between 1940 and 1947 at practically unchanged rates. The relative position of the tax declined somewhat, however, since it now accounts for only 35 per cent of total consumption tax collections while in 1940 its share amounted to more than 50 per cent. The liquor tax is one of the oldest taxes in El Salvador, its imposition in its present form being governed by the Liquor Law of 1916. The law distinguishes two tax rates. One rate is imposed on the so-called obligatory monthly sales quota of each sales outlet as determined by the Bureau of Internal Revenue, and amounts to 2 colones per liter.

[15] The revenue statistics show wide year-to-year fluctuations in the item "exchange difference." Thus in 1940 no exchange differences were recorded while two years later the exchange differences amounted to more than 650,000 colones. The records in the archives of the Court of Accounts do not provide any information concerning the origin of these funds, except the fact of their receipt through the Customs Service. It appears, therefore, that the accounting procedures of the receipts of the Customs Service were changed frequently. A small amount of the "exchange difference" originated with the diplomatic and consular service of El Salvador, which explains the amounts appearing in the statistics after 1945. The foreign service of El Salvador appears to be still applying in some instances the old 2-to-1 conversion rate, and reporting the difference as "exchange difference."

## TABLE 84

### CONSUMPTION TAXES, 1935/36 AND 1940 TO 1948

*(In thousands of colones)*

| | 1935/36 | 1940 | 1941 | 1942 | 1943 | 1944 | 1945 | 1946 | 1947 | 1948[a] |
|---|---|---|---|---|---|---|---|---|---|---|
| **Beverage taxes:** | | | | | | | | | | |
| Liquor tax | 1662.4[b] | 1767.1 | 1664.6 | 2010.9 | 2425.9 | 2982.1 | 2838.6 | 3308.5 | 3662.6 | 3000.0 |
| Liqueur tax (licores confeccionados) | 39.3 | 40.0 | 46.0 | 63.1 | 106.1 | 198.6 | 333.0 | 452.0 | 555.0 | 420.0 |
| Stamp tax on liqueurs | .. | 5.8 | 6.9 | 9.1 | 14.9 | 29.2 | 40.9 | 23.9 | 35.9 | 35.0 |
| Tax on fruit wine | .. | 0.7 | 0.5 | 1.0 | 0.8 | 0.8 | 1.0 | 1.0 | 1.1 | 0.9 |
| Beer tax | } 175.3 | 104.2 | 112.1 | 140.6 | 150.8[b] | 193.8 | 286.5 | 354.8 | 358.9 | 350.0 |
| Beer stamp tax | | 59.8 | 64.6 | 80.0 | 96.3 | 118.2 | 147.8 | 192.6 | 283.4 | 180.0 |
| Soft drink stamp tax | 46.0 | 56.2 | 58.9 | 79.1 | 101.5 | 135.7 | 169.8 | 238.3 | 331.0 | 300.0 |
| Total | 1923.9 | 2033.8 | 1953.6 | 2384.7 | 2896.3 | 3658.4 | 3824.6 | 4571.1 | 5227.9 | 4285.9 |
| **Tobacco taxes:** | | | | | | | | | | |
| Cigarette tax | 390.8 | 390.2 | 408.9 | 380.0 | 383.4[b] | 510.2 | 672.2 | 731.1 | 850.4 | 800.0 |
| Cigarette paper tax | .. | 432.5 | 454.3 | 639.1 | 1082.5 | 1303.7 | 1551.3 | 1755.9 | 1994.9 | 2000.0 |
| Total | 390.8 | 822.7 | 863.2 | 1019.1 | 1465.9 | 1813.9 | 2223.5 | 2487.0 | 2845.3 | 2800.0 |
| **Other consumption taxes:** | | | | | | | | | | |
| Sugar tax | 233.7 | 231.6 | 257.7 | 224.9 | 288.2[b] | 329.1 | 347.8 | 775.3 | 1630.6 | 1400.0 |
| Match tax | ..[c] | 50.2 | 65.3[d] | 103.7 | 160.6 | 182.5 | 210.9 | 327.9 | 391.1 | 180.0 |
| Cotton tax | 26.6[d] | 82.1[d] | 75.8[d] | 158.8[d] | 76.4[d] | 288.2 | 265.4 | 286.4 | 373.4 | 300.0 |
| Cattle stamp tax | 35.8 | 40.3 | 39.1 | 41.0 | 40.6 | 35.1 | 37.1 | 35.9 | 37.8 | 35.0 |
| Entertainment tax | ..[c] | 31.0 | 30.0 | 52.2 | 44.9 | 22.9 | 31.2 | 39.2 | 33.8 | 30.0 |
| Tax on denatured alcohol | 33.3 | 47.8 | 49.3 | 50.0 | 51.4 | 49.2 | 51.0 | 62.5 | 67.5 | 60.0 |
| Tax on boat and airplane fares | ..[c] | 3.1 | 14.1 | 13.2 | 24.4 | 25.0 | 62.1 | 58.8 | 56.0 | 80.0 |
| Total | 329.4 | 468.1 | 541.3 | 643.8 | 686.5 | 932.0 | 1005.5 | 1586.0 | 2590.2 | 2085.0 |
| Grand Total | 2643.2 | 3342.6 | 3348.1 | 4047.6 | 5048.7 | 6414.3 | 7053.6 | 8644.1 | 10,663.4 | 9170.9 |

[a] Budget.  [b] Partly estimated.  [c] Not available.  [d] Henequen tax.

Upon sales in excess of this quota, a tax of 1.15 colones per liter is assessed. These rates have been in effect since March 1945, prior to which the rates amounted to 2.06 colones for the obligatory quota and 1.06 colones for excess sales. The tax is collected through the Liquor Section of the Bureau of Internal Revenue.[16]

## LIQUEUR TAXES

Liqueur (*aguardiente confeccionado*) is subject to two tax levies. To the liquor tax corresponds a liqueur tax which has amounted to 1.80 colones per liter since April 1945; previously the rate was 1.70 colones. As Table 84 indicates, the amount of revenue collected from the liqueur tax has increased much more rapidly than that from the liquor tax. This seems to suggest that with the rising income of the war and postwar years a gradual change in consumption habits has taken place. At present substantially more liqueur is consumed than ten years ago. This increase has occurred at the expense of the consumption of liquor (*aguardiente*), the sale of which has increased at a slower rate.

The second tax on liqueur is a stamp tax (*timbre de garantía*) of 0.20 colones per liter.

## WINE TAX

The tax on fruit wine is not imposed on the production of wine, but on the alcohol added to the fruit juices used in wine production. The tax, which is in effect a reduction of the liquor tax, was introduced in order to foster the consumption of fruit wines and thereby curtail the consumption of hard liquor. As Table 84 shows, the attempt to foster the production of wines with low alcoholic content has been unsuccessful so far.

## BEER TAX

The tax on beer amounts to 18 centavos per liter. Originally it was 12 centavos, of which 10 centavos were allocated to the Mejoramiento Social fund, and 2 centavos for state hospitals, but in 1939 an additional stamp tax of 6 centavos per liter was

---

[16] In July 1948, the sale of liquor was further regulated through the introduction of uniform bottles and caps. Henceforth, *aguardiente* is to be sold only in standard bottles. In this connection, the tax rates were modified.

imposed. At present, both taxes are collected through tax stamps attached to each bottle, but the tax statistics continue to show two distinct taxes.

### SOFT DRINK TAX

The tax on soft drinks (*bebidas gaseosas*) is a stamp tax of 1.5 centavos per bottle of 0.35 liters.

### TOBACCO TAXES

The tax on domestic machine-made cigarettes amounts at present to 0.65 per cigarette or 11.7 centavos for a pack of 18 cigarettes. This rate was introduced in 1942, the previous rate having been 0.2 centavos per cigarette.[17] The production of cigarettes by hand is taxed through the imposition of a tax of 0.2 centavos per cigarette on cigarette paper; prior to 1942, this tax was 0.05 centavos. The pre-1942 rate on imported cigarettes of 5.0 centavos per pack of 20 is unchanged. The cigarette tax is collected entirely through the sale of cigarette paper by the Bureau of Internal Revenue, which watermarks the paper used in the production of cigarettes. The tax statistics, however, continue to show two distinct taxes, on cigarettes, and on cigarette paper.

### SUGAR TAX

The tax on sugar amounts to 4 colones per quintal (46 kilograms) of sugar consumed domestically. This rate was introduced at the end of 1946 when in addition to the prevailing rate of 2 colones per quintal a surtax of 2 colones was introduced. From 1945 to 1947 the export of sugar was likewise subject to a tax of 3 colones per quintal, but this tax was repealed at the end of 1947 because the world sugar price had fallen so low that the exportation of sugar from El Salvador would have been unprofitable. The law repealing the tax on sugar exports provided, however, a schedule according to which such exports become subject to a progressive tax if and when the world market price

[17] The current tax is composed of two levies: 0.4 centavos per cigarette (0.2 prior to 1942) on cigarette paper; and 4.5 centavos per pack of 18 produced (untaxed prior to 1942).

exceeds $6.00 per quintal in the New York market, the rate being determined by the spot quotation of sugar in the New York market. The construction of the tax thus is similar to that of the export tax on coffee, which was repealed only recently.

The sugar tax is collected by special tax inspectors who supervise sugar production in the rural areas and attach a seal (*marchamo*) to each bag of sugar. The sugar tax proceeds were originally reserved for the Mejoramiento Social fund.

### MATCH TAX

Until July 1948 the match tax was imposed upon the domestic production or importation of matches. The match tax amounted to 15 colones per case of matches of 1200 boxes (of 35 to 40 matches each) or 1.25 centavos per box. In August 1948, the tax on domestically produced matches was lowered to 5 colones per case (or 0.417 centavos per box) and imported matches were exempted. At the same time, the import duty on matches of $35.00 per 100 kilograms was changed to $12.00 per case.

### COTTON TAX

The cotton tax was introduced in 1944 in connection with the establishment of the Cotton Cooperative (*Cooperativa Algodonera Salvadoreña*), which is the central sales agent for all Salvadorean cotton growers and enjoys monopolistic powers. The tax, which amounts to 5.50 colones per quintal of clean cotton, is collected through the Cotton Cooperative from the cotton mill owners to whom the cotton is sold. As pointed out above, the payment of the cotton tax absolves the textile producers from the payment of income taxes. Since the production of cotton textiles is protected against the competition of imported textiles through high import taxes, and since the proportion of Salvadorean cotton textile production that is normally exported is negligible, the tax is in effect a tax upon the consumption of cotton goods in Salvador and is passed on to the ultimate consumer.[18]

[18] When the cotton tax was introduced in 1944, cotton goods remained subject to price controls. As long as the controls prevailed, the tax was probably not, or at least not fully, shifted.

Prior to 1943 the production of henequen was taxed. This tax was not strictly a consumption tax since most of the henequen was used in the production of coffee bags which were exported.

## OTHER CONSUMPTION TAXES

The cattle stamp tax (*timbre agro-pecuario*) is a tax imposed upon cattle slaughtering; and is collected through the issuance of stamps.

The entertainment tax is a graduated tax on tickets for public performances, and amounts to from 1 to 20 centavos, depending upon the price of the ticket. The collection of this tax is controlled by special tax inspectors who are attached to the theaters.

The tax on denatured alcohol is imposed upon alcohol made unfit for human consumption. The tax rate is 0.40 centavos per liter of alcohol of 90 degrees. All preparations with an alcohol base are subject to this tax.

The tax on boat and airplane fares amounts to 10 per cent of the price of the fare. The collection of the tax is controlled through inspectors of the Bureau of Internal Revenue who check on the tickets issued and the fares charged to the passengers. The tax is then collected through the issuance of a payment order to the shipping and air transport companies.

## 7. OTHER TAXES, FEES, AND FINES

### OTHER TAXES

This group includes several minor taxes and municipal *arbitrios* originally collected for the benefit of various *juntas* and other public institutions. In most years the major proportion of this group is made up, however, of an item of "unforeseen receipts." The Court of Accounts does not have any detailed records as to the origin of these unforeseen receipts, but incomplete data for a few years suggest that the receipts originate mainly in the imposition of taxes that had not been included in the annual budget of receipts. Thus, for instance, the imposition of a surtax on sugar in 1946 resulted in substantial "unforeseen receipts." Such unforeseen receipts were therefore included in the category of "other" taxes.

Another item included in this group is a percentage share of the General Fund in taxes originally collected for the Mejoramiento Social fund. Since this share, which amounted to 10 per cent of all tax collections in favor of the Mejoramiento Social (on sugar, beer, and cigarettes), was not included among the receipts of the Mejoramiento Social, its inclusion in this group was necessary.[19]

## FEES

This group includes all fees collected by the government for various services, including the issuance of documents and permits. Certain of these fees are collected by the consular service (for passports, authentication of documents, etc.), by the police (drivers' licenses), by the Customs Service (for lending or sailing permits of vessels), and by other government authorities. The group also includes a border-crossing fee of 2 colones per person entering or leaving the country. Some of the fees are collected through the sale of tax stamps.

## FINES

Fines collected by the traffic police account for half of all fines imposed; others are collected by the finance police in prosecuting violations of the liquor law, by the Customs Service for smuggling and improper customs declarations, and by other government authorities exercising administrative jurisdiction.

## 8. LOANS

The only loans that are included in the liquidation of the annual budget are those authorized in the annual budgets in accordance with the Budget Law,[20] i.e., short-term loans from the central bank which must be repaid within the same fiscal year. During the last ten years the Minister of Finance has made use of the blanket authority to contract short-term loans only five times. The following loans were obtained:

| | |
|---|---|
| 1941 | 1,660,000 colones |
| 1942 | 1,440,000 |
| 1943 | 1,260,000 |
| 1944 | 1,000,000 |
| 1945 | 50,000 |

[19] For the amounts of "other" taxes, fees, and fines collected, see Table 11 in Chapter IV.

[20] See above, p. 264.

The loans contracted from 1941 to 1944 were for general government expenditures. The small loan of 1945 was for the purchase of cereals abroad when a temporary shortage of supplies threatened to cause sharp price increases.

Loans obtained by the government from other sources, or on the basis of special legislative authorization, are not included in the budget liquidation figures. The only long-term loan obtained by the government during the period under consideration was the Export-Import Bank loan for the construction of the inter-American highway. This loan was agreed upon in 1941 and increased in 1945. The total amount disbursed by the Export-Import Bank was $1,476,000 (3,690,000 colones). Although this loan is not included among the government receipts shown in the annual liquidation, the payments for interest and amortization thereof (as well as of the National Loan of 1922) are included among the expenditures for public debt service (see Chapter V). The proceeds of the Export-Import Bank loan were recorded as receipts of an extraordinary budget for the construction of the inter-American highway, passed in 1942. This budget has not been liquidated as yet.

## 9. GOVERNMENT ENTERPRISES

As Table 12 in Chapter IV demonstrates, receipts from government enterprises never accounted for more than a small percentage of government receipts. The percentage share of these enterprises has declined somewhat in the recent years, although the absolute amount received has increased considerably in the last decade.

### POSTAL, TELEGRAPH, AND TELEPHONE SERVICES

The receipts of the postal, telegraph, and telephone services (including radio communications) are determined by their respective rate schedules. The basic postal rates were established in 1937, but were amended in later years by the addition of air mail rates. As Table 85 shows, the postal system has operated in most of the last ten years with a small deficit and in two years (1940 and 1946) with a small surplus. The budget for 1948 provides for expenditures considerably in excess of anticipated re-

## TABLE 85

### OPERATIONS OF POSTAL, TELEPHONE, AND TELEGRAPH SYSTEM, 1938–1948[a]

(In thousands of colones)

| | 1938/39 | 1939[b] | 1940 | 1941 | 1942 | 1943 | 1945 | 1946 | 191. | 1948[c] |
|---|---|---|---|---|---|---|---|---|---|---|
| **Postal system:** | | | | | | | | | | |
| Receipts............ | 338.6 | 151.2 | 354.9 | 316.9 | 356.1 | 393.8 | 451.1 | 581.0 | 533.1 | 550.0 |
| Expenditures: Fixed...... | 264.1 | 135.8 | 273.5 | 276.3 | 278.2 | 288.8 | 327.4 | 358.1 | 447.9 | 693.4 |
| Variable... | 79.2 | 37.4 | 80.9 | 60.7 | 116.0 | 211.8 | 161.6 | 201.8 | 146.4 | 227.8 |
| Total...... | 343.3 | 173.3 | 354.3 | 337.0 | 394.2 | 500.6 | 489.0 | 559.8 | 594.3 | 921.2 |
| Surplus (+) or deficit (−) | −4.7 | −22.1 | +0.6 | −20.1 | −38.1 | −106.8 | −37.9 | +21.2 | −61.2 | −371.2 |
| **Telephone and telegraph:** | | | | | | | | | | |
| Receipts............ | 682.6 | 350.7 | 695.8 | 719.3 | 777.5 | 852.2 | 999.4 | 1182.3 | 1155.0 | 1206.0 |
| Expenditures: Fixed...... | 765.2 | 393.0 | 789.4 | 790.0 | 796.5 | 805.0 | 908.1 | 1024.9 | 1231.3 | 1566.6 |
| Variable... | 143.7 | 129.2 | 178.8 | 137.8 | 169.7 | 194.1 | 115.4 | 187.7 | 641.8 | 751.5 |
| Total...... | 909.0 | 517.2 | 968.3 | 927.8 | 966.3 | 999.1 | 1023.5 | 1212.6 | 1873.1 | 2318.1 |
| Surplus (+) or deficit (−) | −226.4 | −166.5 | −272.5 | −208.5 | −188.8 | −146.9 | −24.1 | −30.3 | −718.1 | −1112.1 |

a For years prior to 1938/39, and for 1944, expenditure data are not available.
b Second half of 1939 only.
c Budget.

ceipts. However, if account is taken of the fact that the postal system supplies its services free of charge to the government and that the "variable" expenditures of the postal system include expenditures for improvements and investments, the rate structure appears to have been more or less adequate until recently. The budget law for 1948 and the salary law for the same year provide for a considerable extension of the postal system through the addition of new suboffices and the transformation of existing substations into main stations. Since this improvement of the postal service is not likely to be accompanied by a comparable increase in receipts, it appears likely that the operational deficit budgeted for 1948 will continue for some years unless postal rates are increased.

The operations of the telephone and telegraph services have been much less satisfactory financially than those of the postal system. Even if allowance is made for the free services provided the government authorities, the substantial deficits incurred continuously during the last decade appear to have been the result of inadequate rates. This contention is borne out by the fact that in most years the receipts did not even cover the fixed expenditures for salaries, wages, rents, etc. The inadequacy of receipts of the telephone and telegraph offices seems to be due largely to the fact that the basic tariff schedule has been in effect since 1933, although salaries of telegraph and telephone employees and the cost of equipment have increased sharply in the intervening period.

OTHER GOVERNMENT ENTERPRISES

This group includes receipts derived from the sale of goods and services supplied by facilities owned and operated by the government. The largest single item among these receipts is the fees paid for the use of government-owned docks in La Libertad. Warehousing facilities operated by the Customs Service also have resulted in considerable revenue to the government. Sales of official publications prepared by the government printing office resulted in receipts of approximately 50,000 colones annually in recent years. Smaller amounts were earned by the chemical laboratories.

Many of the minor government enterprises are operated primarily for the benefit of other government agencies, and their gross receipts therefore cover only a small fraction of their operating expenses. For instance, the annual expenditures of the government printing office amounted to 337,000 colones in 1946, while receipts were only 54,000 colones.

### SALE OF GOVERNMENT GOODS

Receipts from the sale of goods owned by the government, usually from stocks of materials, are in most years very unimportant. Only in years 1942 and 1943, when the government sold large quantities of road-building material, did such receipts reach major proportions.

### 10. OTHER RECEIPTS

Under "other receipts" have been included certain amounts that either are nonrecurring or do not fit into the classifications discussed above. In most years "other receipts" were unimportant. The major items in those years when "other receipts" exceeded 100,000 colones were: in 1935–36, a profit of 128,000 colones made by the government on a bulk purchase of sugar abroad; in 1940 to 1943 a participation, first by the special fund of the Mortgage Bank and later by the General Fund, in the profits derived from the production of matches; in 1943 a contribution of 728,800 colones of the United States government for the construction of the inter-American highway and a reimbursement to the General Fund of 188,000 from the funds set aside for the construction of the highway; and in 1947 the proceeds of the sale of sugar imported by the government (535,000 colones).

### TRANSITORY ITEMS

This group includes receipts that are listed in the budget liquidations of the government in order to preserve the comprehensiveness of budgetary accounting procedures. These receipts correspond to expenditures of the same or smaller amounts that appear under various headings on the expenditure side. Thus, for instance, the sale of cigarette paper by the Bureau of Internal Revenue to cigarette factories gives rise to a receipt which is offset by the purchase price paid for the acquisition of paper.[21] Other receipts of the same type are derived from the sale of license plates for vehicles. Another item of relative importance in this group is the receipts from the sale of liquor that is transferred from one administrative area (*departamento*) to another. The intervention of the government in these liquor transactions is necessary because the liquor law prohibits the private sale of liquor from one such area to another. The government purchases liquor in one of these areas and resells it to distributors in others. In the budget of 1948 the group of transitory items included an amount of 1 million colones. This amount was to be obtained from the sale of bottles and caps to be used in the distribution of *aguardiente* in accordance with the new regulations pertaining to the sale of liquor.[22]

#### OFFSET TO EXPENDITURES AND TRANSFER OF FUNDS

The group of receipts included under this heading consists of amounts received by the General Fund of the Treasury from two sources. The first is the reimbursement and rebate of payments made by the government. Receipts of this sort are small, except in the budget for 1948 under which the General Purchasing Office is to obtain 700,000 colones from the General Fund for the purchase of supplies, but must return the same amount after it transfers such supplies to the various government departments. The budgeted expenditure of 700,000 colones is thus offset by budgeted receipts of a like amount in the revenue budget. The second group of receipts are amounts transferred from special funds to the General Fund. An occasion for the transfer of such funds occurred in mid-1939 when most special funds were discontinued and their assets transferred to the General Fund. Thus, in the second half of 1939, 693,700 colones were transferred at once. In 1942–43 a remainder of 45,000 colones was so transferred. To the same group belong contributions of the special funds of the Mortgage Bank and of the Mejoramiento

---

[21] The Bureau of Internal Revenue collects cigarette taxes when the paper is sold to manufacturers.

[22] Cf. above, p. 309.

Social to the General Fund, as reimbursement for expenditures incurred by the tax administration in connection with the collection of taxes for these special funds.

Prior to 1940 there existed a third group of entries under the heading of "Offsets to Expenditures." These entries are the remainders of undisbursed obligated funds (*sobrantes reserva residuos pasivos*) which resulted because the liquidation data for the preceding years included expenditures that had not been approved and completed as yet. The "remainders" thus represent the excess of the amounts shown in the liquidation of disbursements of previous years over the amounts actually disbursed. After 1940 the accounting procedures were changed and the "remainders" were no longer included in budgetary receipts because it was apparently considered more appropriate to treat such remainders as Treasury but not as budgetary receipts.

Since the receipts included under the heading under discussion are in all instances either a deduction from expenditures, or parts of receipts recorded in the same or in previous years under the revenues of special funds, the group has been excluded from the corrected total shown in Table 11, Chapter IV. In those instances in which the deducted amounts correspond to expenditures, the same amounts have been deducted from total expenditures (see Table 18 of government expenditures in Chapter V and Appendix F).

### FUNDS IN CUSTODY

The receipts shown under this heading have been included in the tables of government receipts only because they were included until 1937 as receipts of the General Fund. Thereafter they were, quite properly, treated as receipts that are entirely unrelated to the financial operations of the government. The custody funds, also, come from two sources. One is the fiscal offices (*Oficinas Fiscales*) which deposit funds with the Treasury; the other is the pension funds (*masitas*) of the armed forces.

# APPENDIX E

## (Second appendix to Chapter IV)

### TABLE 86

RECONCILIATION OF OFFICIAL LIQUIDATIONS OF GOVERNMENT RECEIPTS WITH TOTALS SHOWN IN THIS STUDY

(*In thousands of colones*)

| | 1935/36 | 1936/37 | 1937/38 | 1938/39 | 1939ᵃ | 1940 | 1941 |
|---|---|---|---|---|---|---|---|
| Revenues of: | | | | | | | |
| General Fund | 17,716.6 | 19,910.8 | 19,620.7 | 16,873.5 | 9,995.3 | 17,376.7 | 19,493.1 |
| Banco Hipotecario | 983.3 | 1,211.4 | 1,040.4 | 1,308.0 | 247.4 | 1,508.4 | 865.5 |
| Tax receipts of Mejoramiento Social | 758.0 | 898.8 | 753.6 | 808.1 | 254.8 | 726.6 | 779.2 |
| Other special funds | 685.9 | 812.2 | 973.6 | 1,100.5 | ... | ... | ... |
| Funds in custody | ... | ... | 151.0 | 371.5 | 150.5 | 268.7 | 339.5 |
| Total | 20,143.8 | 22,833.2 | 22,539.3 | 20,461.6 | 10,648.0 | 19,880.4 | 21,477.3 |
| Minus: | | | | | | | |
| Offset to expenditure and transfer of funds | 322.2 | 487.0 | 1,143.7 | 202.3 | 801.5 | 157.3 | 23.1 |
| Funds in custody | 412.2 | 183.7 | 151.0 | 371.5 | 150.5 | 268.6 | 339.5 |
| Corrected total | 19,409.4 | 22,162.5 | 21,244.6 | 19,887.8 | 9,696.0 | 19,454.5 | 21,114.7 |

## TABLE 86 (Continued)

|  | 1942 | 1943 | 1944 | 1945 | 1946 | 1947 | 1948[b] |
|---|---|---|---|---|---|---|---|
| Revenues of: |  |  |  |  |  |  |  |
| General Fund............ | 20,146.8 | 24,308.6 | 23,741.5 | 26,502.9 | 34,213.4 | 53,133.6 | 51,702.6 |
| Banco Hipotecario........ | 1,113.1 | 1,148.3 | ... | ... | ... | ... | ... |
| Tax receipts of Mejoramiento Social.. | 746.1 | 823.2 | 1,033.9 | 653.9 | 899.0 | ... | ... |
| Other special funds....... | ... | ... | 4,392.3 | 1,918.9 | 4,414.4 | 535.0 | ... |
| Funds in custody......... | 478.3 | 376.6 | 549.6 | 779.9 | 1,085.6 | 3,220.6 | 350.0 |
| Total............ | 22,484.3 | 26,656.7 | 29,717.3 | 29,855.6 | 40,612.4 | 56,889.2 | 52,052.6 |
| Minus: |  |  |  |  |  |  |  |
| Offset to expenditure and transfer of funds.......... | 265.5 | 98.4 | 15.9 | 18.3 | 24.2 | 28.7 | 719.0 |
| Funds in custody......... | 478.3 | 376.6 | 549.6 | 779.9 | 1,085.6 | 3,220.6 | 350.0 |
| Corrected total........ | 21,740.5 | 26,181.7 | 29,151.8 | 29,057.4 | 39,502.6 | 53,639.9 | 50,983.6 |

[a] Second half of 1939 only.
[b] Budget.

# APPENDIX F

## (*Appendix to Chapter V*)

### TABLE 87

RECONCILIATION OF OFFICIAL LIQUIDATIONS OF GOVERNMENT EXPENDITURES WITH TOTALS SHOWN IN THIS STUDY

(*In thousands of colones*)

| | 1935/36 | 1936/37 | 1937/38 | 1938/39 | 1939[a] | 1940 | 1941 |
|---|---|---|---|---|---|---|---|
| Expenditures of: | | | | | | | |
| General Fund: Fixed | 10,559.9 | 11,097.9 | 11,700.4 | 11,520.7 | 6,622.0 | 13,706.8 | 13,625.8 |
| Variable | 9,312.0 | 8,261.9 | 7,955.5 | 5,617.2 | 3,480.6 | 6,399.9 | 6,217.3 |
| Banco Hipotecario | 983.3[b] | 1,211.4[b] | 1,032.7 | 1,299.1 | 255.0 | 1,497.5 | 836.8 |
| Mejoramiento Social | 758.0[b] | 898.8[b] | 715.0 | 759.3 | 254.8[b] | 726.6[b] | 779.2[b] |
| Other special funds | 685.9[b] | 812.2[b] | 833.8 | 816.2 | ... | ... | ... |
| Total | 22,299.1 | 22,282.2 | 22,237.4 | 20,012.5 | 10,582.4 | 22,330.8 | 21,459.1 |
| Adjustment[c] | 18.6 | 32.0 | 76.8 | 54.1 | 73.5 | 157.3 | 23.1 |
| Adjusted Total | 22,280.5 | 22,250.2 | 22,160.6 | 19,958.4 | 10,508.9 | 22,173.5 | 21,436.0 |

| | 1942 | 1943 | 1944 | 1945 | 1946 | 1947 | 1948[d] |
|---|---|---|---|---|---|---|---|
| Expenditures of: | | | | | | | |
| General Fund: Fixed | 13,997.4 | 14,195.0 | 14,786.8 | 16,954.9 | 19,679.7 | 25,389.6 | 32,592.6 |
| Variable | 6,294.4 | 7,254.4 | 9,363.1 | 9,159.3 | 14,011.3 | 26,486.4 | 24,960.0 |
| Banco Hipotecario | 1,070.6 | 1,141.5 | ... | ... | ... | ... | ... |
| Mejoramiento Social | 746.1[b] | 823.2[b] | 1,033.9[b] | 653.9[b] | 899.0[b] | ... | ... |
| Other special funds | ... | ... | ... | 2,385.7 | 10,436.8 | ... | ... |
| Total | 22,108.5 | 23,414.1 | 25,183.8 | 29,153.8 | 45,026.7 | 51,875.9 | 57,552.6 |
| Adjustment[c] | 265.5 | 98.4 | 15.9 | 18.3 | 24.2 | 28.7 | 719.0 |
| Adjusted Total | 21,843.0 | 23,315.7 | 25,167.9 | 29,135.5 | 45,002.5 | 51,847.2 | 56,833.6 |

[a] Second half of 1939 only.
[b] Tax receipts.
[c] Corresponds to the "Correction" made in the tables on government revenues, but includes only such amounts as are included in the expenditure figures above.
[d] Budget.

# APPENDIX G

## DISTRIBUTION OF THE TAX BURDEN BY
## FAMILY-INCOME GROUPS IN 1946[1]
### (*Appendix to Chapter VIII*)

IN THIS APPENDIX are presented the statistical methods employed in making the estimates of the tax burden upon typical families as given in Table 36 in Chapter VIII. The basic information for the distribution of the tax burden by family income groups was provided by the official revenue statistics and the various tax laws. Before this information could be utilized, however, it had to be supplemented by estimates both of consumers' expenditures and of the distribution of their incomes, because the impact of taxes upon any family depends in general on either the family's consumption or its income.

### 1. THE CONSUMERS' BUDGET STUDY

The study of consumers' budgets presented in Table 88 was made by a group of Salvadorean economists. Part of this budget study had been previously prepared for the Mejoramiento Social in order to ascertain the volume of consumers' expenditures on domestic and on imported textiles. In connection with the present report, the study, based on a limited sample of families, was revised and expanded. Its results were then submitted to a number of persons believed to be familiar with Salvadorean social and cultural habits and customs, who expressed general agreement with the findings of the study. It may therefore be assumed that, despite the limited size of the sample, the results are reasonably representative, even though they may contain a considerable margin of error.

The year 1946 was chosen as the basis of the study because

---

[1] The statistical computations and the development of the various methods of estimate employed in this appendix are the work of Mr. Eugene R. Schlesinger of the Federal Reserve Bank of New York.

## TABLE 88

### CONSUMERS' FAMILY BUDGET EXPENDITURES IN 1946

| Type of Expenditure | Family Income (in colones) | | | | | Total Consumption (in thousands of colones) |
|---|---|---|---|---|---|---|
| | Under 600 | 600–1200 | 1200–2400 | 2400–3600 | Over 3600 | |
| Food | 325.0 | 412.0 | 565.0 | 800.0 | 1,716.0 | 165,000 |
| Imported only | (5.0) | (25.0) | (60.0) | (130.0) | (270.0) | (9,000) |
| Refined sugar | (10.0) | (30.0) | (60.0) | (80.0) | (140.0) | (11,200) |
| Unrefined brown sugar and sugar loaf | (14.0) | (0.0) | (0.0) | (0.0) | (0.0) | (3,390) |
| Beverages | 29.8 | 39.2 | 54.0 | 96.0 | 204.5 | 15,936 |
| Beer | (3.2) | (9.0) | (14.0) | (20.0) | (47.0) | (2,800) |
| Liquor | (18.5) | (21.0) | (25.0) | (23.0) | (12.0) | (7,810) |
| Soft drinks | (3.3) | (8.2) | (10.0) | (14.0) | (23.0) | (2,341) |
| Imported beverages | (0.0) | (1.0) | (5.0) | (39.0) | (122.5) | (1,835) |
| Liquor made in illegal stills | (4.8) | (0.0) | (0.0) | (0.0) | (0.0) | (1,150) |
| Tobacco | 5.8 | 16.0 | 20.0 | 30.0 | 40.0 | 4,470 |
| Cigarettes | (3.0) | (15.5) | (20.0) | (30.0) | (39.4) | (3,674) |
| Raw tobacco | (2.8) | (0.5) | (0.0) | (0.0) | (0.0) | (732) |
| Imported manufactured tobacco products | (0.0) | (0.0) | (0.0) | (0.0) | (0.6) | (64) |
| Clothing, textiles, shoes, and hats | 53.5 | 100.0 | 208.0 | 320.0 | 580.0 | 38,000 |
| Imported textiles and clothing | (14.5) | (35.0) | (90.0) | (180.0) | (450.0) | (15,800) |
| Textiles and clothing from domestic cotton | (33.0) | (45.0) | (90.0) | (90.0) | (60.0) | (16,600) |
| Shoes and hats | (6.0) | (20.0) | (28.0) | (50.0) | (70.0) | (5,600) |
| Household articles[a] | 13.2 | 35.0 | 80.0 | 138.0 | 200.0 | 12,300 |
| Imported only | (1.0) | (3.0) | (25.0) | (60.0) | (160.0) | (3,240) |
| Matches | (1.5) | (2.5) | (5.0) | (9.0) | (15.0) | (1,000) |

## TABLE 88 (Continued)

| Type of Expenditure | Family Income (in colones) | | | | | Total Consumption (in thousands of colones) |
|---|---|---|---|---|---|---|
| | Under 600 | 600–1200 | 1200–2400 | 2400–3600 | Over 3600 | |
| "Articles not primary necessities"b | 4.2 | 24.5 | 58.0 | 94.0 | 380.0 | 9,830 |
| Imported only | (2.0) | (12.0) | (28.0) | (64.0) | (360.0) | (6,800) |
| Luxury articlesᶜ | 0.0 | 0.0 | 0.0 | 40.0 | 601.0 | 6,410 |
| Gasoline | (0.0) | (0.0) | (0.0) | (0.0) | (800) | (800) |
| Medical care | 4.0 | 14.0 | 28.0 | 45.0 | 150.0 | 5,700 |
| Pharmaceuticals | 16.6 | 25.0 | 42.0 | 60.0 | 156.0 | 10,000 |
| Imported only | (6.25) | (12.5) | (26.0) | (38.0) | (110.0) | (5,000) |
| Domestic only | (10.35) | (12.5) | (16.0) | (22.0) | (46.0) | (5,000) |
| Housing | 36.0 | 100.0 | 360.0 | 600.0 | 1,200.0 | 45,840 |
| Transportationd | 5.8 | 18.0 | 30.0 | 40.0 | 20.0 | 4,400 |
| Entertainment | 1.0 | 6.0 | 20.0 | 40.0 | 60.0 | 2,360 |
| Private education | 0.0 | 0.5 | 12.0 | 45.0 | 135.0 | 2,100 |
| Electric power | 0.0 | 9.0 | 28.0 | 60.0 | 90.0 | 3,100 |
| Domestic servants | 0.0 | 0.0 | 60.0 | 170.0 | 220.0 | 5,000 |
| Other expenditures | 36.0 | 60.0 | 100.0 | 180.0 | 400.0 | 23,640 |
| Total | 530.9 | 859.2 | 1,665.0 | 2,758.0 | 6,152.5 | 354,086 |

a Includes furniture, kitchen utensils, household soap, and matches.
b Includes cosmetics, perfumes, radios, refrigerators, watches, jewelry, glassware, and recreational equipment.
c Includes pianos, boats, automobiles and other vehicles, tires, and gasoline, all of which are imported.
d Excludes air transportation.

[ 327 ]

data for later years were incomplete at the time the study was undertaken. Estimated expenditures for specific goods and services were computed for families with annual incomes of 600, 900, 1,800, 3,000, and over 3,600 colones, these incomes being regarded as "typical" of the corresponding income brackets of less than 600 colones, 600 to 1,200, 1,200 to 2,400, 2,400 to 3,600, and above 3,600.[2] The total expenditures for each family budget item were so adjusted as to be consistent with the gross national product estimate of that item.

## 2. DISTRIBUTION OF INCOME

### INCOME DISTRIBUTION AMONG FAMILIES WITH INCOMES OF LESS THAN 3,600 COLONES

In the process of preparing the study of consumers' budgets, the Salvadorean economists computed the estimated distribution of income among families with annual incomes of less than 3,600 colones, and estimated that 10,000 families had earned more than this amount in 1946. These figures are presented in Table 89, the 1946 population of approximately 2,000,000 persons having been assumed to consist of 400,000 families of five members each.

TABLE 89

DISTRIBUTION OF INCOME BY FAMILY IN 1946

| Income Range | "Typical" Family Income | Estimated Number of Families |
|---|---|---|
| Under 600 colones ............... | 600 colones | 240,000 |
| 600–1,200 ........................ | 900 | 120,000 |
| 1,200–2,400 ....................... | 1,800 | 20,000 |
| 2,400–3,600 ....................... | 3,000 | 10,000 |
| Over 3,600 ....................... | . . . | 10,000 |
| Total ........................ | | 400,000 |

[2] Since the subsistence level is believed to be only slightly below 600 colones, it was felt appropriate to consider an annual income of 600 colones or slightly less as "typical" for the lowest income bracket.

INCOME DISTRIBUTION AMONG FAMILIES WITH
INCOME OF MORE THAN 3,600 COLONES

The distribution of income among families with incomes of more than 3,600 colones was computed from the income tax return statistics for 1946 (Table 77 in Appendix D). These taxable-income data were converted to total personal-income data by assuming that all payers of income tax were granted the basic exemption of 3,000 colones, this sum being added to the taxable-income statistics. The resulting figures were adjusted in order to reduce the number of brackets and so to shift their upper and lower limits that the mean income in each bracket would become a round number, such as 4,000, 6,000, or 8,000 colones (see Table 90). In this manner, the figures were put on a comparable basis with those for the lower income groups, as shown in Table 89. The results of these computations are shown in the first three columns of Table 90. Since only 2,435 families paid income taxes in 1946, the number of families in each bracket was then multiplied by 4.1 (the ratio of the Salvadorean economists' estimate of the total number of families with incomes of over 3,600 colones, to the number actually paying income tax).[3] The results, rounded off and adjusted to total 10,000, are given in the last column of Table 90.

TABLE 90

INCOME DISTRIBUTION CONSTRUCTED FROM INCOME TAX RETURNS

| Income Range | "Typical" Family Income | Payers of Income Tax | Estimated Number of Families |
|---|---|---|---|
| 3,600– 4,700 colones... | 4,000 colones | 1,012 | 4,150 |
| 4,700– 7,500.......... | 6,000 | 542 | 2,225 |
| 7,500– 9,000.......... | 8,000 | 254 | 1,050 |
| 9,000– 12,000.......... | 10,000 | 157 | 650 |
| 12,000– 21,000.......... | 15,000 | 211 | 850 |
| 21,000– 35,000.......... | 25,000 | 132 | 550 |
| 35,000– 72,000.......... | 50,000 | 85 | 350 |
| 72,000–150,000.......... | 100,000 | 28 | 115 |
| Over 150,000.......... | ... | 14 | 60 |
| Total.............. | | 2,435 | 10,000 |

[3] This ratio is discussed in the next paragraph.

The derivation of this income distribution from the data of income-tax payers in 1946 is based upon the following three assumptions: (1) an equal accuracy of reporting was assumed for each level of income; (2) the distribution of the income of families with annual incomes of over 3,600 colones who were not liable to payment of the income tax was assumed to be the same as for those who were (and who therefore filed income tax returns);[4] and (3) taxes paid by corporations were treated as income of individuals.[5] In the middle income brackets (i.e. "typical" incomes of 4,000 and 6,000 colones) errors that may arise through these assumptions tend to offset each other. On the one hand, the fact that families which receive at least 80 per cent of their incomes from work rather than from capital, and those that have more than five minor dependents, are granted exemptions of 4,000 and 5,000 colones respectively, instead of the 3,000-colón figure used in the computations, causes an upward bias in the results. On the other hand, the existence of under-reporting, which experience shows is greatest for income recipients just above the exemption level (who, if they under-appraise their incomes, do not even appear on the tax roles), creates a corresponding downward bias. The possibility of large errors in the highest brackets, because of both the small number of reported taxpayers and the inclusion of corporations, is minimized by employing an open-end group of "over 150,000." Moreover, the two adjustments that were made (i.e. as already noted, the shifting of the upper and lower limits of the brackets and the rounding off of the figures and their adjustment so as to total 10,000 families) also reduce this source of error, as a comparison of Table 90 with Table 77 in Appendix D will show. The income distribution in the last column of Table 90 therefore may be considered adequate for the purposes of the present study.

### 3. ALLOCATION OF THE TAX BURDEN

The estimates of the burden of taxes upon typical families, which were given in Table 36 of Chapter VIII, attempt to repre-

---

[4] Income derived from coffee and cotton production is exempt from the income tax.

[5] This was permissible because the number of corporations is so small and their ownership is generally so highly concentrated that no great distortion is introduced.

sent tax liabilities (i.e., the amounts that the families should have borne in 1946) rather than the actual tax burdens (i.e., the amounts that they actually did bear in 1946). The burden of such taxes as those on income, inheritances, and coffee exports, the *cédula de vecindad*, and the *vialidad* series, which are direct functions of a family's income and/or capital, were therefore computed directly from the various tax rates.

Taxes that depend on a family's level of consumption or disposable income, however, could not be thus directly estimated. Accordingly, in the case of consumption taxes, import duties, and shifted business taxes, the burden for a "typical" family in each income group was first calculated on the basis of actual collections in 1946, and these figures were then adjusted in accordance with the particular family's disposable income and estimated consumption pattern. For example, in the case of a family with an annual income of 1,800 colones, the tax burden was first allocated on the basis of the consumption pattern of the "typical" family with such an income and then adjusted to fit the different consumption patterns of the families of a farmer, an industrial worker, and a white-collar worker in this income bracket.

Such taxes as the inheritance tax and the *cédula de vecindad* are not payable every year. In such cases estimates of the frequency of payment were made, and a certain portion of the total tax burden was allocated to 1946.

#### 4. Allocation of the Burden of Individual Taxes

A brief description of the assumptions employed and the methods of computation used in allocating the burden of the major groups of taxes follows.

##### INCOME TAX

Taxable income for income tax purposes was defined as total income minus income from coffee and also minus the basic exemption of 3,000 colones. For example, the combination importer and coffee producer in Table 36 of Chapter VIII had a total income of 25,000 colones. Of this, 50 per cent or 12,500 colones was assumed to be income from coffee. Subtracting the basic exemption of 3,000 colones, this person had a taxable income of 9,500 colones and was liable for a tax of 395.0 colones.

### COFFEE EXPORT TAX

On the basis of production and trade figures, it was found that 97.5 per cent of the coffee produced in 1946 was exported, and this proportion was assumed to hold true for the crop of each individual coffee producer. The productivity of all *fincas* was assumed to be the same, and the physical output of each coffee producer was then estimated by dividing his export coffee income (97.5 per cent of his total coffee income) by 49.26 colones, the average export price per quintal during 1946. This figure was then multiplied by the computed coffee export tax rate of 4.845 colones per quintal, a weighted average[6] of the 4.50-colón coffee tax rate in effect from November 1945 to October 1946 and the 5.19-colón rate in effect from November 1946 to October 1947.

Under the alternative assumption that 50 per cent of the coffee export tax is shifted backward to the workers in the form of lower wages, the burden of the coffee export tax on each coffee producer was reduced by one half. Since coffee is such an important element in the monetary economy, the reduction in coffee wages would produce a commensurate decline in demand throughout the entire economy, which would result in lower incomes for most business units.[7] In order to indicate the order of magnitude of this decline in incomes, 2,207,150 colones (one half the total coffee tax collections in 1946) was allocated to all members of the population in accordance with their total incomes and treated as a burden reflecting the decline in incomes resulting from the 50 per cent shifting of the coffee tax.

[6] Weighted on the basis of the seasonal pattern of coffee exports.

[7] The incomes of coffee producers and exporters would of course be larger, and these additional funds would increase demand to some degree. However, it was assumed that a large proportion of this increased purchasing power would be saved, rather than spent, and that consequently the increased purchases of coffee producers would fall considerably short of offsetting the decreased purchases by coffee workers.

### INHERITANCE AND GIFT TAX

The rates of the inheritance and gift tax vary with respect to both the size of the estate and the degree of consanguinity of the beneficiary. For this analysis no attempt was made to distinguish the tax with regard to the latter, and the effective tax rate was assumed to be equal to the weighted average of the rates levied on the various degrees of consanguinity, the weights assigned to the first and second degrees being four times those given the last three degrees. The taxable estate was defined as total capital minus the basic exemption of 4,000 colones, and the prospective taxpayer was assumed to make provision for death duties over a period of twenty years. Each family was therefore assumed to bear in 1946 one twentieth of its total computed inheritance tax liability.[8]

### VIALIDAD A, B, C, AND D

The *vialidad* tax that each family was assumed to pay was computed directly from the rate schedules on the basis of the income, capital, or occupation of the head of the household (see Appendix D for rate schedules).

### CÉDULA DE VECINDAD

For the *cédula de vecindad*, the head of each household was considered as paying the rate based on his income, capital, or occupation, and two other members of the family were considered as paying the minimum tax of 0.15 colones. Since this tax is payable every four years, in 1946 each family was considered as bearing 25 per cent of its total computed *cédula de vecindad* liability.

### CONSUMPTION TAXES

Total collections of each consumption tax were first allocated among the various income brackets on the basis of the corresponding expenditure item in the consumers' budget study presented in Table 88. For example, in 1946 collections of the beer

[8] The results are therefore independent of the unusually large inheritance tax collections of 1946.

tax were 354,800 colones, and those of the beer stamp tax were 192,600. This total of 547,400 colones was then allocated as follows:

| Family income | Average expenditure for beer per family | Number of families | Expenditure for beer per income group | Per cent of total expenditure for beer of each income group | Beer and beer-stamp tax per income group | Beer and beer-stamp taxes per family |
|---|---|---|---|---|---|---|
| Under 600 | 3.2 | 240,000 | 768,000 | 27.5 | 150,500 | 0.6 |
| 600–1200 | 9.0 | 120,000 | 1,080,000 | 38.6 | 211,300 | 1.8 |
| 1200–2400 | 14.0 | 20,000 | 280,000 | 10.0 | 54,700 | 2.7 |
| 2400–3600 | 20.0 | 10,000 | 200,000 | 7.1 | 39,400 | 3.9 |
| Over 3600 | 47.0 | 10,000 | 470,000 | 16.8 | 92,000 | 9.2 |
| Total | | 400,000 | 2,798,000 | 100.0 | 547,400 | |

No attempt was made to allocate the consumption taxes on individual commodities for incomes in excess of 3,600 colones. Such a computation, however, was made for total consumption taxes. Inspection of these totals for the lower brackets and the "over 3600" group as a whole indicated that these taxes were regressive in the higher brackets, and they were therefore allocated accordingly, their total impact on families with incomes of over 3,600 colones being made equal to that which had already been derived for this group from the consumers' budget study.

The figures thus obtained were then adjusted by interpolation to conform to disposable income rather than to total income. Weights were then assigned to distinguish the different consumption patterns of farmers, industrial workers, and white-collar workers. For example, it was assumed that an industrial worker in general consumes more alcoholic beverages and fewer textiles than a white-collar worker, and the taxes on these items were adjusted accordingly.

### IMPORT TAXES

For the purposes of this analysis import taxes were divided into import taxes on consumers' goods and import taxes on "business goods" by first estimating the total value of the former on the basis of the consumers' budget study presented in Table 88, and then considering the import taxes on "business goods" as the difference between the consumers' goods estimate and the total import taxes collected in 1946.

It was assumed as a reasonable approximation of Salvadorean business practices that domestic handling costs and profit margins amounted to 75 per cent of the value of imports, and the expenditures for imported items given in Table 88 consequently differ from the import values by the sum of these handling costs and profit margins and the various import taxes.

The *ad valorem* rate for each commodity in a family-budget-expenditures account was calculated by dividing the total value of imports of that commodity into the total import taxes (the sum of the tariff, consular fees, 2 per cent surcharge, and consular bill of lading, plus the various special duties in the case of gasoline, pharmaceuticals, and cigarettes) for that commodity. Each commodity within a family-budget-expenditures account was then assigned a weight based upon the estimated consumption of the commodity in each income group.[9] An effective *ad valorem* rate for the entire family-budget expenditures account was then derived by using these weights to arrive at an average of the *ad valorem* rates of the individual commodities.

No attempt was made to allocate the import taxes on individual consumers' goods for incomes in excess of 3,600 colones, but this computation was made for total import taxes on consumers' goods. Analysis of these totals indicated that these taxes were probably progressive in the middle income brackets ("typical" incomes of 4,000, 6,000, and 8,000 colones) and regressive in higher ones. They were allocated accordingly, the total burden for each bracket being so adjusted that the total burden on families with incomes of over 3,600 colones was equal to that which had already been derived for this group from the consumers' budget study.

Total import taxes on consumers' goods were estimated by this method at 7,539,000 colones. Since all import taxes collected in 1946 amounted to 15,028,100 colones, the difference of 7,489,-100 colones was assumed to represent import taxes on "business

[9] The estimates were based on the figures giving the total consumption of all commodities within a particular family-budget expenditures classification in Table 88.

goods." These were assumed to be entirely shifted to the consumer in the form of higher prices, and were then allocated among the income groups on the basis of total consumption. Since on inspection these taxes appeared to be regressive in the brackets over 3,600 colones, they were allocated accordingly, following the method of computation already used for consumption taxes.

The figures for both import taxes on consumers' goods and shifted import taxes on "business goods" were then adjusted by interpolation to conform to disposable income rather than total income. For the examples in Table 36 in Chapter VIII, the differences in the consumption patterns of the various occupations were taken into account.

### BUSINESS-LICENSE AND TRANSACTION TAXES

Business-license and transaction taxes were assumed to be entirely shifted to the consumer, and were allocated by the same general method as was employed for consumption taxes. In the case of some of these taxes, however, corresponding expenditure accounts did not exist in the consumers' budget study, and the taxes had to be allocated on the basis of the most comparable account. For example, the burden of the shifted tax on fire insurance premiums ought to have been allocated on the basis of total use of real estate, but in the absence of such data, it was allocated on the basis of expenditures on residential housing.

No attempt was made to allocate the individual shifted business taxes among families with incomes in excess of 3,600 colones, but this computation was made for the total of such shifted business taxes. For this computation, the same method was used as for import duties on consumers' goods.

### OTHER TAXES

The preceding analysis accounts for all but 2,429,000 colones of the taxes collected in 1946. Fifty per cent of this residue was assumed to be borne directly by the consumer, and since there were no factors that seemed to make it either progressive or regressive, it was allocated proportionately to total income. The other 50 per cent was assumed to be levied on business and then shifted to the consumer in direct proportion to his disposable income.

# APPENDIX H

## CONSTRUCTION OF INDICES OF AVERAGE SALARY AND NUMBER OF NATIONAL GOVERNMENT EMPLOYEES

*(Appendix to Chapter IX)*

THE INFORMATION USED in the construction of the indices of the unit cost (i.e., average salary) and number of government employees was taken from the official salary appropriations (*Ley de Salarios*), a source that lists the number of employees in each pay grade and their respective salaries. A broad representative sample of government employees and their salaries was selected for the second half of 1939, the first period for which the figures were available, and the cost of their employment per employee was traced for 1942, 1946, 1947, and 1948, the other years for which salary appropriations were reported in detail. The sample covered the following fields of government employment: (1) the National Assembly (*Asamblea Nacional*); (2) the National Post Office (*Correos Nacionales*); (3) the several branches of the Treasury Department (*Secretaría de Estado, Servicio de Tesorería, Servicio de Aduanas, Dirección General de Contribuciones*, etc.); and (4) the Secretariat of the Ministry of Education (*Ministerio de Cultura, Ramo de Cultura Popular, Secretaría de Estado*) and the elementary school teachers (*escuelas primarias para toda la República*). Approximately 37 per cent of the salaried employees of the government in 1942 were covered by the sample. It is believed that the selection of that sample was such that all salary grades were adequately represented.

Relevant indices derived from the sample are shown in Table 91. The index of number of government employees (column 3) may be regarded as representing the extent to which the rise in the total sample salary bill (column 1) was caused by an actual increase in government personnel, both to fulfill existing functions more adequately and to fill new jobs resulting from the expansion in functions of the agencies in the sample.

TABLE 91

INDICES DERIVED FROM THE SAMPLE

| Year | Index of Total Salary Bill of Sample | Number of Employees | Index of Number of Employees | Index of Average Salary of Employees[a] |
|------|------|------|------|------|
| | (1) | (2) | (3) | (4) |
| 1939......... | 94 | 3,913 | 96 | 96 |
| 1942......... | 100 | 4,058 | 100 | 100 |
| 1946......... | 148 | 4,999 | 123 | 125 |
| 1947......... | 178 | 5,622 | 139 | 134 |
| 1948......... | 251 | 6,875 | 169 | 159 |

[a] Based on 3,856 jobs.

In the case of 3,856 jobs it was possible to trace their existence in the table of organization throughout the years. The index of the wage bill of this stable number of employees (column 4) was

TABLE 92

INDICES ADJUSTED TO "FIXED" GOVERNMENT EXPENDITURES

(1942 = 100)

| Year | Index of Government "Fixed" Expenditures | Adjusted Index of Average Salary of Government Employees (unit cost of government) | Adjusted Index of Number of Government Employees |
|------|------|------|------|
| | (5) | (6) | (7) |
| 1939................ | 93 | 97 | 97 |
| 1940................ | 98 | 99 | 99 |
| 1941................ | 98 | 99 | 99 |
| 1942................ | 100 | 100 | 100 |
| 1943................ | 102 | 101 | 101 |
| 1944................ | 107 | 104 | 103 |
| 1945................ | 119 | 110 | 108 |
| 1946................ | 140 | 119 | 117 |
| 1947................ | 172 | 129 | 133 |
| 1948................ | 221 | 144 | 153 |

considered to be indicative of the increase in the salary of the average employee, the second factor causing the rise in the total salary bill.

Comparison of the index of the total salary bill of the sample (column 1, Table 91) with an index of the government's "fixed" expenditures (column 5, Table 92), which is composed almost entirely of the government's salary bill, indicated that the sample had an upward bias. Since the wage-bill index for the sample (column 4, Table 91) was constructed with a fixed base of 3,856 employees, a further technical upward bias also resulted.[1] An adjustment was made in order to eliminate both upward biases and thus adjust the indices to "fixed" government expenditures.[2]

The adjusted indices of the average salary (unit cost) and number of national government employees after the upward bias had been eliminated are compiled in Table 92.[3] Since the index of "fixed" government expenditures (column 5) is continuous from 1939 through 1948, the component average-salary and number-of-employees indices (derived from it by means of the indices of the number of employees and of their average wage) were computed by straight-line interpolation for years other than those covered by the sample.

These indices of the number and unit cost of national government employees for the years 1939 through 1948 are considered indicators of the changes in government expenditures due to

---

[1] The product of the average-salary and number-of-employees indices (columns 3 and 4 of Table 91, respectively) for each year exceeded the index of the total salary bill of the sample (column 1, Table 91) for that year.

[2] The following technique was employed:

Given: Index of "fixed" government expenditures (column 5, Table 92)

      Sample index of average salary of government employees (column 4, Table 91)

      Sample index of number of government employees (column 3, Table 91)

Let:   CW = a computed index of average salary of government employees equal to column 5 (Table 92) divided by column 3 (Table 91)

      CN = a computed index of number of government employees equal to column 5 (Table 92) divided by column 4 (Table 91)

Then: Adjusted index of average salary of government employees (column 6, Table 92) is equal to the geometric mean of column 4 (Table 91) and CW.

      Adjusted index of number of government employees (column 7, Table 92) is equal to the geometric mean of column 3 (Table 91) and CN.

[3] The product of the indices in columns 6 and 7 for each year is equal to the index in column 5 for that year.

changes, respectively, in the volume of government services and in average salaries. The unit cost-of-government index (column 6, Table 92) was used in Appendix B (column 10, Table 70) to deflate the estimated gross product of the government sector of the Salvadorean economy.

# INDEX

# INDEX